# JAVA
# FOR
# ALIENS

CLAUDIO DE SIO CESARI

# JAVA
# FOR
# ALIENS

**LEARN JAVA FROM SCRATCH
AND BECOME A PRO**

# Volume 1

# Java for Aliens - Volume 1

Copyright © 2019 by **Claudio De Sio Cesari**

**Proofreader**: Proofreading Guy (http://www.proofreadingguy.com)
**Book Editor and Cover Designer**: Emanuele Giuliani (emanuele@giuliani.mi.it)
**Cover Designers**: Ciro Improta (improta@libero.it)
Riccardo Ferti (riccardo.ferti@gmail.com)
Andrea Massaretti (andrea.massaretti@gmail.com)

**Printed by**: kdp.amazon.com

First Edition (November, 2019)

**ISBN: 979-12-200-4915-3**

## Font licenses

*Libre Baskerville* (https://fonts.google.com/specimen/Libre+Baskerville, Impallari Type): OFL
*Libre Franklin* (https://fonts.google.com/specimen/Libre+Franklin, Impallari Type): OFL
*Cousine* (https://fonts.google.com/specimen/Cousine, Steve Matteson): AL
*Inconsolata* (https://fonts.google.com/specimen/Inconsolata, Raph Levien): OFL
*Roboto* (https://fonts.google.com/specimen/Roboto, Christian Robertson): AL
*Digits* (https://www.1001fonts.com/digits-font.html, Dieter Steffmann): FFC
*Journal Dingbats 3* (https://www.1001fonts.com/journal-dingbats-3-font.html, Dieter Steffmann): FFC
*Musicals* (https://www.1001fonts.com/musicals-font.html, Brain Eaters): FFC

## Image licenses

*Curiosity* icon (https://www.flaticon.com/free-icon/toyger-cat_107975, www.freepik.com): FBL
*Alien* icon (http://www.iconarchive.com/show/free-space-icons-by-goodstuff-no-nonsense/alien-4-icon.html, goodstuffnononsense.com): CC
*Trick* icon (https://www.flaticon.com/free-icon/magic-wand_1275106, www.flaticon.com/authors/pause08): FBL
*Millennium Falcon* image: (https://free-clipart-pictures.com/startdownload.html?id=951327): FCP.com

## License specifications

*Open Free License* (OFL): https://scripts.sil.org/cms/scripts/page.php?site_id=nrsi&id=OFL_web
*Apache License, Version 2.0* (AL): http://www.apache.org/licenses/LICENSE-2.0
*1001Fonts Free For Commercial Use License* (FFC): https://www.1001fonts.com/licenses/ffc.html
*Flaticon Basic License* (FBL): https://file000.flaticon.com/downloads/license/license.pdf
*CC Attribution 4.0* (CC): https://creativecommons.org/licenses/by/4.0/legalcode
*Free-clipart-pictures.com* (FCP.com): https://free-clipart-pictures.com/terms.html

# Table of Contents

# Part III - Java Language Advanced Features

## Chapter 11 - Enumerations and Nested Types

**XV**

# Preface

Java for Aliens is structured in such a way as to facilitate the learning of the Java language (Version 13), even for those who have never programmed, or for those who have programmed with functional languages. The structure, writing and contents have been chosen carefully, based on the experience I have accumulated as a trainer and mentor over a twenty-year career. In particular, for Sun Microsystems, for Oracle, and as a freelancer, I've had the opportunity to deliver about 250 courses, for thousands of learners, on Java technology, architecture, object-oriented analysis, design and UML. This book also covers complex topics that even the most experienced Java programmers might not master. These topics are marked with appropriate icons to warn the reader about the frequency of use, complexity and importance.

This two-volume book represents an evolution of the most popular book on Java in Italy, which since 2006, has been recommended as a reference book in all the most important Italian universities. The "Java Manual", (published by Hoepli), boasts the highest number of reviews on Amazon Italy compared to all other programming books, even those of the most established international authors. Furthermore, my free book on Java 5 (**http://www.claudiodesio.com**), has been downloaded over 450,000 times out of a total of about 2 million Italian programmers of all languages.

The book you have in your hands is therefore the result of years of work, based not only on practical and educational experience, but also on extensive feedback from readers.

## What's New?

From Version 9 of Java onwards, a new six-monthly release cycle has been introduced. This book is being published at the same time as Version 13, and also covers all of the new features in Versions 9, 10, 11 and 12, often with a very high level of detail. Each topic introduced in these versions will be presented with a specific icon that is clearly identifiable. After the Java 8 revolution, Versions 9 to 13 have brought new constructs (switch expressions, text boxes, modules...), new ways to launch applications (JShell, Launch Single Source Files...), new Garbage Collectors (G1, Epsilon, ZGC, Shenandoah...), new syntax words (var, opens, exports...), new application types (Modules, Custom Runtime Images, Modular Jar...), new JDK tools (**jlink**, **jmod**...) and much more ... including loads of challenging insights for more skilled aliens!

# Book Structure

Java for Aliens is divided into 7 parts within two volumes:

1. Part I, "Java Language Basics" (Chapters 1 to 5 of Volume 1), presents all the fundamental concepts of Java programming, such as the development environment, essential components, programming constructs (including novelties such as the switch expression), data types, etc. The study of the first five chapters should therefore allow the reader to write their first programs, and also to be confident in the development environment. Nothing will be taken for granted, and notions of basic computer science will also be introduced. Furthermore, the reader will receive support in the form of simplified examples, exercises and explanations. However, there will also be an in-depth analysis, especially on the latest new features. I have also created a simple, free and open source development tool called EJE, to support the initial learning phases.

2. Part II, "Object Orientation" (Chapters 6 to 10 of Volume 1), explains the fundamental concepts for correctly designing our programs. How do we organize a program from scratch? How many classes do we need to create? What should these classes be called? What methods will they have to define? How can we create a program capable of evolving without changing parts that have already been written? These and many other questions are answered by the theory of Object Orientation with its paradigms (abstraction, reuse, encapsulation, inheritance, polymorphism and then cohesion and coupling, and the principle of inversion of dependence, etc.). In this part, particular emphasis is placed on the support that the language offers to Object Orientation. Usually, the major difficulty that a Java programmer faces is being able to exploit the paradigms of object-oriented programming in practice. This text then strives to provide all the information needed by the reader in order to follow the path of Java programming in the most correct way possible, that is, the object-oriented way. Further, important features such as abstract classes, interfaces, packages, initializers, design by contract with assertions, handling exceptions, errors and warnings, etc. will be presented contextually.

3. Part III, "Java Language Advanced Features" (Chapters 11 and 12 of Volume 1), introduces some more complex topics such as enumerations, generic types, erasure, wildcards, bounded wildcards, bounded parameters, generic methods, intersection types, wildcard capture, helper methods, covariant parameters, nested types, and anonymous classes. These arguments are in preparation for those that will be presented in the chapters that follow. Furthermore, at this point and in other chapters, the discussion is extensively developed with a view to supporting possible Oracle certification (both OCA and OCP).

**4.** Part IV, "Java API Fundamentals" (Chapters 13 to 15 of Volume 2), presents the fundamental standards libraries for language and utilities. These include the *Date & Time API*, the *Reflection API* and all the fundamental classes such as `Object`, `System`, `String`, `Runtime`, `Math`, etc. Further, it introduces APIs for managing string formatting, internationalizing our applications, creating configuration files, using regular expressions. It also explains how to manage *concurrent (multi-threaded) programming* and the related libraries that support it.

**5.** Part V, "Java Language Evolution" (Chapters 16 to 19 of Volume 2), presents the main features introduced in recent years that have revolutionized the language, such as *functional programming* with lambda expressions and method references, the *Fluent API* with streams, *meta-programming* with annotations, and the Java Platform Module System that has changed the way we design Java programs today - a key part for keeping up with the times.

**6.** Part VI, "Java Integration API" (Chapters 20 to 22 of Volume 2), introduces the Java support structures that allow us to interact with other technologies or systems. The Java Native Interface, the `java.io`, `java.nio` packages (and the sub-packages that define *NIO 2 API*), networking support with `java.net`, the JDBC interface to connect with databases, and libraries for interacting with programs and technologies based on XML, are featured in this part of the book.

**7.** Finally, Part VII, "Java Graphical User Interfaces" (Chapters 23 and 24 of Volume 2), presents the libraries that will allow us to create graphical user interfaces with Java. In particular, we will learn to use the AWT, Swing and JavaFX libraries, with a view to creating any kind of user interface for standalone programs.

This is therefore a book that should satisfy the expectations of both the aspiring programmer and the expert programmer.

Moreover, in order not to burden the body and the cost of the work too much, a lot of material (including over 500 exercises) has been moved to a special space available online at this address: http://www.javaforaliens.com.

## Text Styles

The text is stylized to capture attention, highlighting words, sentences or entire paragraphs. In particular: with the *Italic* style, particular or important terms are highlighted; the **Bold** style highlights key words, important concepts of the Java language, names of technologies or other things the author considered important and sought to draw attention to; the Interface style is used, within the text, for links, commands and everything that can be typed in the interfaces of an operating system; the `Code in the text` style is used to distinguish parts of the code in the explanations from the rest of the text. The code lines are inserted in highlighted blocks similar to the following:

```
public class MyFirstJava13Class {
    //This is Java 13 code!
}
```

while the command line inputs and execution outputs are formatted in blocks with a black background:

```
this is the output of my program
```

> Finally, notes like this add information to the topic before or after it. They can be insights, suggestions, or even simple references to other parts of the work.

## Semantic Icons

To help visually identify parts of the text with particular semantic characteristics, the following icons have been used.

| New Feature in Java 9 | New Feature in Java 10 | New Feature in Java 11 | New Feature in Java 12 | New Feature in Java 13 |
|---|---|---|---|---|

Curiosity (Non-essential concept or story)

Trick

Common Error

Rarely Used

| Best Practice | Very Important | Complex Concept | Only for Aliens |
|---|---|---|---|
|  |  |  |  |

> We recommend the novice reader not to dwell on the parts marked with the icon "Only for Aliens" and "Rarely Used", in case they are too complicated. These are not essential parts for language learning, and you can go back to reading them when you feel ready.

## Who Should Read This Book?

Java for Aliens has been structured to meet the expectations of:

- Aspiring programmers who want to become pro: nothing is taken for granted, you can learn to program even from scratch, and enter the world of work from the front door.

- University students: the previous versions of this work have been adopted as a textbook for many university courses in all the major Italian universities.

- Expert Java programmers: who need to upgrade to Version 13 and keep up with the times.

## Online Resources

A lot of resources have been moved online for this edition. This could easily have given rise to a third volume! In particular, in addition to fifteen appendices, the errata, all the source code of the examples, there are about 500 exercises (and their solutions), fundamental for learning the concepts presented in the paper book.

You can download all the exercises and the appendices and the other files in a special space available online accessible at **http://www.javaforaliens.com**.

You can also subscribe to the Telegram channel **https://t.me/java4aliens** in order to be notified about future updates of the online material.

# Source Code

Working with the code examples in this book, you can decide to write the whole code by hand, or to use the source files that come with the book. All of the source code written in this book is available for download at http://www.javaforaliens.com.

# Errata

Every effort has been made to avoid errors in the text and in the code.
However, nobody is perfect, and mistakes happen. If you find a spelling error or a part of the code that is not working, the author would be grateful for the feedback and it will be reported in a new version of the errata. Other readers will thus avoid hours of frustration and, at the same time, it will help to ensure the highest possible standards in terms of quality of information. You can do this by writing to the author at claudio@javaforaliens.com. As usual, the reference address remains: http://www.javaforaliens.com.

# Author

Since 1999, I have worked as a freelance IT consultant. Today I am a specialist in training, technical writing, development, analysis, design, Java technologies, architecture and object-oriented methodologies. I am the author of several technical articles and the "Manuale di Java" series from Version 6 to 9, Italian bestsellers, all published by Hoepli. I have worked with several universities, ministerial authorities and IT companies including Sun Microsystems, as a trainer and mentor. Today, I mainly work as a training consultant for Oracle.

# Contacts

You can contact me through the following channels:

- **Internet**: http://www.claudiodesio.com
- **E-mail**: claudio@claudiodesio.com
- **Facebook**: http://www.facebook.com/claudiodesiocesari
- **Twitter**: http://twitter.com/cdesio
- **LinkedIn**: http://www.linkedin.com/in/claudiodesio
- **YouTube**: https://www.youtube.com/c/claudiodesiocesari

## Acknowledgments

My thanks go to all of the people who have supported me throughout this work, and to all those who, in some way, have contributed to its realization.

A special thanks goes to my editor Emanuele Giuliani (**emanuele@giuliani.mi.it**) and my English guru, 'Proofreading Guy' (**http://www.proofreadingguy.com**) who has taken care of this work with great patience and professionalism.

I would also like to thank (though it's never enough) my parents, for all they have done for me and continue to do, and for their unconditional love.

Finally, I thank my family, who are my reason for living: Rosalia, Andrea and Simone. This book, as always, is dedicated to you. You are everything to me.

*Claudio De Sio Cesari*

To Rosalia, Andrea and Simone...

# Part I
# Java Language Basics

Part I has been designed to allow a "non-traumatic" approach to Java. Even the reader with no programming experience or fundamental computer science concepts can start programming! The concepts are introduced gradually following an educational method perfected in twenty years of providing training courses on Java. No topic will be taken for granted.
Part I consists of 5 chapters:

1. In the first chapter, we introduce ourselves to the development environment so that we may immediately write a simple first program. In the first chapter, after introducing some basic computer science concepts, the Java language and technology are defined. Then the development environment is explained and we'll write a first simple program. The final part of the chapter is dedicated to understanding and solving some of the most frequent errors that newbies face at the beginning of their studies.

2. In the second chapter, there is a comprehensive look at the fundamental concepts of the language such as classes, objects, methods, variables, constructors and packages. The other components such as enumerations, interfaces, annotations, initializers, lambda expressions, nested classes and modules are only introduced, since they will be explained in subsequent chapters.

3. The third chapter is essentially dedicated to the primitive and complex Java data types, for which the degree of detail is particularly high. Memory management, the rules that must follow the identifiers, code conventions, the standard library, and comments are also explained. Two fundamental arguments like arrays, and a new feature introduced with Java 10: the inference of the type for local variables, (i.e. the introduction of the word var), conclude the chapter.

4. In the fourth chapter, all of the tools to manage the control flow of the code (loops, conditions and operators) are presented, including the Java 12 preview novelty: the switch expression.

**5.** Finally, the fifth chapter, first introduces features to allow us to learn and experiment faster: the new Java 11 feature that lets you launch files without compiling them, and JShell (introduced with Java 9). Afterwards the reader is introduced to the software development cycle, to the IDE, to the working reality in a business context and, above all, a process is defined to develop a program from scratch, step by step.

Having studied this first part, the reader should have all the necessary requirements in order to start programming with Java.

The study of this section will be equally useful to expert programmers who only need updates on Java Version 13. The new features introduced in Versions 9, 10, 11, 12 and 13 are distinguished by specific icons, and the more complex insights are characterized by an icon that shows an image of an alien.

# 1

# Introduction to Java

**Goals:**

At the end of this chapter the reader should:

- ✔ Know some basic computer concepts (Unit 1.1).
- ✔ Know how to define the Java programming language and its features (Unit 1.2).
- ✔ Be able to interact with the development environment: The Java Development Kit (Units 1.3, 1.4, 1.5).
- ✔ Know how to type, compile and run a simple application (Units 1.3, 1.4, 1.5).
- ✔ Choose a development environment (Unit 1.6).

The primary objective of this chapter is to allow the reader to immediately see some initial concrete results. After reading this first chapter, you will have created and executed your first Java program. This is a very simple program, but this will allow you to immediately become familiar with Java programming. To achieve this goal, we will not take anything for granted: we will define the language and the Java technology, describe the development environment and detail a process that will allow us to perform our first application step by step. Finally, you'll learn to understand any error messages and solve our first programming problems.

> It is quite probable that, without the basics of programming, it will be hard to understand some concepts, but do not be discouraged. In this first chapter, we have everything that is needed to start from scratch. You don't have to have extra-terrestrial abilities, but you should always be focused on the target, and it is not advisable to skip sentences or even sections. If something is not clear, a re-reading is recommended.

# 1.1 Prerequisites: Basic IT Concepts

To be able to code with Java, you need to know some basic concepts of computer science. In this book, these concepts are described in order to make programming more approachable. So, even someone who completely lacks the basic concepts to make a computer work can start studying Java without always having to research on Google. For this reason, also in the next chapters you will find discussions on basic concepts. Having a common vocabulary is the first step in order to fully understand this book. We will, however, try to limit the explanations only to the concepts that are really necessary, and we will use the synthesis so that we don't bury the desire to learn under the weight of too much superfluous information.

Let's start from scratch by setting out some definitions that we will use extensively in this book. To be able to program in Java, you need a computer, an electronic device that aggregates a series of physical components that are usually referred to, by the term **hardware**. Examples of hardware are all the interface components with which the user interacts: the mouse, the keyboard, the monitor, the printer, and so on. In a computer, however, there are also many other less "visible" hardware components such as the processor, the motherboard and the RAM memory. However, a computer needs **instructions** to be able to operate and perform operations. These instructions are defined by the **programs**, which are generally referred to by the term **software**. So, a computer is defined by its physical part (hardware) and by the programs that run on it (software). Nowadays there are many types of devices that can be defined as computers. In this book, we assume that the reader will use a **desktop** or a **laptop** computer, not a tablet, smartphone, or other device.

## 1.1.1 Hardware

In this context, we will distinguish three types of hardware. The first type deals with collecting **input** data and includes devices, such as a **mouse** or a **keyboard**, that accept input from the computer user. The second type has the task of returning **output** data. Examples of components belonging to this second type are **monitors** and **printers**. These two types are to be considered "interface hardware" and are those with which the user interacts. For this reason, you should already have a basic understanding of these devices. The type of hardware that we will be most interested in, is that with which we do not interact directly: the "inside the box" hardware. Before talking about programs, you need to have at least an idea of how a computer stores data, that is, for example, how the memory and the processor work.

The **processor** or **CPU** ("**Central Processing Unit**"), is the hardware component that executes the instructions of a program. Its main task is to perform elementary arithmetic operations, and to manage the shifting operations of the data in the memory. It may seem strange, but it is the processor that makes everything that we do with a computer possible.

The **memory** preserves the data that is used by the programs and there are two types: a main memory and an auxiliary one. The **main memory** is usually called **RAM** ("**Random Access Memory**"). This is a memory that contains the programs that are running, along with their data. This memory is temporary (it is also called *volatile*) and is deleted when the computer is turned off. The **auxiliary memory** (also called **secondary memory**), on the other hand, preserves data even when the computer is switched off. The auxiliary memory is therefore usually much larger than the main one, but is also less efficient from the point of view of data storage speed. Examples of auxiliary memory are hard drives and other devices such as solid-state memories, USB sticks, etc.

## 1.1.2 Software

To use a computer, we need programs that contain instructions to be executed by the underlying hardware. In particular, there is at least one main program that manages the whole computer, which is often identified as being the computer itself: the **operating system**. Nowadays, the most famous operating systems are Microsoft Windows systems, Apple Mac operating systems, and Linux and Unix systems. When we turn on a computer, it starts its operating system and this manages the entire computer. The operating system, among other things, makes it possible to install and launch other programs. For example, the Microsoft Windows 10 operating system, allows us to install and launch programs such as Microsoft Word, a browser such as Mozilla Firefox or Google Chrome, a Java development IDE such as Netbeans or Eclipse, a media player like VLC, or our own program written in Java.

There are thousands of types of programs, very different from each other. For example, a *browser* is a program that allows us to surf the internet. An *IDE* is a programming environment that integrates different tools ("IDE" stands for "Integrated Development Environment"). A *media player* allows us to view videos or listen to audio. So, each program executes instructions that very often rely on input data, that perform certain activities and that produce a result as output. For example, a browser can take as input an Internet address entered by the user using the keyboard. It can perform a process that includes identifying the requested resource online, retrieving the code that represents the web page and interpreting the languages and technologies that are used in the page code. Finally, it can output the page formatted as the user sees it.

## 1.1.3 Programming Languages

A **programming language** facilitates the communication of instructions to the computer so that it executes these instructions in the context of a program. It is just a language with its own vocabulary and rules. The vocabulary is almost always quite limited, but usually there are a lot of rules.

**The set of rules is sometimes called "language grammar".**

There are many programming languages and their history is often fascinating. Languages like Assembly, Fortran, Basic, COBOL, Pascal, C, C++, LISP, Prolog, SmallTalk, Visual Basic, Javascript, and of course Java, are just some of the languages that are part of the history of programming (the full list would be very long). The question arises: can a computer understand all of these languages? Obviously not! The hardware of a computer is able to understand a single language, called **machine language**. Machine language has a vocabulary defined by the **binary numeral system**, and therefore formed by only two symbols: 0 and 1. By arranging these symbols in sequence, we can obtain "words", and with these words we can create instructions to be performed by the processor.

> **Since there are different types of processors, it is technically incorrect to speak of the existence of one single machine language. Indeed, there are many. Each processor can interpret a particular machine language.**

So how can we create a computer program without knowing which processor it will be executed on and therefore without knowing which machine language must be used? And how does a computer understand a program written in any programming language when it is only capable of understanding machine language? It seems that we require a "translator" and, in fact, that's exactly what we use.

Modern languages like Java are called **high-level languages**, that is, languages that are very similar to the language that we use every day to communicate, and consequently quite different from machine languages (which can only use symbols 0 and 1 to compose instructions). On the other hand, languages like Assembly, that are very similar to machine languages, are called **low-level languages**. But programs written with both Assembly and with Java require a machine language translation to be understood by the processor. This translation is made by a software that is part of the language programming environment, called **compiler**. A compiler is therefore a software that translates instructions written with a programming language into instructions written with a machine language.

The process of developing a program includes the following steps:

1. The developer writes a program using a programming language. By correctly following the language rules, he saves the instructions within one or more text files. We say that these files contain the **source code** of the program, and the text files themselves are called **source files**.

2. The developer uses a compiler to which will pass as input the source files. After having checked the correctness of the source code, the compiler will translate the instructions

from the source code into instructions written in machine language. To do this, the compiler will create the so-called **binary files**. The binary files are directly executable by the processor each time they are launched, and represent the program itself. Programs ready to use are also called **executable files**, or also **object files**.

Languages that have the support of a compiler are called **compiled languages**.

But there are also languages that do not use a compiler to translate the source code into machine language but, rather, use a software that is called **interpreter**. Unlike a compiler, an interpreter is a tool that can launch the program, translating on the fly the source code into object code, instruction after instruction. A language that uses an interpreter instead of a compiler is called an **interpreted language**. An interpreter can represent a more flexible solution within the dynamics of development, allowing us to alternate the writing of the code and its execution without having to perform the compilation phase. But unfortunately, it suffers from an obvious disadvantage. The translation of the source code into machine code is included in the execution phase of the program. This is inevitably slower than the execution of a program that has already been compiled. Furthermore, this alternation between translation and execution occurs every time the program is interpreted.

Each programming language requires a different compiler or interpreter, depending on the hardware where the program is to be executed. In many languages, this can result in different behaviours for programs launched on different computers and generated from the same source. This problem, however, is brilliantly solved by Java as we'll soon see.

## 1.2 Introduction to Java

Having introduced some basic concepts of computer science, now is the time for a brief introduction to Java. But we will not talk about the heroic deeds of the creators of Java, nor about the legends of the past and predictions for the future. In fact, several topics will not feature in these two volumes, because they have been moved into special online appendices to be downloaded. Among these appendices, you will also find one relating to the creation and history of Java: Appendix A. If you are curious to know why the language is called Java, who the creators are and what the conditions are that determined the birth and success of Java, etc., you should read Appendix A. Further you can find important info on the new licence and support model adopted by Oracle. In these pages, instead, we will try to lead straight to our goal, without boring those who cannot wait to get their hands on the code.

> To limit the number of pages and consequently the cost of this book, a lot of material has been moved online! You can download all of the appendices, about 600 pages of exercises, all of the code . . .

> . . . presented in the book and the errata file by visiting the address
> http://www.javaforaliens.com. From here you can download all of the
> material.

## 1.2.1 What is Java?

With the term "Java", we usually refer to:

1. The most used programming language on the planet.

2. A technology that includes several "sub-technologies" that have established themselves
   in different areas of software use. Nowadays, Java technology is the most used on enterprise applications, and there are billions of electronic devices all over the world that use
   Java technology: smartphones, SCADA, mobile phones, satellites, decoders, smart cards,
   robots that roam on Mars, and so on.

In this book, we will focus on the Java programming language which is the starting point for
accessing all Java technologies. We will mention and introduce some of them, but just enough
to arouse curiosity. Then anyone who wants to further study these technologies, can do it later
with other didactic resources.

## 1.2.2 Java Language Features

The language was presented in 1995 by Sun Microsystems, a historic and glorious American
company that since 2010 has been acquired by Oracle.
The main features of Java are:

- **Syntax**: it is similar to that of other historic programming languages such as C and C++.
  Other languages with very similar syntaxes are languages that were born after Java, such
  as C# and JavaScript. This means that if the reader already has knowledge of one of these
  languages, he will have a significant advantage in this first part of the study. However, it is
  a syntax considered to be among the clearest in comparison to those of other programming languages, and is characterized by a high readability (sometimes it seems like writing in a 'natural' language).

- **Robustness**: a language is more robust than another when it has a greater ability to prevent programming errors, and Java is one of the most robust languages around. It defines
  a clear and functioning exception management, and has an automatic mechanism for
  memory management (Garbage Collection) that exempts the programmer from having

to de-allocate memory when needed (one of the most delicate points in programming). Furthermore, the Java compiler is very "severe". The programmer is actually forced to solve all "unclear" situations, guaranteeing the program a better chance to work properly. The logic is: "it is much better to get an error at compile-time than at execution-time".

■■ **Platform Independence**: thanks to the Java Virtual Machine concept, every application, once compiled, can be executed on any platform (for example a PC with a Windows operating system or a Unix workstation). This is definitely the most important feature of Java. In fact, if you have to implement a program designed to run on different platforms, there will be no need to create different specific versions. This is obviously a huge advantage.

■■ **Java Virtual Machine**: what makes the platform independence real, is the **Java Virtual Machine** ("**JVM**"). This is software capable of playing the role of interpreter. Java can actually be considered both a compiled and interpreted language. In fact, after writing our source code with Java, we will have to use the Java compiler first to compile it. We will not directly produce, however, an executable file containing instructions in machine language, but a file that contains the translation of our code in a language very similar to machine language called **bytecode**. Once this file is obtained, the programmer can pass as input it to the JVM which will interpret the bytecode and our program will be finally executed. So, if a platform has a Java Virtual Machine, this will be enough to execute bytecode. This is the case when it comes to the most widespread mobile operating system (Android by Google), where the most of the native applications are written in Java. That's why there are so many different models of smartphones and tablets (and also cookers, washing machines, refrigerators, robots, etc.) that use the Android operating system: the secret is the virtual machine. After translating our source code into bytecode, our program is potentially executable on many types of devices. The Java Virtual Machine is called a "virtual machine" because this software has been implemented to simulate a hardware. It could be said that "the machine language is to a computer as the bytecode is to a Java Virtual Machine". In addition to allowing platform independence, JVM provides Java with many other advantages. For example, it is a multi-threaded language (usually a feature of operating systems), that is, capable of executing several processes in parallel mode. Moreover, it guarantees very powerful security mechanisms, the "supervision" of the code by the Garbage Collector for the automatic management of memory, and much more.

■■ **Object-Oriented**: object orientation is a fundamental programming style that allows us to program in a more "natural" way. We will talk extensively about this topic from the sixth chapter onwards. In fact, Java provides us with some tools that practically "force us" to program with objects. The fundamental paradigms of object-oriented programming (inheritance, encapsulation, polymorphism) are more easily appreciated and comprehensible. Java is clearer and more schematic than any other object-oriented language. If you learn Java, later you can certainly access the knowledge of other object-oriented languages in a more natural way, since you will have an object-oriented way of thinking about programming. However, as the years have passed, the language has evolved, and it has also opened up to other programming paradigms.

■■ **Ease of Development**: before the release of Version 5, Java was advertised as a "simple to learn" language. Since the release of Version 5, the term "simplicity" has been replaced with "ease of development". In fact, with the introduction of revolutionary characteristics such as generic and annotation types, Java has created for itself a clearly outlined path: that of allowing the language to evolve so that it keeps pace with modern developments, even at the expense of simplicity. The language today has become more difficult to learn, but programs should be easier to write. In short, learning Java will not be simple, but once we have understood the basic logic, we will have in our hands a very powerful tool.

■■ **Library and Standardization**: Java has a huge, standard and well documented *software library*. So we can use in our code pieces of already working software. This makes Java a *high level language,* and also allows newbies to create complex applications in a fairly short time. For example, it is relatively easy to create graphical interfaces, database links, and network connections regardless of the computer on which the application is developed. Moreover, thanks to Oracle's specifications, standardization problems as compilers that produce different outputs on different platforms, will not exist.

■■ **Open**: using Java does not mean moving in a closed environment where everything is standard. From the choice of the development tool (Eclipse, Netbeans, etc.) to the interaction with other languages, external libraries and technologies (SQL, XML, open source framework, etc.) you'll never stop learning! The Java code is also *open source*, which means that it is possible to read the source code. Since its inception, Java has always been considered as an "open" language, and interaction with its developers has always been a strong point of its evolution. The reference site today is **http://openjdk.java.net** and it is also possible to actively contribute to the development of Java with tests, proposals and bug fixing. The new features of the latest versions have all been proposed by developers who have contributed with ideas. Java is made by developers for developers.

There are many other features that could be mentioned, but these are the ones that are most relevant for readers of this book.

### 1.2.3 False Beliefs About Java

The following are a series of gossips, prejudices, misconceptions and inaccurate or at least superficial beliefs, concerning the Java language:

- **Java is slow**: in the early years, Java was a slow language compared to other compiled languages. The performance level of the bytecode interpretation by the JVM was not optimized and the slowness was clear. But a few years after Java was created, Sun Microsystems created its first **HotSpot Performance Engine-based JVM**, which became the default JVM from Java Version 1.3 onwards. This is a JVM with **Just-In-Time (JIT)** compilation that, during execution, continuously analyzes the program, identifies the parts of the code that are executed more often (calls precisely **hot spots**) and translates them into machine language, optimizing translation as much as possible. Furthermore, the Java compiler also performs many optimizations when it creates bytecode. Today, after about twenty years of evolution, the JVM has performance levels that are comparable to those of the most performing compiled languages such as C and C ++ which, according to some benchmarks, are even exceeded.

   Oracle is focusing on testing a new type of JVM based on **Ahead-Of-Time (AOT)** compilation. AOT aims to significantly reduce the time of compilation on the fly (JIT), especially in the application startup phase. Oracle has therefore released, with Java 9, **GRAAL** for the 64-bit Linux platform, which is a JIT compiler written in Java, that will allow us to test the feasibility of creating a future AOT compiler written in Java. So, in the future, we could have even better performance levels.

- **Java is not sure**: in the early years there was a sort of competition to find how critical some Java technologies were, such as Applets. This received a lot of publicity, but Sun actually resolved it quite quickly. Even more emphasis was put on some bugs found in the Java Plug-in in the early '10s, so as to remove them from the most important browsers in a matter of a few months. That was nothing compared to the damage caused throughout those years by viruses and worms distributed with programs executable on Windows. Actually, Java is among the most important languages, and undoubtedly the safest, especially after the giant steps made in recent years by Oracle. An ironic video was created about that strange period to publicize the 2013 JavaZone conference in Oslo. You can find it here: **http://www.javaforaliens.com/ext/javapocalypse.html**.

- **Java is verbose**: undoubtedly, compared to other languages, Java is a verbose language. But it was worse at the beginning. It is also true that in recent years, a significant part of the evolution of the language has focused on making its syntax more concise. Multi-catch, try with resources, factory method for collections, Lambda expressions, streams and pipelines, and the local variable types inference are just some of the latest changes that make Java a more modern language. Unfortunately, often the critical nature of some projects, means that developers get stuck on old versions of Java, and are not being able to upgrade to take advantage of the new features.

- **Java is easy to learn**: once Java was really easy to learn. Today, however, it is a complex language, and some features are really difficult to learn. So, Java is not just for aliens, but to study it will not be that simple.

- **You must pay to use Java**: after Java 8, it is true that Oracle has introduced a new payment policy to support of programs running on the Oracle JDK in production, but it is also true that you can download the OpenJDK, which is aligned with the Oracle JDK. The "price to pay" to get the security patches, is to update the JDK every time a new version comes out. You can also choose other JDKs such as those that offer AdoptOpenJDK and Azul (as well as many others), that also propose different solutions for support. So, the response is no, Java is still a language that can be used for free.

- **Javascript is a simplified version of Java**: actually, apart from the name (which was chosen because at the time Java was very popular) and a quite similar syntax, Javascript has nothing to do with Java. Javascript is a scripting language that runs on web pages, thanks to the fact that each browser implements an interpreter. It is an **untyped language** (as opposed to Java which is **strongly typed one**) and does not have a compiler.

# 1.3 Development Environment

**In this book, we will assume that the reader uses a computer on which a Windows 7 operating system or higher is installed (recommended Windows 10), but obviously, it is possible to program on other platforms such as Linux or Mac.**

To write a Java program we need two pieces of software:

1. **A program that allows us to write the Java code**. A simple text editor such as Windows Notepad can be a good start. We do not recommend WordPad, Word or any other editor that handles styles, formatting, etc.

2. **The Java Development Kit Standard Edition** ("**JDK**"). This is the official development environment of Java. It's a suite of software including a compiler and the Java Virtual

Machine we mentioned in the previous section. The version 13 of the JDK can be downloaded for free at this address: **http://jdk.java.net/13 choosing the link of the** choosing the link indicating the reference platform, in the **Builds** section (see Figure 1.1). In Appendix B (available for download at **http://www.javaforaliens.com**) we describe the process to be followed to obtain and correctly install the development environment on a Windows operating system.

> **Other alternative development environments will be discussed at the end of the chapter.**

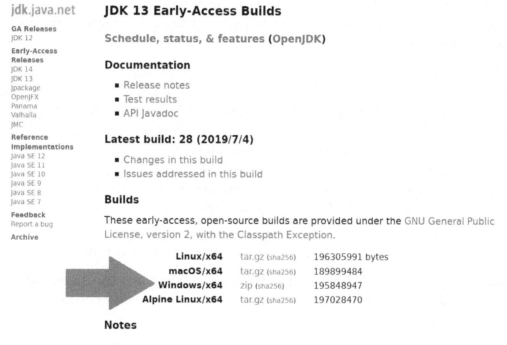

Figure 1.1 – JDK page.

## 1.3.1 Structure of the JDK

Once the JDK is installed correctly, it should be placed in the **C:\Program Files\Java** folder. With the introduction of version 9, the folder structure of the JDK has been radically changed. Compared to the previous version, some folders have been removed, while others have been added. Below is a brief explanation of the current folders:

- **bin**: contains all the executable files of the JDK, for example **javac**, **java**, **jar**, **jlink**, **javadoc** and others, which will allow us to compile, execute, create file archives, etc.

- **conf**: contains configuration files used by the JDK.

- **include** and **lib**: contain libraries written in C and Java that are used by the JDK. With the term "library", we mean a software that makes it possible for other software (in our case the JDK) to use the features it defines.

- **legal**: contains the JDK license files.

- **jmods**: contains the standard Java library reorganized into *modules*. The most important novelty introduced by JDK version 9, concerns the introduction of this new way of organizing our programs: *modularization*. We will see how to use the modules in a dedicated chapter in the second volume of this book.

 Up to Java 10, in addition to the JDK, the Java Runtime Environment (JRE) could also be installed separately. From Version 11 onwards, the JRE is included within the JDK and is no longer downloadable separately. But for a Java application to be executable on a particular machine, as long as only the JRE is installed, there is no need for the entire JDK. With the introduction of the **jlink** tool in Version 9 of the JDK, we can create optimized JRE versions, to be distributed together with our programs. So, in order for a Java program to run on a certain computer, we will not even need to install the JRE anymore as it will be distributed with the application itself.

> **Let's summarize the difference between JVM, JRE and JDK:**
>
> **The JVM is the Java Virtual Machine: the software that simulates hardware capable of interpreting and executing the bytecode contained in a compiled Java file.**
>
> **The JRE is the Java Runtime Environment and consists of software that provides the environment to use the JVM (and, in fact, contains it). To be able to execute Java code, a computer needs the JRE only.**
>
> **The JDK is the Java Development Kit, the software we need to develop Java programs, which contains a suite of tools that support development. So, the JDK is used to develop Java code, while the JRE is used to run Java programs. But the JDK contains the JRE, and thus . . .**

... can be used to run Java applications too. In addition, with the JDK jlink tool, we can create optimized JREs to be distributed with our applications, which will then no longer require a separate JRE installation, as previously.

## 1.3.2 Step by Step Developing Guide

After having correctly installed the JDK and appropriately set any environment variables (see Appendix B), we will be ready to write our first application (see next section).

If you are using a Windows operating system, our recommendation is to enable the display of all the file extensions from the Folder Options, as programmers must always distinguish different types of files. Unfortunately, the default setting of the Windows operating system requires that the extension for the known file types be hidden. To fix this, you have to: open the Control Panel, select the item File Explorer Options (on older Windows systems, select the item Browse Folder), select the View tab and uncheck the checkbox Hide extensions for known file types. Then the extensions of every single file on the hard disk will be visible.

In general, every time we develop, we will have to perform the following steps:

1. **Code writing**: we will write the source code of our application using an editor. As previously stated, we recommend using Windows Notepad for this initial test.

2. **Saving phase**: with the Notepad application, we will save our file with the extension .java in the secondary memory, usually on a hard drive.

3. **Opening a Command Prompt**: after saving our Java file, we need to open a **command prompt window** (also called **DOS prompt**).

If you do not find the link to open the command prompt, you can type the cmd command in the search field of the Windows start menu and press the Enter key. If you are not familiar with the DOS operating system (the Microsoft original operating system that evolved in early versions of Windows), in Appendix C, you can find a short tutorial that will allow you to operate in this environment.

**4. Positioning**: within this prompt, we must move to the folder where our source file was saved. See Appendix C if you're not able to do it.

**5. Compiling phase**: type the compile command:

```
javac fileName.java
```

and press the **Enter** key to execute it. If the compilation is successful, a file named **fileName.class** will be created, in the same folder where the file **fileName.java** exists. The .class file, as we have already said, will contain the translation in bytecode of the source file.

**6. Execution phase**: at this point, we can run the program, invoking the interpretation of the Java Virtual Machine. Just write the following command in the DOS prompt:

```
java fileName
```

(without suffixes). Press the **Enter** key to confirm.

The application, unless there are errors in the code, will be performed by the JVM. In particular, the **class loader** of the Java Virtual Machine will ensure that the bytecode present in the .class file is loaded into the main memory (the RAM memory) to be executed. Then the **bytecode verifier** of the JVM will verify that the code does not violate the security restrictions imposed by Java and does not damage the computer (as a virus could do). Finally, through the **JIT compilation** ("Just In Time"), the JVM will silently execute a second compilation phase, parallel to the interpretation of the bytecode. In fact, it will identify the parts of bytecode that are used several times (called **hot spots**) and translate them into machine language. These parts must no longer be interpreted because they have already been translated into machine code. This behavior improves the performance of our program.

Now we are ready to write our first Java program.

## 1.4 First Approach to the Code

Let's take a look at the classic "Hello World" application. This is the typical first program that is written when learning a new programming language. In practice, it is a simple program that prints the phrase "Hello World!". In this way, we will begin to familiarize ourselves with the syntax and with some fundamental concepts such as that of *class* and *method*.

> Note that, inevitably, some points will remain obscure, and that therefore some parts of the code will have to be taken for granted. This is the didactic approach that this book will follow: instead of trying to explain some concepts prematurely, we will come back to them in later chapters.

We will also see how to compile and run our simple application. As already mentioned, its goal is to print the message "Hello World!" on the screen (in the same command prompt). The code is the following:

```
1 public class HelloWorld
2 {
3     public static void main(String args[])
4     {
5         System.out.println("Hello World!");
6     }
7 }
```

**Line numbers are not part of the application (you do not have to write them) but they will be useful for our analysis.**

This program must be written using the Notepad application. Then it must be saved in a file named exactly as the class that is declared (also paying attention to capitals and lowercase letters) and with the **.java** extension. The name of the file that will contain the Java code just presented must therefore be **HelloWorld.java**.

We do not recommend a "copy - paste" of the code. At least for the first few times, try to write as much code as possible. We recommend writing the program with Notepad line by line after reading the following analysis. In this way you will become more aware of what you're writing.

## 1.4.1 Analysis of the HelloWorld Program

Let's analyze the previous code line by line.

**Line 1:**

```
1 public class HelloWorld
```

This is the declaration of a **class** called HelloWorld. As we will see, each Java application consists of classes. The concept of class will be detailed in the next section. For now, we only need to understand that all operational programming instructions will always be contained in classes (or other similar programming elements). We must also keep in mind that programs consisting of a single class (and therefore of a single file), are usually sample programs (like the one we have just presented). In the real-world, Java programs are frequently composed of several classes, each declared in its own file. Each class has a visibility that determines its usability by other classes. The HelloWorld class has been declared **publicly accessible** (the freest degree of accessibility) using the `public` modifier declaration. In Java, a modifier characterizes a class, just as in a natural language an adjective can characterize a noun. In this case, it can therefore be said that the `HelloWorld` class is public. This topic will also be dealt with in detail in the next chapters.

**Line 2:**

```
2  {
```

This open brace indicates the beginning of the `HelloWorld` class, which will close on line 7 with a closed brace. The block of code included in these two braces defines the `HelloWorld` class.

**Line 3:**

```
3      public static void main(String args[])
```

This line should be memorized immediately since it must be defined in every Java application. This is the declaration of the `main()` method. In Java, the term "method" is synonymous with "action" (methods will be discussed in detail in the next chapter). In particular, the `main()` method defines the starting point for the execution of each program. The first instruction that will then be executed at runtime by the program, will be the one that the JVM will find immediately after opening the block of code that defines this method.

In addition to the word `main`, line 3 contains other words which we will study in detail in the next chapters. Unfortunately, as already stated, when you start to study an object-oriented language like Java, it is impossible to open a discussion without opening many others. For now, the reader will have to settle for the following table:

| Word | Explanation |
|---|---|
| `public` | This is a **method modifier**. Modifiers are used in Java as adjectives are used in human languages. If you place a modifier before the declaration of a Java element (a method, a class, etc.) this will change its properties (depending on the meaning of the modifier). In this case, `public` represents an *access specifier* that actually makes the method accessible, even outside the class in which it has been defined. |
| `static` | This is another **method modifier**. We can mark a Java element with multiple modifiers. The definition of `static` is quite complex. For now, it must suffice that this modifier is essential for the definition of the `main()` method. |

| void | It is the **method return type**, which is the type of data that this method must return as output. The word "void" should be interpreted as "empty", and this implies that this method does not return any type of value. The `main()` method must always have `void` as return type. |
|---|---|
| main | This is the **name** of the method, also called the **identifier** of the method. |
| (String args[]) | To the right of the identifier of a method, we always define a pair of round brackets that optionally encloses a **list of parameters** (also called **method arguments**) that represent the input of the method. The `main()` method always requires an array of type `String` as a parameter (there will be an entire section dedicated to arrays in the third chapter). Note that `args` is the identifier of this array and is the only word that can be changed in the definition of the `main()` method, even if the word `args` is always used by convention. |

**Line 4:**

```
4        {
```

This brace indicates the beginning of the `main()` method that will end at line 6 with a closed brace. The block of code between these two braces defines the method.

**Line 5:**

```
5            System.out.println("Hello World!");
```

This command will print the string "Hello World!". Since we are introducing topics for which the reader is not yet ready, we will postpone a detailed explanation of this command to later chapters. For now, it is sufficient to say that we are invoking a method called `println()` belonging to the standard Java library, passing the string to be printed to it as a parameter. This method takes the string "Hello World" parameter and prints it on the screen.

**Line 6:**

```
6        }
```

This closed brace closes the last one opened, that is, it closes the block of code that defines the `main()` method.

**Line 7:**

```
7 }
```

**19**

This brace closes the block of code that defines the `HelloWorld` class. Note that all of the pairs of brackets have been aligned intentionally.

## 1.4.2 Compiling and Running the HelloWorld Program

Once the code has been written using Notepad, we have to save our file in a folder. You can name this folder for example **java**, and save it in the root folder **C:\**, but you can call this folder whatever you like and save it wherever you want. It is advisable to have a name that does not contain spaces in order to avoid unnecessary complications. So, a folder like **C:\java** would be preferable.

 **Please pay attention when saving the file, since Notepad is a generic text editor, not an editor for Java, so it tends to save files with the .txt extension. So, if we try to save the file with the name HelloWorld.java, Notepad will save the HelloWorld.java.txt file, and this is not what we want. To avoid this behavior, you must include the file name (which we must remember is HelloWorld.java) between quotes in this way "HelloWorld.java". Alternatively, on the save screen, you can select the value All files (*) in the Save as field, located just below the text field where you can write the file name.**

At this point, we can open a command prompt and look inside our folder. After making sure that the **HelloWorld.java** file is placed in the folder (use the `dir` command), we can move on to the compilation phase.

If we run the command:

```
javac HelloWorld.java
```

we're passing our source file (**HelloWorld.java**) as input to the compiler (**javac**) provided by the JDK. If, at the end of the compilation, there is no error message displayed, it means that the compilation was successful.

Then we can see that a file named **HelloWorld.class** has been created in our folder. This is precisely the source file translated into bytecode, ready to be interpreted by the JVM.

So if we run the command:

```
java HelloWorld
```

our program, if no exceptions are raised by the JVM, will be sent for execution, printing the long-awaited message:

```
Hello World!
```

### 1.4.3 Our Interaction with the Computer

Here are the steps we have taken to interact with the computer:

1. We asked the operating system to open the Notepad application by clicking on the corresponding icon with the mouse.

2. We wrote our source code within the Notepad graphical interface using the keyboard.

3. We saved the file on our hard disk (auxiliary memory), in a specific folder (**C:\java**).

4. We opened a session of the "command prompt" program running the **CMD** command from the **Start** menu, then we moved to the folder containing the file just saved.

5. Then we compiled our file by running the **javac** application contained in the JDK bin folder, by running the command "javac HelloWorld.java" directly on the command prompt interface.

6. So, the compiler program has been loaded into the main memory (RAM) along with its input (the **HelloWorld.java** source file).

7. The compiler has executed its instructions thanks to the processor (CPU) and produced, as output, the translation of the source code in bytecode, saving it in a **HelloWorld.class** file.

8. We then ran the interpreter provided by the Java Virtual Machine with the **java** command contained in the JDK **bin** folder, by writing the "java HelloWorld" command directly on the command prompt interface.

9. The JVM was loaded into the main memory (RAM) along with its input (the **HelloWorld.class** source file).

10. The Java interpreter translated the Java instructions into machine language that is understandable to the processor, and then the string "Hello World!" was printed.

## 1.5 Problems That Can Occur During the Compilation and Execution Phases

Usually, in the early days, newbie Java programmers often receive seemingly mysterious messages from the compiler and the Java interpreter. Do not be discouraged! You must be patient and learn to read the messages that are returned. Initially, it may seem difficult but after a short time you'll realize that the mistakes you make are often the same. Knowing how to read the compiler errors will make you a better programmer.

## 1.5.1 Problems That Can Occur During the Compilation Phase

```
"javac" javac is not recognized as an internal or external command.
```

In this case, it is not the compiler that is reporting a problem to us, but the operating system that does not recognize the **javac** command that should run the JDK compiler. Therefore, the latter has not been installed correctly. In this case, it is likely that the PATH environment variable has not been correctly set (see Appendix B).

```
HelloWorld.java:1: error: class Helloworld is public, should be
declared in a file named Helloworld.java
public class Helloworld {
       ^
1 error
```

In this case, we called the file HelloWorld while the class has been called Helloworld (note the lowercase "w"). The compiler is not clever enough to understand that we did not do it voluntarily.

```
HelloWorld.java:3: error: cannot find symbol
        System.out.printl();
                   ^
  symbol:   method printl()
  location: variable out of type PrintStream
1 error
```

If we receive this message, we know that we wrote printl instead of println. The compiler cannot realize by itself that it was simply a typo, and then told us that the printl() method was not found. It is essential to understand the error messages of the compiler, keeping in mind however, that there are limits to the clarity of these messages. The compiler does not always report the problem to us correctly:

```
HelloWorld.java:1: error: class, interface, or enum expected
public Class HelloWorld {
       ^
HelloWorld.java:2: error: class,
interface, or enum expected
    public static void main(String args[]) {
                  ^
HelloWorld.java:4: error: class,
interface, or enum expected
    }
    ^
3 errors
```

In this case, it is not true that there are three errors. In fact, there is only one error: we wrote the word "class" with a capital letter and then the JVM has explicitly requested a class declaration (or interface or enum, concepts that we will clarify later). Remember, "Class" is not the same as "class" in Java.

```
HelloWorld.java:3: error: ';' expected
        System.out.println()
                            ^
1 error
```

In this case, the compiler has immediately understood that we have forgotten the semicolon that is used to conclude every instruction. Unfortunately, our compiler will not always be that precise. In some cases, if we forget a semicolon, or worse, if we forget to close a block of code with a brace, the compiler may report the existence of non-existent errors in successive lines of code.

### 1.5.2 Problems That Can Occur During the Execution Phase

> In this phase, so-called "exceptions" are usually raised by the JVM. The ninth chapter is dedicated to exceptions and related concepts.

```
Error: Main method not found in class HelloWorld, please define the main method as:
    public static void main(String[] args)
```

If we receive this message once the HelloWorld program has been launched, we have probably incorrectly defined the main() method. We probably forgot to declare it static or public, or we mistyped the list of arguments (which must be String args[]) or maybe we did not call the method "main".

```
Error: could not find or load main class
  HelloWorld.class
Caused by: java.lang.ClassNotFoundException: HelloWorld.class
```

In this case we tried to run the command:

"Java HelloWorld.class" instead of "java HelloWorld".

# 1.6 Other Development Environments

Up to now, we have seen how to interact with the command line to invoke the compiler with the **javac** command, and the interpreter with the java command. To write our code, we used a simple text editor such as Notepad. We consider it important to understand how low-level

Java works, and we can continue to study the entire book using these tools, but it is objectively awkward to work with two different windows.

When we start programming seriously, we will probably use an IDE like Netbeans or Eclipse. These fantastic tools, however, are not recommended for those who are just starting to code. Their complexity can distract from the real goal, namely that of studying Java. If we also need to learn how to use the IDE, it may distract us from focusing on the language. Also, using an IDE for the small programs that we will initially write, does not seem appropriate. Finally, the comforts offered by an IDE such as auto-completion of the code or code suggestions, can cause dependence and laziness! It wouldn't be difficult to meet people who completely lack some basic concepts, even though they have been programming with these instruments for years.

So, if you are a newbie, we suggest not using an IDE immediately. In the fifth chapter, we will introduce other development environments including IDEs, explaining how to start using them. From the fifth chapter onwards, it should be easier to start working with IDEs, because you should already have some confidence with the language.

> **Further, in the same chapter, we'll introduce other tools to accelerate the way we write code, like JShell (introduced with Java 9) and the option to launch the single-file programs using only the source-code file, skipping the compilation step (introduced with Java 11).**

Of course, you may disagree and choose to ignore our suggestion to postpone the use of an IDE. In that case, at least try not to forget what your main goal is.

I've created an open source Java editor designed for those who start programming: **EJE (Everyone's Java Editor)**. It is not an IDE, but a simple editor that was created not for writing text files but to code in Java. It offers some smart features compared to a generic text editor. Among its features are the coloring of Java syntax, and text completion for some expressions. Above all, it is possible to compile and execute files, by pressing simple buttons, without having to move to a command prompt and edit boring commands. EJE is a really simple program, and there is no need to study it. You can download if for free at **http://www.claudiodesio.com** and **http://sourceforge.net/projects/eje**.

Conclusion: if you are already familiar with integrated development environments (IDEs) then you may also choose to use Netbeans or Eclipse. If you are starting to program just now, or in any case you want to try to focus only on the study of Java, our suggestion is to use EJE for the first few times, then move on to an IDE after the fifth chapter.

# Summary

We call **hardware** the physical part of the computer. Some hardware components collect **inputs** from the outside (mouse, keyboard, etc.), others provide **outputs** (monitor, printer, etc.), and other components are not used directly by the computer user (motherboard, processor, memory, etc.). The **processor** (CPU) performs mathematical operations and manages the data movements in the memory. The **memory** is divided into **main memory** (RAM memory) where the programs are loaded (with their data) during their execution, and **auxiliary memory** (usually hard drives) that, unlike the main memory, survives after the computer has been shut down.

**Software** is the term we use to refer to programs that run on a computer. The **operating system** is a program that manages a computer in its entirety and also allows for the installation and execution of other programs. A **programming language** always has a vocabulary and a set of rules. A processor cannot interpret a programming language because it is capable of using two symbols only (0 and 1) and a particular **machine language** that uses instructions written with these two symbols. To program we must then write the source code with the programming language in text files, and then translate it into machine language using a software such as a compiler or an interpreter. A **compiler** translates the instructions written in the programming language, into machine language instructions creating executable **binary files**. An **interpreter**, on the other hand, translates the instructions contained in the source code into instructions of machine code on the fly during the runtime. The term "Java" is used both to refer to the programming language, and to the technology generated by it (which branches off into many sub-technologies). Its main features are robustness, standardization, syntax, power and, above all, **platform independence**.

Java is a language both compiled and interpreted. Compiling, however, does not create files containing instructions in machine language, but files containing instructions written in a language similar to the machine language called **bytecode**. The Java interpreter defined within the Java Virtual Machine (JVM) is able to interpret the bytecode with excellent proficiency.

The **Java Development Kit (JDK)** is the official development environment for Java. With a simple text editor such as Notepad, and the basic knowledge of the command prompt, it allows us to program in Java. The steps to be taken to write and run a program are always fixed: write the code, save it, compile it and run the program.

A Java program is written using the **class** concept, which contains all the operating code of the program. Each class must be written in its own **source file** (with suffix .java) and must have exactly the same name as the file. A file to be executed must contain a method called main, which is the starting point of a Java program. The compilation process will create a corresponding file with the extension **.class** that will contain the bytecode. This file can be passed as input to any Java Virtual Machine of any hardware-software platform to be executed. It is particularly important to know how to interpret compiler **error messages**, and those launched by the JVM during program execution. It is not recommended for beginners to start programming directly with an **IDE** so that the focus must be only on the study of the language. It is advisable to postpone the use of an IDE for as long as possible (at least until studying the fifth chapter) in order not to be overwhelmed by the complexity of the IDE itself. For beginners, I've expressly created EJE, a user-friendly editor with basic functionalities that simplify the Java coding.

> Exercises, source code, appendices and other resources are available at http://www.javaforaliens.com.
> Bear in mind that the exercises are an integral part of the text and have only been outsourced in order to minimize the number of pages and consequently the cost of this book. In the exercises, you will modify and create new code, confirm your knowledge, and above all learn new things. It can seem strange but understanding the theory perfectly does not automatically imply that you will be able to program correctly. It is surprising how many difficulties you can find while coding, even when your ideas seem very clear. Without practice, there is no Java programming.

## Chapter Goals

**Have the following goals been achieved?**

| Goal | Achieved | Achievement Date |
|---|:---:|:---:|
| Know some basic computer concepts (Unit 1.1) | O | |
| Know how to define the Java programming language and its features (Unit 1.2) | O | |
| Be able to interact with the development environment: the Java Development Kit (Units 1.3, 1.4, 1.5) | O | |
| Know how to type, compile and run a simple application (Units 1.3, 1.4, 1.5) | O | |
| Choose a development environment (Unit 1.6) | O | |

# 2

# Key Components of a Java Program

**Goals:**

At the end of this chapter the reader should:

✔ Understand what it means to develop a program in Java, what the processes and the paradigms of programming are (Unit 2.1).

✔ Know how to define the concepts of class, object, variable, method and constructor (Units 2.2, 2.3, 2.4, 2.5).

✔ Know how to declare a class (Unit 2.2).

✔ Know how to create objects from a class (Unit 2.2).

✔ Know how to use public members of an object using the dot operator (Units 2.2, 2.3, 2.4).

✔ Know how to declare and invoke a method (Unit 2.3).

✔ Know how to declare a variable and assign it a value (Unit 2.4).

✔ Know how to define and use the different types of variables (instance variables, local variables and formal parameters) (Unit 2.4).

✔ Know how to declare and invoke a constructor (Unit 2.5).

✔ Know what a default constructor is (Unit 2.5).

✔ Know how to define a class belonging to a package and be able to import classes from other packages (Unit 2.6).

✔ Have a basic definition of all the other fundamental components of the Java programming that we will study in the next chapters (Unit 2.7).

In this chapter we start studying the Java language. We will familiarize ourselves with the basic concepts that are fundamental to understanding the language that we will study, both theoretically and practically. This means that we'll understand what to write in our programs.
Here is a list of fundamental concepts that we will study in this chapter:

- Class

- Object

- Variable

- Method

- Constructor

- Package

There are other important components of the Java programming, such as interfaces, annotations, nested classes, enumerations, packages and modules. It was decided to avoid introducing these concepts that are not required at this moment in time, in order to start coding earlier. These concepts will be presented later in the book, when the reader is ready to appreciate their use.
Also, in this chapter, we will not take anything for granted and therefore even the reader who has never written a line of code will be ready for starting Java programming. On the other hand, readers who have experience with functional programming will find huge differences with the basic concepts of object orientation. The advice for them is not to get too attached to what they already know. It is useless, for example, to force a class to play the role that could have a function in functional programming. Better to pretend to start from scratch and not to look for shortcuts that could lead to only a partial learning of the topics.

## 2.1 What It Means to Create a Java Program

In the previous chapter, we approached Java code by creating a very simple first program. Indeed, the example of the `HelloWorld` program has been more useful from the point of view of becoming familiar with the development environment than with the code. In fact, the code has only been partially explained. It was also a program that did not have the right characteristics: it consisted of a single class with a `main()` method that directly printed a string on the screen. Rather, writing a program in Java means creating different files (each usually containing only one class). We can use less than ten classes, but also tens, hundreds or even thousands if the project is large. The classes will not be isolated and will work together to solve problems and each one should have a specific role. Among these classes, there will be only one that will contain the main() method. This is a special class dedicated to working as the application's starting point. It will usually not execute instructions directly (like the HelloWorld class of the previous chapter that printed a string on the screen) but will set up objects within the main() method, which will collaborate to execute the instructions of the methods they are composed of. Each class will declare variables, methods and constructors within them. The methods will contain the instructions to be executed. Finally, the classes will be grouped into folders called *packages*, to be organized with a logical criterion. That's how a Java program works.

But before we study the basic components of a Java program, we need to understand some key programming concepts.

## 2.1.1 Programming and paradigms

Software development is a creative process that leads to the creation of a program that starts from an idea. This process consists of a series of activities to be carried out, but there is no standard process that is perfect for any programming situation. Therefore, these activities change in type, order of execution and number, depending on the program to be created. Moreover, when it comes to these activities, only some concern programming. The big mistake that inexperienced programmers often make, is to think that in order to program, it's enough to know how to program. Knowing how to program will allow us to solve the exercises you will find in the first part of this book, but certainly will not be enough to create a real program starting from scratch. To turn an idea into a program, we need to solve conceptual, mathematical, architectural, functional and, sometimes, philosophical problems. We could also be very good at solving all of these problems with programming only, but it is very likely that the quality of the code and the timing will not be satisfying.

We will start discussing the processes (sometimes wrongly called methodologies), from the fifth chapter onwards. They always define preliminary and preparatory phases to the programming. If we want to represent a minimal process, as an example, we could say that it is composed of the following activities, at least:

1. understanding all the functionalities that the application must implement (i.e. understand *what* our program must do);

2. finding strategies to create the program in the best possible way (understand *how* to implement our program);

3. implementing the hypothesized solutions (i.e. program) with the code;

4. testing the correct execution of our program and fixing all the issues.

These seem to us to be the indispensable steps that must be performed to develop any type of software. For each of these steps, there are many techniques that allow we to arrive at a solution; we will see some of them later. However, for now we must keep in mind that programming is just a piece of the puzzle. Can you imagine being able to write a program without knowing what to do (so skipping step 1 and consequently step 2)? Well, it actually happens so many times, and the results are always disastrous.

So, assuming that we have correctly performed step 1 and that all the features to be implemented are clear to us, how do we know the best way to implement them?

Each programming language offers certain tools for programming. On the basis of these tools, it is possible to use a certain programming paradigm, that is, to use processes that lead to the creation of programs designed with certain characteristics. In other words, a programming paradigm allows we to create a program by performing well-defined activities, which will make sure that our software can enjoy the advantages offered by the paradigm itself. But what are the existing paradigms? There are several but, for now, we will focus on the object-oriented paradigm.

## 2.1.2 Object-Oriented Programming (OOP)

Java was born with the intent of being an **object-oriented language**, which is a language that uses the **object-oriented paradigm**. It can also be said that Java supports **object-oriented programming** (hence the acronym **OOP**). In recent years, evolution has allowed Java to support other programming paradigms but, for now, our goal is to understand how object-oriented programming works.

Object-oriented programming is a programming style based on concepts inspired by the real world. Our aim, therefore, is to understand these concepts well, and then to be able to use them *in a natural way* within a program. Although the basic concepts of class and object will be explained in detail in the next chapter, we can already introduce them by taking a cue from the real world. For example, let's start with the first object you see in front of you: a book. This book has a title ("Java for Aliens"), an author ("Claudio De Sio Cesari") and you will surely be able to list other features of this book by yourself, the price, the number of pages and so on. For each of these characteristics, you would also know how to assign a precise value. But "Java for Aliens" is just one of many books that exist. If you close your eyes and think about what a book is, you do not think about "Java for Aliens" or another particular book but, simply, an object that has pages to read. The difference between "Java for Aliens" and your book idea is that the latter does not exist in the real world: the idea cannot be read! It is only an abstraction, an idealization of many objects that exist in the real world: books. An idea does not exist in the real world, we cannot touch it with our hands. In our mind, a book certainly has a number of pages but does not have a specific number of pages. Instead "Java for Aliens" is a concrete book object with a precise number of pages. Now we already understand the two concepts underlying the OOP: the class and the object. The idea of the book we have in our mind can be represented in Java with a Book class. A class is just a concept, an abstraction, an idea, and we only need to define how the real objects will be made. So, we can create concrete book objects within our programs starting with the Book class model.

Just as an idea of a book represents an abstraction of a series of book objects that exist in the real-world in Java, a class represents an abstraction (which acts as a model) for book objects that can be created and used in our programs. So, in Java we can define the Book class and use it as a model to create specific objects like the javaForAliens book. Let us now try to go into more detail.

## 2.2 The Basics of Object-Oriented Programming: Classes and Objects

An object-oriented language is a language that supports the concepts of class and object. These two concepts are closely related to each other. If we wanted to formally define these two concepts, we should assert:

- ▇▇ definition 1:
    - ▇▇ a **class** is an abstraction indicating a set of objects that share the same characteristics and functionalities;

- ▇▇ definition 2:
    - ▇▇ an **object** is an instance (that is, a physical creation) of a class.

Let's try to understand these two definitions better. Every concept that is part of the Object Orientation Theory exists in the real world. This theory was born precisely to satisfy the human need to interact with software in a more natural way (see section 6.1). It will therefore be only a matter of associating the right idea with the new term. Let's move on to a practical example:

```
public class Point
{
    public int x;
    public int y;
}
```

With Java, we can create code to abstract any concept of the real world. We have just defined a Point class. Clearly, the aim of this class is to define the concept of a (two-dimensional) point by defining its coordinates on a Cartesian plane. This code is intuitive enough to be understood even without much explanation. The x and y coordinates were abstracted by two attributes (called usually variables) declared as integer type (int). This means that they can only assume values of an integer type. For example, it is possible to assign the value 5 to the variable x, but not the value abc or the value 5.2, since these are not integers. The variables x and y have also been declared public, which means that they could also be used by other classes other than the Point class. We can imagine that this class is a part of a Java application, maybe a drawing application. In the previous chapter, we saw that we can save this listing in a file called **Point.java** and compile it using the command:

```
javac Point.java
```

thus, obtaining the **Point.class** file. This time, however, we cannot send it running via the command:

```
java Point
```

in fact, we would get the following error message:

```
Error: Main method not found in class Point, please define the main method as:
    public static void main(String[] args)
or a JavaFX application class must extend javafx.application.Application
```

In this class, the main() method is absent (see the previous chapter), but we defined it as the starting point for the execution of each Java application and this would make the class a *special class*. If we execute the **java Point** command, the JVM tries to find this method to execute it, but since it's not present in the class, the command ends the execution instantly. But would we really want a class called "Point" that can be started to execute some code? Does the *idea of a point on a Cartesian plane* perform something in the real world? It does not seem a good idea to create a class called Point that represents the starting point of an application because, in the real world, the idea of a point does not at all seem to be an entity that performs activities.

This is absolutely in line with the class definition (def. 1). In fact, if we wanted to find, in the real world, a synonym of class, we would think of terms like idea, abstraction, concept, model or definition. Therefore, defining a Point class with Java code implies that we have only defined the concept of point within our future program, according to our interpretation and within the context in which the program will work (for example a drawing program). With the code written so far, we have not yet defined any real point (for example the one with coordinates  x = 5  and  y = 6).

> So, as in the real world, if there are no concrete points (but only the definition of a point), nothing to do with a point can occur. It's also obvious that, in the Java code, the Point class should not be executable!

It is therefore necessary to define the point objects: the physical creations made starting from the definition given by the class.

In the context of object-oriented programming, a class has the task of defining the structure of the objects that will be instantiated from it. Instantiating, as we have already stated, is the object-oriented term that is used instead of physically creating, and the result of an instantiation is just an object.

For example, we will set up objects from the Point class by creating another class that contains a main() method that we will call PointObjectsTest:

```
1  public class PointObjectsTest
2  {
3      public static void main(String args[])
4      {
5          Point point1;
6          point1 = new Point();
7          point1.x = 2;
8          point1.y = 6;
9          Point point2 = new Point();
10         point2.x = 0;
11         point2.y = 1;
12         System.out.println(point1.x);
13         System.out.println(point1.y);
14         System.out.println(point2.x);
15         System.out.println(point2.y);
16     }
17 }
```

Let's analyze the PointObjectsTest class. We assume that it is clear that line 1 has declared the public class PointObjectsTest, which ends at line 17, and that line 3 has declared the main() method ending at line 16. It should be equally clear that the braces delimit the class and method structures, and for this reason they have been aligned (indented) appropriately, to make the link between them explicit.

A **line of code** can contain one or more instructions. Within the main() method, we find the lines of code to be executed, from line 5 to line 15. We distinguish two types of instructions:

▪▪ The **statement** is a generic instruction. An example of a statement is calling a method such as System.out.println(). Another example of a statement is, for example, a **declaration**, which is an instruction that declares a programming element (a variable, a method, etc.). The declarations can end either with a semicolon (for example when declaring a variable), or with a block of code consisting of curly braces (for example when declaring a class or method).

■■ The **expression** instruction, that is, a statement that after being executed returns a value. An example would be that of a call to a method that returns a value, or an arithmetic expression (we'll see several examples later).

The instruction terminators (code block and semi-colon) can also be used in isolation, creating empty instructions. For example, it is permissible (though useless) to write the following in a method code:

```
        ;
;;;;;;;;;
{}
{} {} {}
{{{}}}
```

In line 5, we find the first instruction to execute: the declaration of an object of type Point that is called point1:

```
5           Point point1;
```

Declaring an object does not mean creating it, but only defining its name and associating it with a type. The syntax for declaring an object requires that the name of the object (in this case point1) must be preceded by the declaration of its type (the class of type Point).

At line 6 we find the syntax that creates the point1 object of the Point class:

```
6           point1 = new Point();
```

In this line of code, there are two instructions. In fact, with the new Point() instruction, the object is instantiated while the = operator assigns the object created to the "name" point1. So, the new keyword instantiates the Point class, and to this instance the point1 name is assigned. In this line of code there are two instructions: an assignment (which is a statement), and an expression (which follows the symbol =) new Point(). This expression instantiates the object, while the = operator assigns the object created to the "name" point1.

From line 6 onwards, we can then use the point1 object. In lines 7 and 8, we assign the integer values 2 and 6 to the x and y coordinates of point1:

```
7           point1.x = 2;
8           point1.y = 6;
```

Taking advantage of the definition provided by the Point class, we have created a Point object that is identified by the name point1. Note the use of the **dot operator** in order to access the variables x and y. The instruction point1.x = 2, for example, assigns the integer value 2 to the x variable of the point1 object. Note how the variables x and y have been declared in the Point class, but values are assigned for the point1 object, and therefore belong to the point1 object. The Point class was useful only as a template to instantiate point1. Also, note that, within the Point class, the variables x and y were declared as integer type (int).

Summarizing, we first declared the object at line 5, we instantiated it at line 6, and used it (by setting its variables) at lines 7 and 8.

At line 9 then, we declared and instantiated with another line of code, another object from the Point class, calling it point2:

```
9          Point point2 = new Point();
```

Technically, there were three instructions at line 9: declaration of the point2 object, instance of a Point object, and assignment of the newly created object to point2.

We then set the coordinates of the latter to 0 and 1:

```
10         point2.x = 0;
11         point2.y = 1;
```

We have finally printed the coordinates of both points:

```
12         System.out.println(point1.x);
13         System.out.println(point1.y);
14         System.out.println(point2.x);
15         System.out.println(point2.y);
```

The definitions of classes and objects should be a little clearer: the class has served to define how objects will be made. The object represents a physical realization of the class. In this example, we instantiated two different objects from the same class. Both of these objects are points, but evidently, they are different points (they are in different positions on the Cartesian plane).

> **This reasoning, after all, is already familiar to everyone because it derives from the real world around us. The human being, to overcome the complexity of reality, groups objects into classes. For example, in our mind there is a model defined by the Person class even if, in the real world, there are billions of objects of the Person type, each of which has unique characteristics.**

## 2.2.1 About the Point Class

In the previous example, we commented on the definition of two classes. For the first (the Point class), we emphasized the characteristic of representing data. This class is to be considered a structural part of the application and therefore plays an essential role in the compilation.

The `Point` class does not have an active role in the execution of the application. In fact, it is the objects instantiated by it that influence the workflow of the program.

This can be defined as the standard case. In an object-oriented application, a class should just define the common structure of a set of objects, and it should never "hold" neither variables nor methods, but only declare them. In fact, the `Point` class does not hold the variables x and y but, declaring the two variables, defines the objects that will be instantiated as owners of those variables. Note that, within the scope of the execution of the program, there is never an instruction within the code such as:

```
Point.x
```

that is

```
ClassName.variableName
```

(which anyway would produce an error in compilation) but instead:

```
point1.x
```

that is

```
objectName.variableName
```

> **The operator "." means "belonging". Therefore, the objects hold the variables declared in the class (which we will call "instance variables", that is "object variables"). In fact, the two instantiated objects had different values for x and y, which means that each of the two objects point1 and point2 has its variable x and its variable y. The variables of point1 are absolutely independent from the variables of point2. Since the classes do not have members (variables and methods), they do not execute code and do not play a role in the execution of a program. We have seen that the objects are the absolute protagonists within the scope of the execution. In practice, the relationship between class and object is exactly the same as that between idea and concrete object in the real world.**

It is said that an object in a certain instant is characterized by its *state*. The **state of an object** is defined by the value of its instance variables. This terminology will be useful in the next chapters.

## 2.2.2 About the `PointObjectsTest` Class

As often happens when you approach Java and just defined a new rule, immediately an exception can be noted (a case of the exception confirming the rule?). We are focusing our attention on the `PointObjectsTest` class. It is a class that executes content code only within the `main()` method which, given what has been said, is assumed by default as the starting point of a Java application. In fact, somehow, the creators of Java had to establish a way to start running a program. The choice was made based on a practical and historical question: an application written in C or C++ has, as its default starting point, a so-called "main function": a function that is named `main()`. In Java, main functions do not exist, but there are methods, and in particular static methods, that is methods declared with the `static` modifier. This modifier will be covered in detail in the sixth chapter. For now, let's just know that a declared static member belongs to the class and that all objects instantiated by it will share the same static members.

In conclusion, since the `PointObjectsTest` class contains the `main()` method, it can execute some code.

> In every Java application, there must be a class that contains the `main()` method. This class should have the name of the application itself, abstracting the workflow that needs to be performed. In theory, therefore, the class containing the `main()` method should not contain other members. Usually in a real program, the `main()` method creates objects that take care of executing instructions instead of executing instructions itself.

## 2.2.3 About Objects (Again)

The previous example was used for its simplicity. It is, in fact, mathematical to think of a point on the Cartesian plane as formed by two coordinates called x and y. But there are concepts in the real world whose abstraction is not so simple.

For example, if we want to define the idea (abstraction) of a car, we should talk about the characteristics and functionalities common to each car. But, if we compare the idea (i.e. the class) of a car that would define a car expert as that of a person who does not even have a driving license, there would be significant differences. The latter could define a car as "a transport with four wheels and a motor", but the car expert could give a much more detailed alternative definition by defining features such as insurance, chassis, model, tires, etc. Both of these definitions can be introduced into programming in the form of classes.

For convenience, we will think as if we did not have a driving license, creating a class that declares as attribute an integer called `wheelsNumber` initialized to 4 (assuming all cars have 4 wheels). Furthermore, we will define another integer variable `engineCapacity` and a method that we can call `move()`.

> **In the following sections, methods will be defined in detail. For now, we just need to know that the method should define a functionality that must have a class.**

```java
public class Car
{
    public int wheelsNumber = 4;
    public int engineCapacity; // what's the value?
    public void move()
    {
        // method implementation omitted
    }
}
```

> **The code written after two slashes (as in the `move()` method), is a comment and will not be taken into account by the compiler. The Java comments will be explained in more detail in the next chapter.**

Each car has (usually) 4 wheels, moves and has an engine capacity (the value of which is not definable a priori). A Ferrari California and a Fiat 500 both have 4 wheels, one engine capacity and they move, even if they do so in a different way. A Ferrari California and a Fiat 500 should be considered objects of the `Car` class and, in the real-world, they would exist as concrete objects. In the following class, two objects of the `Car` class are created, they are appropriately set, and the `move()` method will be invoked for both objects.

```java
public class CarObjectsTest
{
    public static void main(String args[])
    {
        Car fiat500;
        fiat500 = new Car();
        fiat500.engineCapacity = 900;
        fiat500.move();
        Car ferrariCalifornia = new Car();
        ferrariCalifornia.engineCapacity = 4300;
        ferrariCalifornia.move();
    }
}
```

It should be clear enough that the two objects will both move, but at different speeds.

## 2.3 Java Methods

When we talk about the characteristics of a class, we refer to the data (variables and constants) while, with the term functionalities of a class, we refer to the methods. In fact, we had already mentioned the fact that the term method is synonymous with action. So, if a program has to execute some instructions, it must contain methods. For example, the main() method, by default, is the starting point of every Java application. A class without the main() method like the Point class, cannot be executed but only instantiated within a method of another class (in the previous example in the main() method of the PointObjectsTest class).

The concept of method is therefore also at the basis of object-oriented programming. Without methods, objects cannot communicate with each other and programs cannot perform actions. In addition, the methods make the programs more readable and easier to maintain, avoid duplication and facilitate code reuse, and the development is faster and more stable.

> **The programmer who approaches Java after experiences in the field of functional programming, often tends to compare the concept of *function* with the concept of *method*. Although similar in form and substance, it will be necessary to bear in mind that a method has a different role with respect to a function. In fact, in functional programming, the concept of function is the basis whereas, in object-oriented programming, the concepts of class and object are the basis. All functional programs have a *main function* and a number of other functions. In fact, these functions have the task of solving certain sub-problems generated by a *top-down analysis*, in order to solve the general problem. As we will see later, in object-oriented programming, sub-problems will be solved by the abstraction of classes and objects, which in turn will define methods. Therefore, although the methods and functions are substantially similar, they differ in their role within the relative programming paradigm.**

It's important to clearly distinguish two phases regarding the methods: declaration and invocation (i.e. definition and use).

### 2.3.1 Method Declaration

The declaration defines a method. The following is the syntax:

```
[modifiers] return_type method_identifier ([parameters]) {method_body}
```

Where it is:

- **modifiers**: Java keywords that can be used to modify the functionalities and characteristics of a method in some way. All modifiers are dealt with in depth in the next chapters. Examples of modifiers are `public` and `static`;

- **return type**: the type of data that a method can return after being called. This could coincide with either a primitive datatype like an `int`, or a complex type (an object) as a string (defined by the `String` class) or as a `Point` object. It is also possible to specify that a method does not return anything (`void`), as in the case of `main()`;

- **method identifier**: the name of the method;

- **parameters**: declarations of variables that can be passed to the method as input and, consequently, can be used in the body of the method during runtime. The number of parameters can be zero but also greater than one. If more than one parameter is declared, their declarations will be separated by commas;

- **method body**: a set of instructions that will be executed when the method is invoked.

> **The pair consisting of the method identifier and the parameter list is called the "signature" of the method.**

For example, a class called `Arithmetic` that declares a trivial method that adds two integer numbers, is presented below:

```
public class Arithmetic
{
    public int sum(int a, int b)
    {
        return (a + b);
    }
}
```

Note that the method presents the keyword `public` as a modifier. This is an access specifier (or access modifier) that we have already encountered in the class declaration. If the `sum()` method is declared `public`, it will become accessible by other classes. Precisely, the methods of other classes can, after instantiating an object of the `Arithmetic` class, invoke the `sum()` method on that object. There are also other access specifiers such as `private` around which we will deepen the discussion in the sixth chapter.

The return type is an `int`, which is an integer. This means that, when this method is invoked, it will return an integer type as output, that is, it will have, as a last instruction, a command (return) that will return an integer.

Moreover, this method declares, as a list of parameters, two integers (called a and b). The parameters of a method represent the input of the method. When this method is called, it will be necessary to pass two values of integer type as arguments.

Within the code block delimited by curly braces, the two parameters will be added together with the + operator and their sum will be returned as output via the return command. In the only instruction contained in the code block, there are two instructions: the sum of the two parameters and the return command. Note that the sum expression was surrounded by two round brackets. Although in this case they were not necessary for the correct execution of the method, we preferred to highlight that the sum would have been executed before the return instruction. The sum between two integers can only be an integer, so it is correct to declare the int type as the return type.

In conclusion, the declaration of a method defines a list of modifiers, a return type, a name (identifier), a list of parameters and a block of code that contains the instructions that will be executed when the method is called. The definition of a method, however, is part of the definition of a class which, as we have seen, does not execute code. In order to execute the instructions contained in a method, we must create an object of the class that declares it and invoke it as shown in the next section.

## 2.3.2 Calling (invoking) a Method

Here is another executable class (that is, containing the main() method) that instantiates an object from the Arithmetic class and calls the sum() method:

```
1 public class SumTest
2 {
3     public static void main(String args[])
4     {
5         Arithmetic obj = new Arithmetic();
6         int result = obj.sum(5, 6);
7         System.out.println(result);
8     }
9 }
```

Let's focus directly on the instructions of the main() method. In line 5, an object called obj of type Arithmetic is instantiated. At line 6 on obj, we call the sum() method that we have declared in the Arithmetic class. Note that the access to the sum() method has occurred using the *dot* operator, as we did with variables. Thus, all public members (attributes and methods) defined within a class will be accessible through an instance of the class itself that uses the dot operator. The syntax is as follows:

```
objectIdentifier.methodIdentifier();
```

and

```
objectIdentifier.attributeIdentifier();
```

The access to the method of an object causes the execution of the corresponding block of code. In this example, we defined an integer variable `result` that stored the result of the sum. If we had not done that, it would not make sense to call a method that returns a value since we could not use it in some way! Instead, after storing it in the `result` variable, we print its value on the screen, to verify the real execution of the sum during the runtime of the program. To do this, we had to pass the `result` variable as a parameter to the method we have already encountered in the previous chapter: `System.out.println()`.

> The `System.out.println(result)` **statement is also a call to a method. It is a method that we did not write but that exists in the huge class library that Java provides to us. Keeping in mind what we said about the methods, objects and the dot operator, we can guess that the** `println()` **method can take an input parameter and it does not return an output result. But we know that methods are called on objects, so** `System.out` **must be an object. In fact, it is, and represents the** *standard output of the system* **which, for the Windows operating system, coincides with the command prompt. That's why the call on this object of the** `println()` **method causes writing to the command prompt of the parameter that is passed to it as argument. Later in this book we will study the** `System.out` **object in more detail.**

Note that we could also have replaced lines 6 and 7 with the following:

```
System.out.println(obj.sum(5,6));
```

With this statement, we would have printed, on the fly, the return value of the call to the `sum()` method on the `Arithmetic` object, which is then the same value as the `result` variable.

There are also methods that do not have input parameters. For example, a (useless) method that always adds the same numbers and therefore always returns the same value such as the following:

```
public class FixedArithmetic
{
    public int sum()
    {
```

```
                return (5 + 6);
        }
}
```

or methods that do not return anything, and therefore declare void as return type, as the main() method does. In fact, the main() method is the starting point of the runtime of a Java application, so it does not have to return a result, since it is not explicitly called by another method. There are also methods that have neither input parameters nor output (void return type), such as a simple method that always displays the same message on the screen:

```
public class Greetings
{
    public void printGreetings()
    {
        System.out.println("Ciao!");
    }
}
```

The following is a trivial class that instantiates an object from the Greetings class and calls the printGreetings() method. As we can see, if the method has a void return type, we do not have to "catch" the result.

```
public class GreetingsTest
{
    public static void main(String args[])
    {
        Greetings object1 = new Greetings();
        object1.printGreetings();
    }
}
```

## 2.3.3 Varargs

It is also possible to use methods that declare, as a parameter list, the so-called variable arguments, more briefly known as varargs. In practice, it is possible to create methods that declare an undefined number of parameters of a certain type. The syntax is a bit special and uses three dots (such as suspensive dots), after the type declaration. For example, we can invoke the following method:

```
public class VariableArithmetic
{
    public void sum(int... integers)
    {
        //complex code omitted. . .
    }
}
```

in any of the following ways:

```
VariableArithmetic obj = new VariableArithmetic();
obj.sum();
obj.sum(1,2);
obj.sum(1,4,40,27,48,27,36,23,45,67,9,54,66,43);
obj.sum(1);
```

So, we can pass it from 0 to n arguments. Note that, for each method declaration, we can declare only one varargs parameter as the last argument. So, the following method declarations would not compile:

```
public void sum(int... integers, int... otherIntegers)
{
    //...
}
...
public void sum(int... integers, int otherInteger)
{
    //...
}
```

# 2.4 Variables in Java

In programming, a variable is a portion of memory in which a certain type of data is stored. We have, so far, met as a simple data type the type int, with which we have declared the variables x and y of the Point class. The types of Java will be explored in the next chapter.

Also, for the use of variables we can distinguish two phases: declaration and assignment. Assigning a value to a variable is an operation that can be repeated many times during program execution. The first assignment is often called initialization of the variable.

## 2.4.1 Variable Declaration

The syntax for declaring a variable is the following:

```
[modifiers] data_type variable_identifier [ = initialization];
```

where:

■■ **modifiers**: Java keywords that can be used to modify the functionality and characteristics of the variable in some way;

■■ **data type**: the data type of the variable;

■■ **variable identifier**: the name of the variable;

■■ **initialization**: default value with which a variable can be evaluated.

Below is a class that defines a rectangle in a superficial way:

```
public class Rectangle
{
    public final int SIDES_NUMBER = 4;
    public int height;
    public int base;
}
```

In this case, we have defined two int variables called height and base, and a constant SIDES_NUMBER. The final modifier (which will be discussed in detail in the seventh chapter), in fact makes a variable's value constant. This means that, if an instruction in our program tries to change the value of the constant, we will get a compile-time error.

It is also possible to define a comma-separated list of variables of the same type with a single instruction, as in the following example:

```
public class Rectangle
{
    public final int SIDES_NUMBER = 4;
    public int base, height;
}
```

In this case, we can see that the code is more compact, obtained avoiding duplications, but with less readability.

 The declaration of a variable is very important. The position of the declaration defines the scope, that is the visibility, and the life cycle of the variable itself. The variables share their life cycle with the block of code in which they are declared. In practice we could define three different types of variables, based on the positioning of the declaration: instance variables, local variables and parameters.

## 2.4.2 Instance Variable

A variable is called an instance variable (or even a member variable or an attribute) if it is declared in a class but outside a method.

> **However, it is not possible to define a variable outside a class.**

The variables defined in the Rectangle class are all instance variables. They share their life cycle with the object (instance) they belong to. When an object of type Rectangle class is instantiated, memory space is allocated for all of its instance variables that are initialized to their null values. In our case, the `height` and base variables will be initialized to the value 0 since they're integers. `SIDES_NUMBER`, on the other hand, is a constant explicitly initialized to 4 and its value cannot change. An instance variable will cease to exist when the object it belongs to will cease to exist.

### 2.4.3 Local Variables

A variable is called local (or stack, or automatic, or even temporary) if it is declared within the block of code of a method. It will cease to exist when the method ends its execution.

In the following example (obtained by modifying the `sum()` method of the `Arithmetic` class previously encountered), the variable z is a local variable:

```
public int sum(int x, int y)
{
    int z = x + y;
    return z;
}
```

A variable of this type, unlike an instance variable, will not be initialized to a null value when the object it belongs to is instantiated. Since local variables are not automatically initialized, we have to do it explicitly. In fact, the compiler could return an error message where there is the possibility that the variable is not initialized at runtime. Local variables share their life cycle with the block of code in which they are declared. For example, the z variable of the previous example is only visible within the `sum()` method.

We could also create blocks of code to declare variables that are only visible inside it. For example, we could write the following code (for purely educational purposes):

```
public int sum(int x, int y)
{
    int z;
    {
        int tmp = x + y;
        z = tmp;
    }
    int tmp = z;
    return tmp;
}
```

We can see how the variable tmp (highlighted in bold), declared in the code block, is visible only within the same block of code. In fact, we were also able to declare another local variable outside the code block with the same name. Note also that it would not be possible to declare it before the code block:

```
public int sum(int x, int y)
{
    int z;
    int tmp;
    {
        int tmp = x + y;
        z = tmp;
    }
    tmp = z;
    return tmp;
}
```

In fact, the previous code would have caused the following compile-time error:

```
error: variable tmp is already defined in method sum(int, int)
        int tmp = x + y;
            ^
1 error
```

in fact, the first declared `tmp` variable, would have been also visible in the code block defined immediately after. So, we could not declare again a variable with the same name in the code block.

> **In the next chapter we will see that we can define also other block of codes within the block of code of a method using *programming constructs* like `if` and `for`. The rule is: a local variable always shares its life cycle with the block of code in which is defined.**

## 2.4.4 Parameters

The variables declared within the round parentheses in a method declaration are called parameters or arguments of the method.

For example, in the following declaration of the `sum()` method two integer parameters x and y are declared:

```
public int sum(int x, int y)
{
    return (x + y);
}
```

The parameters of a method will be initialized when the method is called. In fact, to call the `sum()` method we will have to pass the values to the parameters, for example:

```
int result = arithmeticObject.sum(5, 6);
```

In particular, during the execution of the program, within the sum() method, the variable x will be 5, while y will be 6. We could also write equivalently:

```
int a = 5, b = 6;
int result = arithmeticObject.sum(a, b);
```

and get the same result. In fact, in Java, we can *pass parameters only by value*, which means that the variables a and b are not passed to the sum() method as arguments, but rather their values, which will be stored in the x and y parameters within the method.

It is important to underline that a parameter can also be considered a local variable of the method, being visible only within the method and sharing with it the life cycle. The main difference is only in the position of the declaration. A local variable could be declared at the end of the method, while a parameter is declared contextually to the method itself. There is no difference in the way these types of variables are handled in memory.

Furthermore, since they share their life cycle with the method in which they are declared, it makes no sense (and it is not possible) to mark a local variable with an access modifier like public.

> **The concept and the memory allocation mode of an instance variable differ so much from the concept and memory allocation modes of a local variable (or parameter) that it is possible, in a class, to give the same name to a local variable (or to a parameter) and to an instance variable. As we will see, this practice is widely used.**

## 2.5 Constructors

In Java, there are special methods that have special properties. Among these, there is the constructor method, which has the following characteristics:

**1.** has the same name as the class;

**2.** has no return type;

**3.** is called automatically (and only) whenever an object is instantiated;

**4.** exists always in every class.

Usually a constructor is defined for the purpose of initializing the instance variables.

## 2.5.1 Constructor Features

A constructor always has the same name as the class in which it is declared. Let us remember that it is also important to pay attention to capital and small letters.

The fact that it does not have a return type does not mean that the type of return is void but that does not declare any kind of return! It is also distinguished from ordinary methods because of this.

For example, the following is a class with an explicitly declared constructor:

```java
public class Point
{
    //constructor
    public Point()
    {
        System.out.println("Created a Point!");
    }
    public int x;
    public int y;
}
```

Note that the constructor code block will be executed each time an object is instantiated. Let's analyze, in more detail, the syntax that allows us to instantiate objects. For example:

```java
Point point1; //declaration
point1 = new Point();  //instantiation
```

which is equivalent to:

```java
Point point1 = new Point(); //declaration and instatiation
```

As mentioned earlier, it is the new keyword that formally instantiates the object. Therefore, this syntax would suffice to create an object:

```java
new Point();
```

In this way, however, the new object would not have a "name" (we will call it reference) and therefore would not be usable. Usually, when an object is instantiated, it is assigned a previously declared reference.

It is therefore evident that the last part of the instruction to be analyzed (Point()) should not be interpreted as class name with round brackets, but rather as a call to the constructor method. Anyway, the above-mentioned instruction is enough to make a program produce the following output:

```
Created a Point!
```

This is the only way to call a constructor. A constructor being defined without a return type cannot be considered an ordinary method and cannot be called in other ways.

In the previous example, the call to the constructor caused a sentence to be printed on the screen. Actually, the constructor is usually used to initialize the instance variables of an object. Being a method (albeit a special type) it can have a list of parameters. It is therefore possible to code the following constructor within the `Point` class:

```
public class Point
{
    public Point(int a, int b)
    {
        x = a;
        y = b;
    }
    public int x;
    public int y;
}
```

With this class, it will no longer be possible to instantiate objects with the usual syntax:

```
Point point1 = new Point();
```

In fact, we would get a compile error, since we would be trying to call a constructor that does not exist (the one without parameters).

The syntax to be used to instantiate an object instead, must be, for example, the following:

```
Point point1 = new Point(5,6);
```

We can also provide more than one constructor to a class, but with a different list of parameters list. For example, it will be possible to provide both constructors we saw in the `Point` class:

```
public class Point
{
    public int x;
    public int y;
    public Point()
    {
        // This constructor does nothing
    }
    public Point(int a, int b)
    {
        x = a;
        y = b;
    }
}
```

In this way we can instantiate objects from the `Point` class in two ways. Let's use the first constructor:

```
Point p = new Point();
```

Then we can use the second one:

```
Point p = new Point(12,14);
```

In the first case, the point p will have both the x and y coordinates that are equal to 0. Let us remember that the instance variables are automatically initialized to their null values. In the second case, x will be set to 12 and y will be set to 14.
Notice that the following line of code:

```
Point p = new Point(12,14);
```

is equivalent to the following:

```
Point point1 = new Point();
point1.x = 12;
point1.y = 14;
```

> **The possibility of creating more constructors in the same class is a manifestation of *polymorphism* (discussed in detail in the eighth chapter) which is called *overload*. This allows us to write multiple methods with the same name (but with a different parameter list). There are other rules to study but we will go into more detail in due course.**

## 2.5.2 Default Constructor

When we create an object using the new keyword, there is always a call to a constructor (for example, new Point()). Yet, prior to the previous section, we had never provided constructors to our classes, but as we have just said, we have called constructors whenever we have instantiated objects! In fact, Java has a very important feature that many ignore. Often the compiler automatically and transparently inserts instructions not entered by the programmer. In fact, if we try to compile a class without a constructor, the compiler will provide one implicitly. The inserted constructor does not contain commands that cause some visible consequence for the programmer. It is called default constructor and has no parameters. This justifies the fact that, up to now, we have never instantiated objects passing parameters to the constructor.
For example, if we write the Point class in the following way:

```
public class Point
{
    public int x;
```

```
        public int y;
}
```

At compile time, the compiler would add to it the default constructor:

```
public class Point
{
    public Point()
    {
        //In the default constructor
        //seems there are no instructions ...
    }
    public int x;
    public int y;
}
```

That's why up to now we've instantiated `Point` objects with the syntax:

```
Point p = new Point();
```

even without the explicit presence of constructors. If the default constructor did not exist, we would first have to learn the constructors and then the objects.

> **This is one of the features that led to Java being initially defined as a "simple language to learn". In fact, the fact that a constructor within the classes is implicitly inserted by the Java compiler allowed us to talk about object instances without necessarily having to explain a concept like the constructor first.**

Let's underline once more that the default constructor is inserted into a class by the compiler if, and only if, the programmer does not provide one explicitly. When the programmer supplies a constructor to a class, whether it is with or without parameters, the compiler will not insert the default constructor. This topic will be further explored in seventh chapter where we will discover other "phantom instructions".

> **A constructor without parameters entered by the programmer is not called "default constructor", it is only a constructor without parameters! The terminology is important, we must not confuse two different concepts.**

The order of the members within the class is not important for the purpose of compilation. We can write the methods first, then the constructors and then the instance variables, or alternate a constructor with a variable and a method; it's all legal. In fact, the creation of an object of a class in memory does not cause the class code to be executed in sequence as with old functional languages. Usually, however, the convention first requires the definition of the instance variables, then the constructors, and finally the methods.

## 2.6 Introduction to Packages

A package makes it possible to group logically-related Java classes into a single complex entity. Physically, the package is nothing more than a folder (synonymous with directory) of our operating system, but not all folders are packages. To elect a folder to package, a Java class must declare, in its code, that it belongs to that particular package. Furthermore, the result of compiling the class (file with extension **.class**) must physically reside within it.

### 2.6.1 Package and Import

If we want to let the Point class belong to a package named geometry, we should simply insert the following package declaration as the first instruction of our source file:

```
package geometry;

public class Point
{
    //code omitted
}
```

This would mean that the compiled file (**.class**) should reside in a folder called geometry.
If, instead, we want to create a more structured package tree, we can easily use the dot operator (which also means *belonging*):

```
package study.math.geometry;

public class Point
{
    //code omitted
}
```

In this case, the compiled file will reside within a **geometry** folder which, in turn, is contained in a **math** folder which is, in turn, contained in a **study** folder.
However, we must take into account the visibility rules of the classes contained in the packages. For example, how does a class that is in a certain folder use a class that is in another

folder? If a class called `TestPoint` wants to use the `Point` class and is not in the same package, `study.math.geometry`, it must import the `Point` class with the `import` command, which must be declared after the package declaration, but before the class declaration, as in the following code:

```
package study.math.geometry.test;
import study.math.geometry.Point;

public class PointTest
{
    public static void main (String args[])
    {
        Point p = new Point();
        // . . .
    }
}
```

Suppose the source files **TestPoint.java** and **Point.java** are initially in the same **test** folder. Once compiled, the folders relating to the declared packages will be created, and the **.class** files will be directly moved inside them as shown in Figure 2.1.

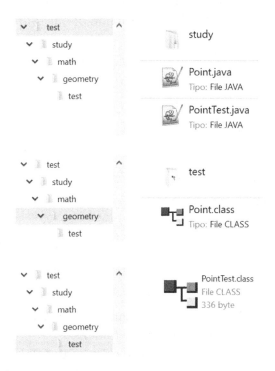

**Figure 2.1 - Compiling files declared with packages.**

## 2.6.2 Manual Package Management

Unfortunately, the situation is not as simple as it seems. In fact, the previous example shows one of the simplest scenarios. With EJE, this kind of scenario would be covered without complications, since EJE would manage file placement and folder creation for you (as long as the **.java** files are both in the same initial folder). If, instead, we try to compile with the command prompt, we should use the following syntax to compile, after we've moved in the **test** folder:

```
javac -d . Point.java TestPoint.java
```

In this way, we would compile both files at the same time, specifying that we want to create directories (synonymous with folders) with the **-d** option (abbreviation of **-directory**) and specifying that these folders must be created starting from the current folder (which is usually identified with the symbol ".").

To run the TestPoint file instead, always from the **test** folder, we should launch the command:

```
java study.math.geometry.test.TestPoint
```

that is, we have to prefix the name of the TestPoint file with the declaration of its package to indicate to the Java Virtual Machine where to find the bytecode. This long version name of the class, is called **fully-qualified name**.

Other scenarios involving the placement of source files in different folders require further measures (explained in detail in the sixth chapter) that could make learning Java a real nightmare for the neophyte. The solution is offered by IDEs, which automatically manage the positioning of source files and **.class** files, thus lightening the programmer's load.

Since using the concept of a package is not essential in order to correctly approach the language, we will set out a detailed treatment of this topic in the sixth chapter. Until then, we will no longer declare the packages in our examples and exercises.

 It is good practice to create source files with the extension **.java**, that have the same name as the public class they define. However, it is possible (but not recommended) to create a non-public class (just do not prefix the public modifier with the class declaration) and use a different name for the file that defines it. Indeed, it is also possible to declare multiple classes in the same file! The requirement that must be respected, is that, if a public class is declared in a file, then the file name must match the public class name. For this reason, if more than one class is defined in the same file, only one can be declared public. For example, we can create the **TwoNonPublicClasses.java** file as follows:

```
package multiclass;
```

```
class NonPublicClass1
{
    public void printName()
    {
        System.out.println("NonPublicClass1");
    }
}
class NonPublicClass2
{
    public void describeClass()
    {
        System.out.println("NonPublicClass2 is not declared as public");
    }
}
```

Note that by compiling this single **TwoNonPublicClasses.java** file, we will get two **.class** files: **NonPublicClass1.class** and **NonPublicClass2.class**, both belonging to the same `multiclass` package. In fact, in each file, it is possible to insert only a package declaration at the beginning (and any import declarations to follow), and all the classes declared below will be declared as belonging to the same package. Also keep in mind that, when a class is not declared `public`, it will not be accessible outside the package it belongs to. For example, if starting from the same root folder, we define the following **PublicClass.java** file belonging to the `otherpackage` package:

```
package otherpackage;
import multiclass.NonPublicClass1;
import multiclass.NonPublicClass1;

class AnotherClass
{

}

public class PublicClass
{
    public static void main(String args[])
    {
        NonPublicClass1 nonPublicClass1 = new NonPublicClass1();
        NonPublicClass2 nonPublicClass2 = new NonPublicClass2();
        nonPublicClass1.printName();
        nonPublicClass2.describeClass();
    }
}
```

then we will get compile-time errors, because we are trying to access the `NonPublicClass1` and `NonPublicClass2` classes that are not declared public and belong to a different package (`multiclass`):

```
PublicClass.java:2: error: NonPublicClass1 is not public in multiclass;
 can not be accessed from outside package
import multiclass.NonPublicClass1;
               ^
. . .
```

In order to compile **PublicClass.java** we should declare both the NonPublicClass1 and NonPublicClass2 classes public, but in that case, they should be defined in the **NonPublicClass1.java** and **NonPublicClass2.java** files respectively.

Finally, we note that we can also declare a non-public class belonging to a package within a file with a different name, and be able to launch that class. For example, consider the following non-public class belonging to a package:

```
package test;

class NonPublicCallTest
{
    public static void main(String args[])
    {
        System.out.println("It works!");
    }
}
```

We can save this class inside a **OtherNameTest.java** file (the name of the file is different from the name of the class), then compile it:

```
javac -d . OtherNameTest.java
```

and also launch it:

```
java test.NonPublicCallTest
It works!
```

# 2.7 Other Key Components of Java Programming

The approach that we will follow is to present the topics at the right time without forcing the reader to learn concepts for which they are not ready. For the sake of completeness, however, in this section we only want to introduce other fundamental components that we will study in depth later.

## 2.7.1 Interfaces

An interface can be saved and compiled in a file with the suffix **.java** that has the same name as the interface, just like a class. However, an interface cannot be instantiated: it is not possible to create objects from an interface. It is possible to define only certain types of methods (usually abstract methods, that is, without a block of code and therefore not directly invokable) and we cannot declare instance variables but only constants.

An example of an interface could be the following:

```java
public interface Playable
{
    public void play(String note);
}
```

As we can see, the syntax is very similar to that of the class, but we use the `interface` keyword instead of the keyword `class`. We also note that the method `play()` declared inside the interface, does not have a code block but ends with a `;` (it is called abstract method). This implies that it is not possible to invoke a method of an interface because it is not defined. The interfaces are closely linked to the concept of inheritance, a paradigm of object-oriented programming that makes it possible to relate more classes to each other. The interfaces will be extended by classes, and these will implement the abstract methods that will be inherited by the interfaces. For example, the class:

```java
public class Ukulele implements Playable
{
    public void play(String note)
    {
        System.out.println("The ukulele is playing the note " + note);
    }
}
```

uses the keyword `implements` to extend and implement methods that are inherited from the interface. But, also, the following class implements the `Playable` interface:

```java
public class Harmonica implements Playable
{
    public void play(String note)
    {
        System.out.println("The harmonica is playing the note " + note);
    }
}
```

In the `main()` method of the following class, we could invoke the `play()` method defined in the `Playable` interface, on objects instantiated by the `Ukulele` and `Harmonica` classes:

```java
public class PlayableTest
{
    public static void main(String args[])
    {
        Harmonica harmonica = new Harmonica();
        Ukulele ukulele = new Ukulele();
```

```
            harmonica.play("C");
            ukulele.play("D");
    }
}
```

The two classes implement the same method `play()` differently, realizing another paradigm of object-oriented programming called polymorphism (see Chapter 8). Interfaces and inheritance will be dealt with in detail in the seventh chapter, and polymorphism in the eighth chapter.

## 2.7.2 Enumerations

An enumeration (also called enum) can be saved and compiled into a file with the extension .java that has the same name as the enumeration, just like a class or an interface. Enumerations define all their instances within themselves. It is not possible to instantiate other objects of an enumeration outside the enumeration itself. Their purpose is to define a type that can be instantiated only with a limited number of objects, which is a typical requirement in programming. For example, if we need an object that represents a day of the week, creating a class would be wasteful and, in some ways, useless. In fact, we should implement the checks so that there are only seven objects to be instantiated from this class. Instead, with an enumeration we can write directly:

```
public enum DayOfWeek
{
    MONDAY, TUESDAY, WEDNESDAY, THURSDAY, FRIDAY, SATURDAY, SUNDAY;
}
```

All the potentialities of enumerations will be detailed in the eleventh chapter.

## 2.7.3 Annotations

An annotation can also be saved and compiled into a file with the suffix .java that has the same name as the annotation, just like a class, an interface, or an enumeration. The concept of annotation is quite complex, and many Java programmers, rather than creating annotations, just use annotations defined in the standard library and in other libraries. Annotations are metadata with which we can characterize other elements such as classes, methods, variables, interfaces, etc. The annotations are read and interpreted by other software (for example the compiler, the Java Virtual Machine or our programs) that can read the annotated elements of code. For example, the annotation of the standard library `@FunctionalInterface`, can annotate interfaces that declare a single abstract method. It has the task of declaring to the compiler that the annotated interface must declare a single method. In case the annotated interface does not respect this constraint, the compiler will report an error to the programmer. For example, if we compile the following interface containing two abstract methods:

```
@FunctionalInterface
public interface TwoMethodsInterface
{
    void method1();
    void method2();
}
```

The compiler will return the following error:

```
TwoMethodsInterface.java:1: error: Unexpected
@FunctionalInterface annotation
@FunctionalInterface
^
  TwoMethodsInterface is not a functional interface
    multiple non-overriding abstract methods found in interface
TwoMethodsInterface
1 error
```

We can also create our own annotations with the following syntax:

```
public @interface MyAnnotation
{
    //...
}
```

The entire sixteenth chapter is dedicated to annotations.

## 2.7.4 Modules

 Modules represent the most important feature introduced with Java 9. They allow us to manage the structure of our applications in a cleaner and more functional way. Like packages, modules are physical folders. These can contain packages, classes, other resources and a descriptor file. In fact, within the folder that represents the module, there must be a .**class** file called by convention **module-info.class** (result of compiling a file called **module-info.java**) which declares the name and characteristics of the module. For example, with the following syntax:

```
module com.cdsc.test
{
    exports com.cdsc.test;
}
```

we're declaring a module named com.cdsc.test. It declares that all classes belonging to the com.cdsc.test package are visible outside (the names of the modules often coincide with the names of a package contained inside). The modules are especially useful for very large applications, which need to be organized well. Modules will be treated in detail in the nineteenth chapter in the second volume.

### 2.7.5 Initializers

Initializers (sometimes called initialization blocks) are infrequently-used components and must be declared internally in the classes. As the name implies, the initializers are used to initialize classes or objects. There are class initializers (also called static initializers) and instance initializers. They have the characteristic of being automatically invoked only once, when the class is loaded (static initializers) or the object (instance initializers). For example, in the class:

```
public class InitializerTest
{
    {
        System.out.println("This is an instance initializer");
    }
}
```

we declared an instance initializer. The syntax is very simple (two curly braces) and this will be called every time an object instantiated by the `InitializerTest` class is loaded into memory, even before a constructor. Initializers will be discussed in the sixth chapter.

### 2.7.6 Nested Classes

Nested classes are classes defined within other classes. They enjoy some properties including having access to all the variables defined within the container class. The following is an example:

```
public class OuterClass
{
    private int i = 0;
    class InnerClass
    {
        public void method()
        {
            System.out.println("I can access to the variable i " + i);
        }
    }
}
```

There are also anonymous nested classes (unnamed) that can be declared on the fly locally within a method. Nested types will be discussed in the eleventh chapter.

### 2.7.7 Lambda Expressions

Lambda expressions were introduced with version 8 of Java, completely revolutionizing the language. With lambda expressions, we can assign a reference to a method and pass it as input to another method as if it were a variable. This is a complex subject that will be dealt with in the seventeenth chapter in the second volume. The syntax is quite specific. A lambda expression allows us to define the code of its only method on the fly and pass it as input to another method. The latter can execute the lambda expression code at any time within a well-defined code stream. For example, if we consider the Consumer functional interface, with the following code:

```
Consumer consumer = ((s) -> System.out.println(s));
```

we have declared a reference to a lambda expression (a function) that can be used as a variable and executed when desired.

## Summary

**Software development** requires that a series of activities (a **process**) be carried out that will allow an idea to become software. A minimal process requires at least four well-defined activities: understanding what to do, understanding how to do it, implementing the software, testing it and fixing any problems.

Java is an **object-oriented language**, which means that it supports **object-oriented programming** (**OOP**) with its features. Underlying OOP programming are the concepts of class and object which, like all other concepts, are inspired by the real world.

A **class** represents an abstraction for a group of objects that share the same features and functionalities. An **object** is a physical creation (also called an **instance**) of the class. Each class is unique, but objects created from the same class are different.

It is said that an object in a certain instant is characterized by its *state*. The **state of an object** is defined by the value of its instance variables.

Java programs consist of many classes referencing each other. In Java programs, however, there will be objects instantiated by the classes that will execute the instructions and the classes will serve, above all, to define the structure of the objects. An exception is the class that contains the static main() method, which represents the starting point for each Java program and then executes instructions (it usually creates objects that execute instructions). The class containing the main() method is the only class that can be executed using the **java** command.

Each file that is part of a Java application will contain the list of one and only one class (except in some exceptional cases that, for now, we can ignore). Furthermore, each class usually contains definitions of variables, methods and constructors.

**Methods** contain operating code and define the functionalities of the objects. They need to be declared within a class and called using the **dot** operator applied to an object. The methods may, or may not, return an output result and may have input parameters, or not.

**Varargs** are a particular parameter that allows passing a variable number of values to a method. It is possible to use a single varargs as a parameter of a method, and in the presence of other parameters it must be positioned as last in the list.

**Variables** are divided into three types, defined by the positioning of the declaration: instance variables, local variables and parameters (which can essentially be considered local). An **instance variable** is declared outside a method and represents a member of the class like a method. In addition to a name (identifier), the variables have a type (for example int) and a value (for example 8). In particular, the instance variables represent the attributes (characteristics) of an object and can be accessed through the dot operator applied to an object. The **local variables** and the **parameters** of a method are declared within a method with which they share their life cycle. This means that when the program is executed, they are created when the method in which they are declared is executed, and once the method is finished, they will no longer be accessible. The parameters in particular are initialized with values that come from outside the method in which they are defined, and these values represent the input of a method.

**Constructors** are special methods that are found within each class. In fact, if the programmer does not provide one explicitly, the Java compiler will add the **default constructor**. The constructor has no return type, has the same name as the class in which it is declared and is called every time an object is instantiated. It can take as input parameters like any other method and, thanks to a feature called *overload*, we can define more constructors within the same class. A constructor is usually used to initialize the instance variables of an object.

A **package** allows us to group classes that are logically related to each other. A package physically coincides with a folder. A class that wants to use another one from a different package must **import** it using the import command. During development, package management can be quite cumbersome if we do not use an IDE.

**Other key components** have only been briefly mentioned. An **interface** usually contains *abstract methods* that are implemented within other classes. **Enumerations** respond to the need to have a finite number of objects or values. **Annotations** are used to write down our code, making it analyzable by other software such as the compiler. The **modules** instead are folders that are self-described by a Java file, and allow packages, classes and other resources to be encapsulated, and expose them to other modules if necessary. **Initializers** are rarely used and are executed when a class or an object is loaded into memory. **Nested classes** are classes declared within other classes that can access all members of the class in which they are declared. Finally, **lambda expressions** allow us to use functions with a reference, as if they were variables.

> **Exercises, source code, appendices and other resources are available at http://www.javaforaliens.com.**

## Chapter goals

Have the following goals been achieved?

| Goal | Achieved | Achievement Date |
|---|:---:|---|
| Understand what it means to develop a program in Java, what the processes and the programming paradigms are (Unit 2.1) | O | |
| Know how to define the concepts of class, object, variable, method and constructor (Units 2.2, 2.3, 2.4, 2.5) | O | |
| Know how to declare a class (Unit 2.2) | O | |
| Know how to create objects from a class (Unit 2.2) | O | |
| Know how to use public members of an object using the dot operator (Units 2.2, 2.3, 2.4) | O | |
| Know how to declare and invoke a method (Unit 2.3) | O | |
| Know how to declare a variable and assign it a value (Unit 2.4) | O | |
| Know how to define and use the different types of variables (instance variables, local variables and formal parameters) (Unit 2.4) | O | |
| Know how to declare and invoke a constructor (Unit 2.5) | O | |
| Know what a default constructor is (Unit 2.5) | O | |
| Know how to define a class belonging to a package and be able to import classes from other packages (Unit 2.6) | O | |
| Have a basic definition of all the other fundamental components of the Java programming that we will study in the next chapters (Unit 2.7) | O | |

# Coding Style,
# Data Types and Arrays

**Goals:**

At the end of this chapter, the reader should:

- ✔ Know the rules and conventions for declaring identifiers for Java code (Unit 3.1).
- ✔ Understand how memory is handled, along with the positional numerical systems and the two's complement method (Unit 3.2).
- ✔ Know how to use all primitive data types (Unit 3.3).
- ✔ Know how to manage casting and promotion (Unit 3.3).
- ✔ Know how to use references and understand how they work (Unit 3.4).
- ✔ Start exploring the standard Java library documentation (Unit 3.5).
- ✔ Know how to use the String class (Unit 3.5).
- ✔ Be able to comment your code and be able to use the javadoc tool to produce external technical documentation (Units 3.1, 3.5).
- ✔ Know how to define, create, and initialize arrays (Unit 3.6).
- ✔ Know how to define the *local-variable type inference* for local variables, and know how to use the special word var (Unit 3.7).

In this chapter, we will first explain some rules that Java programming requires. These rules are very simple but fundamental. Using a standard style simplifies the programmer's life and makes his code more readable. We will also introduce some basic concepts on memory management, fundamental notions for the neophyte.

Subsequently, the types of data defined by the language, and problems related to this, will be presented. Up to now, we have almost always used the data type `int`. After studying this chapter, we will finally be able to master all of the types of data that Java defines. We will also be familiar with the fundamental concept of *reference*. The standard Java library will also be introduced. It will allow us to use high-level objects and exploit them as complex data types within our programs. At the end of the chapter, arrays will be presented and discussed in depth, a topic that is rather difficult for many programmers.

> **An array represents a complex data type that defines a collection of indexed elements of a certain type. With just one name, we will be able to access the elements of the collection through an index.**

Finally, we'll introduce an interesting feature introduced in Version 10, which makes the Java code less verbose: the local variables type inference, an argument better known by the name `var`, from the name of the word used for its implementation.

# 3.1 Coding Style

With the term **coding style**, we mean a series of mandatory and non-mandatory rules, which usually support programming. Naturally, we must follow the mandatory rules, but the optional ones are also very important, because they are used by programmers all over the world, and therefore their use greatly simplifies the readability of the code.
The Java language:

- is a free-form language;

- supports various types of comments;

- defines keywords and other special words;

- is case sensitive;

- has strict rules for data types and some simple naming conventions.

## 3.1.1 Free-Form

Java is a **free-form language**. This does not mean that we can violate the rules of the language. For example, the package declaration statement must always be the first in a file, import statements must follow any package declaration, the declaration of a class cannot precede package and import declarations, classes and methods are bounded by braces and so on. These and other rules cannot be violated because the compiler would return us errors at compile-time.

Java is a free-form language in the sense that we could write an entire program in Java on one line or wrap after each word: the compiler would have no trouble compiling the code if it is correct. The trouble would be for the developer, who would have great difficulty understanding the code!

 There are therefore standard methods of **indenting the code** (**formatting**) that facilitate the reading of a Java program. Below is a simple class that uses one of the two most used formatting methods (the one used in this book, so far):

```java
public class MyClass
{
    public int integer;
    public void method()
    {
        integer = 29;
        int anotherInteger = 7;
        System.out.println(integer + anotherInteger);
    }
}
```

With this style (which is also used by C language programmers), the reader can immediately understand where the class begins and where it ends, since the braces that delimit the block of code are aligned. The same goes for the method: it is clear where it begins, where it ends and the code that defines its behavior. It is the style that we have used up to this point, because it seemed to us more educational for novices. But the style most used by Java programmers is as follows:

```java
public class MyClass {
    public int integer;
    public void method() {
        integer = 29;
        int anotherInteger = 7;
        System.out.println(integer + anotherInteger);
    }
}
```

for which the same observations made for the first method are valid.

A rigorous application of one of the two styles just presented is recommended for the work to be done successfully. The advice is to use the second style that we have presented, which is a standard for Java. Very few Java programmers use the first style, and usually they are developers who previously programmed in C and are more reluctant to change their habits.

> If you are using EJE as editor, you can automatically format your code with both styles using the appropriate menu, or via the . . .

> **. . . corresponding button on the toolbar, or through the** CTRL-SHIFT-F
> **keyboard shortcut. To configure the style to use, choose the** File ⇨ Options
> **menu (or press** F12**) and set the** Braces style **to the desired style in the**
> Editor **tab.**

Some of the typical mistakes that the novice programmer commits are simple omissions. It is common to forget to close a brace of a class, or to forget the "**;**" to end a statement or even the round brackets that follow the invocation of a method. This is why we suggest to the reader to make it a habit to write each instruction in a complete manner, and then think about formatting correctly.

For example, if we declare a class, it is good practice to write both braces, before writing the code contained in them. The following three steps should clarify the concept:

- ▪▪ step 1: declaration:

```
public class MyClass {}
```

- ▪▪ step 2: formatting:

```
public class MyClass {

}
```

- ▪▪ step 3: completion:

```
public class MyClass {
    public int integer;
}
```

## 3.1.2 Comments

Commenting the code properly is a practice that should be considered mandatory by the novice programmer. The comments not only clarify the code, but also force us to understand correctly what we are writing as we have to describe it. So, comments should greatly encourage the learning of the novice. For expert programmers, however, most of the comments should become almost useless because the code should, ideally, be so readable as to make the practice of commenting the written code unnecessary. In fact, the code never lies, but the comments sometimes do!

In any case, Java supports three different ways to comment the code:

**1. Single-line comments**:

```
// This is single-line comment
```

**2. Multi-line comments**:

```
/*
   This is a
   Multi-line comment
*/
```

**3. Documentation comments** also known as **Javadoc comments**:

```
/**
    This comment allows us to produce
    the code documentation in HTML format,
    using the Javadoc standard
*/
```

For single-line comments, everything we write on a line that follows the // symbols will not be taken into account by the compiler. This syntax will allow us to comment briefly on some parts of the code. For example:

```
// This is a method
public void method() {

}

public int a; //This is a variable
```

This type of comment can be particularly useful for beginners to comment, with the right terminology, every instruction that will code. It is a really fundamental practice for those who are starting. The **multi-line comment** might be useful anytime we need to write long comments. The syntax requires us to include the text to be considered as a comment between the symbols /* and */. This type of comment is often used also to comment on parts of code that we are not yet sure need to be deleted permanently. For example:

```
/*
   this method is within a comment, so for the compiler it does not exist
   public void method() {
       ...
   }
*/
```

> These first two types of comments are imported from the C++ language.

**69**

The third type of comment (**Javadoc comment**) is very similar to the multi-line comment. In terms of syntax, the only difference is that the comment opens with the symbols /** (note the two asterisks) but closes in the same way with the symbols */. However, this type of comment offers the possibility to produce the **technical documentation** of a program in standard HTML format, using a command called **javadoc**. By "technical documentation" we mean the documentation that explains the functioning of Java components (mainly the class, the methods and the constructors, but not only these) that describe the input parameters, the output parameters, and the behavior (that is what it does) with a standard syntax. We will see some uses of this type of comment later in the chapter, in section 3.5.4.

### 3.1.3 Rules for Identifiers

The identifiers (synonym of names) of the methods, of the classes, of the objects, of the packages, and of the variables and constants (but also interfaces, enumerations, annotations and modules that we will study later), have two mandatory rules.

1. The first rule to remember to create an identifier for any Java component, is that it can only use a certain set of characters, numbers and symbols. In particular, in an identifier:

   ▪▪ the first character can be **A-Z, a-z, _, $**

   ▪▪ the second and the following can be **A-Z, a-z, _, $, 0-9**

   So: **a2** is a valid identifier, and **2a** is not.

2. The second rule states that an identifier cannot match a **keyword** of Java. In fact, a keyword has a certain meaning for the programming language. The following table lists all the Java keywords in alphabetical order and therefore cannot be used as identifiers:

| | | | | | |
|---|---|---|---|---|---|
| abstract | assert | boolean | break | byte | case |
| catch | char | class | const | continue | default |
| do | double | else | enum | exports | extends |
| final | finally | float | for | if | goto |
| implements | import | instanceof | int | interface | long |
| module | native | new | open | opens | package |
| private | protected | provides | public | requires | return |

| short | static | strictfp | super | switch | synchronized |
|-------|--------|----------|-------|--------|--------------|
| this | throw | throws | to | transient | transitive |
| try | uses | var | void | volatile | while |
| with | yield | @interface | _ | | |

So, we cannot call a variable `class`, or a method, `void`.

We must also remember that Java is a **case sensitive** language, that is, it distinguishes between uppercase and lowercase letters. For example, we cannot declare a class by writing `class` with an initial capital letter, because it does not mean anything to the compiler. The `otherInteger` identifier is different from the `otherinteger` identifier. We must therefore be careful and, especially in the early days, have patience.

> **Note that all the words in the table above contain only lowercase letters (in addition to the _ and @ symbols).**

We should note some keywords that we have already encountered: `package`, `new`, `static`, `import`, `int`, `public`, `void`, `return` and `class`. We already know (or almost know) the meaning of these. However, it should be noted that not all words are just keywords in the table above.

The following: `goto`, `const` and `_` (the latter is intended as an underscore) are known as **reserved words**. In fact, these do not have a meaning in the language, but simply cannot be used as identifiers. These words `goto` and `const` have been reserved words ever since the language was born, while `_` is a novelty of Java 9. Also, other words from the table were introduced with Java 9: `exports`, `module`, `open`, `opens`, `provides`, `requires`, `to`, `transitive`, `uses` and `with`. These are called **restricted words**, as they cannot be used as identifiers only in the context of the declaration of a module (a concept introduced in Java 9), to which the nineteenth chapter in the second volume is dedicated.

So, we could say *that they are keywords only when declaring modules*.

The word `var` is defined as a **reserved type name**. It was introduced with Version 10 of Java, and it is the focus of section 3.7 where we will also investigate its impact on the use of identifiers in the code.

The keyword `yield` has been introduced with Java 13, and is used only in the new `switch` expression construct to yield a value. Unlike other keywords, we can declare variables named `yield` where we want, even within a `switch` expression.

Also note that @interface (word used to declare annotations, which we will discuss later) starting with the symbol @, could not be used as an identifier, as explained at the beginning of this section. So, also in this case, this is technically not a keyword.

### 3.1.4 Standards and Naming Conventions

 If we define the identifiers that respect the two rules described above, we will not get compile-time errors. But there are standard directives provided by Oracle (and originally by Sun Microsystems) in order to achieve a standard in the implementation style. It is very important to use these directives in a language that is as standardized as Java.

The identifiers must be significant. In fact, if we write a program using the class a, which defines the variables b, c, d and the method e, we will surely reduce the comprehensibility of the program itself.

Usually, the identifier of a variable is made up of one or more nouns, for example sidesNumber, or width or even numberOfParticipantsAtTheSymposium. Method identifiers will usually contain verbs, for example, printNumberOfParticipantsAtTheSymposium, or sum.

There are conventions for identifiers depending on the type of component to which we must give a name. They are very simple. They are listed here.

#### ▉ Convention for Classes

An identifier of a class (but this rule also applies to interfaces, enumerations and annotations, which we will study later) must always start with a capital letter. If composed of several words, these cannot be separated, because the compiler cannot guess our intentions. As we have noted before, we must instead combine words in such a way so as to form a single identifier and start each one of them with a capital letter. Examples of identifiers for a class could be:

- ▉ Person
- ▉ RaceCar
- ▉ GeometricFigure

#### ▉ Convention for Variables

An identifier of a variable must always start with a lowercase letter. If the identifier of a variable is to be made up of several words, the same rules for the class identifiers should be applied (except that the first letter must always be lowercase). So, examples of identifiers for a variable could be:

- `specificWeight`

- `totalNumberOfMinutes`

- `x`

## Convention for Methods

The same rules used for variable identifiers apply to an identifier of a method. In any case, we can always distinguish an identifier of a variable from an identifier of a method, since the latter is always followed by round brackets. Furthermore, as already stated, the name of a method should contain at least one verb. Thus, examples of valid identifiers for a method could be:

- `sumTwoNumbers (int a, int b)`

- `findAWord(String word)`

- `print()`

## Convention for Constants

The identifiers of constants, on the other hand, must be clearly distinguished from the others, and all the letters must be uppercase. If the identifier is composed of multiple words, these are separated with an underscore symbol _. For example:

- `SQUARE_SIDES_NUMBER`

- `PI`

## Package Convention

Package names usually contain only lowercase letters (the same convention applies to modules, which we'll study later). If we need compound words, we can create nested packages. For example, if we wanted to create a customer support package, we can create two packages that are nested in the following way:

- `service.customers`

> There is no convention on the maximum number of characters to use for an identifier but, in Java, clarity is preferable to brevity. Obviously, we should use a little common sense here.

# 3.2 Memory Management

In the first chapter, we introduced some basic concepts of computer science. We confirmed that there are two types of memory: the **main memory** (that we associate with RAM memory) and the **secondary memory** (that we associate with the hard disk). Secondary memory is a permanent memory (that is, it survives when the computer is turned off). This is used to save data in the form of **files** and **folders**. RAM memory, on the other hand, is volatile and optimized for writing and retrieving data. Programs with their own data are loaded into RAM memory when they are executed.

It is the **processor** that manages the memory, deciding in which part of it such data must be stored. In fact, we can imagine the memory as a long sequence of cells that can store only one of two values which, by convention, we assume to be 0 and 1. These cells are called **bits**, an abbreviation of **binary digits**.

> Remember that the binary numerical system (which we will discuss very soon) contemplates only the symbols 0 and 1, which also represent the entire vocabulary of machine language.

Data is stored in these cells from the processor. To do this, the memory is divided into eight-bit sequences that are called **bytes**, which have the characteristic of having an **address**, that is to be identified by a number.

## 3.2.1 Bytes

Thus, a **byte** consists of eight bits and is associated with a numerical **address** to be identified. Eight bits are sufficient to memorize every single symbol present on a keyboard. In fact, as we will see in the next section, through the binary numeric system, with a byte we can represent a certain quantity of numbers and each number can be translated into any of the symbols present on the keyboard by means of a decoding standard.

The fact that a byte has a numerical address, allows the processor to keep track of where the data is stored, and then retrieve it quickly in the future.

> The address is chosen not by the hardware but by the program. In the case of Java, the Java Virtual Machine will take care of everything; the programmer will never interact with low-level memory.

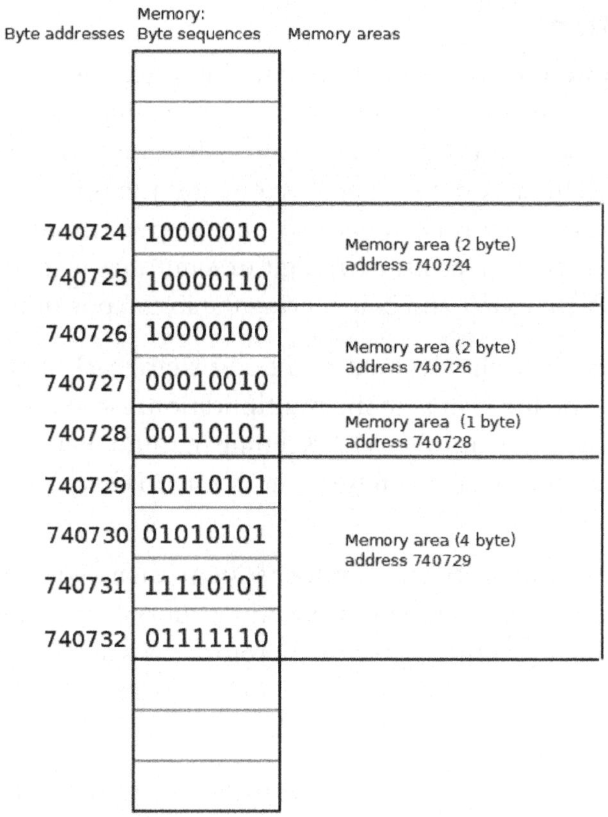

**Figure 3.1 - Representation of the Memory.**

If a data item is too large to be stored in a byte, then it will also be stored on other adjacent bytes, which will be considered a single memory area whose address will coincide with the address of the first byte. In Figure 3.1, an example of how some data could be stored in memory is shown.

> **Modern memory management systems are able to store data in bytes that are not adjacent.**

The 8-bit sequences (bytes) represent numbers. To interpret them, it is necessary to use the **binary number system** and to consider that Java uses the **two's complement method** for representing numbers within bytes.

## 3.2.2 Numeral Systems

The **binary number system** is equivalent to the **decimal number system** that we usually use to represent integers. The decimal number system uses ten digits (0, 1 , 2, 3, 4, 5, 6, 7, 8 and 9) but the binary number system only two digits (0 and 1). It is, nevertheless, capable of representing any whole number. The decimal number system and the binary number system are also called the **positional number system in base 10**, and the **positional number system in base 2**, respectively. In fact, in both systems, each digit of a number is interpreted according to its position. Starting from right to left and considering the initial position with index 0, we have:

1. to interpret a number in the decimal number system, each digit in position n must be multiplied by $10^n$, and the results of the multiplications must then be added together. For example, let's consider the number 127. Keeping in mind that 1 is at position 2, 2 is at position 1, and 7 is at position 0, it will turn out that 127 is equal to $1*10^2 + 2*10^1 + 7*10^0$ which is equal to $100 + 20 + 7$.

2. To interpret a number in the binary number system, each digit in position n must be multiplied by $2^n$, and the results of the multiplications must then be added together. To represent 127 with the binary number system, therefore, we will have to write 1111111. In fact, $1*2^6 + 1*2^5 + 1*2^4 + 1*2^3 + 1*2^2 + 1*2^1 + 1*2^0$ is equal to $64 + 32 + 16 + 8 + 4 + 2 + 1 = 127$.

There are also other systems such as the **octal number system** and the **hexadecimal number system**, also referred to as the **positional number system in base 8**, and the **positional number system in base 16**, respectively. The octal number system uses only eight digits (0, 1, 2, 3, 4, 5, 6, 7), while the hexadecimal uses sixteen digits (0, 1 , 2, 3, 4, 5, 6, 7, 8, 9, A, B, C, D, E, F). The same considerations made for the decimal system and the binary system apply to these systems. So, with the octal number system, 127 will be written 177 ($1*8^2 + 7*8^1 + 7*8^0 = 64+56+7 = 127$). Instead, with the hexadecimal number system we will write 7F ($7*16^1 + F*16^0 = 112+15 = 127$).

## 3.2.3 Two's Complement

To store signed numbers within bytes, Java uses a method called **two's complement**. This method establishes the rules that the processor must use for the representation of signed numbers. With the two's complement method, we will be able to represent an integer from 256 possibilities in a single byte (i.e. 8 bits). In particular, this integer number will be one of 128 positive numbers and 128 negative numbers. So, the **representation range** of a byte is between −128 to +127 (0 is considered a positive number). In fact, the first bit (the leftmost one) is called **sign bit** (or even **more significant bit**) because it is used to declare the sign of the number defined by the following bits. If this bit contains the value 0 it means that the number represented by the successive bits is positive, while if it contains the value 1, it means that it is negative. So, if the sign bit is 0, it is equivalent to the + symbol, while if it is 1 it is equivalent to the - symbol. Using a bit for the sign, in a byte we have 7 bits left to represent a number. As we saw in the example in the previous section, the highest 7-bit representable number is 127, represented as 1111111. Ultimately, the highest value that can be represented in a byte is 01111111, where 0 is the bit of the sign and is +.

To represent a negative number with the two's complement method, we must invert all the values of the bits of the relative positive number and then add the value 1. For example, let's consider the number 9 which has the following binary representation:

$$00001001 \; ([+] \; 0*2^6 + 0*2^5 + 0*2^4 + 1*2^3 + 0*2^2 + 0*2^1 + 1*2^0 = + \; 0+0+0+8+0+0+1 = +9)$$

To obtain the value -9, we must first invert all the values of the bits, obtaining what is called "one-complement" (which is another method of representing the numbers with a sign) 11110110. Then we must add 1 (which is written in binary 00000001) to this result, obtaining 11110111, which is the representation of -9 in two's complement. Note that the sign bit this time is 1, which implies the sign - before 9.

If we want to store a number greater than 127, or less than -128, the data will automatically extend to a larger memory area that will comprise more bytes, but which will consider the first bit of the first byte (the farthest to the left) as the sign bit. For example, if we wanted to store the 2004 value, then we would need two bytes (16 bits): 0000011111010100, where the first bit is the sign bit (positive).

> **The two's complement is the most used method of representation in modern computing for its efficiency in some types of operations, but we will not go into the subject further, as this is not the right place to do it. In fact, with Java, we will never have to deal with memory directly. These last topics have been dealt with only to better understand how data types are represented in Java.**

## 3.3 Primitive Data Types

Java defines only eight types of **primitive data types**, i.e. simple data types that differ from complex types. As we have already seen, they are used to represent:

■■ Integer types: byte, short, int, long.

■■ Floating point types: `float` and `double`.

■■ Textual type: `char`.

■■ Boolean type (also known as logical type): `boolean`.

> In this chapter (and also later), we will often use what are called *snippets*, i.e. fragments of non-contextualized code that should reside within classes and/or methods. In the fifth chapter, we will find out that Java also offers the ability to run the snippets using the JShell tool. For now, if you want to try to execute the snippets, you must always create a class with a `main()` method. In any case, it is possible to download all of the code of this book (both for the examples you find in these pages and for the online exercises) at: http://www.javaforaliens.com.

Before going into details, we should give the following definition: **Literals** are defined as values that are specified in the source code rather than at runtime. They can represent primitive variables or strings and can appear only on the right-hand side of an assignment or as arguments when invoking methods. It is not possible to assign values to literals, literals are constant values that can be assigned to variables.

The following are some examples of literals assigned to variables of the various types that we will see in this chapter:

```
boolean isBig = true;
char c = 'w';
String a = "\n";
int i = 0x1c;
short s = 0;
float f = 3.14f;
double d = 3.14;
int oneBillion = 1_000_000_000;
```

> The definition of literal could be considered useless, but it is one of those definitions that is often mentioned in the standard documentation.

### 3.3.1 Integer Data Types

There are four **integer data types**: byte, short, int and long. They share the same functionality (each one can store positive or negative integers) but they differ in their representation range. In fact, a byte can store an integer using one byte (eight bits), while a short type uses two bytes (16 bits), an int type four bytes (32 bits) and a long type eight bytes (64 bits). The following diagram summarizes the various representation ranges in detail:

| Type | Representation range |
|------|----------------------|
| Byte | 8 bit (from -128 to +127) |
| Short | 16 bit (from -32.768 to +32.767) |
| Int | 32 bit (from -2.147.483.648 to +2.147.483.647) |
| Long | 64 bit (from -9.223.372.036.854.775.808 to 9.223.372.036.854.775.807) |

Note that the representation range of the integer primitive types is always between a minimum of -2 raised to the number of bits minus one, and a maximum of 2 raised to the number of bits minus one, and finally subtracting a unit. So, we could rewrite the previous table as follows:

| Type | Representation range |
|------|----------------------|
| Byte | 8 bit (from $-2^7$ to $2^7-1$) |
| Short | 16 bit (from $-2^{15}$ to $2^{15}-1$) |
| Int | 32 bit (from $-2^{31}$ to $2^{31}-1$) |
| Long | 64 bit (from $-2^{63}$ to $2^{63}-1$) |

> **Note also that, for each numerical type, there is an even number of positive numbers and negative numbers. In fact, the number 0 is considered a positive number.**

To store an integer in Java, we can use four types of numerical systems: decimal (or natural notation), binary, octal, and hexadecimal (see section 3.2.2).

For **binary notation**, it is necessary to put before the integer a 0 (zero) and a b (uppercase or lowercase). For **octal notation**, it is necessary to prefix the integer with a 0 (zero). For **hexadecimal notation** 0 and x (indifferently upper or lower case). For **decimal** (or **natural**) **notation**, there is no need to use prefixes. Here are some examples of using integer types:

```
byte b = 10; // decimal notation: b is 10
short s = 022; // octal notation: s is valid 18
long l = 0x12aCd; // Hexadecimal notation: l is 76493
int i = 1000000000; // decimal notation: i is 1000000000
int n = 0b10100001010001011010000101000101; // binary notation: n is -1589272251
```

> **In the third example, we note that the use of hexadecimal characters in uppercase or lowercase does not make a difference.**

There are some observations to make regarding the primitive data types. Let's immediately give an example, considering the following assignment:

```
byte b = 127;
```

The compiler is able to understand that 127 is a number belonging to the byte representation range and therefore the previous expression is correct and can be compiled without problems. Instead, the following instructions:

```
byte b = 128; // the maximum for byte is 127
short s = 32768; // the maximum for short is 32767
int i = 2147483648; // the maximum for int is 2147483647
```

cause compile-time errors.

### 3.3.1.1 Automatic Promotion in Expressions

Let's consider the following statement:

```
byte b = 50;
```

This statement is correct. The integer 50 is within the representation range of one byte, ranging from −128 to +127. The compiler determines the size of the numerical value and checks if it is compatible with the declared data type.
Now let's consider this other statement:

```
b = b * 2;
```

This will cause a compile-time error! In fact, the compiler will not perform the multiplication operation to check the compatibility of the result value with the declared data type. Instead, it will automatically promote the two operands to int. Thus, if 50 * 2 is an int, it cannot be stored in b which is a byte. The phenomenon just described is known as **automatic promo-**

**tion in expressions** (or simply **promotion**). For binary operators, there are four rules, which depend on the types of the operands involved:

**1.** if one of the operands type is double, the other operand will be converted to double;

**2.** if the "widest" of the operands type is a float, the other operand will be converted into float (float is considered wider than int);

**3.** if the "widest" of the operands type is a long, the other operand will be converted to long;

**4.** in any other case, both operands will be converted into int.

> **The automatic promotion of all the operands to integer takes place before any binary operation is performed.**

### 3.3.1.2 Type Casting

But, clearly, 50*2 can be stored in a byte. There is a technique for forcing a certain amount to be stored in a certain type of data. This technique is known as **cast**. The syntax to use to solve our problem is:

```
b = (byte) (b * 2);
```

that is, we need to put, before the expression to be converted ("cast"), the type of data to which we want to restrict the result between two round brackets. In this way, the compiler will be warned that a possible loss of precision is calculated and under control.

However, one must be very careful in using the cast correctly. In fact, if we wrote:

```
b = (byte) 128;
```

the compiler would not report any type of error as the cast acts by truncating excess bits. In our case, since an int uses 32 bits, while a byte only 8, the first 24 bits of the int will be truncated. So, since the representation of the number 128 within an int type (32 bit) is as follows:

```
00000000000000000000000010000000
```

truncating the first 24 bits we will have:

```
10000000
```

which represents the number –128, so the variable b will store the value of –128 and not 128!

### *3.3.1.3 Operations with Integers*

Another typical problem to worry about is the **sum of two integers**. For the same reasons as above, if the sum of two integers exceeds the allowed range, it is still possible to store the result in an integer without errors in the compilation, but the result will be different from the expected one. For example, the following instructions will be compiled without errors:

```
int a = 2147483647; // Maximum value for an int
int b = 1;
int result = a + b;
```

but the value of the result variable will be -2147483648!

Even **division between two integers** is a critical point! In fact, the final result, as mentioned already, can only be stored in an integer, thus ignoring any decimal figures. So, in Java, unless there's an explicit cast, 3 divided by 2 will result in 1 and not 1.5 as we would expect.

Also, if we use a long variable, unless explicitly cast, it will always be initialized with an integer. So, if we write:

```
long l = 2000;
```

we must bear in mind that 2000 is an int by default, but the compiler will not report errors because an int can be safely stored in a long. To be precise, we should write:

```
long l = 2000L;
```

which represents the from int to long cast with a more **compact syntax**. Thus, a cast to long is obtained with a different syntax than usual, postponing an uppercase or lowercase "L" to the assigned whole value.

> We prefer to use uppercase notation, since a lowercase "L" can be confused with the number "one" in some development environments. Note that we would be forced to a do a cast to long if we wanted to assign a value outside of the representation interval of an int to the variable 1. For example:
>
> ```
> long l = 3000000000;
> ```
>
> would produce a compile-time error. We need to perform the cast as follows:
>
> ```
> long l = 3000000000L;
> ```

Despite this, int is the whole type that is used most often.

### 3.3.2 Floating-Point Data Types, Cast and Promotion

To store decimal numbers, Java defines two **floating-point types**: float (that uses 32 bits) and double (with double precision using 64 bits). We talk about 'floating point' because a decimal number can be represented by moving the comma, using engineering notation. For example, 0.0001 is equivalent to $1*10^{-4}$, which is written with the scientific notation 1E4. The two floating-point types are shown below with their representation range (based on the standard IEEE-754):

| Operator | Representation range |
|----------|---------------------|
| Float | 32 bit (from +/-1.40239846E-45 to +/-3.40282347E38) |
| Double | 64 bit (from +/-4.94065645841246544E-324 to  +/-1.79769313486231570E328) |

A first example of a double declaration could be the following:

```
double d = 0.0126;
```

We can also use **exponential** or **engineering notation** (the "e" can be either uppercase or lowercase) to specify a literal, for example:

```
double d = 1.26E-2; // equivalent to 1.26 divided by 100 = 0.0126
```

Regarding cast and promotion, the situation changes when compared to the case of integer types. While the integer values are assumed by the compiler as int (32-bit type) by default, floating-point values are considered to be double (64 bit) by default, and not a float (32 bit) as you might expect. This implies that if we want to assign a floating-point value to a float type, we cannot do so without a cast. For example, the following line of code would cause an error at compile-time:

```
float f = 3.14;
```

Also, in this case, the language helps us out, allowing us the cast with the **short syntax**:

```
float f = 3.14F;
```

The "f" can be either uppercase or lowercase.
There is, however redundant, even the short syntax of the cast for the double:

```
double d = 10.12E24D;
```

which is equivalent to writing:

```
double d = 10.12E24;
```

Further, some mathematical operations could give results that are not included in the set of real numbers (for example "infinite"). In the standard library, there are defined classes called **wrapper classes**, which are nothing more than classes that represent the primitive data types. For example, there is the Integer class for the primitive type int, the Short class for the short data type, and so on. Objects instantiated by these classes are interchangeable with primitive data, thanks to the Java feature known as **autoboxing-autounboxing**. That's why the Double and Float wrapper classes provide the following static constants:

- Float.NaN
- Float.NEGATIVE_INFINITY
- Float.POSITIVE_INFINITY
- Double.NaN
- Double.NEGATIVE_INFINITY
- Double.POSITIVE_INFINITY

where NaN stands for "Not a Number". For example:

```
double d = -10.0 / 0.0;
System.out.println (d);
```

will produce the following output:

```
NEGATIVE_INFINITY
```

We will meet the wrapper classes several times while reading this book.

> **As an aside, we should mention the** final **and** static **modifiers. A static constant in Java is a variable declared** final **and** static. **In particular, the** final **modifier applied to a variable will ensure that any attempt to change the value of that variable (already initialized) will produce an error at compile-time. So, a** final **variable is just a constant.**
> **As for the** static **modifier, as we have already asserted previously, the description is more complicated. When we declare a** static **variable, this variable will be shared by all the instances of that class, i.e. it is as if it belonged to the class itself rather than to its objects. That's why we access the static constants by using** ClassName.StaticConstantName **syntax (for example** Float.NaN**) instead of** objectName.StaticConstantName. **The** static **and** final **modifiers will be discussed in detail in the sixth Chapter.**

### 3.3.2.1 Floating Point Numbers Precision (IEEE-754)

The representation of floating-point numbers is not accurate, and will often be done with rounding. In particular, in the float consisting of at least 9 digits, rounding may occur, as can be seen in the following example:

```
int i = 123456789;
float f = i;
System.out.println(f);
```

This will produce the following output:

```
1.23456792E8
```

which highlights the fact that the number 123456789 is represented inside a float with an inaccurate decimal representation that makes use of the scientific notation 1.23456792E8. In fact, printing the value of f, casting again to int,

```
System.out.println((int)f);
```

will print the value:

```
123456792
```

So, the original number is increased by three units!

For double types (whose name indicates a doubled precision) there is precision for much higher numbers, but the substance does not change. The following snippet:

```
long l = 9999999999999991L;
double d = l;
System.out.println(d);
System.out.println((long)d);
```

will produce the following output:

```
9.999999999999992E15
999999999999992
```

where it is highlighted that the original number, in the representation passage from integer to floating point, has been increased by one unit.

In addition, the rules are complex, and what will happen when we use certain floating-point numbers is not always predictable, especially when working with arithmetic expressions. For example, consider the following snippet:

```
System.out.println((0.1+0.3));
System.out.println((0.1+0.2));
```

The output is amazing:

```
0.4
0.30000000000000004
```

The first expression was calculated precisely, while the second wasn't!

> These floating-point behaviors are not unique to Java, but they are common to all the major programming languages that use the standard IEEE-754 for representing floating-point numbers, for example C, C ++ or Javascript. If you want to deepen the discussion on `float` numbers (single precision) and `double` (double precision), you can consult the following addresses: https://en.wikipedia.org/wiki/Single-precision_floating-point_format and https://en.wikipedia.org/wiki/Double-precision_floating-point_format.

It seems obvious that performing calculations with primitive types is not that trivial. It is often convenient to use only `double` types in the case of arithmetic expressions involving decimal numbers. But, as we already noted, even using only `double` variables, it's not certain that we'll get accurate results with arithmetic expressions. In fact, having doubled a numeric representation, however limited, it sometimes must be rounded. Furthermore, the rounding depends on the architecture of the platform on which the calculation is performed.

> There is a very rarely used modifier in Java, called `strictfp`, and most Java programmers have probably never used it. Declaring the variables `float` and `double` as `strictfp`, would allow us to truncate the bits that would change these rounds on different platforms, thus ensuring uniformity of results on all platforms (unfortunately the results could still be wrong!). The `strictfp` modifier can mark, not only the `float` and `double` variables, but also classes or methods. In these cases, all operations performed within these classes or methods will follow `strictfp` truncation rules.

To get precise results in operations, we need to use a Java library class: `BigDecimal` (package `java.math`, see Java standard documentation) in place of the `double` type.

### 3.3.3 Underscore in Numeric Data Types

To improve the readability of the values assigned to our variables, we can also use the symbol "_" (called **underscore** or **underscore symbol**). For example:

```
int i = 1000000000;
int n = 0b10100001010001011010000101000101;
```

can be reported as follows:

```
int i = 1_000_000_000;
int n = 0b10100001_01000101_10100001_01000101;
```

When we want to use underscores within numbers, we need to know that we cannot use them:

1. at the beginning or end of a number;

2. adjacent to a decimal point for floating-point data types;

3. before the suffixes F , D or L (both upper and lower case) that are used for the cast to float, double and long types;

4. in positions where a string of characters is expected.

With some examples taken directly from the JDK documentation, we will make things clearer:

```
float pi = 3.14_15F;
long bytesHex = 0xFF_EC_DE_5E;
long maxLong = 0x7fff_ffff_ffff_ffffL;
long bytes = 0b11010010_01101001_10010100_10010010;
float pi1 = 3_.1415F;          // Error: rule 2 violated
float pi2 = 3._1415F;          // Error: rule 2 violated
long socialSecurityNumber = 999_99_9999_L;    // Error: rule 3 violated
int x1 = _52;                  // Error: rule 1 violated
int x2 = 5_2;
int x3 = 52_;                  // Error: rule 1 violated
int x4 = 5_____2;
int x5 = 0_x52;                // Error: rule 4 violated
int x6 = 0x_52;                // Error: rule 1 violated
int x7 = 0x5_2;
int x8 = 0x52_;                // Error: rule 1 violated
int x9 = 0_52;                 // OK! (note that this is an octal representation)
```

### 3.3.4 Boolean-Logical Data Type

The boolean data type can store only two valid literal values: true and false. For example:

```
boolean b = true;
```

To store only two values, it can be sufficient to use just one bit, but the Java Specifications say this is not certain, and that developers don't have to worry about it.

### 3.3.5 Primitive Character Data Type

The char type allows us to store characters (one at a time).

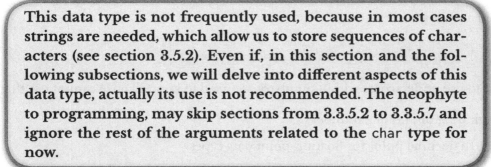

**This data type is not frequently used, because in most cases strings are needed, which allow us to store sequences of characters (see section 3.5.2). Even if, in this section and the following subsections, we will delve into different aspects of this data type, actually its use is not recommended. The neophyte to programming, may skip sections from 3.3.5.2 to 3.3.5.7 and ignore the rest of the arguments related to the char type for now.**

Below is a simple example where the character value is assigned to a char type:

```
char firstCharacter = 'a';
```

Note that each literal character type must be included between two single quotes, not to be confused with double quotes that are used for string literals. We have already used strings previously, for example:

```
String s = "Java melius semper quam latinam linguam est";
```

A typical mistake when starting to program in Java is to confuse single quotes (used for characters) with double quotes (used for strings). For example, the following instructions are both incorrect:

```
char c = "C";
String s = 'Meum filium maxime amo, sed ille me latinam linguam studere compellit';
```

Actually, there are three ways to assign a value (literal) to a char type, and all three modes require the inclusion of the value between single quotes:

■ use a single character on the keyboard (for example '&');

■ use the Unicode format with hexadecimal notation (for example '\u0061', which is equivalent to the number 97 and which identifies the 'a' character);

■ use an escape character (for example '\n' which indicates the *line feed* character (wrap).

Let's see these cases in detail in the next few sections.

### 3.3.5.1 Printable Keyboard Characters

We can assign a char to any character found on our keyboard, provided that the operating system supports the required character, and that the character is *printable* (for example the delete keys, or **Enter** etc. are not printable). In any case, we must include the value to be assigned between single quotes (i.e. the literal assignable to a char primitive type is always included between two single quotes). Here are some examples:

```
char aUppercase = 'A';
char minus = '-';
char at = '@';
```

The char data type is stored in 2 bytes (16 bits), with a range consisting only of positive numbers ranging from 0 to 65535. In fact, there is a 'mapping' that associates a certain character to each number. This mapping (or encoding) is defined by the **Unicode** standard (further described in the next section). So, we can say that the char type is a numeric type.

The fact that each character is represented by an integer is important, because we can use characters in arithmetic expressions. For example, we can add a char to an int. In fact, each character is decoded by Unicode starting from an integer:

```
int i = 1;
char a = 'A';
char b = (char)(a+i); // c = 'B'!
```

Note that if we had not used the cast:

```
char b = a+i;
```

we would have obtained the following compile-time error:

```
error: incompatible types: possible lossy conversion from int to char
        char b = a+i;
                 ^
1 error
```

In fact, with the automatic promotion in expressions rule (see section 3.3.1.1), the sum between a (of type char) and i (of type int) returns a value of type int. So, the following instruction:

```
int ii = a+i;
```

is valid, and the value contained in ii will be 66, which is the number representing the B character in the Unicode encoding. Thus, in arithmetic operations involving char types, integers representing the character type are used, not the characters themselves.

### *3.3.5.2 Unicode Format (Hexadecimal Notation)*

We said that the char primitive type is stored in 16 bits, and therefore can define as many as 65536 different characters. **Unicode** encoding deals with standardizing all the characters (and also symbols, emojis, ideograms, etc.) that exist on this planet. Unicode is an extension of the encoding known as **UTF-8**, which in turn is based on the old 8-bit **Extended ASCII** standard, which in turn contains the oldest standard known as **ASCII code** (acronym for **American Standard Code for Information Interchange**).

 Since version 11, Java has supported version 10.0 of Unicode, which contains many more characters than 65536 which can store a char. In fact, originally, it was designed as a 16-bit encoding that was considered sufficient to represent the characters of all the languages of the world. Now instead, the Unicode standard, allows us to represent potentially over a million characters, although 137,929 numbers have already been assigned to a character. But the standard is constantly evolving. Just to give you an idea, Java 10 implemented Unicode 8.0. With Unicode 9.0, 7500 characters were added and with Unicode 10.0 another 8518 more. So, with Java 11, there are 16018 new characters that can be used, if necessary, with respect to Java 10.

 Now Java 13, supports Unicode Version 12.1 (the latest Unicode version), that have added other 1239 characters.

For more information, see **http://www.unicode.org**.

Unicode can be used in three ways:

1. UTF-8: 8-bit that contains the ASCII encoding and therefore all the most used characters.

2. UTF-16: 16-bit, which contains all of the characters of most alphabets in the world. Also, the char type uses 16 bit and therefore with it, we are able to represent practically all of the most significant characters that exist.

3.  UTF-32: 32-bit that contains encodings of other characters including those that could be considered less used. Java supports the use of UTF-32 with a ruse based on an int (that is to concatenate two Unicode characters), but the use of this UTF-32 can be considered very rare. To use Unicode values that are outside the 16-bit range of a char type, we usually use classes like String (which will be introduced in section 3.5.2) and Character (the wrapper class relative to the primitive type char).

We can directly assign a char a Unicode value in hexadecimal format using 4 digits, which uniquely identifies a given character, prefixing it with the prefix \u (in this case always lower case). For example:

```
char phiCharacter = '\u03A6';
char nonIdentifiedUnicodeCharacter = '\uABC8';
```

In this case we're talking about **literal in Unicode format** (or **literal in hexadecimal format**). In fact, using 4 digits with the hexadecimal format, exactly 65536 characters are covered. Please note that, with this syntax, we indicate the number that identifies a certain character in the Unicode encoding. Since there are also integers from 0 (which corresponds to the number 48) to 9 (which corresponds to the number 57) in the coding, if we want to print the number 0 with the syntax just seen, we should write:

```
char zero = '\u0030'; //the hexadecimal number 30 is equal to the decimal 48
System.out.println(zero);
```

The value '\u0000' is equivalent to the null **character**, i.e. a character that does not print anything. Obviously, it is also possible to write:

```
char zero = '0';
```

### 3.3.5.3 Special Escape Characters

In a char type it is also possible to store **special escape characters**, that is, sequences of characters that cause particular behaviors in the printing:

- \b is equivalent to a *backspace*, that is a cancellation to the left (equivalent to the **Delete** key);
- \n is equivalent to a *line feed* (equivalent to the **Enter** key);
- \\ equals only one \ (just because the \ character is used for escape characters);
- \t is equivalent to a horizontal tab (equivalent to the **TAB** key);
- \' is equivalent to a single quote (a single quote delimits the literal of a character);
- \" is equivalent to a double quote (a double quote delimits the literal of a string);
- \r represents a *carriage return* (special character that moves the cursor to the beginning of the line);
- \f represents a *form feed* (disused special character representing the cursor moving to the next page of the document).

Note that assigning the literal '"' to a character is perfectly legal, so the following statement:

```
System.out.println('"');
```

which is equivalent to the following code:

```
char doubleQuotes = '"';
System.out.println(doubleQuotes);
```

is correct and will print the double quote character:

```
"
```

If we tried not to use the escape character for a single quote, for example, with the following statement:

```
System.out.println(''');
```

we will get the following compile-time errors, since the compiler will not be able to distinguish the character delimiters:

```
error: empty character literal
        System.out.println(''');
                           ^
error: unclosed character literal
        System.out.println(''');
                             ^
2 errors
```

Since the string literal delimiters (see section 3.5.2) are represented with double quotes, then the situation is reversed: it is possible to represent single quotes within a string:

```
System.out.println("'IQ'");
```

that will print:

```
'IQ'
```

On the other hand, we must use the \" escape character to use double quotes within a string. So, the following instruction:

```
System.out.println(""IQ"");
```

will cause the following compilation errors:

```
error: ')' expected
        System.out.println(""IQ"");
                             ^
error: ';' expected
        System.out.println(""IQ"");
                                 ^
2 errors
```

Instead, the following instruction is correct:

```
System.out.println("\"IQ\"");
```

and will print:

```
"IQ"
```

> In the next four sections, we will examine a series of extreme cases that may arise during the use of char primitive data types. As the alien icon tells you, if you are on your first experience with Java, you can safely skip these sections and come back later when you feel ready. This is not immediately necessary information for novices, and only a small percentage of professional Java programmers already know about it.

### 3.3.5.4 Write Java Code with the Unicode Format

The Unicode literal format can also be used to replace any line of our code. In fact, the compiler transforms the Unicode format into a character, and then evaluates the syntax. For example, we could rewrite the following statement:

```
int i = 8;
```

in the following way:

```
\u0069\u006E\u0074 \u0069 \u003D \u0038\u003B
```

In fact, if we add the following to the statement in the previous line:

```
System.out.println("i = " + i);
```

it will print:

```
i = 8
```

Undoubtedly, this is not a useful way to write our code. But we have to know this feature in order to understand some mistakes that rarely happen.

### 3.3.5.5 Unicode Format for Escape Characters

The fact that the Unicode hexadecimal format is transformed by the compiler before it evaluates the code, has some consequences, especially when dealing with escape characters. For example, let's consider the *line feed* character (which can be represented with the escape character \n, which corresponds in the Unicode encoding to the decimal number 10 (which corresponds to the hexadecimal number A). If we try to define it using the Unicode format:

```
char lineFeed = '\u000A';
```

we will get the following compile-time error:

```
error: illegal line end in character literal
        char lineFeed = '\u000A';
                       ^
1 error
```

In fact, the compiler transforms the previous code into the following before evaluating it:

```
char lineFeed = '
';
```

that is, the Unicode format has been transformed into the *newline* character, and the previous syntax is not a valid syntax for the Java compiler.

In the same way, the single quote character (') that corresponds to the hexadecimal number 27 (equivalent to the decimal number 39) and that we can represent with the escape character \', cannot be represented with the Unicode format:

```
char apex = '\u0027';
```

Also in this case, the JVM will transform the previous code in this way:

```
char apex = ''';
```

which will give rise to the following compile-time errors:

```
error: empty character literal
        char apex = '\u0027';
                   ^
error: unclosed character literal
        char apex = '\u0027';
                        ^
2 errors
```

The first error is due to the fact that the first pair of quotes does not contain a character, while the second error indicates that specifying the third apex is an unclosed character literal.

Also, with regard to the *carriage return* character, represented by the hexadecimal number D (corresponding to the decimal number 13), and already representable with the escape character \r, there are problems. In fact, if we write:

```
char carriageReturn = '\u000d';
```

we will get the following compile-time error:

```
error: illegal line end in character literal
        char carriageReturn = '\u000d';
                              ^
1 error
```

In fact, the JVM has transformed the number in Unicode format into a *carriage return* by returning the cursor to the beginning of the line, and what was supposed to be the first apex became the second.

As for the character \, represented by the hexadecimal number 5C (corresponding to the decimal number 92), and, represented by the escape character \\, if we write:

```
char backSlash = '\u005C';
```

we will get the following compile-time error:

```
error: unclosed character literal
        char backSlash = '\u005C';
                         ^
1 error
```

This is because the previous code will have been transformed into the following:

```
char backSlash = '\';
```

and therefore the \' pair of characters is considered as an escape character corresponding to an apex ', and therefore the literal closure is missing another single quote.

On the other hand, if we consider the character ", represented by the hexadecimal number 22 (corresponding to the decimal number 34), and, represented by the escape character \", if we write:

```
char quotationMark = '\u0022';
```

there will be no problem. But if we use this character within a string:

```
String quotationMarkString = "\u0022";
```

we will get the following compile-time error:

```
error: unclosed string literal
        System.out.println("\u0022");
                           ^
1 error
```

since the previous code will have been transformed into the following:

```
String quotationMarkString = """;
```

**95**

### 3.3.5.6 Unicode Format and Comments

 An even stranger situation is found when using single-line comments for Unicode formats such as *carriage return* or *line feed*. For example, despite being commented, both of the following statements would give rise to compile-time errors!

```
// char lineFeed = '\u000A';
// char carriageReturn = '\u000d';
```

This is because the hexadecimal formats are always transformed by the compiler with the *line feed* and *carriage return* characters, which are not compatible with the single line comments, because they print characters outside the comment!

To solve the situation, use the multi-line comment notation, for example:

```
/* char lineFeed = '\u000A';
   char carriageReturn = '\u000d'; */
```

Another mistake that can cause a programmer to lose a lot of time, is when the sequence \u is used in a comment. For example, with the following comment, we will get a compile-time error:

```
/*
 * The file will be generated inside the C:\users\claudio folder
 */
```

If the compiler does not find a sequence of 4 hexadecimal characters valid after \u, it will print the following error:

```
error: illegal unicode escape
 * The file will be generated inside the C:\users\claudio folder
                                             ^
1 error
```

### 3.3.5.7 Casting Between short and char

 In section 3.3.5.2, we saw a cast between an int type and a char type. The rules of casting between int and char are obvious, because int is a type of data that stores data in 32 bits, while char stores them in 16. So, the following snippet is valid:

```
int i = '\n';
System.out.println(i);
```

and will print the value 10 representing the *line feed* character.

But what is the cast relationship between char and short since both store 16-bit numbers? A

**96**

clear difference between the two types is that char is a type that can be defined without a sign. In fact, it is represented only by positive numbers ranging from 0 to 65535. Instead the short type has a range that varies from -32768 to +32767. So, not all short values can be stored in a char, and not even all the char values can be stored in a short. For this reason, if we want to assign a short to a char or vice versa, a cast is required in any case. This is also necessary when it is certain that a value of one type falls within the representation range of the other type. For example, we have already seen that it is possible to assign a value to a certain integer type that is included in its representation interval. For example, the following are valid statements:

```
char c = 'a'; //the character is equal to the decimal number 65
short s = 65;
```

But although s can hold the value 65, to assign c to s there is still a need for a cast not to get a compile-time error:

```
s = (short)c;
```

Instead, let's consider an example, where we force, using cast non-compatible values in the two types we are examining:

```
char cc = '\uffff'; // the hexadecimal FFFF corresponds to the decimal 65535
short ss = (short)cc;
```

In this case, for the same rule used with the byte type in section 3.3.1.2, the variable ss will have value −1. Instead, in this case:

```
short sss = -32768;
char ccc = (char)sss;
System.out.println(ccc);
```

the ccc character will have an undefined value, and a question mark will be printed.

# 3.4 Non-Primitive Data Types: Reference

We have already seen how to instantiate objects from a certain class. We must first declare an object of this class with a syntax of this type:

```
ClassName objectName;
```

and then instantiate it using the keyword new:

```
objectName = new ClassName();
```

To declare an object is therefore very similar to declaring a type of primitive data. The "name" we give to an object is called a **reference**. We are not talking about a traditional variable, but rather, a variable that some define as a **pointer**. We can define a pointer as a variable that contains an address in the memory.

There is a subtle and powerful difference between the declaration of a primitive data type and a non-primitive one. Let's consider an example starting from the definition of a class that trivially abstracts the concept of date:

```
public class Date {
    public int day;
    public int month;
    public int year;
}
```

For our example, Date will therefore be a non-primitive data type. Now, let's take a double as a primitive data type, and consider the following lines of code assuming that they are inside a main() method of a class:

```
double aNumber = 5.0;
Date aDay = new Date();
```

It could help us to schematize how the data will be represented in the memory when the application is running, but faithfully reporting this information is a difficult and perhaps even useless undertaking. In fact, we will never have to deal directly with memory management if we program in Java.

In any case, it may be useful to imagine the situation in the memory with the type of schematization, the result of a convention, illustrated in Figure 3.2.

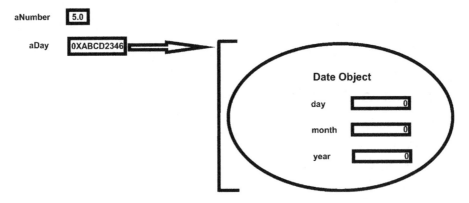

**Figure 3.2 - Convention for Schematization of Memory (Declarations).**

The practical difference between a reference and a primitive variable becomes evident in the assignments. Consider the following snippet:

```
double aNumber = 5.0;
double anotherNumber = aNumber;
Date aDay = new Date();
Date anotherDay = aDay;
```

For both the primitive and the complex data, we have created an equivalent behavior: a declaration and an assignment of a value, and a declaration of another variable of the same type and an assignment to this of the type previously created.

The variable anotherNumber will assume the same value as the variable aNumber, but the two variables will remain independent of each other. The value of the variable aNumber will be copied into the variable anotherNumber. If the value of one of the two variables is changed later, the value of the other variable will not change.

Instead, the reference anotherDay will simply assume the value (i.e. the address) of the reference aDay. This means that anotherDay will point to the same object to which aDay is pointing. Figure 3.3 shows the situation represented graphically.

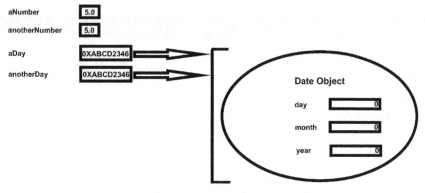

**Figure 3.3 - Convention for Schematization of Memory (Assignments).**

Therefore, if a modification on the common object is made later by one of the two references, this will also be verifiable by the other reference. To be clear:

```
aDay.year
```

is certainly equivalent to:

```
anotherDay.year
```

## 3.4.1 Passing Parameters by Value

"The passage of parameters in Java always takes place by value".

> This statement is contradicted in some texts but reading the entire section will dispel any doubt.

**99**

When invoking a method that takes a variable as input, only the value (a copy) of the variable is passed to the method. So, the variable remains unchanged even after the method is executed. For example, let's consider the class:

```java
public class ITry {
    public void changeValue(int value) {
        value = 1000;
    }
}
```

The following snippet:

```java
ITry obj = new ITry();
int aNumber = 10;
obj.changeValue(aNumber);
System.out.println("The value of the number is " + aNumber);
```

will produce the following output:

```
The value of the number is 10
```

During the execution of the changeValue() method, the parameter value did not coincide with the variable aNumber, but only stored the copy of its value (10). Thus the variable aNumber has not been changed.

The same goes for the reference types: the reference value is always passed, but as we said, the value of a reference coincides with the address in the memory. Let's consider the following class:

```java
public class ITryWithReferences {
    public void changeReference(Date date) {
        date = new Date();
        //The attributes of a new created object
        //are set automatically to their null values
    }
}
```

The following snippet:

```java
ITryWithReferences obj = new ITryWithReferences();
Date birthday = new Date();
birthday.day = 14;
birthday.month = 4;
birthday.year = 2004;
obj.changeReference(birthday);
System.out.println("Birthday = "
 + birthday.day + "-" + birthday.month + "-" + birthday.year);
```

will produce the following output:

```
Birthday = 14-4-2004
```

So, the same rules apply to both primitive and reference types.

However, if we rewrite the changeReference() method in such a way that it changes the values of the object's instance variables:

```
public void changeReference (Date date) {
    date.day = 12; // date and birthday reference to the same address
    date.month = 11;
    date.year = 2006;
}
```

the output will change:

```
Birthday = 12-11-2006
```

In fact, within the method, we would have changed the original object's variables, since the reference data (the parameter of the changeReference() method) would have pointed to the same address as the input object (i.e. the same address as the obj object).

The fact that the parameters are always passed by value, ensures that an object can be modified within the called method, and at the same time, we will be sure that, after the method has been called, the original reference always points to the same object.

In other languages, such as C, the passage of parameters *by reference* is also permitted. In that case, the whole reference is passed to the method, not only its address, with the consequent possibility of being able to change the addressing. This feature was not imported into Java because it was considered (rightly) a security threat. Many viruses, worms etc., exploit the technique of passing by reference.

In this case, Java has chosen the path of robustness and simplicity, instead of expanding the power of the language.

> **Some authors of other texts state that the passing of parameters in Java takes place by value for primitive data types, and by reference for complex data types. But it should be clear that this is only an issue of terminology. If we ignored the C language, we would probably give a different meaning to "passage by reference". The important thing is to understand the concept without making a mess.**

### 3.4.2 The Initialization of Instance Variables

We have already asserted that, when an object is instantiated, all of its instance variables (which share the life cycle with it) are initialized to their respective null values. Below is a table that gives each type of data the value with which an instance variable is initialized at the moment of its creation:

| Variable | Value |
|---|---|
| byte | 0 |
| short | 0 |
| int | 0 |
| long | 0L |
| float | 0.0f |
| double | 0.0d |
| char | '\u0000' **(null value – no character)** |
| boolean | False |
| **Any reference type** | Null |

It is quite logical to consider those present in this table as null values. We can see the cast notations near the null values of long, float and double. Furthermore, the null value of the char is expressed in hexadecimal notation and represents "no character". Finally, for each reference type the literal null value implies that the reference does not have an address to point to, and points to the null address (where there are no objects). Unfortunately, we will see that a typical error in Java programming (probably the most common) concerns the nullity of references.

## 3.5 Introduction to the Standard Library (Java API)

As already mentioned, several times, Java has a huge and luxurious library of standard classes, which is one of the strengths of the language. It is also known as the **Java API**, where API is the acronym for "Application Programming Interface". It is organized into various packages (but also in modules as we'll see at the end of this book) that collect classes according to an organization based on the field of use. The main "historical" packages (that have been around since the first version of Java) are the following:

- java.io contains classes to perform input and output operations.

- java.awt contains classes that represent the components to create graphical user interfaces, such as Button (rarely used), but above all the classes that manage the layout and the events of the graphical interfaces contains classes to create graphical user interfaces (GUIs).

- java.net contains classes to perform net connections as Socket.

- java.applet contains a single class: Applet. This allows us to create applets. With version 9, however, this library has been **deprecated**. This means that Oracle has decided that it is no longer in its plans for the future of the language, and therefore it will, sooner or later, be eliminated.

- java.util contains many utility classes as Date.

- java.lang is the package that contains the core classes of the language, such as System and String.

We will address these packages in later chapters.

## 3.5.1 The import Command

To use a library within a class that we intend to write, we must first import it. Suppose we want to use the Date class of the java.util package. Before declaring the class in which we intend to use Date, we must write:

```
import java.util.Date;
```

or, to import all the classes in the java.util package:

```
import java.util.*;
```

By default, every java.lang package is **automatically** imported into every Java file, without which we could not use fundamental classes such as System and String. We note that this is another example of how Java is also thought to favor initial learning. So, when we compile a Java class, the compiler prefixes the instruction:

```
import java.lang.*;
```

to the declaration of our class.

> The asterisk does not imply the importation of the classes belong-ing to the sub-packages; for example, import java.* does not include java.awt.* nor java.awt.event.*. So the import java.* statement does not import all the basic packages.

To give an idea of the power and simplicity of Java, a simple class is presented below. By in-stantiating some object from some classes of the java.awt package (which we will discuss in the twentythird chapter in the second volume) and assembling them with a certain criterion, we will obtain, with a few lines, a window with a button. The window, taking advantage of the java.awt library, will inherit the graphic style of the operating system on which it runs. Then we will see the Windows style on Windows, the Motif style on Solaris operating system and so on. We can get an idea of how we use the standard library along with its power, by analyzing the following code:

```java
import java.awt.*;

public class FrameWithButton {
    public static void main(String args[]) {
        Frame frame = new Frame("Title");
        Button button = new Button("Click me");
        frame.add(button);
        frame.setSize(200,100);
        frame.setVisible(true);
    }
}
```

It's very easy to interpret these lines of code, even if we don't know the library.

> The FrameWithButton **class has been reported for didactic purposes only. Pressing the button will not cause any action, nor will the attempt to close the window. Only a resizing of the window is allowed because it falls within the characteristics of the** Frame **class. So, to close the application we have to move to the DOS prompt, where we executed it, and terminate the running process by using the** CTRL-C **command (simultaneously press the** CTRL **and** C **keys). If you use EJE, press the "interrupt process" button (or press the** ESC **button). Another solution is to block the Java process directly from the Windows task manager.**
>
> ...

. . .

**Although the topic may have intrigued you, the advice is not to waste time creating unnecessary and useless graphical user interfaces: you must first learn Java! However, you can check the last part (Part VII) included in the Volume II dedicated to the graphical user interfaces.**

### 3.5.2 The `String` class

We have seen that the primitive type char allows us to store one character at a time. In a string type instead, it's possible to store a text composed of characters, numbers and symbols. In our programs, we will almost always use strings and, very rarely, the char type.

In Java, strings are objects, and therefore should be instantiated with the usual syntax using the keyword new. For example:

```
String name = new String("Salvatore Quasimodo");
```

This takes advantage of the concept of constructor introduced in the previous chapter.

Java, however, as often happens, simplifies the programmer's life by allowing us to use a string as if it were a primitive data type. For example, we can instantiate a string as follows:

```
String name = "Salvatore Quasimodo";
```

which is equivalent to:

```
String name = new String("Salvatore Quasimodo");
```

**To assign a value to a string, it must be in double quotation marks, unlike characters, for which single quotation marks are used.**

Also, in this case, we can appreciate the simplifications that Java provides us with. The fact that it is permitted to use a class as important as String, as if it were a primitive data type, has allowed us to approach the first examples of code without the additional difficulty of understanding how a constructor works.

The fact that String is a class, guarantees us a series of utility methods, easy to use and always available to perform operations with strings. Some examples are the toUpperCase() method, which returns the string on which the method is called with each character uppercase (on the other hand there is also the toLowerCase()), the trim() method, which returns the string on which the method is called but without the spaces that precede the first letter and those that follow the last one, and the fundamental equals(String) that allows to compare two strings. The String class is evidently a particular class. Another feature to underline is that a String object is **immutable**. This means that once a string is instantiated, its contents cannot change. The above methods, in fact, do not change the object on which they are called, they just return another. For example, the following lines of code:

```
String a = "claudio";
String b = a.toUpperCase();
System.out.println(a); // a does not change
System.out.println(b); // b is uppercase
```

would produce the following output:

```
claudio
CLAUDIO
```

In general, if we try to print a reference to a string that points to null, the null string will be printed.

> The String **class will be discussed in detail in the thirteenth chapter in the second volume, where we will discuss also a new feature introduced with Java 13 named** *Text Blocks*.

### 3.5.3 Java API Documentation

To know all about the String class and all the other classes, just read the documentation. It is available online at address **https://docs.oracle.com/en/java/javase/13/docs/api/index.html** but things are always changing, so if you can't find it at this address, please search with Google for *Java 13 API Documentation*. If you followed Appendix B to download and install the JDK, you should already have downloaded it to the **Docs** folder within the JDK installation folder. You may have created a shortcut on the desktop too.

 Up to Java Version 8, many programmers preferred not to download the documentation and consult it directly online. In fact, to find the page regarding a certain class, it was easier to perform a search on Google than exploring the package tree. With Version 9, the documentation itself finally provides a field to perform searches in the upper right part of the interface as shown in Figure 3.4.

It is absolutely essential that the reader immediately begins to explore and study the documentation. The real Java programmer is very familiar with it, and knows how to take advantage of its ease of consultation in the best way. In this text, unlike others, topics relating to classes of the

**Figure 3.4 - Java 9 documentation with the search field.**

standard library will be addressed, but in an essential way. So, we will not waste time describing all the methods of a class (except in some cases). Rather, we will strive to understand how to use the various packages in the best way. In fact:

1. We consider the official documentation irreplaceable.

2. The Internet is an inexhaustible source of information and examples.

3. The libraries are constantly evolving.

4. The documentation is in HTML format and allows quick consultation.

> If you use EJE, you can consult the documentation directly from EJE if you install the docs folder inside the JDK folder (parallel to bin, lib, etc.). Otherwise, you can choose the location of the documentation later by configuring it in the EJE options.

## 3.5.4 The javadoc Tool

In the section dedicated to *comments*, we mentioned the possibility of generating the documentation of our classes in HTML format, based on the model of the standard Java classes documentation. In fact, there is a "trick" for automatic generation: the **javadoc** tool. It allows us to generate hypertext in the style of the standard library, with information on the classes that we will write. We only have to:

1. Write the appropriately commented code in the source file. We have to use comments of the third type, those between /** and */.

2. Use the javadoc tool. It's very simple. From the prompt, type:

```
javadoc fileName.java
```

and all the HTML files we need will be generated automatically.

We will only be able to generate documentation for types (classes, interfaces, enumerations, annotations) declared public. We can comment also methods, constructors, variables, constants (if declared public). In addition, the comment must precede what we want to comment. For example:

```
/**
 This is a method!
*/
public void method() {
    // code omitted
}
```

> With EJE, you can generate the javadoc documentation simply by clicking on the appropriate button. The documentation will be generated in a docs folder created on the fly in the folder where the source file is located.

## 3.6 Arrays in Java

An **array** is an indexed collection of primitive data, or of references or other arrays. Arrays allow us to use just one name to identify a collection made up of various elements, which will be accessible through indexes.

> Usually one of the advantages of the use of arrays, is to be able to exploit the index within *loops*, but we will deal with this topic in the next chapter.

In Java, arrays are objects. However, the syntax of the arrays differs from that of the other objects. To use an array, we have to go through three steps: declaration, creation and initialization.

### 3.6.1 Declaration

Below, we present two array declarations. In the first, we declare an array of char (primitive type), and in the second we declare an array of instances of File (class belonging to the java.io package):

```
char alphabet [];        or        char [] alphabet;
File files [];           or        File [] files;
```

So, to declare an array, just postpone (or prefix) a pair of square brackets to the identifier.
To use an array identifier, we do not need to specify square brackets anymore, as we will see in the next section.

### 3.6.2 Creation

An array is a special object in Java and, as such, needs to be instantiated in a special way. The syntax is as follows:

```
alphabet = new char[25];
files = new File[3];
```

As we can see, it is mandatory to specify, at the time of the instance of the array, the size of the array itself in square brackets (a sort of constructor). This dimension, once declared, can no longer be changed. At this point, however, all of the elements of the two arrays are automatically initialized to their null values. Remember that the null value for a char type matches the '\u0000' character, while the null value for an object matches the null value. So, let's see how to explicitly initialize the elements of the array.

### 3.6.3 Initialization

To initialize an array, we must initialize each element individually:

```
alphabet [0] = 'a';
alphabet [1] = 'b';
alphabet [2] = 'c';
alphabet [3] = 'd';
// Let's omit for a few lines of code ...
alphabet [24] = 'z';

files [0] = new File("HelloWorld.java");
files [1] = new File("HelloWorld.class");
files [2] = new File("HelloWorld.html");
```

**109**

The index of an array always starts from zero. So, an array declared to 26 places will have a minimum index of 0 and a maximum of 25 (an array of size n implies the maximum index at n-1).

Notice the difference between a declared array of primitive data type and a declared complex type array. The first contains its elements. The second contains only references, not the elements themselves.

### 3.6.4 Alternative Syntaxes

The reader will have surely noticed that it can be very verbose to initialize an array, especially after having first declared and instantiated it. But Java helps us out, allowing us to perform all three main steps to create an array through a particular **short syntax** that we present below:

```
char alphabet [] = {'a', 'b', 'c', 'd', 'e', 'f', 'g', 'h', 'i', 'l',
    'm', 'n', 'o', 'p', 'q', 'r', 's', 't', 'u', 'v', 'z'};
File files [] = {new File("HelloWorld.java"), new File("HelloWorld.class"),
    new File("HelloWorld.html")};
```

Actually, it is also possible to use the following syntax:

```
char alphabet [] = new char []{'a', 'b', 'c', 'd', 'e', 'f', 'g',
    'h', 'i', 'l', 'm', 'n', 'o', 'p', 'q', 'r', 's', 't', 'u', 'v', 'z'};
File files [] = new File [] {new File("HelloWorld.java"),
    new File("HelloWorld.class"), new File("HelloWorld.html")};
```

### 3.6.5 Characteristics of an Array

As we have already said, arrays are objects, and therefore define variables and methods implicitly within them. For example, they define a constant called length that returns the actual size of the array itself. Then:

```
alphabet.length
```

will have value 26. Remember that the size of an array, once set, cannot be changed. If we wrote:

```
alphabet = new char[27]; // initially the length was 26
```

the result will be that the reference alphabet will target a new object of size 27, with all its elements set to null. The array of size 26 that was previously initialized with the letters of the alphabet will no longer be targeted by the reference alphabet, and will therefore be eligible for erasing from memory by the garbage collector. In fact, being no longer targeted by a reference, it will no longer be usable by the program.

As we will see in the seventh chapter, all objects have some implicit methods like, for example toString(), clone(), equals(), hashCode() and others, that are defined in a class called Object. The argument is premature, but we can also invoke these methods on arrays, just because they are objects. For example, by executing the following statement:

```
System.out.println(alphabet.hashCode());
```

An integer number that represents the address in memory where the array was allocated will be printed.

> In general, arrays are not often used in Java. The objects of the *Collections* library are preferred and these will be dealt with in detail in the next chapters.

Arrays also define a variable called length that returns the actual size of the array itself. Then:

```
alphabet.length
```

will have the value 25.

### 3.6.6 Multidimensional Arrays

There are also multidimensional arrays that are arrays whose elements are other arrays. Unlike most other programming languages, in Java, a two-dimensional array does not have to be rectangular. An example is shown below:

```
int nonRectangularArray [][] = new int[4][];
nonRectangularArray [0] = new int[2];
nonRectangularArray [1] = new int[4];
nonRectangularArray [2] = new int[6];
nonRectangularArray [3] = new int[8];
nonRectangularArray [0][0] = 1;
nonRectangularArray [0][1] = 2;
nonRectangularArray [1][0] = 1;
nonRectangularArray [3][7] = 10;
```

or, equivalently:

```
int nonRectangularArray [][] = {
    {1,2},
    {1,0,0,0},
    {0,0,0,0,0,0},
    {0,0,0,0,0,0,0,10}
};
```

Note that, in the first line, when we instantiated the nonRectangularArray object, we specified only the first dimension (4). This means that there will be four elements in this array, and each element will, in turn, be another array of length yet to be chosen. Beware that a graphical representation of an array is just a convention that helps us to schematize the concept. So, we should not talk about rows and columns for a two-dimensional array, the rows and columns are just in our mind. Actually, Java is also able to create ten-dimensional arrays, which we could never represent graphically.

### 3.6.7 String `args[]`

Usually, when you start learning a new programming language, one of the first topics that the aspiring developer learns to manage, is the input and output operations. When you start learning Java, the *output command* remains mysterious for a while:

```
System.out.println ("String to be printed");
```

and an instruction that allows us to acquire input data remains unknown for a long time! This is due to a very precise reason: the classes that allow us to perform input/output operations are part of the `java.io` package of the standard library, to which a specific chapter is dedicated in the second volume. This package has been designed with a very specific philosophy, based on the **Decorator** design pattern (for information on patterns see Appendix D). This results in an initial difficulty in approaching the topic, but is offset by an eventual simplicity and effectiveness. For example, an aspiring programmer may find it difficult to understand why, to print a string on screen, the Java creators have implemented such a complex mechanism (`System.out.println()`). For a Java programmer, on the other hand, it is very simple to use the same methods to perform complex output operations, such as writing to a file or sending messages over the network via a socket. In the twentieth chapter in the second volume, input-output topics will be explored further.

In order not to jump ahead too much, here is a procedure that allows us to provide only a minimum of interactivity with our first applications. When we encode the `main()` method, the programmer is forced to provide a signature that defines an array of strings (usually called `args`) as input parameter. This array will store command line strings as follows. If, in order to run our application, instead of writing at the command line:

```
java MainClassName
```

we wrote:

```
java MainClassName Andrea De Sio Cesari
```

within our application, we would have available the string `args[0]` which has the value Andrea, the string `args[1]` which has the value of De, the string `args[2]` which has the value Sio, and the string args[3] whose value is Cesari. We could also write:

```
java MainClassName Andrea "De Sio Cesari"
```

In this case, within the application we could use only the string args[0] which has the value Andrea, and the string args[1] which has De Sio Cesari as its value.

> In order to pass parameters from the command line with EJE, you have to run the application from the menu build - execute with arguments. Alternatively, you can use the shortcut made by pressing the SHIFT-F9 keys. A form will be presented to insert the arguments (and only the arguments).

Depending on how many arguments we pass from the command line, the JVM will instantiate the array of strings args of a length equal to the number of arguments passed and will initialize it as we said. For example, the following code:

```java
public class ArgsTest {
    public static void main(String args[]) {
        System.out.println(args[0]);
    }
}
```

will print only the first possible argument passed from the command line. However, if we do not pass any command line arguments, the program will end with the following exception:

```
Exception in thread "main" java.lang.ArrayIndexOutOfBoundsException: 0
    at ArgsTest.main(ArgsTest.java:3)
```

We will study the exceptions in depth in the ninth chapter. But already, in the next chapter, where we will study loops and conditions, we will learn how to write programs that do not break so easily.

# 3.7 Local Variables Type Inference: var

This section talks about the most important new feature introduced with Java 10. In spite of the complicated name, actually it is a rather simple feature. First, let's try to understand what we mean by **local variables type inference**.

### 3.7.1 Verbosity and readability

In recent years, an important part of the evolution of the Java language has been dedicated to making the syntax more concise (in programming we prefer to say "less verbose"). To do this, we have tried to add further tasks to the compiler. With *type inference for local variables*, the compiler can automatically infer the type of the local variable we are declaring, allowing us to use the word var, instead of the variable real data type. For example, suppose we have the JavaBook class, we know how to instantiate an object with the following syntax:

```
JavaBook ogg1 = new JavaBook();
```

Taking advantage of the local variables type inference, we can write instead:

```
var obj1 = new JavaBook();
```

The compiler is able to inference the type of the variable obj1 by reading its initialization, that is the **right-hand side (RHS)** of the declaration. In particular, in the case of the example of obj1, we can say that it is a **manifest type**. The advantage is that we have written less code, reduced the risk of mistakes and all without compromising readability. In fact, by reading the declaration, we can understand the type of the variable ourselves, just looking at the right-hand side of the declaration, rather than on the left-hand side.

The type inference, however, would take place even in the case where, instead of assigning an instance of the JavaBook class to the obj1 variable, we would assign it the return value of a method. For example, suppose we have the following method available in the same class:

```
public JavaBook getInstance() {
    return new JavaBook();
}
```

we could still exploit the type inference like this:

```
var obj2 = getInstance();
```

Of course in the case of the manifest type (obj1), reading the right-hand side of the declaration, we would never have had doubts about the type of obj1. In the case of obj2, instead, if we do not read the declaration of the method, we cannot be sure that it will return an instance of the JavaBook type. So, do not unjustifiably use this feature. We can have cases in which the *verbosity* of our code is improved to the detriment of *readability*, and despite the subjectivity of the meaning that each of us can give to this word, we must be aware that the code we write should be easily readable by others developers. We should therefore always choose the maintenance of our programs above saving a few keystrokes on the keyboard. In this regard, the use of this feature increases exponentially the importance of choosing the name of this variable. The obj2 identifier does not seem to be acceptable, because it will never give us information about its type. If we decide to use the getInstance() method and the word var, then it may be acceptable to change the name of the identifier, for example:

**114**

```
var javaBook = getInstance();
```

At that point, we could reasonably guess the type of the variable.

## 3.7.2 Applicability

We can also use var with other types, for example the following snippet compiles without problems:

```
var bool = false; // type boolean inferred
var string ="Foqus";// type String inferred
var character= 'J'; // type char inferred
var integer = 8; // type int inferred
var byteInteger = (byte)8; // type byte inferred
var shortInteger = (short)8; // type short inferred
var longInteger = 8L; // type long inferred
var floatingPoint = 3.14F; // type float inferred
var doublePrecisionfloatingPoint = 3.14; // type double inferred
```

If not already clear enough from the name, the type inference only works for local variables that are initialized, as well as in other scenarios we have not yet approached, such as within loops (see next chapter), and with lambda expressions (see seventeenth chapter in the second volume). Therefore, it is not applicable for instance variables, for return types of a method, for type of parameter of a method, etc.

Furthermore, the word var cannot be used for local variables that are not initialized, as in the following example:

```
var notInitialized;
```

which will produce the following output:

```
error: cannot infer type for local variable notInitialized
        var notInitialized;
            ^
  (cannot use 'var' on variable without initializer)
1 error
```

The word var, is not even usable if the variable is initialized to null. Indeed:

```
var nullInitialized = null;
```

will print:

```
error: cannot infer type for local variable nullInitialized
        var nullInitialized = null;
            ^
  (variable initializer is 'null')
1 error
```

**115**

The inference cannot be used even if multiple variables are declared. Indeed:

```
var var1 = 1, var2 = 2;
```

will produce the following output:

```
error: 'var' is not allowed in a compound declaration
        var var1 = 1, var2 = 2;
            ^
1 error
```

Finally, not even a scenario involving an array is valid. For example:

```
var varArray[] = new int[3];
```

will print:

```
error: 'var' is not allowed as an element type of an array
        var varArray[] = new int[3];
            ^
1 error
```

As regards the type inference for an array, the compiler is already designed to see the variable type on the **left-hand side** of the declaration (**LHS**), while the word var is used to exploit the right part (RHS) of the declaration.

### 3.7.3 Others uses of var

We will go back to this topic several times in both the first and second volumes. In fact, the applicability of the word var, is also extended to other topics that we have not yet addressed. For instance, in the next chapter, we will see how to use the word var with loops. Later, we will also explore the use of var with particular data structures in particular scenarios. We can, in the meantime, introduce a new definition. All the types we have seen so far, such as int, double and String, are called **denotable types**, since these types can be written explicitly in a Java program. But there is another category of types that defines the so-called **non-denotable types**, that is, types that we cannot explicitly write within our programs, as we have done so far, but that the compiler can define internally, thanks to its capacity for inference. For some of these types, it is possible to use the word var, while for others it is not.

### 3.7.4 The var Reserved Type Name

The word var, is not a *keyword*, but a ***reserved type name***. A keyword cannot be used for any type of identifier, while a *reserved type name* has fewer limitations (see section 3.1.3). In order not to impact too much on the pre-Java 10 code, it was decided that the var identifier can be used for variables (both for instance and for local variables), it is even possible to declare a variable in this way:

```
var var = 0;
```

where the first var is the reserved type name, and the second is the identifier of the variable. We can also use the var identifier to declare a method. In fact, the method:

```
public void var() {
}
```

is syntactically correct.

The word var can also be used as a package identifier without problems:

```
package var;
//code omitted
```

and, also, as an identifier for modules.

However, it is not possible to declare a type (classes, interfaces, enumerations and annotations) with the var identifier. For example, the following statement:

```
class var {}
```

would produce the following compile-time error:

```
error: 'var' not allowed here
class var {}
      ^
  as of release 10, 'var' is a restricted local variable type and cannot be used for type
  declarations
1 error
```

> **Note that for the convention that requires that the type names start with a capital letter (see section 3.1.4), the possibility of the introduction of the word var causing damage to the code written before the advent of Java 10, is really minimal.**

## Summary

Java is a **free-form language** but the code indentation is fundamental for the readability of our programs. It supports three types of **comments** (**single line**, **multi-line** and **Javadoc**). It is a **case sensitive** language and defines **keywords** and **reserved words** that cannot be used as **identifiers**, and **restricted words** and a **reserved type name** that, in some cases, cannot be used as identifiers. These can only be composed of certain **characters** and **symbols** and must be declared respecting the **standard Java conventions**.

Memory is a sequence of memory units called **bytes**. Each byte is made up of 8 **bits** and each bit can store a single value between 0 and 1.

The **decimal**, **binary**, **octal** and **hexadecimal systems** are positional systems and can represent any integer data. Java uses the representation method known as a **two's complement** to represent signed numbers. Within a byte, the **bit of the sign** will contain the value of the sign of the number, and each byte can represent a number between –128 and 127. The bytes have an **address** that the program uses to save and subsequently retrieve the data. A number greater than 127 or less than –128 will be stored in several adjacent bytes.

There are four **integer types**, and they differ, not in functionality, but only in how they are stored in the memory. The most used is undoubtedly the int which is 32-bit long. Less used are the byte (8-bit), the short (16-bit) and the long (64-bit).

There are two **floating-point types**: float (32-bit), and the most used, double (64-bit). With this data, there are various problems (such as **promotion**) as far as arithmetic operations are concerned. The **cast** allows to adapt a certain type of data to be treated as another type of data.

The **logical-boolean data type** is the boolean, which can only take two literals: true or false. The values that are specified in the source code instead of the runtime are defined as **literals**. They can represent primitive variables or strings and can appear only on the right side of an assignment or as arguments when invoking methods. It is not possible to assign values to the literals. In practice, these are the constant values that are assigned to the variables.

The only type of literal primitive data is the char **character**, which can be used to store a single character included between a pair of single quotation marks. We can use three types of different formats, the ordinary format (with a printable character), the Unicode format, and the escape characters. However, a character is represented by an integer and uses the Unicode decoding standard.

On the other hand, a **string** can store whole sentences and its value must be included between two double quotation marks. A string is an object included in the java.lang package that has the characteristic of being immutable and can be instantiated by means of a short syntax that does not use the constructor; this is very useful as it is probably the most widely used object in Java programs.

A **reference** is the "name we give to an object", a particular variable that contains, as a value, the address to which it must point, and which must know the type that will point. When an object is instantiated, all of its instance variables are automatically initialized to their **null values**.

The **passing of parameters** to a method always takes place **by value**, in the sense that, at the moment when a primitive value is passed to a parameter of a method, this value will be copied into the parameter. Even when passing a reference, its value (the address of the reference) is passed and copied to the method parameter.

When instantiating an object, all instance variables are initialized to their null values. Consultation of the **standard library documentation** is crucial. We can also create documentation on our software with the same style as Java documentation, commenting the code with documentation (Javadoc) comments and using the command line **javadoc** command. We can import the standard library classes within our programs using the import command.

An **array** represents a type of complex data (objects) that defines a collection of elements of a certain type, indexed. With just one name, we can access the elements of the collection through an index. It is possible to create reference arrays, two-dimensional arrays (not necessarily matrices) and multidimensional arrays. The String args[] array of the main() method can be used to pass some data from outside to **input into the program**.

The **local variables type inference**, allows us to use as type the word var, instead of the real type of the variable, which will be inferred from the initialization in the right part (**RHS**) of the declaration. If used well, this feature allows us to reduce the verbosity of the application without reducing its readability. Its applicability is limited to local variables correctly initialized, and to a few other cases that we will study in the chapters that follow. Because var is a **reserved type name** (and not a keyword), it can be used as an identifier for variables, methods, packages, and modules, but not for types (classes, interfaces, enumerations, and annotations).

> **Exercises, source code, appendices and other resources are available at http://www.javaforaliens.com.**

## Chapter goals

Have the following goals been achieved?

| Goal | Achieved | Achievement Date |
|---|---|---|
| Know the rules and conventions for declaring identifiers for Java code (Unit 3.1) | O | |
| Understand how memory is handled, along with the positional numerical systems and the two's complement method (Unit 3.2) | O | |
| Know how to use all primitive data types (Unit 3.3) | O | |
| Know how to manage casting and promotion (Unit 3.3) | O | |

| | | |
|---|---|---|
| Know how to use references and understand how they work (Unit 3.4) | O | |
| Start exploring the standard Java library documentation (Unit 3.5) | O | |
| Know how to use the String class (Unit 3.5) | O | |
| Be able to comment your code and be able to use the javadoc tool to produce external technical documentation (Units 3.1, 3.5) | O | |
| Know how to define, create, and initialize arrays (Unit 3.6) | O | |
| Know how to define the *local-variable type inference* for local variables, and know how to use the special word var (Unit 3.7) | O | |

# 4

# Operators and Execution Flow Management

**Goals:**

At the end of this chapter, the reader should:

✔ Know how to use all the Java operators (Unit 4.1).
✔ Know how to use simple programming constructs (Unit 4.2).
✔ Know how to use advanced programming constructs (Unit 4.3).
✔ Know how to use the preview feature for Java 12 and Java 13: the switch expression (Unit 4.4).
✔ Understand that before starting to code we must first clear all the requirements and have a plan to proceed with the development (Unit 4.5).

In this chapter, we will finally discuss all the topics that will allow us to start programming. We will talk about the operators and the programming constructs (loops and conditions). And, we will begin to understand how important the type of approach is when it comes to development, by introducing important topics such as the UML modeling language.

## 4.1 Basic Operators

In this first part, we will present the complete list of **operators** that Java makes available. The operators are divided into **binary** (that do operations with two operands) and **unary** (that do operations with only one operand).

> Java inherits, in bulk, all the operators of the C language and therefore, for some of them, they are rarely used.

### 4.1.1 Assignment Operator

The **assignment operator** = allows us to assign a value to a variable. We can assign different values to a variable during code execution. For example, the following assignments can be made:

```
int variable1 = 1;
int variable2 = 2;
variable1 = variable2;
```

After these instructions, the integer value 2 will be stored in both `variable1` and `variable2`.

### 4.1.2 Arithmetic Operators

The following table summarizes the simple **arithmetic operators** defined by the language:

| Description | Operator |
|---|---|
| Sum | + |
| Subtraction | - |
| Multiplication | * |
| Division | / |
| Modulo | % |

The only operator that may be unfamiliar to the reader is the `modulo operator %` (also known as **modulus** or **remainder** operator).

The result of the modulo operation between two numbers coincides with what remains after dividing them. For example:

- The expression 5 % 3 returns 2.
- The expression 10 % 2 returns 0.
- The expression 100 % 50 returns 0.
- The expression 5.5 % 3.3 returns 2.2.

The + and - operators can also be used as **unary** operators (i.e. they can be applied to a single operand) to specify the sign of a number. For example, the following lines are perfectly valid:

```
int i = -1;
int j = +1;
```

We can use the + and − operators even with the number 0:

```
int negativeZero = -0;
int positiveZero = +0;
```

Obviously, the value of 0 does not change!

### 4.1.2.1 Compound Assignment Operators

In addition to performing an operation, the **compound assignment operators** also assign the value of the result to the first operand, making the code less verbose:

| Description | Operator |
|---|---|
| Sum and assignment | += |
| Subtraction and assignment | -= |
| Multiplication and assignment | *= |
| Division and assignment | /= |
| Module and assignment | %= |

For example, let's consider the following statement:

```
int i = 5;
```

Writing:

```
i = i + 2;
```

is equivalent to writing:

```
i += 2;
```

In fact, at compile-time, the instruction:

```
i += 2;
```

will be translated into the following:

```
i = (i + 2);
```

> **Note that the round brackets that we used in the last example above, are important (see section 4.1.7).**

There are also other compound assignment operators which have to do with operations on the bits of the representation of an integer type (they're called *bitwise operators*), to which section 4.1.3 is dedicated. These operators are rarely used.

We note that, in cases where it is needed, this operator implies an implicit cast. For example, if we consider the following declaration of a variable b (byte type):

```
byte b = 0;
```

the following statement:

```
b += 8;
```

will be implicitly translated into the following:

```
b = (byte)(b+8);
```

In fact, as seen in the previous chapter, the sum between byte b and the integer 8, would give rise to the phenomenon of *automatic promotion in expressions*, which would promote the result of the operation to the int type, which could not be stored in a byte without a cast.

Therefore, compound assignment operators, by implicitly applying the cast, could impact on the result of the operation. In fact, as we saw in the previous chapter, the following snippet:

```
byte b = 127;
b += 1;
System.out.println(b);
```

will print the incorrect result:

```
-128
```

### 4.1.2.2 Pre and Post-Increment (and Decrement) Unary Operators

The following table describes these unary operators:

| Description | Operator | Example |
|---|---|---|
| Pre-increment of a unit | ++ | ++i |
| Pre-decrement of a unit | -- | --i |
| Post-increment of a unit | ++ | i++ |
| Post-decrement of a unit | -- | i-- |

If we want to increase a numerical variable by one unit, we could equally write:

```
i = i + 1;
```

or:

```
i += 1;
```

but also:

```
i++;
```

or:

```
++i;
```

obtaining the same result anyway. In fact, in all cases, we will see that the value of the variable i has been increased by one unit and assigned again to the variable itself. So, these operators also perform two tasks (increment and assignment). We will talk about a **pre-increment operator** where we put the increment operator ++ before the variable. Also, we will talk about a **post-increment operator** where we put the increment operator after the variable. The difference between these two compound operators, is about the priorities they have with respect to the assignment operator, when they are within the same instruction. The pre-increment operator has higher priority with respect to the assignment operator =. The post-increment operator has lower priority than the assignment operator =. Naturally, the same rules apply to the **pre-decrement** and **post-decrement operators**.

Let's take a couple of examples to make the difference between the two operators clear. The following code uses the pre-increment operator:

```
x = 5;
y = ++x;
```

After the execution of the previous instructions, we will get:

```
x = 6
y = 6
```

On the other hand, the following code uses the post-increment operator:

```
x = 5;
y = x++;
```

In this case, we will get:

```
x = 6
y = 5
```

**125**

These operators are also *compound assignment operators* such as those we have seen in the previous section. So even for these operators, in cases where it's needed, an implicit cast could take place. For example, the following snippet is compiled and executed correctly (avoiding any automatic promotion to `int`):

```
byte b = 1;
b++; // equivalent to b += 1 which is equivalent to b = (byte)(b + 1)
```

### 4.1.3 Bitwise Operators

The following table shows all the **bitwise operators**, that is, they perform operations directly on the bit representation defined in Java:

| Description | Operator |
|---|---|
| NOT | ~ |
| AND | & |
| OR | \| |
| XOR | ^ |
| Left shift | << |
| Right shift | >> |
| Unsigned right shift | >>> |
| AND and assignment | &= |
| OR and assignment | \|= |
| XOR and assignment | ^= |
| Left shift and assignment | <<= |
| Right shift and assignment | >>= |
| Unsigned right shift and assignment | >>>= |

All these binary operators are very efficient since they act directly on bits but, in Java, they are rarely used. In fact, in Java, there is no *pointer arithmetic* (as in other programming languages like C and C++) and, as a consequence, the developer is not used to *thinking in bits*.

### 4.1.3.1 The NOT Operator ~

The **NOT operator** ~ is a unary operator, since it applies to only one operand. For example, knowing that the binary representation of 1 is 00000001, we will see that ~1 will be 11111110 or −2.

This operator, applied to an integer number, will overturn the representation of its bits by exchanging all the 0s with 1 and vice versa.

### 4.1.3.2 Bitwise Logic Operators

The **logical bitwise operators** (either **boolean** or **logical-boolean operators**) **AND** &, **OR** | and **XOR** ^, apply to pairs of operands (binary operators), and perform the related logical operations of bit conversions summarized in the following truth table:

| Operand1 | Operand2 | Op1 AND Op2 | Op1 OR Op2 | Op1 XOR Op2 |
|----------|----------|-------------|------------|-------------|
| 0 | 0 | 0 | 0 | 0 |
| 0 | 1 | 0 | 1 | 1 |
| 1 | 0 | 0 | 1 | 1 |
| 1 | 1 | 1 | 1 | 0 |

There are also corresponding versions of **compound assignment with bitwise logical operators**: &=, |= and ^=.

### 4.1.3.3 Shift Operators

**Shift operators** cause a certain number of bits to shift in a certain direction. The number of bits to shift is represented by the operand to the right of the operation. The bits that, after shifting, are outside the binary representation of the number are deleted. The bits that instead "remain empty" are filled with the values 0 or 1 depending on the case. In particular, the shifting on the left causes a filling with the 0 values of the bits left empty on the right of the binary representation of the number. Also right-hand shifting without a sign fills the bits left blank with 0. Right-hand shifting with a sign, on the other hand, causes a filling of 0 or 1, depending on whether the last digit on the left before scrolling (sign bit) is 0 or 1, meaning that the number before scrolling is positive or negative. Consider the following examples, if we have:

```
int a = 35; //binary representation 00100011
```

and a right shift of two positions:

```
a = a >> 2;
```

we will get:

```
a = 8 //binary representation 00001000
```

If, on the other hand, we have:

```
int b = -8; //binary representation 11111000
```

and shift one position to the right:

```
b = b >> 1;
```

we will get:

```
b = -4 //binary representation 11111100
```

The following is an example of an unsigned right shifting:

```
int a = -1;
a = a >>> 24;
```

```
11111111111111111111111111111111 i.e.   -1
>>> 24
00000000000000000000000011111111 i.e   255
```

> **Remember that automatic promotion in expressions is done for all binary operators and therefore also for the unsigned right shift operator.**

 There are also corresponding versions of **compound assignment with shift operators**: <<=, >>= e >>>=.

The right shift operation is equivalent to *dividing the left operand by 2, raised to the right operand of the expression*. The result is rounded down in operations with rest, i.e.: op1 >> op2 is equivalent to op1 divided by (2 raised to op2).

Similarly, the left shift operation is equivalent to *multiplying the left operand by 2, raised to the right operand of the operation*, i.e.:

op1 << op2 is equivalent to op1 multiplied by (2 raised to op2).

> **Given the execution speed of shift operators, it is advisable to use them in situations like these.**

### 4.1.4 Relational or Comparison Operators

The result of operations based on **relational operators** is always a boolean value that is true or false.

| Operator | Symbol | Applicability |
|----------|--------|---------------|
| Equal to | == | All types |
| Different from | != | All types |
| Greater than | > | Only numeric types |
| Less than | < | Only numeric types |
| Greater than or equal to | >= | Only numeric types |
| Less than or equal to | <= | Only numeric types |

 **A classic error of the aspiring programmer is to write =** instead of ==.

To understand how they work, let's read the following examples:

```
boolean b = (9 == 9); // b is equal to true
```

Note that the round brackets are superfluous (even if they help the readability of the code) because, in a statement, the assignment operator always has less priority than the other operators, so it will be executed last (see section 4.1.7).
If we consider the following snippet:

```
int i = 10;
double d = 10.0;
boolean b1 = (i != d); // b1 is equal to false
boolean b2 = b1 == (i >= 11); // b2 is equal to true
```

the variable b1 is false because i is not different to d (they have the same value although they are of different types). So i != d is false, and this value is assigned to b1. Considering the last statement, we will, instead, end up with b2 being true. In fact, i >= 11 is false, as is b1 as we have just seen. So, the last statement is equivalent to the following:

```
boolean b2 = false == (false);
```

**129**

But `false == false` is `true`, so then the value `true` will be assigned to b2.

If we compare two references with the `==` operator, the result will be `true` if, and only if, the two references point to the same object, otherwise the result will be `false`. The value of the variables involved is always compared. The value of a reference variable, as we saw in the previous chapter, is the address of the object it points to in the memory.

So, if we consider the following class,

```
public class Student {
    public String name;
    public Student(String n) {
        name = n;
    }
}
```

the following snippet:

```
Student student1 = new Student("Simone");
Student student2 = new Student("Simone");
System.out.println(student1 == student2);
```

will print `false`. In fact, the boolean comparison will be made on the address of the two created objects, which point to two different objects (even if they contain the same value for the variable name).

 **A typical error by the aspiring programmer is to confuse the assignment operator = and the comparison operator ==.**

### 4.1.5 Boolean - Logical Operators

The following are operators that use only boolean operands, which are called **boolean - logical operators** (or even **logical operators** or **boolean operators**). The result of an operation based on these operators is always of the `boolean` type:

| Description | Operator |
|---|---|
| Logical NOT | ! |
| Logical AND | & |
| Logical OR | \| |

| Logical XOR | ^ |
|---|---|
| Short circuit AND | && |
| Short circuit OR | \|\| |
| AND assignment | &= |
| OR assignment | \|= |
| XOR assignment | ^= |

It's easy to find contact points between the above list of operators and the list of bitwise operators. However, the operands to which the boolean operators apply can only be boolean.

It is customary to use the **short circuit** versions of AND and OR. For example, the following line of code shows how to take advantage of the logical short circuit evaluation:

```
boolean flag = ( (a != 0) && (b/a > 10) );
```

In order for the expression in brackets to be true, both the AND operands must be true. If the first among them is false, it makes no sense to go and check the other operand. In this case, it would be even harmful because it would lead to a division by zero (an error that will be found only at runtime and not in the compilation phase). This short circuit && operator, unlike its traditional version &, will not perform the second check in case the first one fails. Equivalently, the short circuit operator ||, when the first expression to be tested is verified, validates the whole expression without any other (superfluous) verification. For example, with this code:

```
boolean flag = ( (a == 0) || (b/a > 10) );
```

the division will not be executed.

## 4.1.6 String Concatenation with +

In Java, the + operator, in addition to being an arithmetic operator, is also an **operator for concatenating strings**. For example, the following code fragment:

```
String name = "James ";
String surname = "Gosling";
String fullName = "Mr. " + name + surname;
```

will cause the string fullName to have Mr. James Gosling as its value.

If we "add" any type of data to a string, the data type will automatically be converted into a string, which can often be useful.

**131**

But we must be careful about some situations. For example:

```
System.out.println(1 + 1 + "3" + 7);
```

will print:

```
237
```

In fact, first, the sum between two integers 1 + 1 occurs, which returns 2, but this last value is added to the string "3", and then it is also transformed into the string "23". The last operator is to be considered a concatenating operator, thus it adds the string "23" to the integer 7 which is transformed into the final string "237".

### 4.1.7 Operator Priority

The following table shows, in order of priority, all of the Java operators. Some of them have not yet been discussed.

| separators | . [] () ; , |
|---|---|
| from left to right | ++ -- + - ~ ! (data_type) |
| from left to right | * / % |
| from left to right | + - |
| from left to right | << >> >>> |
| from left to right | < > <= >= instanceof |
| from left to right | == != |
| from left to right | & |
| from left to right | ^ |
| from left to right | \| |
| from left to right | && |
| from left to right | \|\| |
| from right to left | ?: |
| from right to left | = *= /= %= += -= <<= >>= >>>= &= ^= \|= |

It is important to memorize the priority of the operators if you need to prepare for an Oracle certification exam. Fortunately, it is not necessary to know the full list to code. When you're not sure, in fact, you can always use the round brackets as we would do in traditional arithmetic. Not being able to take advantage of square brackets and braces (since, in Java, these are used for other purposes) we will always replace them with round brackets. So, if we have the following instructions:

```
int a = 5 + 6 * 2 - 3;
int b = (5 + 6) * (2 - 3);
int c = 5 + (6 * (2 - 3));
```

the variables a, b and c will have the following values: 14, −11 e −1.

As we have already noted, all of the composite assignment operators (*=, /=, %=, +=, −=, <<=, >>=, >>>=, &= and ^=) are actually transformed in two operations, one of which is the assignment. For example, given the following variables:

```
int a = 2;
int b = 10;
```

the statement:

```
a *= a + b;
```

is transformed by the compiler into the statement:

```
a = a * (a + b);
```

The round brackets that we have specified are important, because they make us understand what the priorities are, and therefore how we calculate the final value. In fact, first, we must execute the sum (a + b), which returns 12, then multiply this result with the value 2 contained in the variable a, and, to finish off, assign the final result 24, to the same variable a.

If we had not specified the round brackets, we would have had a different result. Indeed:

```
a = a * a + b;
```

would assign 14 to a.

## 4.2 Simple Programming Constructs

In any programming language, there are constructs that allow the programmer to control the execution sequence of the instructions. This means that such constructs will be used essentially within methods, constructors, or other fundamental components of the language that execute instructions, such as initialization blocks (which we mentioned in section 2.7.5, and which we will explore further in the sixth chapter). We can divide these constructs into two main categories:

■ **Conditions**: allow, during runtime, a choice between the execution of different instructions, depending on whether a specified condition is verified or not.

■ **Loops**: allow, at runtime, to decide the number of executions of certain instructions.

In Java, there are essentially two conditions that can be used: the `if` construct and the `switch` construct (which evolved with Java 12 and updated with Java 13). Further, there is the ternary operator that can sometimes be used as a condition. There are four constructs of the loop type: `while`, `for`, `do` (also called do-while) and the *enhanced* `for` *loop* (also called *foreach*).

The main constructs (at least from a historical point of view) should be the `if` condition and the `while` loop, so we will start with their description. A programmer able to use these two constructs will be able to code any type of instruction. The syntax of these two constructs is rather trivial and, for this reason, they are also called **simple programming constructs**.

## 4.2.1 The `if` Construct

The `if` construct is a condition that allows us to take simple decisions based on a boolean expression. A **boolean expression** is an expression that can only return values of the type boolean, that is, `true` or `false`. It usually makes use of relational operators and, if necessary, of logical operators. The syntax of the construct is as follows:

```
if (boolean-expression) {
    instruction_1;
    instruction_2;
    .............;
    instruction_i;
}
```

With a single instruction, we can omit the braces:

```
if (boolean-expression)
    statement;
```

> **This rule applies to all programming constructs. However, it is advisable to use a block of code (using braces) to surround a single instruction. In fact, this practice adds legibility and promotes the evolution of the code. We should also remember that a variable shares its lifecycle with the code block in which it is defined. So, a local variable declared within a code block of an `if` clause will not be visible outside it.**

Let's immediately give an example:

```
if (sidesNumber == 3)
    System.out.println("This is a triangle");
```

which is equivalent to:

```
if (sidesNumber == 3) {
    System.out.println("This is a triangle");
}
```

In the example, the print statement would be executed if, and only if, the variable sidesNumber had the value 3. In that case, the boolean expression sidesNumber == 3 would be true and then the statement following the expression would be executed. If, on the other hand, the expression is false, the first possible statement following the construct would be directly executed. We can also extend the potential of the if construct using the else keyword:

```
if (boolean-expression) {
    istruction_1;
    istruction_2;
    ............;
    istruction_i;
} else {
    istruction_i+1;
    istruction_i+2;
    ............;
    istruction_n;
}
```

For example:

```
if (sidesNumber == 3) {
    System.out.println("This is a triangle ");
} else {
    System.out.println("This is not a triangle ");
}
```

So, if the boolean expression is true, the string This is a triangle will be printed; if it is false the string This is not a triangle will be printed. Translating the previous code into English, we have:

```
if the number of sides is equal to 3
    print "This is a triangle"
otherwise
    print "This is not a triangle"
```

That should be very clear.

We can also compose multiple constructs in the following way with `else if` clauses:

```java
if (boolean-expression1) {
    istruction_1;
    istruction_2;
    ............;
    istruction_i;
} else if (boolean-expression2) {
    istruction_1+1;
    ............;
    istruction_j;
} else if (boolean-expression3) {
    istruction_j+1;
    ............;
    istruction_k;
} else {
    istruction_k+1;
    ............;
    istruction_n;
}
```

The behaviour should be fairly intuitive. If boolean-expression1 is `true` then the instructions of the first block of code will be executed, and all other instructions will certainly not be executed in all other blocks of code. In fact, the other boolean conditions will be ignored and the code execution flow will move out of the whole construct (after the last brace that defines the code block of the `else` clause). If boolean-expression1 was `false`, then we would evaluate boolean-expression2 and if this were `true`, we would execute the relative statements and ignore all the other lines of code we wrote. Thus, if boolean-expression2 were also `false`, then we would evaluate boolean-expression3 and if this were `true`, the related statements would be executed and the rest of the code would be ignored. Finally, if all three boolean expressions were not verified (i.e. they were `false`) then all of the statements contained in the block of code corresponding to the `else` clause would be executed.

We can also nest more constructs. The following two code fragments may seem equivalent.

| | |
|---|---|
| ```java<br>. . .<br>if (x != 0)<br>    if (y < 10)<br>        z = 5;<br>    else<br>        z = 7;<br>. . .``` | ```java<br>. . .<br>if (x != 0) {<br>    if (y < 10)<br>        z = 5;<br>} else<br>    z = 7;<br>. . .``` |

In fact, the code snippet on the left shows an `if` that surrounds an `if` - `else` construct. The code fragment on the right shows an `if` - `else` construct that surrounds an `if` construct.

**136**

Instructions within the code block of an `if` clause are optional. For example, it is valid to declare constructs that do not execute code, such as the following:

```
if(true) {}
if(false) {}
if(true) {} else if(true) {} else if(false) {} else {}
```

Of course, such instructions are not useful.

## 4.2.2 The `while` Construct

The `while` loop allows us to execute an instruction statement (or a set of instructions included in a block of code) several times (iterate) - as many times until a certain boolean condition is verified.

The syntax is the following:

```
[initialization;]
while (boolean-expression) {
    istruction_1;
    istruction_2;
    .............;
    istruction_i;
    [istruction-update;]
}
```

As an example, let's see a small application that prints the first ten numbers:

```
public class WhileDemo {
    public static void main(String args[]) {
        int i = 1;
        while (i <= 10) {
            System.out.println(i);
            i++;
        }
    }
}
```

Let's analyze the instructions that would be executed at runtime sequentially (so we'll limit ourselves to considering the instructions inside the `main()` method). First, an integer variable i is first declared and initialized to 1. Then the loop begins where the boolean value of the expression in parentheses is examined. Since i is equal to 1, i is also less than 10 and the condition is verified. Then the block of code where the value of the variable i will be printed (i.e. 1) is executed and then the variable will be incremented by a unit. When the execution of the code block is finished, the value of the boolean expression will be tested again. During this second attempt, the variable i will be 2. Then, even in this case, the code block will be executed again. The value of the variable i (i.e. 2) will be printed and the variable itself increased by one unit.

This block of code is executed repeatedly until the variable i assumes the value 11. When this happens, the code block will not be executed, since the boolean expression will not be verified. The program will then execute the instructions following the block of code, but in this example, there are none, so it will end.

> **Also, for the while construct, we can avoid the use of braces if the code to be iterated consists of a single statement. However, it is preferable to use braces in any case.**

# 4.3 Advanced Programming Constructs

In the next sections, we will cover all the other programming constructs that regulate the flow of an application. It is true that with if and while, we can solve practically all of the problems with programming, but it is also true that sometimes they are inconvenient to use, compared to other constructs. Some of those that we will see in this section are used a lot. For example, the for loop is used more often than the while loop. Others are used less frequently (break, continue, ternary operator) but are nevertheless essential for programming.

### 4.3.1 The for Construct

The **for loop** is probably the most complete loop that the language offers. The following is its syntax when using one or more instructions to iterate.

**One statement:**

```
for (initialization; boolean-expression; update)
    instruction;
```

**More statements:**

```
for (initialization; boolean-expression; update) {
    instruction_1;
    ...........;
    instruction_i;
}
```

> **It's recommended to always use the blocks of code anyway, even with a single statement.**

Here is an example that prints the first 10 numbers starting from 10 and ending at 1:

```java
public class ForDemo {
    public static void main(String args[]) {
        for (int n = 10; n > 0; n--) {
            System.out.println(n);
        }
    }
}
```

> Note that the update in a `for` loop (which, in this case, is defined by the decrement of the variable n) will occur only after the first iteration. That's why the previous code prints the numbers ranging from 10 to 1, and not the numbers ranging from 9 to 0.

In this case, we note that the syntax is more compact than the syntax of the `while` loop. Within the round brackets related to a `for` loop, we even declare a local variable (which will cease to exist at the end of the loop). We could even declare it before the loop, if we want to use it outside of it.

For example, the following code defines a method that takes, as an input parameter, an integer j, which is used in the boolean expression. We can see how the variable i is declared externally to the `for` loop, since it is also used after it to print:

```java
public void forMethod(int j) {
    int i;
    for (i = 0; i < j; ++i) {
        System.out.println(i);
    }
    System.out.println("Number of iterations = " + i);
}
```

The syntax of the `for` loop is therefore very flexible and compact. In fact, if we use the round brackets to surround only the boolean expression in the `while` loop, in the `for` loop we use round brackets to surround the initialization of a variable first, then the boolean expression to be verified and then the update that will be executed at each iteration following the first one. Note that these three instructions can also be completely independent from each other.

We can also use the reserved type name var we studied at the end of the previous chapter, as type for the index in the loop initialization. For example, we can write:

```
String [] strings  = {"Antonio", "Ludwig", "Johann Sebastian", "Piotr"};
for (var i = 0; i < strings.length; i++) {
    System.out.println(strings[i]);
}
```

 We could also declare multiple variables within, more updates and, using conditional operators, even more conditions.

For example, the following code is valid:

```
public class For {
    public static void main(String args[]) {
        for (int i = 0, j = 10; i < 5 || j > 5; i++, j--) {
            System.out.println("i="+i);
            System.out.println("j="+j);
        }
    }
}
```

As we can see, the declarations must be separated by commas, and have the constraint of having to be all of the same type (in this case `int`). Updates also need to be separated with commas, but there are no constraints in this case. Note that in this "sector" of the `for` construct, we could have also executed other statements, for example invoking methods:

```
for (int i = 0, j = 10; i < 5 || j > 5; i++, j--, System.out.println("update")) {
    //...
}
```

### 4.3.1.1 `for` vs `while`

The `for` loop is probably the most used loop, given its great versatility. Moreover, it is the only loop that allows us to declare a variable-counter with scope within the loop itself. When it is necessary to loop using an index (for example on an array, whose elements are characterized by an index), the for loop is undoubtedly more suitable.

The `while` loop is used mostly when it is not known how long the statements to iterate will be executed, and there is no index to update at each iteration. For example, in infinite loops, where the syntax is trivial, we get:

```
while (true) {
    //...
}
```

While the equivalent syntax for an infinite `for` loop is a bit weird:

```
for (;true;) {
    //...
}
```

which is equivalent to:

```
for (;;) {
    //...
}
```

> **Beware that statements such as the following:**
>
> ```
> for (; false;) {
>     // ...
> }
> ```
>
> **or:**
>
> ```
> while (false) {
>     // ...
> }
> ```
>
> **will produce compile-time errors! In fact, any statement within the code block can never be executed.**

More generally, the while loop is suitable for declaring boolean expressions with *state-based logic*. For example:

```
while (object != null) {
    // code omitted
}
```

or:

```
while (object.variable == 100) {
    // code omitted
}
```

### 4.3.2 The do Construct

The do loop (also called the do-while loop) is the least used loop. It is essential, however, if we want to be certain that the instructions in a loop are executed at least in the first iteration. The syntax is as follows:

```
[initialization;]
do {
    instruction_1;
    .............;
```

```
        instruction_i;
        [iteration update;]
    } while (boolean-expression);
```

In this case, the code block is executed first and then the boolean expression (termination condition) that is located to the right of the while keyword is evaluated. If the boolean expression is verified, the code block is executed again, otherwise it ends.

> **Note the semicolon located at the end of the construct.**

The output of the following mini-program:

```java
public class DoWhile {
    public static void main(String args[]) {
        int i = 10;
        do {
            System.out.println(i);
        } while(i < 10);
    }
}
```

is:

```
10
```

So, the first iteration was performed anyway. As with the other constructs seen so far, as there is only one instruction to iterate, it would have been possible to avoid using braces as well.

### 4.3.3 Enhanced for Loop

With Version 5 of Java, a fourth type of loop has been introduced: the so-called **enhanced** for **loop**. However, the adjective that better suits this loop is not "enhanced" but "simplified". This loop is, in fact, no more useful than a traditional for loop and can only replace it in some cases. In other languages, the enhanced for loop is called **foreach**, and for this reason, even in Java we tend to use this name. It's certainly easier to pronounce and probably more appropriate. But the foreach keyword, however, does not exist in Java and, moreover, in the Collections framework, a very important method named foreach() is defined (which we'll see later). So be careful not to make a mess!

The syntax is very simple and compact, and reuses the for keyword:

```
for (temporary_variable : iterable_object) {
    instruction_1;
    ..........;
    instruction_i;
}
```

where `iterable_object` is the array or any other object (that we will see later) on which is possible to iterate, on whose elements we want to execute iterations. Instead, `temporary_variable` declares a variable to which, during the execution of the loop, the value of the i-th element of `iterable_object` in the i-th iteration will be assigned. Thus, within the code block of this loop, `temporary_variable` represents an element of the `iterable_object`; presumably the instructions inside the code block of the loop will use this variable. Note that there is no boolean expression for which the loop should terminate. This is already indicative of the fact that this loop is used especially when we need to iterate all of the elements of the iterable object.
Let's take an example:

```
int [] arr = {1,2,3,4,5,6,7,8,9};
for (int tmp : arr) {
    System.out.println(tmp);
}
```

The previous code fragment prints all of the elements of the array on the screen.

> **It seems superfluous to add that, even with this construct, it is possible to avoid the use of braces when there is a single instruction to iterate.**

The foreach loop has different limits compared to the traditional for loop. For example, it is not possible to run backwards, nor it is possible to loop on several objects at the same time. It is also not possible to access the array index of the current element. Actually, it is always possible to declare a counter outside the loop and increase it inside, but in cases like this, it is perhaps better to use a simple `while` loop.

The temporary variable can also be marked `final`. So, we could rewrite the previous construct like this:

```
for (final int tmp : arr) {
    System.out.println(tmp);
}
```

It can sometimes be useful to emphasize that the temporary variable should not be changed within the construct's code block. In fact, it is useless and discouraged.

Note that the temporary variable is local to the current iteration of the loop construct, and then is re-declared with each iteration. This is different If it were not so, then the `final` modifier would prevent the reassignment of a second value (so the loop could not be executed). This behavior is different from that of the variable that we usually initialize in a `for` loop, which has loop-level scope instead of iteration scope.

**143**

We can also use the word `var`, instead of the data type of the temporary variable. So, we can rewrite the previous loop like this:

```
for (var tmp : arr) {
    System.out.println(tmp);
}
```

### 4.3.4 The `switch` Construct

The `switch` construct is a condition, as is the `if` construct. It allows us to execute certain instructions rather than others, based on the value that will be passed to the runtime at the construct. For example, consider the following method:

```
public void switchTest(byte test) {
    switch (test) {
        case 1:
            System.out.println("case 1");
        break;
        default:
            System.out.println("default");
        break;
    }
}
```

If, at runtime, we call this method, passing it the value 1, we would get as output:

```
case 1
```

If we had passed to the method any value other than 1, then the following would have been printed:

```
default
```

At runtime, instructions are then executed that follow the `case` keyword which defines the same value the parameter `test` has. If the `test` value does not match any of the declared case values, then the instructions that follow the `default` clause are executed (if it is present, since it is optional).

#### 4.3.4.1 Syntax

The syntax of the `switch` construct is quite complex, as it uses four keywords (`switch`, `case`, `break` and `default`):

```
switch (test) {
    case value_1:     // optional case clause
        statement_1;
    break;            // optional break
```

**144**

```
    case value_2:
        statement_2;
        ...........;
        statement_k;
    break;
    case value_3:
    case value_4: { // optional block of code
        statement_k+1;
        ...........;
        statement_j;
    }
    break;
    default:          // optional default clause
        statement_j+1;
        ...........;
        statement_n;
    }
    break;
}
```

The switch keyword defines the construct itself, and is bound to a block of code. In round brackets, it declares a variable or an expression (that is, an instruction that returns a value, such as a method or an operation), which plays the same role as the *boolean expression* does for the if construct. The difference is that, with the boolean expression of the if, for instance, we could define expressions as a < 10, while for the switch, we only have a value, and not a boolean expression. In Java Version 13, this value must be of one of the following types:

- A primitive integer type such as byte, short, char, or int (see example, SwitchTest), while the type long is not allowed.

- A wrapper class such as Integer, Short, Byte, or Character. As we have already mentioned in section 3.3.2, these classes can be used in place of the respective primitive types thanks to the Java feature known as *autoboxing-unboxing*. The latter allows us to interchange the primitive type with an object of the corresponding wrapper class or vice versa (we will develop this discussion in detail in the thirteenth chapter in the second volume).

- A class of type String. But we must be careful to make equality checks when using strings, because they are case sensitive and can contain spaces, so it will be easier for bugs to be introduced.

- Any kind of enumeration (a concept we have only mentioned in the second chapter, and which we will detail further in the eleventh chapter).

The keyword case, on the other hand, is followed by a constant value that identifies it (it is called **label**), and after the colon symbol (:), the instructions that will be executed are specified if the test value coincides with the value of the case.

> ## Naturally, it is not possible to declare two cases with the same label.

The default keyword plays the role that else plays in the if construct. In practice, it is the equivalent of a case clause that defines the instructions which will be executed if the value of the test parameter does not coincide with any label of the defined cases.

 The case and default clauses are, in theory, optional. For example, it is legal to declare an empty switch construct such as the following:

```
switch(test) {}
```

Obviously, such an instruction is not useful.

The keyword break causes an immediate exit from the construct, but it is also optional.

### 4.3.4.2 Fallthrough

If after having executed all of the instructions for a specific case, there is no break statement, all of the statements that follow the other cases will be executed, until a break occurs (this technique is known as **fallthrough**). The following is an example of a switch construct that uses an Integer wrapper type as a parameter:

```
public class SeasonSwitch {
    public static void main(String args[]) {
        Integer month = 4;
        String season;
        switch (month) {
            case 12:
            case 1:
            case 2:
                season = "winter";
                break;
            case 3:
            case 4:
            case 5:
                season = "spring";
                break; //without this break: season = summer
            case 6:
            case 7:
            case 8:
                season = "summer";
                break;
            case 9:
            case 10:
```

**146**

```
            case 11:
                season = "autumn";
                break;
            default:
                season = "not identifiable";
                break;
        }
        System.out.println("The season is " + season);
    }
}
```

> **The type of the test variable** month **could also be declared with the primitive type** int, **without modifying other lines of code.**

Let us now consider the enumeration Month of the java.time package (discussed in detail in the fourteenth chapter in the second volume). This enumeration defines, as its elements, the months of the year (JANUARY, FEBRUARY, etc.). We can use it to modify the previous example using the Month enumeration as a test variable:

```
import java.time.Month;

public class SwitchEnumTest {
    public static void main(String args[]) {
        Month month = Month.APRIL;
        String season;
         switch (month) {
            case DECEMBER:
            case JANUARY:
            case FEBRUARY:
                season = "winter";
                break;
            case MARCH:
            case APRIL:
            case MAY:
                season = "spring";
                break;
            case JUNE:
            case JULY:
            case AUGUST:
                season = "summer";
                break;
            case SEPTEMBER:
            case OCTOBER:
            case NOVEMBER:
                season = "autumn";
                break;
```

```
        default:
            season = "not identifiable";
            break;
    }
    System.out.println("The season is " + season);
    }
}
```

Here it is another example of fallthrough: a method that declares a switch with a string parameter:

```java
public static String getTypeOfWeekDay(String dayOfWeek) {
    String typeOfWeekDay;
    switch (dayOfWeek) {
        case"Monday":
            typeOfWeekDay ="Start week";
            break;
        case"Tuesday":
        case"Wednesday":
        case"Thursday":
            typeOfWeekDay ="Mid week";
            break;
        case"Friday":
            typeOfWeekDay ="End work week";
            break;
        case"Saturday":
        case"Sunday":
            typeOfWeekDay ="Weekend";
            break;
        default:
            typeOfWeekDay ="Indefinite!";
            break;
    }
    return typeOfWeekDay;
}
```

> **Remember that the strings are case sensitive and therefore a small typo will cause a bug that is not always easy to find.**

### 4.3.4.3 How to Use the switch Construct

The switch construct should be used in the simplest and most complete way possible. In practice, it is always better to use all four keywords that characterize its syntax, anytime we can. Indeed:

■ In general, it is good practice to avoid the fallthrough (due to its complexity and lack of readability) and for each case always use the corresponding break. If we really need a fallthrough, we should probably consider converting the switch construct to an if.

■ It is always advisable to use a default clause even when it does not seem necessary. In fact, a priori, we do not know if our switch will evolve and expand the possible number of cases. The default clause could be used both to manage new cases with a standard behaviour, and to discover that the switch construct must be modified to accommodate new cases. As we said, the default clause in the switch construct is the equivalent of the else clause in the if construct.

■ Although it is possible to sort the various cases randomly (for example, by moving the default clause to the top of the list) without altering the functioning of the construct, it is always advisable to keep a logical order of the various cases in order to avoid forgetting and making the readability worse.

■ Also, for the default clause, it is recommended to use break, even if it is positioned as the last clause of a switch construct. In fact, it is possible that, in a future code update (maybe performed by a different person), a new case will be added, after the default clause. In cases like this, we could incur an involuntary fallthrough.

■ Remember that the local variables share the lifecycle with the block of code in which they are defined. If we define a local variable within a switch case, it will be visible within all of the cases of the same construct declared later. If we want to avoid this behavior, we can arbitrarily use blocks of code inside a case.

> **If you are using EJE as an editor, you can take advantage of shortcuts when creating the main programming constructs. You can use the Insert menu or any keyboard shortcuts (CTRL-2, CTRL-3, CTRL-4, CTRL-5, CTRL-6, etc.). In particular, it is also possible to select a piece of code and then automatically surround it with a construct.**

## 4.3.5 The Ternary Operator

There is an operator we haven't covered so far, which can sometimes replace the if construct. This is the so-called **ternary operator** (also called a **conditional operator**), which can control the flow of execution as a condition. Below, we have the syntax:

```
variable = (boolean-expression) ? expr1 : expr2;
```

**149**

where, if the value of the boolean-expression is true, the value of expr1 is assigned to the variable; otherwise the value of expr2 is assigned to the variable. The indispensable requirement is that the type of the variable and the one returned by expr1 and expr2 are compatible. The void type is excluded.

The ternary operator cannot be considered a substitute for the if construct, but it is very useful in some situations, because it defines an *expression*, and therefore can be used on the fly within complex instructions. A practical example for those who have already dealt with a database is the following:

```
String query = "select * from table" +
    (condition! = null? " where " + condition: "");
```

We have created a string containing an SQL query and, if the condition string is not null, it adds a condition to the query, otherwise it adds an empty string.

## 4.3.6 Support for Programming Constructs break and continue

In this section, we will talk about two keywords, which support the constructs we have seen so far: break and continue. The role of these two keywords is to somehow modify the execution flow within the loop type constructs. We will also introduce the concept of *label*, which is a technique for "skipping" certain parts of the code.

> **In general, the use of break and continue is not encouraged, and the use of labels is not recommended. However, programming situations can occur where these tools represent acceptable solutions.**

### 4.3.6.1 The break Keyword

The keyword break has just been presented as a command capable of terminating the switch construct. But break can also be used to terminate any loop. The following code shows an alternative way to print the first ten integers:

```
int i = 0;
while (true) { //infinite loop?
    if (i > 10) {
        break;
    }
    System.out.println(i);
    i++;
}
```

In this example, after checking the boolean expression i > 10, the loop is interrupted by the break keyword and the execution flow continues after the end of the loop.

**150**

### 4.3.6.2 The `continue` Keyword

In addition to break there is a keyword `continue`, which does not cause the entire loop to terminate, but only the current iteration (i.e. it skips to the next iteration).

The following code fragment causes the first ten numbers to print, excluding the fifth:

```java
int i = 0;
do {
    i++;
    if (i == 5) {
        continue;
    }
    System.out.println(i);
} while(i <= 10);
```

### 4.3.6.3 Labels

Both break and `continue` can use **labels** to specify, only in the case of nested loops, which loop they are to be applied to. The following code fragment only prints the usual first ten integers once:

```java
int j = 1;
foo: //we can name the label as we want
while (true) {
    while (true) {
        if (j > 10)
            break foo;
        System.out.println(j);
        j++;
    }
}
```

Therefore, a label has the following syntax:

```java
labelName:
```

A label can only be placed before a statement, probably a block of code which is usually defined by a loop (as in the previous example); but we could also place a label outside an `if` or a block of code, as in the following example:

```java
int j = 1;
codeBlockLabel: //we can name the label as we want
{
    while (true)
    {
        if (j > 10)
            break codeBlockLabel;
        System.out.println(j);
```

**151**

```
            j++;
        }
//    System.out.println("This will never be printed!");
    }
```

In the previous example, we could not use `continue` since the label is not related to a loop. It is also clear that `break` and `continue` when used with labels must be inside the "labeled" code block.

A label can actually mark any statement, and not necessarily a construct or a block of code. We can write for example:

```
statementLabel: System.out.println ("label");
```

or even

```
statementLabel:;
```

since an isolated semicolon is itself a statement.

If this statement does not coincide with a block of code or a construct, then it is not useful on a practical level. In fact, it is not easy to find space to correctly use a `break` within a single line of code.

## 4.4 Experimental Programming Construct (Feature Preview)

 The choice of Oracle to accelerate the Java development process through the six-monthly release of the new versions, brings many improvements to Java programming. The platform is enriching itself with new, very interesting features, after a few years where its development had undergone a significant slowdown, probably due, above all, to the operational transition from Sun Microsystems to Oracle. A more modern approach, based on the proposals of the developers, is giving new life to the language. With Version 12, a new **feature preview** has been introduced. In practice, a new construct (the `switch` expression) will be usable as a preview, to allow developers to test it, with a view to improving it in future versions, thanks to feedback from the developers themselves.

> In fact, Java 13 has brought an update to the switch expression introducing the yield statement, but it remained a preview feature, so it can change again in the future.

Let's see what it is.

### 4.4.1 The `switch` Expression

 We have already said that the historical Java constructs (`while`, `for`, `do`, `if`, `switch` in addition to the ternary operator) were imported from the C/C ++ languages, and have existed since the first version of Java. A "modern" construct was only introduced with Java 5: the enhanced `for` loop. In Version 12, it was felt that there was a need to evolve the `switch` construct. In fact, it was suitable for a certain type of low-level programming written in C and C ++, but in Java, it has always been considered a less important construct, due to its singular syntax. With Java 12, therefore, a new construct is presented to Java developers: the `switch` **expression**.

> The switch expression is a *feature preview*, it is not a "definitive" construct. In fact, it was introduced in Version 12 in order to gather feedback from developers, perhaps to improve its usefulness in future versions (in fact, Java 13 has an update). To be able to use it, we must specify options from the command line, both for the compilation phase and for the execution phase (see section 4.4.5.1). For this reason, and given the level of difficulty of the discussion, the novice could decide not to develop this topic. It is certainly preferable, in a first stage of learning, to prioritize pre-existing programming constructs.

### 4.4.2 Syntax and Arrow Notation

The `switch` expression evolves the `switch` construct, which indeed suffers from some defects. For example, forgetting a `break` means causing an unintentional fallthrough. Furthermore, the applicability scenarios are limited compared to a classic `if`, and the syntax is rather verbose. For these and other reasons the `switch` is a relatively rarely-used construct.

Remember that with the term *expression*, we mean an instruction (a literal, a method invocation, an operation, etc.) that returns a value. So, a `switch` expression is a construct that returns a value. Below is the example `SeasonSwitchEnumTest`, rewritten with a `switch` expression:

```
import java.time.Month;

public class SeasonSwitchExpressionEnumTest {
    public static void main(String args[]) {
        Month month = Month.APRIL;
        String season = switch(month) {
            case DECEMBER, JANUARY, FEBRUARY -> "winter";
            case MARCH, APRIL, MAY -> "spring";
            case JUNE, JULY, AUGUST -> "summer";
```

```
            case SEPTEMBER, OCTOBER, NOVEMBER -> "autumn";
        };
        System.out.println("The season is " + season);
    }
}
```

The syntax is intuitive with respect to the syntax of the original `switch`. First of all, note that the various cases can declare multiple labels separated by commas. This way, there is no need to use fallthrough to have the same instructions run for different cases. Rather, this syntax prevents us from using fallthrough. Furthermore, the **arrow notation** `->` (which is also used by lambda expressions that we mentioned in section 2.7.7, and that we will explore further in the seventeenth chapter in the second volume), substitutes the symbol of the two points (`:`) used in the ordinary `switch` construct.

There was no need to use the keyword `break`. The most interesting feature, however, is that, being an expression, the `switch` can now return a value. In the example, the returned value is the literal that follows the arrow symbol, and it is stored in the `month` variable. A literal is itself an example of an expression.

**As an expression, it must end with a semicolon symbol.**

 The arrow symbol can then "point" to an *expression* (in our example it was a literal), but it can also point to a *block of code* that may contain different instructions. In the latter case, to return a value from the block of code we can use a `yield` **statement** which, with the new syntax, can specify a value to be returned. Let's immediately give an example. The following `switch` expression is equivalent to the one presented in the previous example:

```
String season = switch(month) {
    case DECEMBER, JANUARY, FEBRUARY -> {yield "winter";}
    case MARCH, APRIL, MAY -> "spring";
    case JUNE, JULY, AUGUST -> {yield "summer";}
    case SEPTEMBER, OCTOBER, NOVEMBER -> "autumn";
};
```

Note that we have used simple literals as expressions (`spring` and `autumn`), while in the code blocks, we have used the so-called `yield` statement, which allows us to return a value. In practice, the `yield` statement in a `switch` expression is very similar to a `return` statement in a method.

Actually, the notation -> can also point to an instruction that throws an exception, a discussion that we will postpone until the ninth chapter.

Note that in version 12 of Java the yield statement did not exist. Instead of yield, the break keyword was used. In practice the previous code can be compiled with Java 12 only if we replace break to yield in this way:

```
String season = switch(month) {
    case DECEMBER, JANUARY, FEBRUARY -> {break "winter";}
    case MARCH, APRIL, MAY -> "spring";
    case JUNE, JULY, AUGUST -> {break "summer";}
    case SEPTEMBER, OCTOBER, NOVEMBER -> "autumn";
};
```

User feedbacks has led to the introduction of yield, judging the *new use* of the break keyword as confusing.

### 4.4.3 Feature Preview

The switch expression is a **feature preview**. This means that it was introduced in order to gather feedback from developers, perhaps to improve their usefulness in future releases. If we tried to compile the class of the previous example in an ordinary way, we would get compile-time errors:

```
javac SeasonSwitchExpressionEnumTest.java
SeasonSwitchExpressionEnumTest.java:9: error: switch expressions are a preview feature
 and are disabled by default.
        String season = switch(month) {
                        ^
  (use --enable-preview to enable switch expressions)
SeasonSwitchExpressionEnumTest.java:10: error: multiple case labels are a preview feature
 and are disabled by default.
            case DECEMBER, JANUARY, FEBRUARY -> "winter";
                 ^
  (use --enable-preview to enable multiple case labels)
SeasonSwitchExpressionEnumTest.java:10: error: switch rules are a preview feature and are
 disabled by default.
            case DECEMBER, JANUARY, FEBRUARY -> "winter";
                                             ^
  (use --enable-preview to enable switch rules)
3 errors
```

In order to use the switch expression, then we must specify options from the command line. In particular --enable-preview to enable preview functionality, and -source 13 to specify the version of Java for which we want to enable them (the options are highlighted in bold):

```
javac --enable-preview -source 13 SeasonSwitchExpressionEnumTest.java
```

We can also specify the -release option in place of the -source option:

```
javac --enable-preview -release 13 SeasonSwitchExpressionEnumTest.java
```

On the other hand, to launch the example we only need to enable the preview features:

```
java --enable-preview SeasonSwitchExpressionEnumTest
```

> If you use EJE with JDK 13, these options will be enabled by default.

### 4.4.4 Arrow vs Colon

Even with switch expressions, we can still use fallthrough. In fact, there is an alternative syntax to the one we saw in the first example, where the arrow notation -> "points" the value to be returned (which can be defined by an expression, or by a block of code). Actually, by simply substituting the arrow notation ->, with the notation that was used with the ordinary switch (i.e. the colon :), we get the same result. We have also seen that the keyword yield (that was break in Java 12) in a switch expression can specify the value to be returned:

```
String season = switch(month) {
    case DECEMBER, JANUARY, FEBRUARY: yield "winter";
    case MARCH, APRIL, MAY: yield "spring";
    case JUNE, JULY, AUGUST: yield "summer";
    case SEPTEMBER, OCTOBER, NOVEMBER: yield "autumn";
};
```

With this syntax, the yield can also be used outside a block of code, and it is the only way to return a value (we can no longer use a literal, like with the arrow notation). The most important difference between the two types of syntax, however, is that, with the latter, it is still possible to use the fallthrough. Here is an example:

```
String season = switch(month) {
    case DECEMBER:
    case JANUARY:
    case FEBRUARY: yield "winter";
    case MARCH, APRIL, MAY: yield "spring";
    case JUNE, JULY, AUGUST: yield "summer";
    case SEPTEMBER, OCTOBER, NOVEMBER: yield "autumn";
};
```

**156**

Remember that we have already seen that, even with the syntax that uses the notation arrow ->, we can use the `yield` statement, but only within blocks of code. For example, this code is valid and equivalent to the other examples seen:

```
String season = switch(month) {
    case DECEMBER, JANUARY, FEBRUARY -> {yield "winter";}
    case MARCH, APRIL, MAY -> {yield "spring";}
    case JUNE, JULY, AUGUST -> {yield "summer";}
    case SEPTEMBER, OCTOBER, NOVEMBER -> {yield "autumn";}
};
```

However, it is not possible to mix the two notations (arrow notation and colon notation) in the same construct. For example:

```
String season = switch(month) {
    case DECEMBER, JANUARY, FEBRUARY: yield "winter";
    case MARCH, APRIL, MAY: yield "spring";
    case JUNE, JULY, AUGUST: yield "summer";
    case SEPTEMBER, OCTOBER, NOVEMBER -> "autumn";
};
```

would cause the following compile-time error:

```
error: different case kinds used in the switch
            case SEPTEMBER, OCTOBER, NOVEMBER -> "autumn";
            ^
Note: SeasonSwitchExpressionEnumTest.java uses preview language features.
Note: Recompile with -Xlint:preview for details.
1 error
```

## 4.4.5 Poly Expression

The `switch` expression is called a **poly expression**, because it is a construct that can define multiple expressions.

There are two scenarios to distinguish:

- The type, to which the expression is assigned, is explicitly defined.

- The keyword `var` is used in place of the real type.

### 4.4.5.1 First Scenario (Explicit Type)

When the type to be returned by the `switch` expression is known, then all of the cases must return values consistent with the type. This means that the following snippet:

```
String integer = "2";
int index = switch(integer) {
    case "1"-> {
        byte b = 1;
        yield b;
    }
    case "2"-> {
        short s = 2;
        yield s;
    }
    case "3"-> 3;
    default -> -1;
};
```

will be compiled without errors, since all the cases return compatible values with the int type. Note that, in this case, the compiler uses the left-hand side (LHS) of the declaration, to determine if the types that return all of the cases are compatible.

### 4.4.5.2 Second Scenario (var)

On the other hand, if the index variable was declared with the word var:

```
var index = switch(integer) {
    // code omitted (see code of the previous section)
```

its type would be deduced as int, because, in that case, the compiler would have checked the right-hand side (RHS) of the expression (see switch expression code of section 4.4.5.1). Note that also the following code:

```
public class PolyExpression2 {

    public static void main(String args[]) {
        PolyExpression2 po2 = new PolyExpression2();
        String integer = "2";
        po2.method(
            switch(integer) {
                case "1" -> {
                    byte b = 1;
                    yield b;
                }
                case "2" -> {
                    short s = 2;
                    yield s;
                }
                case "3" -> 3;
                default -> -1;
            }
        );
    }
```

```
    public void method(int index) {
        System.out.println(index);
    }
}
```

would have compiled without errors. In fact, being an expression, we could pass the `switch` expression to the method `method()`. The type to be returned for the `switch`, in this case is then inferred by the type of the `index` parameter of the method `method`.

> Within a `switch` **expression, we cannot use the** `return` **command, which is usually used to exit a method. In fact, the purpose of a** `switch` **expression is to exit the construct by returning a value, for example with a** `yield` **statement. We will see in the ninth chapter that, instead, it will be possible to exit the construct by throwing an exception.**

## 4.4.6 Switch as a Statement

The syntax of the `switch` expression can also be used to define a `switch` statement, which is a `switch` that does not return a value, as in the case of the ordinary `switch` construct.

For example, suppose we have the following enumeration that defines colors for a traffic light:

```
public enum Color {
    GREEN, YELLOW, RED;
}
```

and then consider the following class that represents a traffic light:

```
public class TrafficLight {
    public String changeColor(Color lightColor) {
        switch(lightColor) {
            case GREEN -> System.out.println("The light is green");
            case YELLOW -> System.out.println("The light is yellow");
            case RED -> System.out.println("The light is red");
        }
    }
}
```

In the `changeColor()` method, we have written a `switch` construct with arrow notation, which, however, does not return values, but executes a statement for each case. Note that when the `switch` is used as a statement, there is no need for a final semicolon, as with expressions.

> The definition of a "switch expression", in this case, seems inappropriate. We could instead say that "future switch" can be used as a statement and as an expression, and that it can use the arrow notation, and the colon notation, obviously, if it isn't modified further in upcoming versions.

When the switch is used as a statement, as mentioned in the previous section, it is not possible that its cases can return some value. So, if we tried to compile the following snippet:

```
switch(lightColor) {
    case GREEN-> {
        String message = "The light is green";
        System.out.println(message);
        yield message;
    }
    case YELLOW -> {
        String message = "The light is yellow";
        System.out.println(message);
        yield message;
    }
    case RED -> {
        String message = "The light is red";
        System.out.println(message);
        yield message;
    }
}
```

we would get the following compile-time errors:

```
.\TrafficLight.java:7: error: undefined label: message
            yield message;
            ^
.\TrafficLight.java:12: error: undefined label: message
            yield message;
            ^
.\TrafficLight.java:17: error: undefined label: message
            yield message;
            ^
```

Since a switch used as a statement does not return a value, it is possible to use the return command (which cannot be used if the switch is used as an expression). So, the following method is compiled without problems:

```
public String changeColor(Color lightColor) {
    switch(lightColor) {
        case GREEN -> {
```

```
            String message = "The light is green";
            System.out.println(message);
            return message;
        }
        case YELLOW -> {
            String message = "The light is yellow";
            System.out.println(message);
            return message;
        }
        case RED -> {
            String message = "The light is red";
            System.out.println(message);
            return message;
        }
    }
}
```

## 4.4.7 Exhaustiveness

If we use a switch expression, the compiler will not accept situations where a value will not be returned by the construct, due to the lack of a case clause to execute. For example, we modify the TrafficLight class so that it has a state variable, which is set by a switch expression. But we do not insert the Red case, (in the example the relevant line has been commented-out with a single line comment and highlighted in bold):

```
public class TrafficLight {
    public String state;
    public void changeColor(Color lightColor) {
        state = switch(lightColor) {
            case GREEN -> "The light is green";
            case YELLOW -> "The light is yellow";
//          case RED -> "The light is red";
        };
    }

    public void printState() {
        System.out.println(state);
    }
}
```

As we would get the following compile-time error:

```
javac --enable-preview -source 13 TrafficLight.java
TrafficLight.java:4: error: the switch expression does not
 cover all possible input values
        state = switch(lightColor) {
                ^
```

which warns us that not all cases have been contemplated by the construct. To compile the previous file, it would be enough to re-enable the RED case by removing the comment symbol //. We note, however, that this is possible because we are using an enumeration (Color). In fact, when compiling the **TrafficLight.java** file, the compiler can check the enumeration to evaluate what all of its elements are. But this would not have been possible if, instead of an enumeration, we had a string, an integer or a wrapper type. In fact, in these cases, we do not have a finite number of values to assign, so the only way to cover all cases is to add a default clause. In a switch expression then, the default clause is always mandatory, except when using an enumeration as the value to be tested.

Referring to the previous example, no one forbids us from using a default clause in place of the missing RED case, but it does not seem to be the most correct choice.

Rather, the best solution would be to add both clauses (RED and default cases) as below:

```
public void changeColor(Color lightColor) {
    state = switch(lightColor) {
        case GREEN-> "The light is green";
        case YELLOW -> "The light is yellow";
        case RED -> "The light is red";
        default -> "The light is off";
    };
}
```

In fact, suppose we have not defined the default clause, and then let's consider the following code:

```
public void changeColor(Color lightColor) {
    state = switch(lightColor) {
        case GREEN-> "The light is green";
        case YELLOW -> "The light is yellow";
        case RED -> "The light is red";
    };
}
```

where the Color enumeration will evolve to define the BLACK color, which will be used to manage the situations in which the traffic light is off:

```
public enum Color {
    GREEN, YELLOW, RED, BLACK;
}
```

Then we must distinguish two scenarios:

- Both the TrafficLight class and the Color class are recompiled.

- Only the Color class is recompiled.

In the first scenario, compiling the `TrafficLight` class will cause the following error:

```
javac --enable-preview -source 13 TrafficLight.java
TrafficLight.java:4: error: the switch expression does
 not cover all possible input values
        state = switch(lightColor) {
                ^
```

In the second scenario, however, the problem will occur at runtime with an exception (the topic of the ninth chapter). By launching the following test class:

```
public class TrafficLightTest {
    public static void main(String args[]) {
        TrafficLight trafficLight = new TrafficLight();
        trafficLight.changeColor(Color.RED);
        trafficLight.printState();
        trafficLight.changeColor(Color.YELLOW);
        trafficLight.printState();
        trafficLight.changeColor(Color.GREEN);
        trafficLight.printState();
        trafficLight.changeColor(Color.BLACK);
        trafficLight.printState();
    }
}
```

we will get the following error:

```
java --enable-preview TrafficLightTest
Exception in thread "main" java.lang.NoSuchMethodError: TrafficLight.changeColor(LColor;)V
        at TrafficLightTest.main(TrafficLightTest.java:4)
```

In practice, the `default` clause helps us to better manage a `switch` expression, even when using an enumeration that evolves over time. By adding the `default` clause we had deleted, we will get the following output:

```
java --enable-preview TrafficLightTest
The light is red
The light is yellow
The light is green
The light is off
```

# 4.5 Better Programming

Loops and conditions are just tools that will allow us to manage the control flow of our applications. Mastering these tools is essential but not enough. It will be the way we approach programming that will be decisive.

## 4.5.1 Approach to Programming

When it's time to start a new program, the instinct of the programmer is to write the code as soon as possible. It may seem right, but as we have already mentioned in the second chapter, *programming* means performing a process like this:

1. understand well what should be done;

2. decide how to do it;

3. implement the solution;

4. test the program and return to the code to fix any issues or make improvements.

The first step must necessarily be to understand all the functionalities that the software must implement, and understand what to do. This may seem obvious, but we will see that often, it is not at all. To define all of the functionalities that a program must implement, specific techniques can be used, otherwise we risk not having the prerequisites to proceed correctly. In the sixth chapter, we will develop this topic when we talk about *Object-Oriented Analysis*.

The second point is to decide how to implement the code (before writing it). Many programmers, however, prefer to skip the second point and go directly to the third. The practice of "throwing yourself directly on the code" can be done correctly when you have the necessary experience, but it is more difficult when this is missing. When we program in Java, in fact, we will write classes from which we will create objects that will solve the problems during the runtime. Objects will collaborate together by calling methods, then performing actions. So, it does not seem that simple to write a Java program and, in fact, that's correct: it's not easy! Although the object orientation theory is clear and immediately familiar because it is inspired by the real world, the practice may instead be rather difficult, depending on the *forma mentis* of the programmer. Beginning with the sixth chapter, we will also investigate these topics when we talk about *Object-Oriented Design*. In the meantime, in order to correctly approach the problem by carrying out point two of the process recommended above, we now introduce, in a simplified and informal way, a fundamental definition for programming: the algorithm.

## 4.5.2 Algorithms

An **algorithm** is a succession of instructions or steps that define the operations to be performed on **data** to solve a given **problem**.

Many people identify programming itself with the concept of the algorithm. In fact, one of the pivotal activities in programming consists of exactly this, solving problems by performing steps, even though, actually, we will see that modern programming is not only made up of algorithms. The concept of an algorithm is not exclusive to the computer field and can be applied to every field, even in everyday life. A real example of an algorithm are the instructions for assembling a piece of furniture. With a series of instructions to be executed in sequence, they allow us to make a piece of furniture using various objects (screws, wooden planks of different sizes, various work tools, etc.). In this case, the problem is "building the furniture", the data are the available materials, the algorithm is represented by the instruction booklet. Once the algorithm is defined, solving the problem just means executing the instructions given in it. Without an instruction booklet, and without adequate experience, it will not be easy to put together the piece of furniture, just as in programming it will not be easy to create a program without first deciding which activities to perform.

In the example of section 4.2.1, we wrote:

```
if (sidesNumber == 3)
    System.out.println("This is a triangle");
else
    System.out.println("This is not a triangle ");
```

and we said we could translate this code into natural language like this:

```
if the number of sides is 3 then
    print "This is a triangle"
otherwise
    print "This is not a triangle"
```

Note that, if we had written an algorithm for this example, this would not have been very different from this translation.

Let's continue with another example: the algorithm written in natural language to "prepare a cup of tea":

■ Input data: cup, water, electric kettle, tea (various types)

**1.** fill the cup of water up to the desired level

**2.** pour the water from the cup into the electric kettle

**3.** turn on the electric kettle

**4.** choose the type of tea

**5.** place the tea bag in the cup

**6.** when the water in the kettle is hot enough, pour the water into the cup

**7.** wait for the length of time necessary for the correct infusion and remove the bag from the cup

**8.** add sugar to taste

■ Output: cup of tea ready.

This is just one of the possible algorithms for making a cup of tea. It is likely that, in preparing tea without algorithms, points 1 and 2 would be replaced by the following:

1. Fill the electric kettle with at least enough water to fill the cup as desired.

Also points 4 and 5 may have been anticipated or perhaps postponed. With this algorithm, however, we tried to optimize the desired water level and eliminate possible waste with points 1 and 2. In addition, we tried to optimize our time by doing points 4 and 5 while waiting for the kettle to complete its task. This should make us think that the creation of an algorithm allows us to think about how to optimize the activities to be performed. If, instead, you prepare tea directly without having an algorithm to follow, you should probably focus on the practice (take the cup without dropping it, be careful not to burn yourself with hot water, etc.) and you would not have the time and the concentration to optimize preparation. This is the fundamental point. Create a plan before executing it. Even when programming, the programmer dedicates part of his mental resources to other things related to programming, such as using the keyboard correctly, interacting with the development environment in the most profitable manner, documenting the libraries to be used and so on. So, it is best to start with clear ideas.

To write an algorithm, you can use various tools, natural language, a programming language, pseudocode or even a notation language. Writing an algorithm in natural language (i.e. in English or in another language) will probably be your first choice initially (see the example of preparing a cup of tea). Writing an algorithm directly in a programming language, on the other hand, is often an overly complex choice, especially if we're newbies. Using the **pseudocode**, or creating the algorithm by explaining some parts with natural language and other parts with the programming language, is the right compromise. We could also use a modeling language like **UML** to graphically represent an algorithm.

### 4.5.3 Introduction to UML

**UML**, which stands for **Unified Modeling Language**, is a language whose constituent elements are mostly elementary graphs such as rectangles, ovals, stylized men, arrows and so on. These elements are used in *diagrams*, following certain rules. It is a language based on the object-oriented paradigm, and provides different types of diagrams that can be used in situations and for different purposes.

More formally, we can define UML as a language that allows a software system to:

1. create specifications: it can help to define what the system must do.

2. Building: can help us understand how the system is to be built.

3. View: allows us to view the software from other points of view, other than the code.

**4.** Documenting: with UML diagrams, we can explain our software without reading the code.

The definition of UML is very abstract and complicated, so we will try to understand it by using it in this book for our examples. In Appendices F and G, you will find other interesting information about UML.

In short, we can say that UML can be used in many different ways. With UML, we can create **implementation specifications**, or create documents so complete and accurate that, in the hands of a programmer, they will be transformed into a working code in a short time - a situation that is, unfortunately, rare but, all in all, feasible. The main initial goal of UML was to become an **executable language**: designing very detailed solutions without being distracted by a programming language, and then using tools that transform our diagrams into working code. It was a promise realized only in part, actually, and it now looks a lot more like a utopia ideal.

In this book, on the other hand, we will limit ourselves to using *UML with just a few details*, to the extent that we need to clarify our ideas, to draft solutions, to anticipate errors, but without the need to solve programming problems without programming. We will use UML by making it functional for our purposes, avoiding falling into the trap of acting like a know-it-all as an end in itself. That is, despite the knowledge of exciting, advanced syntax elements, we will not force ourselves to use it. For this reason, we will not use specific tools to draw our diagrams, and feel free to draw on simple sheets of paper when needed.

UML defines different diagrams (we will only see the most used) within which elementary graphical elements are used. We can divide them into two types: static diagrams and dynamic diagrams.

**Static diagrams**, which together define the **static model** of the system, represent the static aspects of the software system. This type includes the **use case diagram**, the **class diagram**, the **deployment diagram** and the **component diagram**.

**Dynamic diagrams**, which together define the **dynamic model**, represent the behaviors of the software system. The **sequence diagram**, the **collaboration diagram**, the **state diagram** (also called **state transition diagram**) and the **activity diagram** belong to this typology.

For example, an algorithm, which describes a system functionality, can be represented with a UML activity diagram. For example, in Figure 4.1, a simplified algorithm shows how to play a scale with a musical instrument by reading from a music sheet.

The notation is very simple and intuitive. The black circle represents the starting point of the activity, the white circle, with the concentric black circle inside, represents the end of the activity. The ovals represent the actual activities, the rhombus a condition (in this case the condition of a loop), and the arrows represent the transitions that lead from one element of the diagram to another.

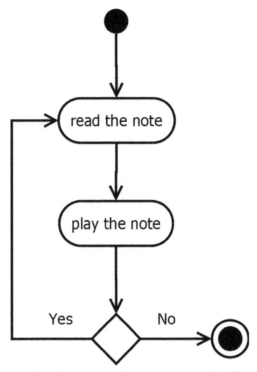

**Figure 4.1 - Activity Diagram "Playing a musical scale".**

> **Appendix G is entirely dedicated to the basic syntax of UML. In this example, we have simplified the syntax.**

Rewriting the algorithm in natural language:

1. read the note
2. play the note
3. if there are other notes on the music sheet go back to point 1

We can use (although it is not mandatory) an activity diagram to describe our algorithms. In any case, we will learn to use them in the examples and exercises of this book.

# Summary

The **assignment operator** = allows assigning a value to a variable. The **arithmetic operators** +, -, * and /, work exactly the same as in traditional arithmetic, while the modulo operator % returns the remainder of a division. The + symbol is also used as a **string concatenator**.

**Pre and post-increment operators** ++ and -- allow a number to be increased or decreased by one unit. They differ only with respect to the priority within an expression that contains an assignment, otherwise pre or post-increment operators work in exactly the same way.

The **bitwise operators** (~, &, |, ^, <<, >>, >>>, &=, |=, ^=, <<=, >>=, >>>=) allow us to directly modify the bits representation of the operators in order to achieve a very high performance, but these are rarely used.

The result of operations based on **relational operators** (==, !=, <, >, <=, >=) is always a boolean value.

The operands and the result of an operation based on **boolean – logical operators** (!, &, |, ^, &&, ||, &=, |=, ^=) is of the boolean type. **Short-circuit operators** are more often used because they are more powerful and efficient. They allow us to avoid evaluating the second operand if it is not necessary.

All operators present in a statement are executed via a **priority table**. Priority can be forced through the use of round brackets.

We need **conditions** and **loops** to manage the execution flow.

The most used condition construct is the if construct. Together with its else clause, it allows us to control the execution flow of the application. Depending on one or more conditions, a certain piece of code may be executed rather than another. The same goes for the switch construct which, however, is better suited to situations where the conditions to be verified are based on the comparison operator. The **ternary operator**, on the other hand, allows us to create conditions on the fly very dynamically.

The for is the most complete of the loops, also allowing the definition of one or more local variables within its own definition. The while loop is more suitable for simpler loops, for example infinite loops. The **enhanced** for loop, on the other hand, is the most practical and less verbose (or more synthetic) but does not allow the use of indices within it.

The do loop, instead, is recommended when it is desired that its block of code is executed at least once, since the condition is evaluated only after the first iteration.

The keyword break, allows us to exit the loop in which it is located, while the keyword continue, allows us to jump out of the current iteration and continue with the next. Both these keywords can use **labels** to even jump outside the loop where they are declared (discouraged implementation).

The switch **expression** is a **preview feature** for Java 12 and Java 13, which can be used by specifying some command line options, both during compilation and at run time. With a more modern syntax, it allows us to exploit switch as an expression (but also as a statement), evolving a construct that has always been little appreciated by Java programmers.

When starting out, it is important to know that, before writing the code, we need to understand **what** to implement, and **how** to implement it. The **algorithm** defines a series of steps that can be performed to implement the software. We can write it with natural language, programming language, pseudocode or a modeling language.

**UML** is the de facto standard of modeling languages; it defines diagrams in which it is possible to use simple graphic elements, to construct, create specifications, visualize and document a software system.

> **Exercises, source code, appendices and other resources are available at http://www.javaforaliens.com.**

## Chapter Goals

Have the following goals been achieved?

| Goal | Achieved | Achievement Date |
|------|----------|------------------|
| Know how to use all the Java operators (Unit 4.1) | O | |
| Know how to use simple programming constructs (Unit 4.2) | O | |
| Know how to use advanced programming constructs (Unit 4.3) | O | |
| Know how to use the preview feature for Java 12 and Java 13: the switch expression (Unit 4.4) | O | |
| Understand that before starting to code we must first clear all the requirements and have a plan to proceed with the development (Unit 4.5) | O | |

# 5

# Real Development with Java

**Goals:**

At the end of this chapter, the reader should:

- ✔ Launch simple applications and scripts without compiling (Unit 5.1).
- ✔ Know how to interact with JShell so as to experiment, explore and discover Java (Unit 5.2).
- ✔ Understand the potential of IDEs (Unit 5.3).
- ✔ Understand the difficulties of working in a company (Unit 5.4).
- ✔ Know how to use a process that will allow a program to be started from scratch (Unit 5.5).

The main purpose of this chapter is to help us understand what it really means to develop in Java, beyond programming. Although this book is dedicated to programming, it is essential to have at least an idea of the context around it, in order to get better results. The first part of the chapter is dedicated to describing some tools that can help us to both speed up our language learning process and improve the final quality of our development. So, we'll see how we can launch Java files without compiling them by using the **java** command (updated in JDK 11). Then JShell will be presented, a JDK tool introduced in Version 9 that allows us to write and quickly execute code fragments (snippets) without specifying the context represented by the encoding of classes and methods. Then we will briefly introduce what the IDEs are and what the advantages of using them are. We will not go into details, we will only try to give an idea of what the potential of an IDE is. In the second part of the chapter instead, we will introduce some aspects regarding dealing with a company. This should be useful for preparing you to face the world of work without too much trauma. The last part of the chapter is the most important - in a practical way, we will try to define a process to create software from scratch.

# 5.1 Executing a Program Using the Source File (Without Compiling)

Yes, Java 11 introduced a new way to execute Java code directly from the source file. For example, let's consider this class:

```java
public class GreetingsFromAliens {
    public static void main(String args[]) {
        String arg = "humans";
        if (args.length != 0) {
            arg = args[0];
        }
        System.out.println("Greetings " + arg + "!");
    }
}
```

We can save the class within a **GreetingsFromAliens.java** file and without compiling it, run the command:

```
java GreetingsFromAliens.java
```

getting the output:

```
Greetings humans!
```

So, starting with JDK 11, the **java** command has been revised to directly support the launch of a source file. Here, we say that we have launched it in **source file mode**. This feature is known as **Launch Single-File Source-Code Programs**.

> **Note that no .class files will be created, but the compiling will be done by the JVM in the memory, and the file launched directly.**

You can also specify the various classic options we use with the **java** command, such as **-d**, **-classpath** (or **-cp**), **-module-path** or (**-m**), etc., and command-line arguments can be passed. The GreetingsFromAliens class can print the first argument specified on the command line instead of the word humans. So, if we launch our program in source file mode with the following instruction:

```
java GreetingsFromAliens.java "from Ziltoid"
```

we will get the following output:

> **Remember that more words in quotation marks are considered as a single argument.**

### 5.1.1 When to Use This Technique

Java has not become an interpreted language, compilation is still a fundamental and unavoidable process for our "real" programs. In fact, it is possible to launch a program without compiling it, but only if it consists of a single file. Since a Java program consists of many files organized in packages (and maybe in modules), the applicability of this feature is limited to some situations, for example doing fast experiments, or launching the examples we have presented so far in this book, often consisting of a single file.

> **Some might think that it would have been preferable to introduce this feature from the first chapter, thus simplifying the execution of most examples and exercises. But we preferred to postpone it for educational reasons. Having said that, we must consider the possibility of avoiding the compilation, not as a rule, but only as an option for speeding up our tests when we use a single file. Introducing this concept from the beginning could have been counterproductive for some.**

Note that we are talking about a single file, not a single class, and we already know that it is possible to create multiple classes in the same file. Thus, we can also test, without compiling, a set of classes that collaborate with each other. In section 2.6.2, however, we saw that there are some constraints to be taken into account:

1. Of the classes defined in the same file, only one can be declared public and, in this case, the file must have exactly the same name as the public class (and obviously .**java** file extension).

2. The classes declared within the same file, however, will all belong to the same package (if the package declaration is present).

The first constraint however, is valid only in the compilation phase! For the **java** program, on the other hand, we can also declare all public classes in the same file and use an arbitrary name for the file. In fact, as we will see in the next chapter, the name of the file will be passed to the **java** command, not a class contained in it. The **java** executable file will then only look for the `main()`method in the first class defined within the file.

 The advice is to use this technique only when we want to run tests quickly, and not to force the inclusion of multiple classes within a single file, in order to avoid compilation. Since we have previously recommended creating a single class for each .java file, we will use this technique probably only if we have one simple class to invoke with its `main()` method.

## 5.1.2 Launching Files Instead of Classes

We have said that we can call the file whatever we want, and that it can contain an arbitrary number of classes (public or not). For example, consider a **SingleFile.java** file that contains the following classes:

```java
class IslandTest {
    public static void main(String args[]) {
        Region campania = new Region("Campania", new Island("Capri"),
                            new Island("Ischia"), new Island("Procida"),
                            new Island("Nisida"), new Island("Vivara"));
        campania.printDescription();
    }
}

public class Island {
    String name;
    Island(String n) {
        name = n;
    }
    void printName() {
        System.out.println(name);
    }
}

public class Region {
    String name;
    Island[] islands;
    Region(String n, Island... i) {
        name = n;
        islands = i;
    }
    void printDescription() {
        System.out.println("The " + name + " region "
            + (islands.length != 0 ?
                "have the following islands:":"has no islands!"));
```

```
        for(Island island: islands) {
            island.printName();
        }
    }
}
```

> **Note that the class with the `main()` method is defined first and is the only non-public one.**

By launching the following command:

```
java SingleFile.java
```

we will get the output:

```
The Campania region have the following islands:
Capri
Ischia
Procida
Nisida
Vivara
```

This is really innovative. For the first time, we are launching a file and not a class! The fundamental requirement for executing our command is that, among the classes present in the file, the first in declaration order contains the `main()` method. In fact, if, for example, we put the declaration of the `Island` class before that of `IslandTest`, and try to re-launch the execution command without compiling, we would get the following output:

```
java SingleFile.java
error: can't find main(String[]) method in class: Island
```

 With Java 11, if we launched a source file and a **.class** file was available with the same name as one of the classes contained in the file, we got an error at runtime. For example, if, in the same folder as the **SingleFile.java** file (or within the specified CLASSPATH, see Appendix E), there was a file called **Island.class**, then launching the **SingleFile.java** file, we would have had:

```
java SingleFile.java
error: class found on application class path: IslandTest
```

This limitation with Java 12 has been removed, and it is therefore possible to launch the **SingleFile.java** file in source file mode, even when we have compiled files that have names that coincide with the classes included within **SingleFile.java**.

### 5.1.3 Shebang Files

The fact that the concept of file has replaced the concept of class with regard to the source file mode, allows not only the .**java** files to be executed, but also the so-called *shebang files*. **Shebang files** are files that can be executed directly on **Unix-like** operating systems (that is, in addition to Unix, also on derived operating systems such as Mac OS and Linux). These files are text files (that some simply call **scripts**) that, in their first line, declare the executable program to be used, with a syntax of the type:

```
#!/path/executable_program
```

and in the subsequent lines, Unix commands.

Now, we can specify shebang files that contain Java code! For example, the following file, has been saved with the name **ShebangFileTest** (without a file-extension):

```
#!java --source 13

public class GreetingsFromAliens {
    public static void main(String args[]) {
        String arg = "humans";
        if (args.length != 0) {
            arg = args[0];
        }
        System.out.println("Greetings " +  arg + "!");
    }
}
```

> **Note that we also had to specify the  --source 13  option (it must be specified as at least release 11 to work).**

We can run this script from a Unix-like system, using the **shell** (the equivalent of the DOS prompt that exists on Windows, which is a command line terminal).

> **On Windows, we can use a Shell Unix emulator, such as the "Bash Shell" which offers us the installation of the Git software (http://git-scm.com), probably the most popular *version control system*, i.e. software which manages the issues that arise when versions of the code are shared by multiple developers.**

Just move to the folder where the shebang file resides within a shell session, and run the command:

```
./ShebangFileTest
```

You can also pass command-line arguments to the class defined in the shebang file as follows:

```
./ShebangFileTest Developers
```

## 5.2 JShell

 One of the most important pieces of news that Java 9 brought with it does not concern the language, but the JDK. The JShell console has been added to the suite of historical applications such as **java**, **javadoc**, **javac**, etc. It's a **REPL** software, ("**Read Evaluate Print Loop**"). In fact, a REPL software is usually implemented as an interactive console which, when activated, opens a loop with which it puts itself on hold waiting for input from the user. With each input that is confirmed by the user, the software reads it, evaluates it and prints a result.

To test how a given piece of code works, we usually have to write an entire program, which requires at least the execution of a class that contains the main() method (but usually also the compilation). Then, we must fix any errors by repeating the write(-compile)-execute-evaluate cycle, many times until the problems are gone.

With Jshell, we can write various snippets such as statements, expressions, methods, variables, classes, imports and so on, without having to write the expressions in the methods, or the methods in the classes or write a main() method. You do not even need to compile: every input passed to JShell is immediately read and evaluated, so an evaluation response message is printed. You will not even need to use the print commands as we have done so far. JShell will save us time and will encourage us to experiment more easily with our code, to create prototypes, to discover standard libraries as they really work, and more. It can therefore speed up the learning process.

JShell does not replace an IDE, but we can copy the code from an IDE and paste it into JShell to simplify our test. Of course, it is also possible to copy the code from JShell and paste it into an IDE.

### 5.2.1 HelloWorld **with JShell**

To **open a session** with JShell, simply open a command prompt (**cmd** program) and, from there, run the command:

```
jshell
```

(You can also execute the **jshell** command directly from the Windows **Start** menu, without first opening the command prompt).

JShell will welcome us and invite us to execute a command to get more information. Then by typing the suggested command:

```
/help intro
```

JShell will briefly describe how it works, also showing some simple examples, as we can see in Figure 5.1.

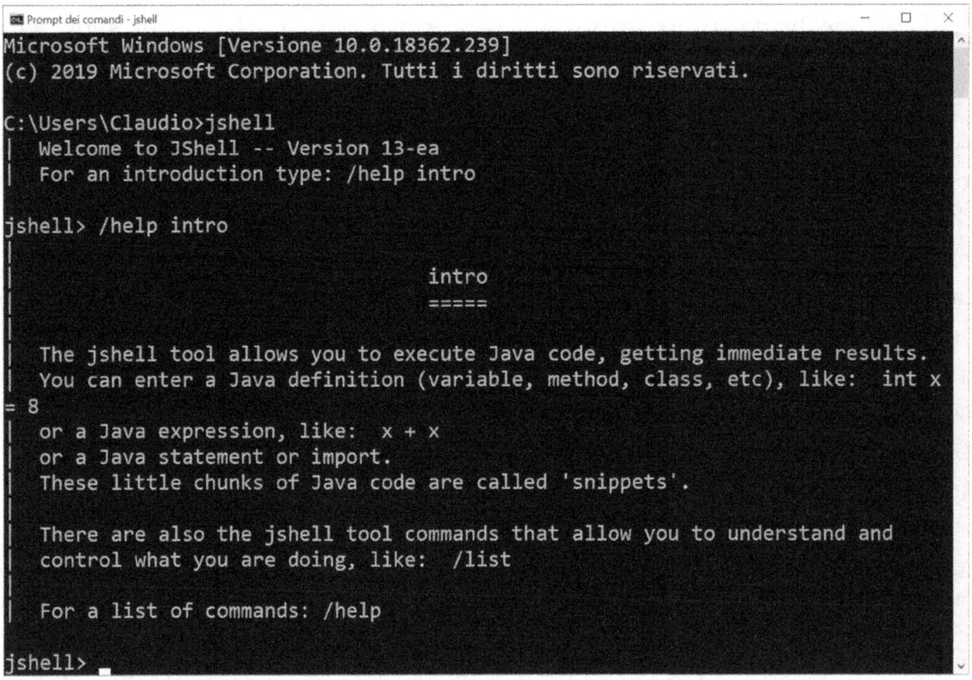

**Figure 5.1 - JShell session opening and "/help intro" command execution.**

In the introduction message, a distinction is made between the **JShell commands** (for example **/help intro**) and the so-called **snippets** (that is, the fragments of Java code that JShell reads, evaluates and prints). The JShell commands all start with the symbol **/**, and we can read the complete list by simply typing the command:

```
/help
```

or more briefly:

```
/?
```

We can write any Java instruction within a JShell session, and let it process by pressing the **Enter** key. For example, we can print the `Hello World!` string on the fly in the following way:

```
jshell> System.out.println("Hello World!")
```

and get the answer:

```
Hello World!
```

> Note that there was no need to even use the final ; symbol, as with all the statements written so far. This is because JShell, as we will see in the next section, has less restrictive rules than the classic Java compiler.

If we type our code incorrectly:

```
jshell> System.out.PRINTLN("Hello World!")
```

we will get an error from JShell:

```
|  Error:
|  cannot find symbol
|    symbol:   method PRINTLN(java.lang.String)
|  System.out.PRINTLN("Hello World!")
|  ^---------------^
```

To exit a JShell session (and be greeted), just type the command:

```
jshell> /exit
|  Goodbye
```

## 5.2.2 JShell and Java Code

We have seen that, within a JShell session, it is possible to alternate **Java code** (snippets, classes, methods, and so on) and **JShell commands**. As for the Java code, JShell aims to represent a tool to test it as fast as possible. As we have already noted, we do not necessarily need to create classes and methods nor follow all the classic Java rules, but this tool tries to facilitate coding and therefore there are some rules that are a little different from the classical ones. Let's start immediately with examples.

> The reader is advised to write the following instructions step by step to familiarize themselves with JShell. Between one example and another, we can also test other instructions. You can also safely work with two separate JShell sessions.

### 5.2.2.1 Practical Examples

We have already noted the **first rule** that is different from classical Java programming: with the expressions on a single line there is no need to use the final ; symbol. We can then declare an integer variable one, initialized with the value 1 in the following way:

```
jshell> int one = 1
one ==> 1
```

Notice how JShell returned the snippet evaluation by printing:

```
one ==> 1
```

which should be interpreted as "the value of the one variable is 1". Now we declare a boolean variable without initializing it:

```
jshell> boolean b
b ==> false
```

In this case, the b boolean variable is automatically initialized to its default value false (as an instance variable when an object is instantiated). We have therefore found the **second rule** that is different from the Java compiler, concerning the initialization of the variables. Uninitialized snippet variables are automatically set to their null values, as if they were instance variables.

Now, if we try to declare another variable with the same name as the previous one (b) in the following way:

```
jshell> byte b
b ==> 0
```

JShell will have no problems using it. In fact, the new declaration of the b variable goes to overwrite the previous declaration. Within ordinary Java code, this situation would have caused a compile-time error, because two variables with the same name cannot be declared. So, this is a **third rule** to follow when using JShell that is different with respect to the Java compiler: declaring the same variable twice (or the same method) causes the first declared variable (or the first declared method) to be overwritten. In standard programming this situation would cause a compile-time error. Also, in this case, not having provided an initialization to the variable b, the null value is automatically assigned for the data type, which for a byte type is equivalent to 0. Then we assign the value 128 to the variable b. Remember that the maximum value that a given byte type can take is 127, so we will get an error:

```
jshell> b = 128
|  Error:
|  incompatible types: possible lossy conversion from int to byte
|  b = 128
|      ^-^
```

> **JShell messages always follow a "|" symbol.**

So, let's force the assignment with a cast to the byte type:

```
jshell> b = (byte)128
b ==> -128
```

As explained in the third chapter, the value 128 stored in the byte b variable becomes −128 because of the truncation of the first 24 bits of the binary representation of 128. So, let's try to subtract a unit from the number that was supposed to be 128, but instead appears to be represented in a byte as −128, and assign it again to the variable b. Also, in this case we must use the cast operator, since an expression between a byte type and an int type (the b−one subtraction) returns an integer result:

```
jshell> b = (byte)(b-one)
b ==> 127
```

The value is now correctly stored in the byte variable. Now let's execute the print command by adding b and again the one variable:

```
jshell> System.out.print(b+one)
128
```

This time the correct value is printed, since b+one is an expression between a byte and an int, and then the result is promoted to int, and 128 is a value that can be easily represented as an int type.

> **Up to now we have always used the `println()` method on the `System.out` object, but this time we used the `print()` method. The difference lies in the fact that `println()` prints the input value and then . . .**

> ...wraps it ("println" is the abbreviation of "print line"). In our example it was useless to wrap and so we took the opportunity to introduce the `print()` method.

We can also define classes, enumerations, annotations and even isolated methods - it will probably not be possible to write these on a single line, as with the snippets written so far. Every time we go to the next line, without syntax errors, JShell will not evaluate what we have written, but it will wait for the completion of the data structure we are defining. We have to take into account that, for the non-nested types (classes, interfaces, enumerations and annotations) all modifiers (except `abstract`) will be ignored, and that it is not possible to declare packages or modules. Finally, if we call a method that we have not yet defined, JShell will warn us with a warning, but will allow us to go on considering our code as being valid (as we see in section 5.2.4.2).

### 5.2.2.2 JShell Rules

Writing code in JShell, therefore, presents some differences compared to writing it in Java classes. These differences are intended to simplify the coding experience but, at the same time, they also place limits on programming. We summarize the main differences below:

1. Although it is possible to declare methods, it is not mandatory to declare one to write snippets.

2. Although it is possible to declare classes, it is not mandatory to declare one to write methods or variables.

3. If we write instructions in a single line, it is not necessary to use the ; symbol.

4. It is not possible to declare packages or modules.

5. All non-nested types and all fundamental modifiers, apart from `abstract`, are ignored or not allowed by JShell.

6. The `synchronized` keyword (explained in the sixteenth chapter in the second volume) is always ignored.

7. Declaring the same variable twice (or the same method) causes the overwriting of the first declared variable (or of the first declared method); in standard programming this situation would cause a compile-time error.

8. Declaring a variable in a snippet without initializing it, implies that it is automatically initialized to its null value.

**182**

### 5.2.3 JShell Commands

JShell commands can be distinguished from Java code because they are always preceded by the prefix /. Until now we have only executed two commands: the **/help** command (equivalent to **/?**) And the **/exit** command. Let's take a brief overview of the main JShell commands.

#### 5.2.3.1 Exploratory Commands

Let's try to execute the command **/history**:

```
jshell> /history

int one = 1
boolean b
byte b
b = 128
b = (byte)128
b = (byte)(b-one)
System.out.print(b+one)
/history
```

This command shows us the history of everything we've typed in this session (both snippets and JShell commands). If we are only interested in the snippets, we can use the **/list** command:

```
jshell> /list

   1 : int one = 1;
   3 : byte b;
   4 : b = (byte)128
   5 : b = (byte)(b-one)
   6 : System.out.println(b+one)
```

A numbered list of valid snippets we have performed is shown. Each snippet has its **snippet id**. As we can see, the snippet id 2 is missing, where we had declared b as a boolean variable, but we then overwrote this with the definition of b as a byte variable (snippet id 3). The snippet that caused an error has not been reported. We also note that the ; symbol is added only for the snippet ids 1 and 3. This is because JShell highlights the ; only when it comes to a declaration. The id snippets can be called with the syntax:

```
/snippetId
```

If we call up a snippet id, relative to a declaration of a variable, it will be redesigned by over-writing the value it might have taken previously. The **/help** command executed without adding options, lists all the possible commands that we can execute with a brief explanation. You can instead have some more details on how the various commands work by following the command **/help** the name of the JShell command for which information is desired. In general, we can therefore type:

```
/help commandName
```

For example:

```
jshell> /help /list
|
|   /list
|
|   Show the source of snippets, prefaced with the snippet id.
|
|   /list
|        List the currently active snippets of code that you typed or read with /open
|
|   /list -start
|        List the automatically evaluated start-up snippets
|
|   /list -all
|        List all snippets including failed, overwritten, dropped, and start-up
|
|   /list <name>
|        List snippets with the specified name (preference for active snippets)
|
|   /list <id>
|        List the snippet with the specified snippet id
```

Thus, we find out that it is possible to pass options to the **/list** command. In particular, to see all the details of our session, including invalid snippets and instructions that implicitly added JShell, we can run the **/list -all** command:

```
jshell> /list -all

   s1 : import java.io.*;
   s2 : import java.math.*;
   s3 : import java.net.*;
   s4 : import java.nio.file.*;
   s5 : import java.util.*;
   s6 : import java.util.concurrent.*;
   s7 : import java.util.function.*;
   s8 : import java.util.prefs.*;
   s9 : import java.util.regex.*;
  s10 : import java.util.stream.*;
    1 : int one = 1;
    2 : boolean b;
    3 : byte b;
   e1 : b = 128
    4 : b = (byte)128
    5 : b = (byte)(b-one)
    6 : System.out.println(b+one)
```

From this output we can understand various things. For example, JShell imports some libraries automatically to make life easier. In fact, there is a **startup script** that automatically imports the libraries listed in the previous example, and that runs when the JShell session starts. The libraries are identified with an id consisting of the letter "s" (initial of "start") and a sequential number, i.e. s1, s2, s3, etc. We will see in the next section how it is possible to change these settings. If we want to only see the imported packages, we can use the command:

```
jshell> /list -start
```

or the command **/imports**:

```
jshell> /imports
```

that will not show us the numbering s1, s2, s3, etc. next to each import statement. The difference between the two commands lies, above all, in the fact that the latter will also report any other import instructions typed as a snippet, while the first will only report the default JShell imports.

We can also note that, in this output, there is also the snippet with id 2, even if it has been overwritten by the snippet with id 3. Furthermore, the instruction that caused the error (b = 128) is also listed, and the snippet id e1 (the letter "e" stands for "error") has been assigned to it. The **/types**, **/vars** and **/methods** commands, have the same function as **/list**, i.e. to list what we have already typed. The difference is that the **/types** command only shows the declared types (interface classes, annotations and enumerations), the **/methods** command only shows the declared methods (not those declared in the classes), the **/vars** command only shows the variables declared (not those declared in classes and methods). These commands share the same options with the **/list** command: for example **-all** to see all valid and invalid occurrences (of types, variables, methods), **-start** to see what belongs to the session startup script (of types, variables, methods), or we can specify the snippet id or the name (of types, variables, methods).

### 5.2.3.2 Executive Commands

We have already asserted that there is a startup script that automatically imports some packages, and that runs when the JShell session starts. In particular we have seen that, by default, JShell executes a script that imports the most common packages (see previous example).

This import list can be configured using the **/set start** command. Three different configurations are already available, but it is also possible to create new ones. In addition to the default configuration (which is called DEFAULT), there are two other predefined configurations: JAVASE and PRINTING. With the command:

```
jshell> /set start -retain PRINTING
```

the **PRINTING** script will be set as startup script for the sessions that follow.

> **If we do not specify the** -retain **option, the startup script will not be kept for the sessions that follow.**

If we want to apply the script set in the current session immediately, we must execute the command **/reload**, which also re-executes all the valid instructions executed in the session. The **PRINTING** script will provide methods with short names for printing, and we can use, in place of System.out.println(), System.out.print() and System.out.printf() (which we'll see later), respectively the println(), print() and printf() methods. The third **JAVASE** script imports all the possible Java Standard Edition packages. In this way we will not be forced to import anything, but we will have to wait a few more seconds before JShell starts. You can also set up more than one startup script at a time, for example:

```
jshell> /set start -retain DEFAULT PRINTING
```

To set custom scripts instead, we can write:

```
jshell> /set start -retain C:/MyFolder/MYScript
```

Or to write, in a file, the current startup configuration with the **/save** command:

```
jshell> /save -start C:/MyFolder/MyScript
```

With the **/save** command, we can also save other information in a file. For example, we can save the whole list of valid instructions that we have typed, with the following command:

```
jshell> /save C:/MyFolder/MyScript
```

or the whole list of valid and invalid instructions:

```
jshell> /save -all C:/MyFolder/MyScript
```

or the entire history of the current session:

```
jshell> /save -history C:/MyFolder/MyScript
```

On the other hand, with the **/open** command, we can open a previously saved file. It can also be a **.java** file. For example:

```
jshell> /open C:/MyFolder/HelloWorld.java
```

With **/env** we can set the **CLASSPATH** variable to make it point to some library (**.jar** file), with the syntax:

```
jshell> /env –class-path C:/MyFolder/MyLibrary.jar
```

> The concepts of **CLASSPATH** (introduced in the first chapter) and JAR files, are presented in Appendix E.

With **/env,** it is also possible to set up the so-called **MODULEPATH** which, however, will be the subject of the nineteenth chapter in the second volume.

The **/drop** command can delete a snippet, specifying its name or id.

With the **/reset** command, the **/list** command will be cleaned of all the instructions executed. Instead, the **/history** command will continue to function as previously, even after running the command /reset.

You also can recall the last line (valid or invalid) edited with the /! command.

## 5.2.4 JShell Auxiliary Tools

Because JShell runs within a DOS prompt, we can take advantage of some of its convenience. For example, we can call up **previously entered lines** using the **arrow Up** key ⬆ (and go back with the **Down Arrow** key ⬇). You can also copy, paste, and search using the DOS prompt features, as described in Appendix C.

But these are not the only tips we can use using JShell.

### 5.2.4.1 Implicit Variables

JShell assigns a reference or a primitive variable implicitly, in case we do not explicitly assign one to it, deducing its type automatically. We are talking about **implicit variables with inferred type**. For example, if we write:

```
jshell> 1
$1 ==> 1
```

we can see that 1 is implicitly assigned the integer variable $1 (the type has been deduced automatically). We can recall the variable and use it, for example:

```
jshell> $1 + $1
$2 ==> 2
```

note how a second implicit variable was also created ($2).

### 5.2.4.2 Forwarding Reference

We have already asserted that we can also declare types or methods and that, maybe, we can also copy them in JShell from already written code. In cases like these, it may happen that we invoke methods, or use classes that are not yet defined. For example, if we were to declare a reference to a class that has not yet been declared:

```
jshell> User u;
|  created variable u, however, it cannot be referenced until class User is declared
```

JShell would create it, but would also warn us that it will not be possible to use it until the User class is declared. If we created the User class later:

```
jshell> class User {}
|  created class User
|    update replaced variable u, reset to null
```

the variable u would be initialized to its default value (null). A similar discussion is repeated if we try to call an undefined method:

```
jshell> void testForward() {
  ...> print();
  ...> }
|  created method testForward(), however, it cannot be invoked until method print()
   is declared
```

### 5.2.4.3 Auto-Completion

The **TAB** key can be used for **auto-completion**, both for snippets and for JShell commands. For example, if after writing **Strin** we hit the **TAB** key, we will get the following output:

```
jshell> Strin
String                          StringBuffer
StringBufferInputStream         StringBuilder
StringIndexOutOfBoundsException StringJoiner
StringReader                    StringTokenizer
StringWriter
jshell> String
```

So, we are offered all the possible options to complete our code but, in the meantime, the most probable one is chosen. **TAB** can be used whenever we want help or want to explore a particular class, library or method, and even a JShell command. By double pressing the **TAB** key we get the **official documentation** of the last declaration, to be scrolled page by page always with the **TAB** key.

JShell offers more help to automatically complete our code with an unusual combination of keys. To **automatically import** a class that has not yet been imported, for example, we must first use that class. Then press the **SHIFT** and **TAB** keys together, release them and then press the i key (which stands for "import"). For example, if we use this key combination after typing:

```
jshell> new JButton
```

then JShell will propose us to choose between the possible imports or to do nothing (option 0):

```
0: Do nothing
1: import: javax.swing.JButton
Choice:
Imported: javax.swing.JButton
```

Or, if after declaring a value we want to **declare a reference** (or a primitive variable), simply press the **SHIFT** and **TAB** keys at the same time, release them, then press the **v** key (which stands for "variable"). JShell will deduce the variable type, declare it and position the cursor immediately afterwards to allow us to define the reference. In fact, after instantiating an Integer, using the aforementioned combination of keys, we obtain:

```
jshell> new Integer(1);
jshell> Integer = new Integer(1);
```

where the cursor is positioned before the = symbol. We just have to write the name of the reference and confirm:

```
jshell> Integer integer = new Integer(1);
integer ==> 1
```

### 5.2.4.4 The /edit Command

The **/edit** command opens a simple editor called **JShell Edit Pad** (see Figure 5.2) which, in some cases (like copy-paste), simplifies code development.

Everything we write in JShell Edit Pad can be reported on the fly on JShell by clicking on the **Accept** button (JShell will be updated with the new edited values) or it will automatically be restored after JShell Edit Pad has been closed by clicking on the **Exit** button.

> Deleting existing instructions does not mean deleting them as if we were using the /drop command. We will simply not see them in the editor.

The changes will be ignored if we click on the **Cancel** Button.

If we want to exploit another more complete editor (for example Notepad++) it is possible

**Figure 5.2 - JShell Edit Pad in action.**

to set it as default for the current session (for the permanent setting use the **-retain** option) with the **/set** command:

```
jshell> /set editor C:\Program Files (x86)\Notepad
++\notepad++.exe
|  Editor set to: C:\Program Files (x86)\Notepad++\notepad++.exe
```

By saving the file in Notepad++, we will get the same effect as the **Accept** button in the JShell Edit Pad. You can also configure other features with the **/set** command. For example, with the **feedback** option, it is possible to increase the verbosity of the analysis messages by specifying the **verbose** value (the operations performed will be described verbatim), or decrease it by specifying the **coincise** value (only the results of the operations and not the declarations will be printed), or avoid them altogether with the **silent** command. For the most demanding, there are also the **mode**, **format**, **prompt** and **truncation** options, to further customize JShell. Please refer to the documentation (command **/help**) if you are interested in these details.

### 5.2.4.5 Keyboard Shortcuts

JShell offers some **keyboard shortcuts** to automate predefined commands. Below is an explanatory table of the available commands (the keys must be pressed simultaneously):

| Shortcut | Description |
|----------|-------------|
| CTRL a | Move the cursor to the beginning of the line |
| CTRL e | Move the cursor to the end of the line |
| ALT b | Move the cursor a character backwards |
| ALT f | Move the cursor a character forward |
| CTRL b | Move the cursor to the beginning of the previous word |
| CTRL f | Move the cursor to the beginning of the next word |
| CTRL r | Search for the last command or snippet that contains the characters typed immediately after **CTRL r** |
| CTRL t | Switch the two characters to the left of the cursor |
| CTRL w | Delete the word to the left of the cursor |
| ALT d | Delete the word to the right of the cursor |
| CTRL k | Delete everything to the right of the cursor to the end of the line |
| CTRL u | Delete everything to the left of the cursor to the end of the line |

## 5.3 Integrated Development Environment (IDE)

An **Integrated Development Environment**, or an **IDE** for short, is software that integrates various tools for developing. As with Java, the most used free IDEs are definitely **Eclipse** and **Netbeans**. They provide a compiler, an advanced editor, code completion tools, a JVM, a debugger, an archive generator and so on, all within a relatively simple tool to be used with an intuitive graphical interface. The latter consists of many different areas, tabs, menus, drop-down menus, buttons and dialog boxes that can be displayed or not if necessary.

Both software are *free* and *open source*. With *free* we mean that we can use them without buying it, and with *open source* we mean that the source code is freely downloadable. Both currently (March 2019) support Java 11.

**Eclipse** is developed by the Eclipse Foundation and can be downloaded at **http://www.eclipse.org**. Starting from its core, many other professional commercial IDEs have been created by various companies, which provide even more advanced tools to develop and integrate with other proprietary software. They allow extreme customization, continuous updates, integrations with software of all kinds through plug-ins, and an excellent basic stability.

**Netbeans** was the official development tool recommended by Oracle until 2016, when its project was donated to the Apache Software Foundation. It can be downloaded at **https://netbeans.org**. This transition has caused a stasis in terms of the revisions of the IDE which has not been updated for months. The strength of Netbeans is simplicity. Compared to Eclipse, it seems be less powerful, but the learning curve is much less steep than that of Eclipse.

Another widely used IDE is the **IntelliJ IDEA** by JetBrains (downloadable at **https://www.jetbrains.com/idea**). This, however, makes only the Community version available for free download (there is an evaluation version that, after a period of time, must be purchased). For the purposes of this book, the Community version is fine. The choice of IDE is personal, but it is highly probable that, throughout our programming career, we won't deal with just a single IDE.

### 5.3.1 Project

When we use an IDE, we cannot create code on the fly as easily as we saw with JShell. The concept of unity of development that IDEs share, is the concept of **project**. You must first create a project, which resides in a certain folder with a certain name, and the IDE automatically develops (according to its philosophy) the tree of the subfolders that will contain the sources, the **.class** files, resources, libraries, configuration files and so on. From a certain point of view, this is a great advantage, because the IDE deals with files, in a semi-automatic way, freeing us from some responsibilities, and giving us the opportunity to focus only on programming. The **compilation** is often done **in line**, i.e. while writing the code the IDE will report any errors or warnings on the fly, without the need to press a button for an explicit compilation (in Eclipse, there is not even a button to compile).

### 5.3.2 Editor

The **editor**, which is the text area where the code can be written, supports dozens of techniques that allow faster and more accurate coding. There are many combinations of keys that allow us to create even quite complex code fragments. The most famous is the combination of the **CTRL** and **SPACEBAR** keys, which causes the auto-completion of the code that was being written or, where there are more options available, the choice between them (similar to the **TAB** key for JShell). Furthermore, pressing the right mouse button on the editor (on each IDE) displays a drop-down menu with various options. Among these are also several that perform **code refactoring** techniques of the code, or standard techniques that modify the appearance of the code without changing its functionality. It's a bit like applying programming patterns to improve the readability and quality of the code.

### 5.3.3 Debugger

Undoubtedly, one of the most useful tools of an IDE is the **debugger**. It is a tool that allows us to run the application in a special mode, which allows the introspection of variable values at runtime. In fact, it is possible to insert the so-called **breakpoints** on the left side of our editor (in line with the line numbers). When the flow of the application reaches a line marked with a breakpoint, the program freezes, as if it stopped time. At that point, the IDE will offer us various possibilities: from the inspection of the values of the variables and the objects available at that point of code, to the possibility of evaluating expressions that we have not written (for example calling a different method than the one defined in the code). From the possibility to explore the queue of calls between the various objects (to understand which object has called the method in which we stopped with the debugger), to the possibility of changing the values of the variables to continuing the execution of the program in a different way. Then we can move with the debugger: we can go to the next line, to the next debugging point, enter a method called in the current line, or exit the method where we are to return to the calling method, and so on. In complex programs and professional applications, a debugger is an indispensable tool.

### 5.3.4 Integrations

An IDE allows us to integrate with other development tools and use them directly from its graphical interface. A Java programmer does not write only code, especially if they work in a company with other developers. Most of the applications, for example, interact with a database in which it stores and retrieves the data to be stored. Whatever the **database** (Oracle, MySQL, Postgres, etc.), an IDE will provide a way to connect, consult and update it from one of its interfaces. Eclipse, for example, can completely change the display layout with dedicated buttons called **debugging**, **databases**, **servers**, etc. Another typical integration that an IDE offers is an **application server**, a software with which particular types of applications can be executed. An example would be the Oracle Weblogic server, which is a Java EE (Enterprise Edition) compliant application server. This is capable of running Java EE technology applications, such as servlets, EJBs, JSPs and so on, and managing their life cycle. In fact, these applications do not define a main() method, but their lifecycles are usually managed by an application server. An IDE can start, shut down and configure an application server from its graphical interface. Among the many other integrations that can be found in an IDE, there are the **version control systems** (for example GIT, Mercurial, Subversion, etc.), which help to manage the versions of the code shared by more developers (and the problems related to them).

## 5.4 Business Reality

To become a developer in an IT company, unfortunately it is not enough to know how to program in Java. When a enter the company, even if you may have a degree in computer science or computer engineering, it is easy to get in trouble. So, it is better to have a picture of the situation as soon as possible and to make the best decisions.

## 5.4.1 Architecture

When you begin to work in a company, an aspect of software that is sometimes ignored is the **architecture**. When we program, we usually focus on the functional part of the application. We identify the functionality of the program, we try to understand the best way to solve the problems, and implement a solution. The architecture contains all the activities that solve the problems of **non-functional requirements**. Let's try to clarify with an example using UML, in particular, a component diagram embedded in a deployment diagram. The **component diagram** is a static diagram that describes the software components and their dependencies. The **software component** (often simply called **component**) is the main notation of this diagram, and can represent any type of program (or part of a program, library, technology, etc.). Its graphic notation consists of a rectangle with two smaller rectangles that protrude from the upper left corner. The **deployment diagram** shows the hardware components where the software will be installed. In this diagram, the main element is called a **node**, it is depicted as a cube, and represents a **hardware component**. The dashed arrows imply **dependency** of the component from which the arrow starts on the component indicated by the arrow. The dependency notation in UML is generic and can be used in all diagrams but, in this case, we mean that the component from which the arrow starts needs the component indicated by the arrow to work.

With the diagram in Figure 5.3, we show essentially where the software components that make up a management application are installed and executed. A management application is an application that supports the management of a business with a warehouse (such as a shop).

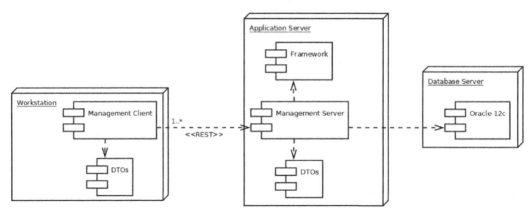

**Figure 5.3 - Deployment Diagram of a Management System.**

Notice how this diagram gives a high-level view of the architecture of this application. You can understand various things. First of all, the application consists of two distinct parts, a *client part* and a *server part*. By definition, a **client** is a program that requires services from another program called server. By definition, a **server** is a program that is always running, and which makes services available. A client and a server usually communicate over the network, with a well-defined protocol (in the example, the "REST" protocol was specified).

> The term "server" often also refers to the machine where the server application runs, because usually this machine is dedicated to hosting only that program.

The multiplicity notation 1..* (see Appendix G) indicates that there is a server and one or more clients. They also share a component called **DTOs** on which both client and server components depend. Note how the server component accesses a database while clients cannot access it. Instead they can ask the server for the various services that it makes available through the REST protocol. In addition, the server depends on a framework (we didn't specify a name). A **framework** is a software layer on which an application can be based, following its functionality and features, so as not to start working from scratch. Frameworks often simplify development, but this does not always happen! The **DTO** acronym in particular stands for **Data Transfer Object**, which is the name of a famous architectural pattern used to minimize client-server network interactions, creating objects to transport data that aggregate information from different objects. So, with the name **DTOs** (the final "s" indicates the plural of DTO) we add further information to the diagram. The architecture has among its purposes the fulfillment of the non-functional requirement of performance optimization. A programmer of the system shown in Figure 5.3 must fully understand the architecture he's working on. For example, by developing a class within the **DTOs** component, it must be aware that it will be used by both the client program and the server program. It may seem obvious, but actually, it is not at all.

## 5.4.2 Knowledge

Java is a very successful language because it adapts and integrates with other languages and technologies. So, in the first place, it is almost impossible not to have other **important IT notions**. For example, knowing a minimum of theory about relational databases, and the basics of SQL to query them is almost mandatory. Therefore, it is very likely that knowledge of frameworks that are considered standard for interaction with databases such as EJB or Hibernate (JPA standard) is required. Knowing the basic theory of XML is also fundamental (see the twentysecond chapter in the second volume). If you work in the web field, you must have basic knowledge about the HTTP protocol, HTML, Javascript and CSS, libraries like Bootstrap, and frameworks like Spring or Angular.

Another aspect that should not be underestimated is having a **knowledge of the business**.

When creating a program for a client, you usually need to learn the business in which the software will be used in a short time, how the customer's business works, and find solutions that can simplify his work. You learn new terminology and gain insights into the workflow of the client during the entire duration of the project.

Finally, it should be emphasized that developing together with **other people** can be complicated. Divergences always exist, sometimes a lack of empathy, and often work on code written by others may not be intuitive, not readable, out of the known standards or, in some cases, may have to be rewritten!

### 5.4.3 Types of Programs

So far, we have essentially created short programs in order to learn the various concepts. The type of applications that we have developed all fall under a certain category: **standalone applications** (also called **desktop applications**). These types of applications are run on desktops and laptops and usually have a graphical interface. As we have learned, they start by executing a `main()` method, which we know must be executed from the command line via the JVM. However, when we deploy software, we cannot expect the user to run a Java application by opening a command prompt. Rather we must provide a file capable of running our code, with a simple double click. The easiest way is to release an execution script within a batch file (file with suffix .**bat**). An example of a standalone program is EJE, which runs through the batch file called **EJE.bat**. This file contains the following script:

```
start /MIN "EJE running..."
   javaw -splash:resources/images/splash.png com.cdsc.eje.gui.EJE
```

that runs EJE with the **javaw** command (which is the specialized version of the **java** command for GUI applications) specifying a *splash screen* (that is, an image that appears when loading the resources when the program starts) and hiding the prompt DOS used to execute the command.

Nowadays however, standalone applications are only a small part of the set of professionally developed applications. The term "standalone" can be translated as "autonomous". In fact, a standalone application, apart from the installation of the JVM, does not require anything else to be performed. The other types of applications instead run within execution contexts. **Web applications** for example, are applications that have an architecture divided into a client part and a server part. A **web client** requires web pages and coincides with the programs we commonly call **browsers** (Mozilla Firefox, Google Chrome, etc.). A **web server** on the other hand, is an application that makes network services available. A famous example of a web server is Apache HTTP Server (**HTTP** is the main communication protocol on the network, used by browsers). Within the web server, applications are executed that create web pages with various technologies including Java, Javascript, HTML and others, known as **web applications**. The life cycle of a web application is managed by the web server (that is, they do not start by executing a main() method) as well as its configuration.

**Enterprise applications** are an evolution of web applications, and usually provide more complex services such as downloading resources, **web services** (i.e. communication applications between heterogeneous systems that use the HTTP protocol), reporting services, etc. So, the enterprise applications can also define as **enterprise client**, a standalone program specifically created to interact with the **enterprise server** layer. The latter consists, in turn, of various layers that use different technologies to fulfill various purposes (the management application shown in Figure 5.3 can be considered of enterprise type).

But the type of application that is probably the most developed today is the **mobile application**. In recent years, with the incredible spread of tablets and smartphones, billions of so-called **apps** have been developed, which have revolutionized the way we develop and conceive software. This type of application can have both a client-server architecture and a client-only architecture. The client part is particularly important, and although sometimes it is developed with web pages to ensure maximum portability between the various mobile devices, other times it is developed in the native language of the platforms to which it is intended (as already said, the most of the native Android apps are programmed in Java).

## 5.4.4 Roles

When developing in a company, programming is only one of the activities that are carried out. **Software engineering** defines various activities that contribute to the creation of a functioning software. In a company, there are not only developers, but there are many people who play various roles, each of which should have precise responsibilities within the various stages of the software development cycle. The **project manager** should plan the work on time, assign the work to the resources, interact with all of the main members of the development team, with the management and with the client. The **business analyst**, on the other hand, aims to collect customer requirements, and to formulate and resolve functional doubts. The role of the **software architect** is to manage non-functional requirements, that is, to choose technologies, to supervise the quality of the code, to improve the usability of the software, to decide the architecture to be used, to decide the structure and the application installation, to improve performance, to train developers and so on. The **IT manager** (also known as the **system administrator**) deals with preparing the environments, installing the software, and configuring the network, the machines, the permissions, etc. The **deployer** (or **release manager**) is responsible for creating and installing software versions for the various environments in which it is to be used. The **tester** takes care of finding bugs in the testing environment and reports them to the managers of the development team in order to find fixes. The **database administrator** (or **DBA**) is the database expert and takes care of everything related to the interaction and configuration of the database. The **graphic designer** is responsible for the appearance of the application graphics. The same **developer** will have various activities to perform, depending on how the business is organized. If the company is not very structured, it often happens that the developer must be able to do analysis, design and documentation in addition to development. The smaller the company, the easier it is for multiple roles to be assigned to one person. In short, how the various activities are assigned depends on how the company is organized and the resources available to it.

## 5.4.5 Methodology

These activities include: **gathering the system requirements** with the customer, formalizing in a document, such as an **SRS (Software Requirement Specification)**, an **analysis of the scenarios**, the **choice of technologies**, the choice and preparation of the development, the testing and maintenance **environments**, the **feasibility plan** with respect to the available resources, the **project plan** which includes all activities and related time schedules, the design of the **architectural solution**, the **design** of the functionalities, the **database design**, the creation of **internal technical documentation**, the creation of the **information sharing environment**, (obviously) the **development**, the **deployment**, the **testing**, the **bug fixes phase**, **user training**, the creation of the **user manual**, and the **maintenance** and the **evolution** of the software. So, as you can see, learning to program is only a small part of everything!

Furthermore, all these activities must be organized and performed with certain standards, in a particular order, using appropriate timing and the right techniques. All of this is usually regulated by a **company methodology**. In fact, each company adopts its own methodology, which can be more or less inspired by standard methodologies. An **object-oriented methodology**, in its more general definition, could be understood as a *pair consisting of a process and a modeling language.*

In turn, a **process** could be defined as a series of indications regarding the steps to be taken to successfully complete a project.

A **modeling language** is the tool that the methodologies use to describe (possibly in a graphic way) all the static and dynamic characteristics of a project. **UML** is nothing more than a modeling language, and is considered the de facto standard by most established methodologies. As we have seen, it is made up of general lines from a series of diagrams whose elements are simple lines, triangles, rectangles, stylized men and so on. These diagrams have the task of clearly describing everything that may be difficult or too long during a project with textual documentation.

Since this is not a book on software engineering, we cannot dedicate too much space to theory. So, among the exercises in this chapter, we have introduced a case study where we will try to start developing. In this way, we will have practical examples of how these activities can be addressed. Since, so far, we have spoken almost exclusively about Java programming, starting from the next section we will introduce, with a practical example, one of the many ways to approach the problem. Although we can feel we understand well the concepts studied so far, we do not yet have a method to use them correctly. Though you may have diligently studied, you may not yet be able to develop a program properly. In fact, in the exercises, the implementation of an application from scratch has never been requested, even if it is simple. For example, do you feel able to create an application that simulates a phone book? Which classes would you create? How many classes would you create? It seems very difficult to start! So, let's introduce a possible **process** that can lead us to some concrete result.

# 5.5 Case Study

Imagine you're a programmer employed by a small computer company that we will call **Noumeno Ltd**. This small company is commissioned to create a web application to support the business of **Panta Rei Clothing**, a chain of five clothing stores that are scattered across various cities. A contract is signed with the target of having it online within six months. It will be the new internal management application for Panta Rei, which will be called **Logos**. A **management application** is a type of application with a client-server architecture (usually), which supports the management of a business that uses a warehouse. This application must facilitate the searching of all products for sale, showing their availability in all of the chain's stores. The employees of the various stores will be users of the application and will also be able to insert new products, change their availability, and delete them.

A description like the previous one (which we could call a **problem statement**) is insufficient to start writing the code. What classes do we have to create to start? Are you able to use previous experience (perhaps using frameworks like Spring) to start throwing together a rough solution? From our point of view... absolutely not!

The requirements are too few and too generic to be able to start writing code, choose a framework, and to define the basic functionalities that the application must have. Let's therefore introduce the first step of our process.

## 5.5.1 Requirements Gathering with Use Cases and Scenarios

Without identifying the functionality of the application, it's impossible to create a program. So, our first purpose is to identify this, talk to the customer, understand how the business currently works and what we want to improve with the required system. We can, in the meantime, introduce a technique called use case analysis.
We will use, in this regard, the Use Case UML diagram. This diagram is useful to represent the interactions between the system and the users of the system itself. Users of the system are represented as stylized men, and are called actors, but this term should be interpreted as roles

and not as physical persons. The use cases which, for simplicity, we can identify as the functionalities of the application, are represented by simple ovals. Furthermore, on this diagram it is possible to report some dependencies (dashed arrows) and other complex relationships between use cases, such as the include relationship, which implies that the use case from which the arrow starts could use the use case pointed to by the arrow (see Appendix G). Where we want to express a concept in a textual way we can use a note (sheet with a bent corner), which is an element common to all UML diagrams. Finally, there is the so-called system boundary that represents the system itself, which is represented with a rectangle (containing the use cases).

### 5.5.1.1 Use Case Diagram

In Figure 5.4 we report the final diagram deriving from our analysis.

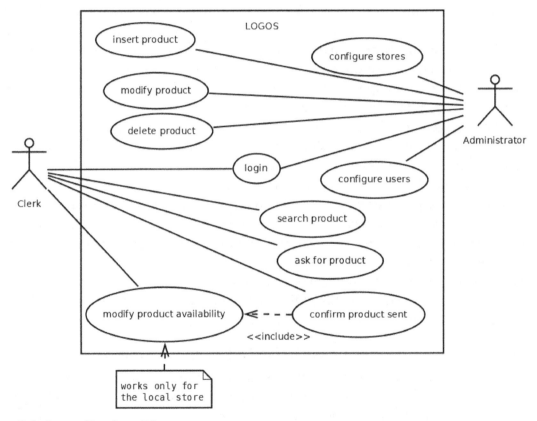

**Figure 5.4 - Logos Use Case Diagram.**

How is it possible to have obtained so many features? Let's explain the steps we performed. We asked several questions of the client, and discovered new requirements. From time to time, we updated the diagram which statically showed the interaction between users and the system, and helped us to reason in a simple way. Our analysis started with doubts about the problem statement. In fact, first of all, this sentence sounded ambiguous: "This application must facilitate the searching of all products for sale, showing their availability in all of the chain's stores." If we're talking about availability and there are five stores, maybe we're talking about **availability per store**. And, in fact, the customer has confirmed this. And why do they want to know the availability at other stores? The client explained to us that it would be very useful when other stores have more availability on certain products compared to the local store. We have proposed a solution based on the following process. A clerk can look for the availability of a given product that is not available or scarce in the local store, using the **search product** feature. He can then request it from another location using the **ask for product** feature. A clerk in another location will receive this request through Logos and will be able to confirm (or not) the sending of the requested product to the other location through the **confirm product sent** function. This feature will, in turn, automatically decrease the availability of the product at the other location, automatically using the **modify product availability** feature. Once the request has been received, the clerk of the requesting office will have to update the availability of his office, also using the **modify product availability** function. A **constraint** shown in the diagram with a **note** (a leaflet with a bent corner) is that a clerk can update the availability of products only in their own office. Our proposal was accepted by the customer with enthusiasm. So, we added all the use cases to the diagram and, at first, we had only one actor: the **Clerk**, as suggested by the problem statement. Then we realized that the functionality of **insert product**, **update product**, **delete product**, cannot be assigned to a clerk, because the products are shared by all locations and not by one in particular. So, we proposed adding a new actor called **Administrator**, that has to deal with defining the products. He must also have the capacity to define the stores (**configure stores** feature) and their details and, using the **configure users** feature, the users' employees (clerks), who will have to authenticate themselves in the system in order to perform operations (**login** feature, also used by the administrator himself). The result of our analysis is represented in the diagram in Figure 5.4.

### 5.5.1.2 Use Case Scenarios

After having identified all of the use cases, our analysis must go on to explain the so-called **use case scenarios**. The **scenario**, by definition is a sequence of steps that describes the interaction between the user and the system. It is said that the scenario is an *instance of a use case*. The use case, in fact, is defined in UML as a set of scenarios linked to a common goal for the user (we had previously identified the use case with a functionality, but this definition is more precise). So, the next step is to explain all of the possible scenarios for each use case. A scenario contains no conditions, there is a standard scenario that is what is expected to be done if everything goes as it should go, and then any conditions give rise to other scenarios. The description of the scenarios helps to identify all of the critical points in the system without writing a single line of code. This passage can easily be done with some text. For example, let's go into the details of the use case **search product**. The **standard scenario** could consist of the following steps:

1. the clerk searches for a certain product specifying the type of product = "scarf", and brand = "Columbia";

2. the system returns three results with products that match the search, showing for each of them all the details (id, price, color, etc.);

3. the clerk selects the desired product clicking on it;

4. the system offers a screen that shows the availability of the product for each store, showing, next to each result, an **ask for product** button and, at the bottom of the page, a **search product** button.

There are dozens of alternatives to this scenario and for each it is worthwhile to fill in a new scenario. To identify them, start from the main scenario and, for each point, look for an alternative. For example, here is a possible **second scenario**:

1. the clerk looks for a certain product, specifying the type of product = "scarf";

2. the system finds 505 results, but only shows the first ten, while paging all the others.

Let's stop here, because we have already found an interesting result, without effort and in a very short time: if the research produces too many results, we want to page them to make the user's life easier! Would we have thought about this if we had jumped straight to the code?
Let's continue with the third scenario:

1. the clerk searches for a certain product specifying id = "741231";

2. the system, having found a single result, directly proposes the screen referred to in point 4 of the standard scenario.

Even this solution seems very interesting! If the system finds a single result, it skips steps 2 and 3 of the main scenario. Also, in this case: would we ever have arrived at the same solution without describing the scenarios? The answer seems obvious and the analysis of the scenarios seems absolutely essential in order to start planning with clear ideas. We will continue the description of other scenarios in the exercises. You can also use a UML activity diagram to specify all scenarios with a single diagram.

## 5.5.2 High Level Architecture

Parallel to the use case analysis, in our process, an architect could identify and propose the non-functional requirements of the Logos application. For example, with the deployment diagram depicted in Figure 5.5, let's define a **high-level architectural solution** (i.e. without specifying too many details).

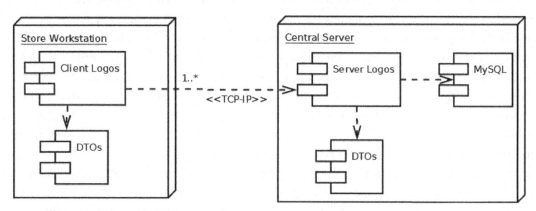

**Figure 5.5 - High Level Deployment Diagram of Logos.**

In agreement with the customer, it was decided to minimize the infrastructure costs as the risks of possible hardware and software malfunctions would not cause any particular damage to Panta Rei Clothing. So, we chose to have a single central server that will be installed in the office with the best internet connection. It will be a single machine where the Logos server module and the MySQL database will run. Communication with the clients will take place via the TCP-IP protocol. What happens if for some reason a client fails to communicate with a server (non-functional requirement)? It was decided to allow the client to record some data locally, which will be synchronized with the server when the connection will be available again.

## 5.5.3 Key Abstractions

The next step, after the use case analysis, is to finally define which are the fundamental classes that will certainly be implemented in our program, the so-called **key abstraction**. The list of these key abstractions can be derived from a list of all the words that seem to make some sense for our analysis. This list is called a list of **candidate classes**, and is obtained simply by reporting all the words that seem to have some relevance within the use case analysis and the high-level deployment diagram. We have not completed the analysis (we have just started), so a complete list is not easy to draw but, based only on the product research use case, we can report the following candidate classes: clerk, research, product, scarf, result, pagination, product type, identifier (id), price, color, availability, screen, client and server. How do we extract the sub-list from the key abstraction? Simply consider that a key abstraction must already have *clear responsibilities*, otherwise it is discarded. This does not mean that it will not become a class of the system later, but simply that it is not a key abstraction. Furthermore, a good rule says that no matter how big the project is, the initial list of key abstractions must not consist of more than seven entities. In our case, we will try to minimize this number even further. On the basis of what has been said, we immediately exclude the concepts of identification, price, color, product type, and also availability, which seem more like attributes of the first key abstraction product (the Product class is naturally essential for the application business). The concepts of screen and pagination seem to belong more to the client's graphical interface, while scarf seems to be a possible value of the product type attribute. The clerk, instead of a key abstraction is, more than anything else, the user of the system. Furthermore, research looks more like the name of a method than the name of a class (although it might also fit). In fact, the only secure key abstraction is Product, since we have partially explored a single use case. Although very general to be considered key abstractions, to start, we will use the Client and Server classes. We will assign to them the executive responsibilities of the functionalities of the application, given that Product represents application data. It is possible that these classes will then split into more specific classes going forward in the development cycle.

### 5.5.4 Design with Interaction Diagrams

The next step is therefore to use the UML dynamic diagrams such as the **sequence diagram** or the **collaboration diagram** (see Appendix G), to simulate all the scenarios realized through assigning the responsibilities of the actions to the objects created for this purpose. These diagrams have the task of defining the exchange of messages between objects that will realize the use case, and to demonstrate the actual feasibility of implementing the scenarios using the classes identified so far. Figure 5.6 shows the third scenario that we have analyzed with a **sequence diagram**, which shows how groups of objects interact in a given period of time (in our case within a scenario).

The syntax of this diagram shows the system **objects** at runtime and an **actor** who starts the scenario with one of his actions, at the top. The names of the objects have the syntax: objectName:ClassName, with both parts being optional (we have omitted the objectName). The dotted lines that descend from objects are called **life lines** and represent the existence of the object. You can see how the Product object begins to exist when the database is queried and a result is returned. Note that the <<create>> label indicates that the constructor was called. The strings enclosed in editorial quotation marks in UML are called **stereotypes**, they can be used on all diagrams and are useful for providing further information to the reader. The rectangles covering the life lines are called **activity lines**, and show the period of time in which a certain object is active. Finally, the arrows that join the objects are called **messages** and represent the method calls, as we can guess from their labels. Messages that return to the same object represent private method calls.

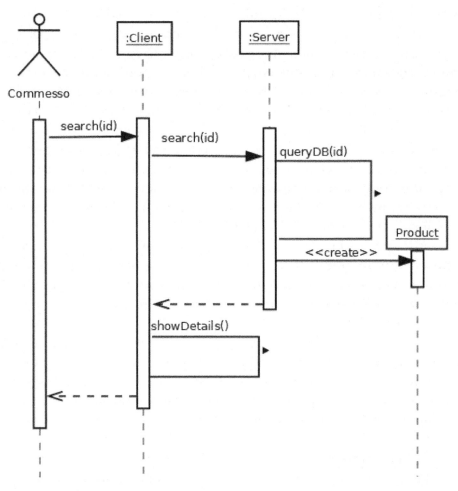

**Figure 5.6 – Sequence diagram of the third scenario of the "search product" use case.**

## Summary

Java 11 has updated the java JDK command, so that it can be used to launch applications written in a single file with a new feature called Launch Single-File Source-Code Programs. Within a single file, we can put more classes (but we'll probably put only one), and they can all be public. In fact, we will pass the file name to the java command and not the name of a class. It is essential, however, that among the classes contained in the file, the first one declares the main() method. You can also create shebang files containing Java code, that can be launched as typical Unix scripts.

**JShell** is a **REPL** software, an acronym of read-evaluate-print loop. It is possible to edit both code snippets and JShell commands that must always be executed with the prefix **/**. The commands can be divided into exploratory commands (**/list**, **/history**, **/help**, **/imports**, **/types**, **/vars** and **/methods**) and executive commands (**/set**, **/env**, **/exit**, **/drop**, **/edit**, **/open**, **/save**, **/reload** and **/reset**). As for the code that can be edited in JShell, there are some **rules** that differ from classic Java programming: it is possible to declare methods but it is not mandatory to declare one in order to write a statement; it is possible to declare classes but it is not mandatory to declare one to write methods or variables; it is not necessary to use the symbol ; to declare an instruction in a single line; we cannot declare packages and modules; apart from abstract, all other basic modifiers are ignored or not allowed for all non-nested types; the synchronized keyword is always ignored; declaring the same variable twice (or the same method) causes the overwriting of the first declared variable (or of the first declared method); and a declared and uninitialized variable is automatically initialized to its null value.

JShell also offers several auxiliary tools, such as **implicit variables** that are automatically declared, the **forwarding reference** that allows us to use undefined data structures, **auto-completion** of the code, import and variable declaration, the possibility to open **JShell Edit Pad** (or other editors) and **keyboard shortcuts**. Being executed from the command line, JShell also benefits from tools such as copy-paste, search, etc.

The **IDEs** allow us, once we have more confidence, to develop more quickly and correctly. Among the many advantages that they offer are the automatic management of the **project**, an advanced **editor** with various refactoring features, an integrated **debugger** that represents a fundamental tool for the programmer, and **integration** with other fundamental software for development as a database, application server, version control system, and different frameworks.

When you **work in a company**, you run into various difficulties, and unfortunately it is not enough to just know how to program. We need to understand the **architecture** of the project, to orient ourselves with the code, and to be aware of what we are developing. In this regard, UML diagrams such as **component** and **deployment diagrams** can be used. Other **basic knowledge** is required, such as databases, networks, XML, the web, and so on. There are different **types of programs** such as standalone, web, enterprise and mobile applications.

In the company, the various activities necessary for development are carried out by different people who have certain **roles**. Depending on the organization and size of the company, it often happens that some people can even play more than one role.

A **methodology** consists of a **process** (i.e. the steps to be performed) and a **notation language**

(**UML** which is considered a standard by the most important methodologies).

We have also introduced a **case study** (with a short problem statement) that can be progressively developed. We took the opportunity to introduce a **process** that defines some simple techniques that allow us to start a program from scratch. In particular, the **use case analysis** allows us to identify the functionalities of the application, and the actors who will use them, thanks to the help of the **use case diagram**. Writing the scenarios for each use case, we will be able to identify all the critical points of the system before even starting to write code. This step can be done using simple **text**, or even with dynamic diagrams like the **activity diagram**, with which it would be possible to describe all the scenarios with a single diagram. In the meantime, a **high-level architecture** for the application can be chosen, also based on customer needs and constraints, describing it with a **component diagram** inserted into a **deployment diagram**. You can get the list of **key abstractions** of the program (i.e. the classes that will surely be implemented from the beginning) extracting it from the list of all the **candidate classes** (a list consisting of any term that has any relevance for the analysis made so far). Finally, it is possible to validate, with **interaction diagrams** (**sequence** or **collaboration diagram**), the actual applicability of the scenarios with the identified key abstractions and eventually add new abstractions.

> **Exercises, source code, appendices and other resources are available at** http://www.javaforaliens.com.

# Part I Conclusions

Here ends the first part of the book. Now we have all the necessary information to be able to code any type of program in Java. We know the development environment, the fundamental components of the language, all the types of data, all the operators and control structures, as well as having some extra-programming information, such as programming in a business environment, UML, processes, tools that facilitate learning, etc. If we have done all the exercises, then our preparation should be sufficient. In fact, in the exercises, very precise tasks have been assigned, and if we have been able to apply the concepts learned, we are already at a very good point. However, if we were to create a program from scratch, the task would still be quite difficult. In the second part, we will mainly study techniques that will allow us to write code in a more natural and functional way for our purposes.

## Chapter Goals

Have the following goals been achieved?

| Goal | Achieved | Achievement Date |
|---|:---:|---|
| Launch simple applications and scripts without compiling (Unit 5.1) | ○ | |
| Know how to interact with JShell so as to experiment, explore and discover Java (Unit 5.2) | ○ | |
| Understand the potential of IDEs (Unit 5.3) | ○ | |
| Understand the difficulties of working in a company (Unit 5.4) | ○ | |
| Know how to use a process that will allow a program to be started from scratch (Unit 5.5) | ○ | |

# Part II
# Object Orientation

Part II is entirely dedicated to the support that Java offers to object-oriented programming paradigms and other related mechanisms. This is perhaps the most important part of this text. In fact, after studying the first few chapters, even a neophyte should already be able to write Java code. But "tweaking" with a programming language is not enough, even when you have great skills. How do we organize a program from scratch? How many classes do you need to create? What should these classes be called? What methods will they have to define? How can we create a program capable of evolving without changing parts that have already been written and verified? The theory of Object Orientation answers these and many other questions. The paradigms of OO will be presented in such a way that the reader learns to appreciate its usefulness in practice. In addition, an attempt has been made to outline the more complex subjects (in particular, polymorphism) in order to facilitate learning. We will also address the mechanism of exception handling and design by contract with assertions.

Part II consists of 5 chapters:

1. **1.** In the sixth chapter, the object-oriented paradigms of abstraction, reuse and encapsulation will be introduced. The rest of the chapter focuses on other topics relating to the visibility of our components, such as access modifiers, the reference this, packages, the static modifier, and also the Singleton design pattern will be introduced.

2. **2.** In the seventh chapter, the inheritance paradigm will be introduced and explored. We will also deal with fundamental related topics such as interfaces, abstract classes, multiple inheritance, initializers, and the final modifier.

3. **3.** The eighth chapter is entirely dedicated to polymorphism and its sub-topics: overload, varargs, overrides, polymorphic parameters, heterogeneous collections and the virtual invocation of methods.

**4.** The ninth chapter mainly explains exception handling. Related topics such as the `try` with resources construct, warnings and errors will also be discussed in depth. We will also introduce *design by contract* and assertions, a powerful method for implementing robust software.

**5.** Finally, the tenth chapter contains a guided example for the realization of a simple program. Step by step, we will discuss the ideal choices, errors, and solutions we can find in order to reach our goal. Furthermore, two important topics will be introduced, Unit Testing and Logging.

At the end of this part, the reader should have learned the basic notions of Object Orientation applicable to Java, and therefore will be able to access the third part of the book concerning the advanced features of the language. However, we recommend the study of this section to anyone, even those who have been programming in Java for some time. Often, Object Orientation does not receive so much attention in programming books.

# 6

# Encapsulation and Scope

**Goals:**

At the end of this chapter, the reader should:

- ✓ Understand the reasons for the birth of object-oriented programming (Unit 6.1).
- ✓ Know how to list the fundamental paradigms and concepts of object-oriented programming (Unit 6.2).
- ✓ Know how to create a basic class diagram (Units 6.2, 6.9).
- ✓ Know how to define and use the concepts of abstraction and reuse (Unit 6.2).
- ✓ Understand the use and usefulness of encapsulation (Units 6.3, 6.4, 6.5).
- ✓ Understand how the use the reference this (Unit 6.3).
- ✓ Understand when and how to use encapsulation (Units 6.4, 6.5).
- ✓ Understand how to use packages (Units 6.6, 6.7).
- ✓ Understand how to use access modifiers (Unit 6.7).
- ✓ Understand how to use the static modifier (Unit 6.8).
- ✓ Understand the concept of design pattern and be able to implement with code the Singleton pattern (Unit 6.8).

This is the first chapter that deepens the support offered by Java to Object Orientation. In particular, the first paradigms of this science will be introduced, such as encapsulation, reuse and abstraction. We will try to introduce the reader to the topic starting with a look at the historical reasons for the birth of Object Orientation. The chapter also contains other concepts that are preliminary to the study of the chapters that follow.

# 6.1 Brief History of Object-Oriented Programming

 Writing a program means simulating, in some way, concepts from the real world, along with physical and mathematical models on a computer. In its early days, programming was conceived as a series of linear steps. Instead of considering the whole purpose of the program by creating an abstract model, developers tried to arrive at the solution to the problem by overcoming intermediate steps. This process-oriented programming model, with the passage of time, and with the consequent increase in the size of the programs, has laid bare its shortcomings. In fact, by increasing the number of variables and the interactions to be managed between them, the troubled programmer began to make reckless use of the tools he had available, in particular of the **global variables** and the goto command.

> The goto **construct allowed the program execution flow to jump to an arbitrary line at any time. Global variables, on the other hand, are variables that are visible to all parts of the program and can therefore be changed at any time and in any situation.**

The indiscriminate use of the goto construct and of the global variables, however, has often compromised the functionality of the programs. In fact, when it was necessary to evolve the software, or fix bugs, these tools have always represented shortcuts that are too inviting to not be used. In this way, at the beginning of the seventies, for some functional programming, the derogatory term "spaghetti code" was used, since the programs, growing in size, more and more resembled a mass of tangled pasta.

Object-oriented programming was born in the 1960s with the **Simula-67** language. It was not a *pure* object-oriented language but, with it, fundamental programming concepts such as classes and inheritance were introduced. It was developed in 1967 by Kristen Nygaard of the University of Oslo and Ole Johan Dahl of the Norwegian Computing Center and, despite the historical importance, we cannot assert that Simula was really popular in the developers' world.

In the early '70s, the **SmallTalk** language was born, initially developed by Alan Kay at the University of Utah and later by Adele Goldberg and Daniel Ingalls of the Xerox Park, Palo Alto research center in California. SmallTalk can be considered a *pure* object-oriented language. It introduced the encapsulation paradigm and the SmallTalk-80 release had some success in the United States. In the long run, however, although considered by many as an ideal programming environment, it remained confined (like Simula) to university research centers all over the world, considered as an environment of study rather than development.

The introduction, in the developers' world, of the concepts of class and object, which make the programs more easily manageable, did not therefore immediately provoke a revolution in information technology. This was due to the fact that, at the beginning of the seventies, languages such as **C** were achieving many successes. One example above all was the **Unix** operating system, still used today, which was born during those years, and its kernel (core) was written in C. Let's imagine the scenario of the time. Languages like C, Cobol and Fortran, were widely used in many professional applications with excellent and exciting results. Criticism, from the theoretical point of view, focused on the procedural paradigm being *out of place* but today we can see that this focus should have been on it being *out of time*! In fact, the increasingly frenetic progress of the hardware, was accompanied by an uncontrollable evolution of the software that, using new resources, had to manage an ever-increasing quantity of variables and functions. The limits of the procedural paradigm were evident at the end of the seventies, when the philosophy of creating software had taken a definitive path. The software had to be extensible, in order to adapt to new technologies that were born one after the other. Software was published in subsequent versions (1.0, 1.1, 1.2, 2.0 etc.) called **releases**, and this required a continuous updating of the code.

To make changes to the software, languages such as C, offered tools such as global variables and the goto command, which, as we said, can be considered error prone. Then, the extension of the C language, created by Bjarne Stroustrup, known as **C++**, was providentially introduced. This new language has effectively revolutionized the world of programming. It was chosen as the standard language among many object-oriented languages by large corporations (Microsoft, Borland, etc.) which, in turn, began to produce development tools that extended C++ by creating their own version.

Being an extension of C, any program written in C must be able to be compiled by a C++ compiler. This, even if it has encouraged the mass migration of C programmers to C++, has also turned out to be one of the main limitations of C++. In fact, the C programmer who migrates to C++ could easily end up writing mainly functional programs with little object orientation. Hence the idea of creating a new language that had to be truly object-oriented. Java proposes a programming style that almost obliges us to correctly program with objects. Moreover, compared to C++, all the ambiguous and dangerous tools have been eliminated, such as goto, **pointer arithmetic** (tool to interact directly with memory, both powerful and dangerous) and it's more difficult to use something that can look like a global variable.

We can conclude that, if C++ has the merit of having made object-oriented programming known to the general public, Java has the merit of having made it clear!

 **Object-oriented programming** is a science or, rather, a philosophy that is adaptable to programming. It is based on concepts that exist in the real world, which we deal with every day. We have already pointed out that human beings have always known the concepts of class and object. The abstraction of real objects in classes makes us overcome the complexity of reality. In this way, we can observe completely different objects, recognizing in them characteristics and functionalities that join them, and then associate them with the same class. For example, although completely different, a saxophone and a piano both belong to the class of musical instruments. Moreover, object-oriented programming, using the concept of **encapsulation**, makes programs composed of classes that hide implementation details behind public interfaces, which allow communication between the objects that are part of the system. The **reuse** of already written code is favored thanks to concepts such as **inheritance** and **polymorphism**, which will be presented to the reader in the following chapters.

It must be emphasized that, with Java 8, a revolutionary step has been taken. After almost twenty years, typical constructs of functional programming have been introduced to allow the programmer to have greater freedom, and to have a more powerful language. However, Java remains, and will remain forever, a language especially object-oriented.

# 6.2 Object-Oriented Paradigms

From the reading of the previous section, we can deduce that object-oriented programming will allow us to create programs that are easier to evolve and maintain, which reuse well-defined parts of code, and which facilitate the interaction between the programmer and the code. The advantages are not limited to these characteristics alone, and we will discover new benefits when reading the chapters that follow.

What characterizes an object-oriented language is its support for the so-called **object-oriented paradigms**:

- **Encapsulation**
- **Inheritance**
- **Polymorphism**

Unlike other object-oriented programming languages, Java clearly defines the concepts just mentioned. Even programmers who consider themselves to be experts in other object-oriented languages such as C++, by studying Java could interpret differently some concepts that were previously unclear.

In this and future chapters, we will introduce the three fundamental paradigms. Note that not all books speak of three paradigms. Abstraction and reuse should certainly be considered paradigms of object-oriented programming. But these paradigms are considered secondary to others, not because they are less powerful or useful, but because they are not specific to object-oriented programming. In fact, abstraction and reuse are concepts that also belong to functional programming.

> **The fundamental paradigms of Object Orientation are many, but we will discuss the subjects gradually.**

## 6.2.1 Abstraction

 **Abstraction** could be defined as "the art of knowing how to focus only on the truly essential details in the description of an entity". Abstraction is a very clear concept to all of us, since we use it in every moment of our life. For example, while you are reading this book, you are concentrating on correctly learning its contents, paying no attention to the shape, colors, style and all the physical and theoretical details that make up the page you are viewing (or at least we hope so!) .

To formalize a discussion that is too "abstract", we could talk about at least three levels of abstraction in terms of its implementation in object-oriented programming:

- ▪▪ functional abstraction

- ▪▪ data abstraction

- ▪▪ system abstraction.

We use **functional abstraction** every time we implement a method. In fact, through a method, we are able to bring into the application a dynamic concept, synonymous with action and operation. To write a method, we should limit ourselves to its most robust and clear implementation possible. In this way, we will have the possibility to invoke that method to obtain the desired result, without having to take into account the implementation of the method itself.

> **The same concept is also valid in functional programming, thanks to the functions.**

We use **data abstraction** every time we define a class, gathering in it only the essential characteristics and functionalities of the objects that it must define, in the context in which the application works.

> **We could say that the abstraction of data "contains" functional abstraction.**

**215**

We use the **system abstraction** every time we define an application in terms of the essential classes that must satisfy the purposes of the application itself.

> We could say that the abstraction of the system "contains" the data abstraction, and for the transitive property, the functional abstraction.

Implementing abstraction in Java sometimes means simply knowing how to find an appropriate name for the entities (methods, variables, classes, etc.) that we define. Examples of correct abstraction are: a Poet class that defines the method writePoem(), a method printResult() that prints a result and does nothing else, a package called cinema.genre which defines the classes Drama, Fantasy, Thriller, Comedy. Examples of bad abstraction, on the other hand, could be a Poet class that, in addition to the method writePoem(), defines the method printResult() (the poets do not print results), the method printResult() which performs a complicated algorithm before printing the result (in that case it would be advisable to create two separate methods, one that executes the algorithm, and another one for printing), and a cinema.genre package that also defines the FilmScript class (which is not a genre and therefore should not be in that package).

## 6.2.2 Reuse

With the term **reuse**, we refer mainly to the concept of reuse we have in the real world, which is imported into the Java world as the reuse of programming elements such as classes and methods, and also concepts and processes that we usually use when we develop a program. Reuse is a consequence of abstraction and other paradigms of object-oriented programming (encapsulation, inheritance and polymorphism). These paradigms in fact, intrinsically favor reuse.
In this case also, we can talk about three levels of abstraction regarding its implementation in object-oriented programming:

- functional reuse

- data reuse

- conceptual reuse.

We use **functional reuse** whenever we create a very abstract method that is invoked, in many parts, by our code. Above all, this means not to duplicate code. When we duplicate code with a copy-paste from one method to another, we are probably doing something wrong. We should take the time to evaluate the creation of a sub-method that is called by both methods that have the code in common.

> Reuse is, in fact, a paradigm that is also valid for functional programming.

We use **data reuse** whenever we create a very abstract class with a usable public method interface, which is instantiated, in several parts, by our code. In the case of data reuse, it is also the case in which a **software component** is created, that is, a set of classes with a well-defined interface, which provide functions that can be performed independently from the context. Finally, we use **conceptual reuse** when we can reuse an already known technique, algorithm or approach to the problem, design or architectural solution.

### 6.2.3 UML: Class Diagram

At the end of the fourth chapter, we introduced the UML notation language. To get a new perspective on code visualization, we now introduce a new type of diagram: the **class diagram**. As already stated, we will use UML without pretending to create precise specifications to program. We will simply limit ourselves to creating "sketches" to obtain information that by reading the code directly would not be so clear.

The class notation in UML is very intuitive, a rectangle divided into three sections: in the first one, the name of the class is written, in the second, the list of attributes and, in the third, the list of methods.

| AClass |
|---|
| -aVariable: int |
| +aMethod(aParameter:int): String |

**Figure 6.1 - Class Diagram Sample.**

UML is a modeling language, independent of the programming language it wants to represent. This means that we should not expect attributes and methods described with the Java syntax. As we can see from Figure 6.1 the attributes are defined with the following UML syntax:

```
scope_symbol attributeName : attributeType
```

In Figure 6.1, it can be seen that the scope symbol of the variable aVariable that we have defined in the diagram is -, which is equivalent to the private modifier.
So, the syntax:

```
- aVariable : int
```

**217**

in UML, is equivalent to the syntax:

```
private int aVariable;
```

in Java.

Regarding the methods, the UML syntax is the following:

```
scope_symbol methodName(parametersList) : returnType
```

where with `parametersList` we mean a list of parameters that uses the comma symbol as a separator, where each parameter uses the syntax:

```
parameterName : ParameterType
```

Referring to Figure 6.1, it is easy to guess that the + symbol corresponds to the `public` modifier. So, the syntax:

```
+ aMethod(aParameter:int) : String
```

in UML, is equivalent to the syntax:

```
public String aMethod(int aParameter)
```

in Java.

Note that the body is not specified for methods in UML. The class diagram, in fact, allows the definition of the public interface of the objects we want to create, hiding the internal implementation. The reason for this is to separate the public interface from the internal implementation, which is the subject of the next section.

> We can define many other elements in the class diagram that sometimes use a fairly cryptic syntax. With the basic syntax, however, almost all the needs of development can be covered. We will introduce new syntax elements whenever they are useful to us.

## 6.3 Encapsulation

 **Encapsulation** is the key to object-oriented programming. Through it, a class is able to acquire characteristics of robustness, independence and reusability. Furthermore, its maintenance will be easier for the programmer. Any class is essentially made up of data and methods. The encapsulation philosophy is simple. It is based on controlled access to data, using methods that can prevent errors at the implementation level, this simply translates into declaring the attributes of a class private and therefore inaccessible outside of the class itself. For this purpose, we will introduce a new modifier: `private`.

Access to **private data** may be provided by a **public interface** consisting of methods declared **public** and therefore accessible by other classes. In this way, such methods could, for example, make it possible to carry out checks before confirming access to private data.

If the encapsulation is intelligently managed, our classes can be used in the efficiently, and for the longest time, since the modifications and revisions can only concern parts of code not visible from the outside.

If we want to give an example based on the reality that surrounds us, we could consider a telephone. Most users know how to use the phone, but they do not know how it works. Anyone can choose a contact from the phone book or dial a phone number and converse with another person, but few know in detail the sequence of processes triggered by these few simple actions. Evidently, to use the telephone, it is not necessary to have a degree in telecommunications engineering: it's just sufficient to know its public interface (consisting of the display, the telephone keypad, the speaker and the microphone), not its internal implementation.

Let's move on to an example of code. Suppose we want to write an application that uses the following class, which simply abstracts the concept of date:

```
public class Date {
    public int day;
    public int month;
    public int year;
}
```

How can our application use this abstraction? Whenever we need a `Date` object, the code to be written will look like this:

**(Code 6.1)**

```
...
Date aDate = new Date();
aDate.day = 14;
aDate.month = 4;
aDate.year = 2004;
...
```

What's the problem? It is not uncommon for the object variable values to be set to the runtime dynamically, probably by the user. Suppose our application allows the user to enter his date of birth, perhaps through a graphical user interface. In this case, the code to be written will be similar to the following:

**(Code 6.2)**

```
...
Date aDate = new Date();
aDate.day = interface.getConfirmedDay();
```

**219**

```
aDate.month = interface.getConfirmedMonth();
aDate.year = interface.getConfirmedYear();
...
```

where the getConfirmedDay(), getConfirmedMonth(), and getConfirmedYear() methods of the interface object return an integer entered by the user through the application's graphical user interface (GUI). Suppose the user has entered the values 32 for the day, 13 for the month and 1800 for the year; here the problems of the code start to be evident. How can we permanently avoid problems like this for the Date class? We list some possible solutions.

1. We could limit the user to use only particular values on the graphical interface. The problem would be solved, but only when setting the date always takes place via the graphical user interface. Moreover, the problem will be solved only for that particular functionality and therefore not in a definitive way. But if we wanted to reuse the Date class in another function (reuse should be a fundamental paradigm of object-oriented programming), without reusing the same GUI, we would be forced to write the code that handles the problem again.

2. We could delegate to the code of the methods getConfirmedDay(), getConfirmedMonth(), and getConfirmedYear() of the GUI object, the necessary checks in order to set the date correctly. But even in this case, all the problems exposed in the previous point would remain.

3. Use encapsulation by modifying the Date class as follows:

**(Code 6.3)**
```java
public class Date {
    private int day;
    private int month;
    private int year;
    public void setDay(int d) {
        if (d > 0 && d <= 31) {
            day = d;
        }
        else {
            System.out.println("Invalid day");
        }
    }
    public int getDay() {
        return day;
    }
    public void setMonth(int m) {
        if (m > 0 && m <= 12) {
            month = m;
        }
```

```
            else {
                System.out.println("Invalid month");
            }
        }
        public int getMonth() {
            return month;
        }
        public void setYear(int y) {
            year = y;
        }
        public int getYear() {
            return year;
        }
    }
```

Implementing encapsulation with Java code most of the time consists of declaring private data and providing the public methods of the type **set** and **get** to access them in writing and reading respectively.

> These methods usually follow a convention that is also used in the standard library. If we have a private variable, we should call these methods with the syntax `setVariableName()` and `getVariableName()`. There is only one exception to this convention when we are dealing with a `boolean` variable. In this case, the `getVariableName()` method should be called `isVariableName()`.

So, although at first, it may seem boring (the second version of the Date class is much more extended than the first), implementing encapsulation does not require a lot of inventiveness on the part of the developer. In addition, all IDEs (also EJE) offer tools for the automatic generation of the set and get methods. In Figure 6.2, the non-encapsulated version and the encapsulated version of the Date class are represented with UML.

We note, in this diagram, the comment notation. A **comment** in UML is accepted in any diagram, and is used to comment on anything we want. In our case, we simply specified information about the defined classes. But it is possible to write in the comments: algorithms, requirements, codes, descriptions, etc. Notice that the comment is linked to the element to which it is related by a dashed arrow. This dashed arrow is called **dependence**, and implies dependence from the source to the destination (in our case from the comment to the class, because the comment without the class would not have made sense). Dependencies notation, such as comments notation, can also be used on all types of UML diagrams.

**221**

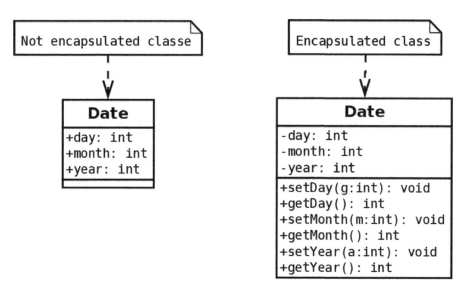

**Figure 6.2 - Class Diagram "Date Class".**

For now, we can emphasize the documentation value of the class diagram, which shows us an encapsulated version of a class without specifying details. This, especially in the design phase of the class, can give us many advantages. In fact, the graphic view of a class can helps us to think about classes more easily than looking at Java code. When we read the code of a class it is easy to get lost in the implementation details.

Let us now try to clarify why it is so important to use encapsulation. When we have declared private data, according to the definition of the private modifier, they will no longer be accessible through the dot operator, unless the code that wants to access the private data is not in the class that declared it. This implies that code 6.1 and code 6.2 would produce a compile-time error, since they would attempt to assign values to variables not visible in that context (classes other than the Date class). The codes 6.1 and 6.2 must be replaced respectively by the following:

**(Code 6.1 bis)**

```
...
Date aDate = new Date();
aDate.setDay(14);
aDate.setMonth(4);
aDate.setYear(2004);
...
```

**(Code 6.2 bis)**

```
...
Date aDate = new Date();
```

```
aDate.setDay(interface.getConfirmedDay());
aDate.setMonth(interface.getConfirmedMonth());
aDate.setYear(interface.getConfirmedYear());
...
```

When implementing encapsulation, to exploit the private data of the Date object, we will be forced to use the public interface of the object consisting of the public methods *set* and *get*, just as when we want to use a phone, we are forced to use the public interface consisting of the display, the microphone, etc. In fact, the set and get methods have implementations that are inside the Date class and therefore can access private data. Furthermore, in code 6.3, it can be noted that, for example, the setDay() method sets the day variable with the parameter passed to it if it is between 1 and 31, otherwise it prints an error message. So, a priori, every Date object works correctly! This implies greater opportunities for reuse and robustness of the code.

Another big advantage: the code is much easier to maintain and adapts to changes. For example, the reader will surely have noticed that the code 6.3 only partially solves the problems of the Date class. In fact, it would allow the setting of the day to the value 31, even if the variable month for example is 4 which is equivalent to the month of April which has only 30 days. Nor does it solve the problem that February has only 28 days, and in leap years 29. The good news is that we can evolve the Date class, introducing all the improvements we want within the 6.3 code, but we should not change a line for the codes 6.1 bis and 6.2 bis. For example, if the setDay() method is changed as follows:

```
public void setDay (int d) {
    if (d > 0 && d <= 31 && month != 4) {
        day = d;
    } else {
        System.out.println("Invalid day");
    }
}
```

only the Date class will have to be recompiled, but the codes 6.1 bis and 6.2 bis will remain unchanged.

We should now be clearer about the usefulness of the set methods that we can now call **mutator methods**, that is, methods that mutate the value of the variable. However, there may still be some reservations about the get methods, that we will now call **accessor methods** or **access methods**.

> Sometimes, these methods are also referred to as "setter" and "getter" methods.

With a couple of examples, we should dispel any doubts.

Suppose we want to add, to code 6.2 bis, a check on the effective success of setting data of the aDate object, printing the data on the screen. From the moment in which:

```
System.out.println(aDate.day);
```

will return an error in the compilation, and:

```
System.out.println(aDate.setDay());
```

it makes no sense because the type of return of the setDay() method is void, it seems clear that the only solution remaining is:

```
System.out.println(aDate.getDay());
```

In addition, an accessor method could also perform checks like a mutator method.

For example, in the following class, the accessor method manages access to a personal bank account, by entering a secret code:

```java
public class BankAccount {
    private String money = "50000 Euro";
    private int code = 1234;
    private int insertedCode;

    public void setInsertedCode(int cod) {
        insertedCode = cod;
    }

    public int getInsertedCode() {
        return insertedCode;
    }

    public String getMoney() {
        if (insertedCode == code) {
            return money;
        }
        else {
            return "wrong code!!!";
        }
    }
    // . . .
}
```

## 6.3.1 Functional Encapsulation

Until now we have seen examples of quite classical encapsulation, where we hide, within the classes, the attributes using the private modifier. Nothing prevents us from using private, even as a modifier of methods, thus obtaining a functional encapsulation. A private method, in fact, can be invoked only by a method defined in the same class, which could, in turn, be declared public. For example, the previously defined BankAccount class could evolve as follows:

```java
public class BankAccount2 {
    // code omitted
    public String getMoney(int codeToCheck) {
        return checkCode(codeToCheck);
    }

    private String checkCode(int codeToCheck) {
        if (codeToCheck == code) {
            return money;
        }
        else {
            return "wrong code!!!";
        }
    }
}
```

This would favor the reuse of code since, by introducing new methods (as will probably happen in a project that is maintained), these could reuse the checkCode() method.

Figure 6.3 shows the BankAccount class. Notice how class notation can clearly represent the concept of class without specifying details.

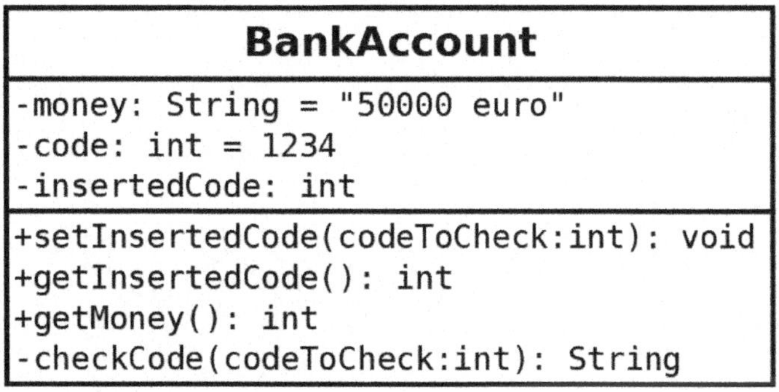

| **BankAccount** |
| --- |
| -money: String = "50000 euro"<br>-code: int = 1234<br>-insertedCode: int |
| +setInsertedCode(codeToCheck:int): void<br>+getInsertedCode(): int<br>+getMoney(): int<br>-checkCode(codeToCheck:int): String |

**Figure 6.3 - Class Diagram "BankAccount Class".**

## 6.3.2 Encapsulation and Reuse

Usually it is thought that a member of a class declared private becomes "inaccessible from other classes". This sentence is reasonable with regard to the scope of compilation, where the declaration of classes is the problem to be overcome. But if we operate in the context of the Java Virtual Machine where, as we said, the key protagonists are not the classes but the objects, we must re-evaluate the previous statement. In fact, encapsulation will allow two objects instantiated by the same class to access the respective private members in "public mode". Consider the Employee class represented in UML in Figure 6.4:

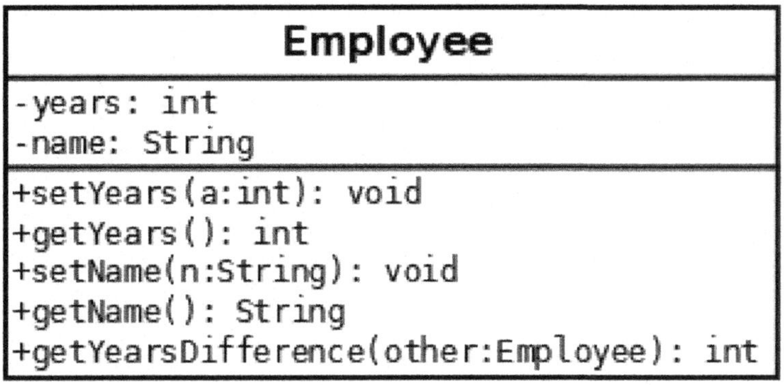

| Employee |
|---|
| -years: int |
| -name: String |
| +setYears(a:int): void |
| +getYears(): int |
| +setName(n:String): void |
| +getName(): String |
| +getYearsDifference(other:Employee): int |

**Figure 6.4 - Class Diagram "Employee class".**

The implementation in Java could be the following:

```java
public class Employee {
    private int number;
    private int hireYear;

    public void setNumber(int number) {
        this.number = number;
    }

    public int getNumber() {
        return number;
    }

    public void setHireYear(int hireYear) {
        this.hireYear = hireYear;
    }

    public int getHireYear() {
        return hireYear;
    }

    public int getYearDifference(Employee other) {
        return (hireYear - other.hireYear);
    }
}
```

In the getYearDifference() method, we notice that we can directly access the private variable hireYear of the other object, without having to use the getHireYear() method.
The previous code is therefore valid for compilation, but the following method:

```
public int getYearDifference(Employee other) {
    return (hireYear - other.hireYear);
}
```

would certainly favor the reuse of code, and therefore should be considered preferable. In fact, the getHireYear() method could evolve by introducing checks (or perhaps replace the hireYear variable with the yearsOfExperience variable), which should be recalled rather than rewritten.

> **The reuse of methods is very important. If we copy and paste the code from one method to another, we are probably making a mistake. In fact, as we have said several times, the software evolves and having two methods that contain the same code in our program will not favor its evolution. If, for example, we discover that we have a bug in either of these methods, it is easy to forget that there is another method that probably contains the same problem.**

## 6.3.3 The this Reference

The getHireYear() method of the previous example may have caused some doubts in the reader. Up to now, we have assumed that accessing an instance variable within the class where it is defined was a "natural process" that did not need to be referenced. For example, within the getDay() method in the Date class, we accessed the day variable directly without using a reference. After having read the last example, and considering that many objects could be instantiated from the Date class, we might ask: if day is an instance variable, to which instance does it belong? The answer to this question is: it depends on the **current object**, that is, on the object on which the getDay() method is called. For example, during the execution phase of a certain application, two particular objects could be instantiated, which we assume are called myBirthday and yourBirthday. Both of these objects have their own day variable. At some point, the following instruction may appear within the program:

```
System.out.println(myBirthday.getDay());
```

The value of the day variable of the myBirthday object will be printed. Then the getDay() method, which is defined by the following code:

```
public int getDay() {
    return day;
}
```

**227**

must, in some way, use a reference for the day variable, because when this method is called on the myBirthday object, it returns the day variable of the myBirthday object, and not that of the yourBirthday object. That is, as if the method was defined as follows:

```
public int getDay() {
    return myBirthday.day;
}
```

As it is easy to understand, it would not be possible to write this code, since we do not know how the objects that will be instantiated from this class will be called, and if we will have visibility on them.

Also in this case, the compiler takes the initiative independently. If the programmer does not use a reference for a certain instance variable, at the time of compilation, the code will be modified by the compiler itself, which will add a reference to the current object in front of the variable. But which reference to the current object? The class cannot know, a priori, the references for the objects that will be instantiated by it at runtime!

Java introduces a keyword that, by definition, coincides with the reference to the current object: this. The reference this is then implicitly added to the bytecode compiled, to refer to each instance variable not explicitly referenced.

So the getDay() method that will have the JVM available after compiling will be modified as follows:

```
public int getDay() {
    return this.day; //the reference this is added by the compiler
}
```

 Also, in this case, we see another one of those language points that once led to Java being defined as "simple" to learn. If, up to this point, we have not noted the problem of using the reference this with the instance variables, it is also because this time "Java has given us a hand". We repeat, today Java is a complex language, but at least its creators created some mechanisms that facilitate its initial learning.

### 6.3.3.1 Using this with Variables

In the second chapter, we distinguished the instance variables from the local variables. The difference between the two concepts is such that the compiler allows us to declare, in the same class, a local variable (or a parameter of a method) and an instance variable with the same identifier. In fact, the JVM allocates local variables and instance variables in different memory areas, called respectively **Stack Memory** and **Heap Memory**. In the Stack Memory, the data defined by a running method is temporarily stored, and once the method is finished, the data will be removed from the memory. In the Heap Memory, on the other hand, the objects and their data are stored, and they will be deallocated by the garbage collection automatically when the latter ensures that they are no longer usable by the program.

The keyword this fits into this speech in the following way. We have repeatedly dealt with the passing of parameters in methods, in order to initialize instance variables. Up to now, for method parameters, we have been forced to contrive an identifier different from that of the instance variable to be initialized. Consider the following class:

```
public class Customer {
    private String name, address, phoneNumber;

    public void setData(String n, String add, String num) {
        name = n;
        address = add;
        phoneNumber = num;
    }
    //...
}
```

Note that the use of the identifier n to initialize the name, number to initialize the phoneNumber, and add to initialize the address. There is nothing wrong with this. However, knowing the existence of the reference this, we could equally write:

```
public class Customer {
    private String name, address, phoneNumber;

    public void setData(String name, String address, String phoneNumber) {
        this.name = name;
        this.address = address;
        this.phoneNumber = phoneNumber;
    }
    //...
}
```

In fact, through the keyword this, we specify that the referenced variable belongs to the instance. As a consequence, the non-referenced variable will be the parameter of the method, without any ambiguity.

This style of programming is generally considered preferable, but it should be considered a standard. In this way there is no chance of confusing the variables with similar names. In our example, it could happen, by mistake, that the parameter n is assigned to the instance variable phoneNumber, or the parameter num to the variable name. We could state that using the reference this adds clarity to our code.

Figure 6.5 shows the Customer class in a diagram of the UML classes.

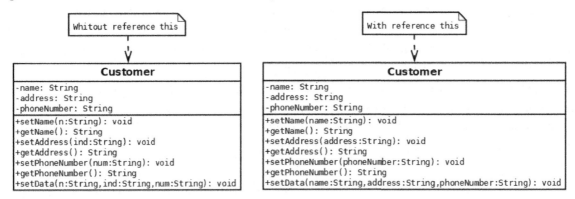

**Figure 6.5 - Class Diagram "Customer Class".**

The reader can note that if we wrote:

```
public class Customer {
    private String name, address, phoneNumber;

    public void setPhoneNumber(String phoneNumber) {
        phoneNumber = phoneNumber;
    }

    public void setAddress(String address) {
        address = address;
    }

    public void setName(String name) {
        name = name;
    }
    //...
}
```

the compiler, not finding explicit references, would consider the variables always local and therefore we would not get the desired result.

### 6.3.3.2 Use of this with Methods

As stated, this represents the current object and can therefore access the instance variables. Of course, with this it is also possible to invoke methods. For example:

```
public class Customer {
    private String name;
    private String address;
    private String phoneNumber;
```

```
        public Customer(String name, String address, String phoneNumber) {
            this.setName(name);
            this.setAddress(address);
            this.setPhoneNumber(phoneNumber);
        }

        public void setPhoneNumber(String phoneNumber) {
            this.phoneNumber = phoneNumber;
        }

        public void setAddress(String address) {
            this.address = address;
        }

        public void setName(String name) {
            this.name = name;
        }
        // . . .
    }
```

In the constructor, we invoked the setter methods using the reference this. In this case, however, if we did not put the reference this before the setter methods, we would have obtained the same result, since, in Java, this is an implicit reference as seen with the variables.

### 6.3.3.3 Use of this with Constructors

 More interesting is the use of the reference this when we have more constructors in the same class (*overload of constructors*), and from one constructor if we want to call another (*reuse of constructors*). The syntax changes slightly since a constructor is not an ordinary method and the dot operator is not usable. Let's take an example:

```
public class Customer {
    //...
    public Customer (String name, String address) {
        this(name, address, "unknown");
    }
    public Customer(String name, String address, String phoneNumber) {
        this.setName(name);
        this.setAddress(address);
        this.setPhoneNumber(phoneNumber);
    }
    //...
}
```

Focus on the first constructor code. Note that we have passed three string parameters to this (not having received the phone number as input, we called the second constructor passing as third parameter the default value unknown (we reused code). In the event of overloading constructors, therefore, the recommendation is to make them call each other to avoid rewriting the same lines of code several times. In Figure 6.6, we can see in the representation of the last version of the Customer class, the syntax of the constructors in the class diagram. A so-called **UML stereotype** is used, that is a word (usually a noun or an adjective) that characterizes what we are declaring. In our case, with the <<constructor>> stereotype, the fact that we are declaring a constructor and not just an ordinary method, is more evident.

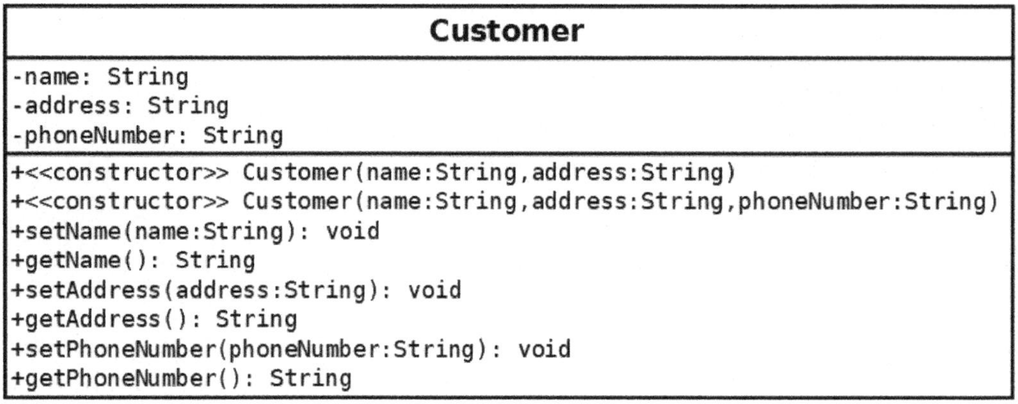

| Customer |
|---|
| -name: String<br>-address: String<br>-phoneNumber: String |
| +<<constructor>> Customer(name:String,address:String)<br>+<<constructor>> Customer(name:String,address:String,phoneNumber:String)<br>+setName(name:String): void<br>+getName(): String<br>+setAddress(address:String): void<br>+getAddress(): String<br>+setPhoneNumber(phoneNumber:String): void<br>+getPhoneNumber(): String |

**Figure 6.6 - Class Diagram "Customer Class with Constructors".**

### 6.3.3.4 this *and assignment*

The reference this, therefore, is not a reference like any other. It is not possible to assign another value to the reference this, because it must always point to the same current object. This means that if we try to assign the reference this another object as in the following constructor:

```java
public Customer() {
    this = new Customer();
}
```

we will get the following compilation error:

```
Customer.java:6: error: cannot assign to 'this'
        this = new Customer();
        ^
1 error
```

Another bad practice is to declare a reference, and point it to the object this. For example:

```java
public class Customer {
    private Customer customer;
    public Customer () {
        customer = this;
        //code omitted
    }
```

**232**

This time the compiler will not report errors, but the practice is all in all useless, because we will have two references that always point to the current object. We will see in section 6.8.5, how a reference to which we have assigned the value of this can be exploited.

## 6.4 When to Use Encapsulation

 Applying encapsulation is never wrong. Any class of any application could, and should, be developed using encapsulation. We should never allow the sacrificing of encapsulation to save a few seconds of programming. Sometimes, it may seem to us that taking advantage of encapsulation is superfluous to certain classes, but experience teaches us that encapsulating our classes is never a mistake. Let's take a trivial example. We have already mentioned that, to implement an application at any level (assuming it is not really elementary), incremental changes must be made. The software evolves and it is difficult to create a program that doesn't change anymore. For example, suppose we want to write a simple application that, assigned two points, draws the segment that unites them. Suppose also that the following non-encapsulated point class is used (class already encountered in the second chapter).

```
public class Point {
    public int x, y;
    //...
}
```

At first, the application will instantiate and initialize two points with the following code fragment:

**(Code 6.4)**
```
Point p1 = new Point();
Point p2 = new Point();
p1.x = 5;
p1.y = 6;
p2.x = 10;
p2.y = 20;
//...
```

Suppose that the evolution of our application makes it necessary for the two points to not lie outside a certain well-defined flat area. It is evident that the best solution is to implement the encapsulation within the Point class in this way:

```
public class Point {
    private int x, y;
    private final int MAX_VALUE_FOR_X = 10;
    private final int MIN_VALUE_FOR_X = -10;
    private final int MAX_VALUE_FOR_y = 10;
```

```
        private final int MIN_VALUE_FOR_Y = -10;
        public void setX(int a) {
            if (a <= MAX_VALUE_FOR_X && a >= MIN_VALUE_FOR_X) {
                x = a;
                System.out.println("X is OK!");
            }
            else {
                System.out.println("X is not valid");
            }
        }
        public void setY(int a) {
            if (a <= MAX_VALUE_FOR_y && a >= MIN_VALUE_FOR_Y) {
                y = a;
                System.out.println("Y is OK!");
            }
            else {
                System.out.println("Y is not valid");
            }
        }
        //   . . .
}
```

Unfortunately, after making these changes to the Point class, we will be forced to also modify the code fragment 6.4 of the application in the following way:

**(Code 6.5)**
```
Point p1 = new Point();
Point p2 = new Point();
p1.setX(5);
p1.setY(6);
p2.setX(10);
p2.setY(20);
...
```

We would have started better if the Point class had been encapsulated a priori:

```
public class Point {
    private int x, y;
    public void setX(int a) {
        x = a;
    }
    public void setY(int a) {
        y = a;
    }
    ...
}
```

since we would only have modified the code within the access methods and would have been forced to use the code 6.5 within the application that uses Point.

> Note that a code similar to 6.5 could be used in many other parts of the application. In a real program, composed of many classes, if we do not use encapsulation but use a code similar to 6.4, the changes to be made (such as adding controls to the coordinates of the point) would be numerous and located in many different classes.

We conclude that encapsulation is always advisable in Java.

A "pure" object-oriented language would not even allow the declaration of public attributes. However, Java was intended to be a simple language to learn, and by allowing the declaration of public instance variables, it does not force the aspiring programmer to learn a concept such as encapsulation prematurely. In particular, in the early days, it would not fully appreciate its use, having to approach too many new concepts at the same time.

## 6.5 How to Use Encapsulation

In general, if we only talk about the language and not the object-oriented philosophy, encapsulation is simply reduced to creating classes that declare their variables as `private` and the related set and get methods as `public`. So, let's start immediately and get used to this good habit. The variables of our classes must always be declared `private`, providing the setter and getter methods to make them usable outside the class.

### 6.5.1 IDEs

Although fundamental, it is obvious that this activity can be boring and, above all, it is not uncommon to write incorrectly the setter and getter methods. Just a lower-case in place of an upper-case letter, and we end up losing a lot of time. Fortunately, various development tools are very helpful in automating the creation of these methods. Netbeans and Eclipse have contextual menus that open by clicking on the editor with the right button of the mouse, where the **Refactoring** entry is (in Eclipse there is also a **Source** menu). This contains various items to automate the creation of parts of the code. The **Encapsulate Field (s)** entry will automatically generate the setter and getter methods. Even EJE allows us to automatically create these methods, starting from the definition of the variable to be encapsulated. Just open the **insert** menu and click on **JavaBean Properties** (or press **CTRL-9**). With JavaBean Properties, we mean an encapsulated instance variable. A simple wizard will ask us to insert the variable type first (for example "String") and then the name (for example "name"). Once this information is provided, EJE will fulfill its task. Netbeans also has another fast context menu that is obtained by pressing the **ALT + INSERT** keys at the same time and offering several items to create code quickly, among which is **Add Property** which allows the creation of an encapsulated variable from scratch.

 The name "JavaBean Property" comes from the term *Java-Beans*, a technology that in the early years of Java was very successful, currently shelved. The name JavaBean, however, is still on everyone's lips, thanks to the reuse of this term in EJB (*Enterprise JavaBeans*) technology. The term "JavaBean" should be intended as a bean of Java (remember that Java is the name of a type of coffee, see appendix A on line for more information).

## 6.5.2 Other Forms of Encapsulation

But is it necessary to declare both the set and get methods for each variable? Usually yes but if, for example, we want to limit the access of the instance variable outside the class, it is also possible to avoid declaring the set method (if we do not want it to be set outside the class), the get method (in case we want to prevent the reading outside the class), or even both methods (in this case the variable will exist and will be managed only within the class where it was defined). For example, there are cases in which it is necessary to declare classes whose instance variables can be set only once, when they are instantiated, and whose value will not change over time. In that case, it will not suffice to provide the set methods, exploiting a constructor for the first (and only) assignment. For example, the following `Point` class abstracts the concept of fixed point:

```java
public class FixedPoint {
    private int x,y;

    public FixedPoint (int x, int y){
        this.x = x;
        this.y = y;
    }

    public int getX(){
        return x;
    }

    public int getY(){
        return y;
    }
}
```

The value of the x and y variables cannot be changed once an object has been instantiated, as follows:

```
FixedPoint fixedPoint = new FixedPoint(3,5);
```

This is because there are no set methods.

# 6.6 Package Management

The meaning of public is clear when applied to variables and methods. But why have we defined all the classes public so far? To understand this, we must better introduce the concept of a package. We have seen how the standard Java library is organized in packages. Thanks to this concept, the programmer therefore has the possibility to organize his own classes as well. It's very easy to declare a class belonging to a package. With the package keyword we can declare the package to which the class we are declaring belongs. Here is a snippet of code that shows us the syntax to use:

```
package programs.customermanagement;
public class CustomerSupport {
    . . . . .
```

> The package **declaration must be the first one in a Java file.**

In this case the CustomerSupport class belongs to the customermanagement package, which in turn belongs to the programs package. Declaring CustomerSupport as a public class, will allow all classes that are declared externally to the package programs.customermanagement to use it. If we did not prefix the CustomerSupport class with the public keyword, only classes belonging to the same package could have used the CustomerSupport class.

Physically, packages are just folders (directories). This means that, after declaring the class belonging to this package, we will have to insert the compiled class inside a folder called **customermanagement**, located in turn in a folder called **programs**. Usually the source file must be kept separate from the compiled class as shown in Figure 6.7, where we have represented the files as ovals and the directories as rectangles.

However, the Java Development Kit allows us to realize the correct insertion of the files in the folders and the automatic creation of the same folders, by means of the command:

```
javac –d . CustomerSupport.java
```

**237**

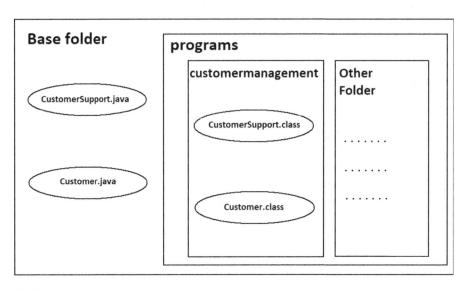

**Figure 6.7 – Package Management.**

By executing the above command from the base folder (where is located the file **CustomerSupport.java**), the folders **programs** and **customermanagement** will be automatically created, and the file **CustomerSupport.class** placed in the right folder, but without moving the source file from the base folder. At this point, assuming that the `CustomerSupport` class contains the `main()` method, we could launch it only running the following command from the base folder:

```
java programs.customermanagement.CustomerSupport
```

in fact, at this point, the file is associated with a package, and can no longer be called by moving to the folder where it resides using the command:

```
java CustomerSupport
```

Furthermore, we must use an `import` command to use this class from a different package.

> **There are other problems related to the use of the packages that the aspiring programmer can meet and solve with the help of error messages received from the compiler. For example, it could be problematic to use classes belonging to a package, from a folder not directly linked to the package itself, i.e. where there is no root package shared.**
>
> ...

> . . .
>
> This can be solved by setting the "classpath" environment variable of the operating system, which should point to the base folder relative to the package in question. The appendix E is dedicated to the "class-path" topic.

## 6.6.1 Manual Management

 Although it is easy to explain, package management can be difficult and, above all, unnecessarily boring if done "by hand". If you have arrived at this point using a tool like EJE or Notepad to practise, it means that you are ready to move to a more sophisticated editor. Any Java IDE manages the organization of packages automatically.

> Currently, EJE allows you to specify the output directory where the classes have to be generated. By default, however, EJE compiles the classes in the same directory where the sources are located. There are cases in which to compile your files correctly, you will need to compile all the files that make up your application together. You should not have any problems if you specify another folder other than the default directory as the output directory (F12 - Options). In general, complex tools such as Eclipse and Netbeans manage packages in a transparent manner.

If you want to continue using Notepad for educational purposes, and start using the packages, it is advisable to follow the following guidelines.

■■ When starting a project, it is advisable to create a folder with the name of the project itself. For example, if the project is called POS, name the folder **POS**.

■■ Then you have to create at least two subfolders, called **src** (where we will put all the source files) and **classes** (where we will put all the compiled files). In this way, we will separate the development environment from the executable environment. As an option, we recommend creating other parallel folders such as **docs** (for all of the documentation), **config** (for the configuration files), etc. For example, in the **POS** folder, insert the **src** folders, **classes**, etc.

**239**

- Whenever a class needs to belong to a package, create the package-folder by hand, and insert the source file inside. For example, if the `BankAccount` class must belong to the bank package, create the **bank** folder inside the **src** folder and insert the **BankAccount.java** file in the **bank** folder.

- Whenever you need to compile, you must always position ourselves via the DOS prompt in the **classes** folder, and from there execute a command like:

```
javac -d . ..\src\packagename\*.java
```

If we wanted to compile all the classes in the bank package, we would have to run the following command:

```
javac -d . ..\src\bank\*.java
```

We advise the reader to create batch files (files with `.bat` suffix) to store such long commands or, better still, use a tool like Ant, Maven or Gradle.

**This development strategy is very similar to the one implemented automatically by the most important tools such as Eclipse and Netbeans.**

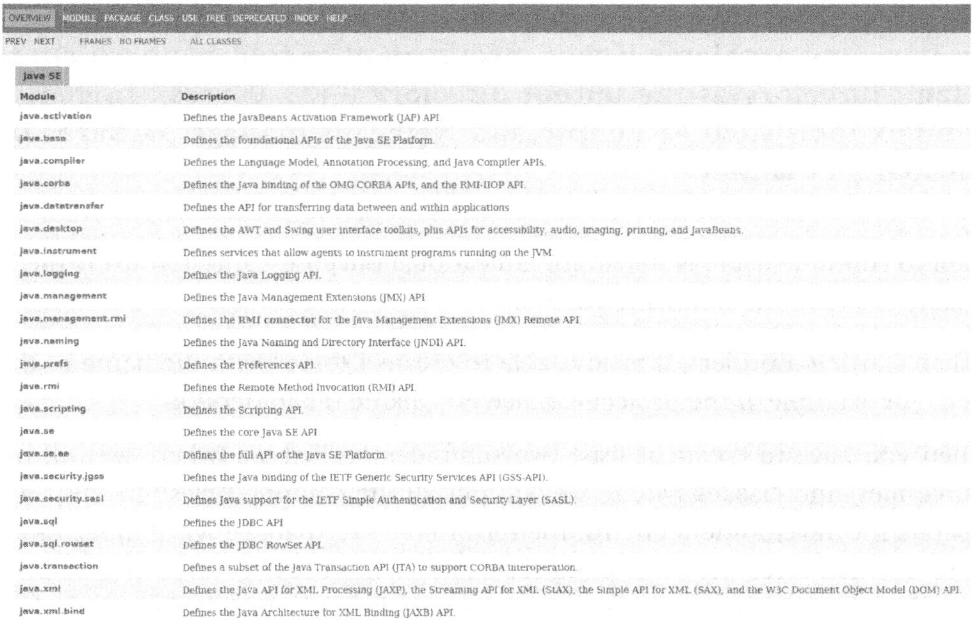
OVERVIEW MODULE PACKAGE CLASS USE TREE DEPRECATED INDEX HELP

PREV NEXT FRAMES NO FRAMES ALL CLASSES

Java SE

| Module | Description |
|---|---|
| java.activation | Defines the JavaBeans Activation Framework (JAF) API. |
| java.base | Defines the foundational APIs of the Java SE Platform. |
| java.compiler | Defines the Language Model, Annotation Processing, and Java Compiler APIs. |
| java.corba | Defines the Java binding of the OMG CORBA APIs, and the RMI-IIOP API. |
| java.datatransfer | Defines the API for transferring data between and within applications. |
| java.desktop | Defines the AWT and Swing user interface toolkits, plus APIs for accessibility, audio, imaging, printing, and JavaBeans. |
| java.instrument | Defines services that allow agents to instrument programs running on the JVM. |
| java.logging | Defines the Java Logging API. |
| java.management | Defines the Java Management Extensions (JMX) API. |
| java.management.rmi | Defines the RMI connector for the Java Management Extensions (JMX) Remote API. |
| java.naming | Defines the Java Naming and Directory Interface (JNDI) API. |
| java.prefs | Defines the Preferences API. |
| java.rmi | Defines the Remote Method Invocation (RMI) API. |
| java.scripting | Defines the Scripting API. |
| java.se | Defines the core Java SE API. |
| java.se.ee | Defines the full API of the Java SE Platform. |
| java.security.jgss | Defines the Java binding of the IETF Generic Security Services API (GSS-API). |
| java.security.sasl | Defines Java support for the IETF Simple Authentication and Security Layer (SASL). |
| java.sql | Defines the JDBC API. |
| java.sql.rowset | Defines the JDBC RowSet API. |
| java.transaction | Defines a subset of the Java Transaction API (JTA) to support CORBA interoperation. |
| java.xml | Defines the Java API for XML Processing (JAXP), the Streaming API for XML (StAX), the Simple API for XML (SAX), and the W3C Document Object Model (DOM) API. |
| java.xml.bind | Defines the Java Architecture for XML Binding (JAXB) API. |

**Figure 6.8 –Java API Main Page.**

### 6.6.2 Modules

 The most important innovation of Java 9 is certainly the introduction of modules. If the packages are a tool to manage the scope of the classes, the modules instead represent a more powerful tool, which allows us to expose packages with greater control, and to implement what is called **strong encapsulation**. With Java 9, the standard library has also been completely reorganized using modules. This can also be seen from the official documentation, as we can see on the main page index.html, shown in Figure 6.8.

We decided to dedicate a whole chapter of the book to the topic. If we do not declare modules, we can use Java as it was used up to Java 8. So, for now, we will explain which scope rules are valid without using the modules. When we address the modules topic, we will come back to some topics covered in this chapter.

# 6.7 Access Modifiers

Up to now, we have seen that there are `private` and `public`, two keywords that represent the adjectives with which we define characteristics for the members of our class. These adjectives are called **modifiers** and we have already met others, such as `final` or `static`. A modifier is a keyword that can change the meaning of a component of a Java application. As already stated in the first chapter, a modifier is a component of a Java application like an adjective is a noun in human language. Each modifier applies to one or more types of Java components. These include classes, methods, instance variables, local variables, methods arguments, and constructors, but there are also others that we have not yet talked about, such as interfaces, enumerations and annotations.

The modifiers explained in this chapter so far (`public` and `private`), are better defined as **access modifiers** (or even **access specifiers**) because they essentially regulate the scope and the access to a Java component. There is also a third access modifier called `protected`, and another option is **not to use access modifiers** (in this case we are talking about **package scope**).

### 6.7.1 The `public` Modifier

The `public` modifier has been used repeatedly so far. We already know that it can be applied either to a member (attribute or method) of a class, or to a class itself. We also know that a public declared member will be accessible from any class located in any package, and that, to support encapsulation, the instance variables should never be declared `public`. A public class will also be visible from any package (unless being hidden by a module).

For example, consider the following public class declaring a public variable and a public method:

```
package com.cdsc.test;

public class PublicWithinClass {
    public int publicVariable;

    public void publicMethod() {
        System.out.println("Public method invoked");
    }
}
```

The class is declared public and declares public members, so the following class will compile without problems:

```
package com.cdsc;

import com.cdsc.test.*;

public class PublicClassOutsidePackage {
    public void methodThatUsesPublic() {
        var publicWithinClass = new PublicWithinClass();
        publicWithinClass.publicMethod();
        System.out.println(publicWithinClass.publicVariable);
    }
}
```

## 6.7.2 The protected Modifier

Although subclasses will be the main topic of the next chapter dedicated to inheritance, in order to deal with the protected access modifier, it is useful at least to have an idea of what a subclass is. A **subclass** is a class that *extends* another class, inheriting its characteristics. For example, suppose we have an Employee class and a Programmer class that share some characteristics. In particular, suppose that both classes declare the number and hireYear variables, but that the Programmer class also declares an array named certifications. These classes can be linked among themselves through **inheritance**, by simply writing that the Programmer class extends the Employee class. So, the Programmer class does not have to redefine all the characteristics in common with the Employee class (because they will be inherited). The Employee class could be coded as follows:

```
public class Employee {
    private int number;
    private int hireYear;

    public void setNumber(int number) {
        this.number = number;
    }
}
```

```
    public int getNumber() {
        return number;
    }

    public void setHireYear(int hireYear) {
        this.hireYear = hireYear;
    }

    public int getHireYear() {
        return hireYear;
    }
}
```

The Programmer class uses the extends keyword to inherit the public methods of the Employee class, and uses them within the constructor:

```
public class Programmer extends Employee {
    private String[] certifications;

    public Programmer(int number, int hireYear) {
        setNumber(number);
        setHireYear(hireYear);
    }

    public void setCertifications(String[] certifications) {
        this.certifications = certifications;
    }

    public String[] getCertifications() {
        return certifications;
    }
}
```

The protected access modifier defines, for a member, the most accessible degree after the one defined by public. A protected member will, in fact, be accessible within the same package and in all subclasses of the class in which it is defined, even if it doesn't belong to the same package. For example, consider the following class declaring a protected variable and a protected method:

```
package com.cdsc.test;

public class ProtectedWithinClass {
    protected int protectedVariable;

    protected void protectedMethod() {
        System.out.println("Protected method invoked");
    }
}
```

The following class belonging to the same package will compile without problems:

```
package com.cdsc.test;

public class ProtectedClassWithinPackage {
    public void methodThatUsesProtected() {
        var protectedWithinClass = new ProtectedWithinClass();
        protectedWithinClass.protectedMethod();
        System.out.println(protectedWithinClass.protectedVariable);
    }
}
```

On the other hand, compiling the following class, belonging to another package:

```
package com.cdsc;

import com.cdsc.test.*;

public class ProtectedClassOutsidePackage {
    public void methodThatUsesProtected() {
        var protectedWithinClass = new ProtectedWithinClass();
        protectedWithinClass.protectedMethod();
        System.out.println(protectedWithinClass.protectedVariable);
    }
}
```

will get the following compile-time error:

```
ProtectedClassOutsidePackage.java:8: error:
  metodoProtected() has protected access in
  ProtectedWithinClass
        protectedWithinClass. protectedMethod();
                    ^
ProtectedClassOutsidePackage.java:9: error:
  protectedVariable has protected access in
  ProtectedWithinClass
        System.out.println(protectedWithinClass.protectedVariable);
                    ^
2 errors
```

> **Unlike the public modifier, the** `protected` **modifier is not applicable to a class declaration.**

 The fact that the protected members are inherited in all the subclasses, even if belonging to other packages, does not mean that a subclass belonging to a different package, can instantiate an object of the superclass and use protected members.

Protected members in fact, are accessible only by the classes belonging to the same package. We will deepen the discussion in the next chapter when discussing inheritance.

 All in all, as mentioned, under encapsulation it is not necessary to use this modifier for the instance variables in order to let them inherit in the subclasses. It is a common mistake of newbies to use protected instance variables. As we can see in the `Programmer` class, instead, we can use the private variables of the superclass using the setter (and the getter) methods without breaking the encapsulation.

 Another common mistake is to think that `protected` makes class members only accessible to subclasses, and not also to classes in the same package.

### 6.7.3 No Access Modifier

We can avoid using modifiers either to mark a member (attribute or method) of a class, or a class itself.

If we do not place access modifiers on a member of a class, it will only be accessible by classes belonging to the package where it is defined. There is only one difference between members declared without the access modifier and members declared with the `protected` modifier: protected members will be inherited even in subclasses outside the declaration package.

If, instead, we declare a class belonging to a package that is not public, the class itself will be visible only from the classes belonging to the same package. In this case, we talk about **package scope** (or also **default scope**).

For example, consider the following class declared without modifiers:

```
package com.cdsc.test;

class ClassWithoutModifier {
}
```

Compiling the following class (declared outside the package com.cdsc.test) that tries to use ClassWithoutModifier:

```
package com.cdsc;
import com.cdsc.test.*;

public class ClassWithoutModifierTest {
    public static void main(String args[]) {
        var c = new ClassWithoutModifier();
    }
}
```

will obtain the following error message:

**245**

```
javac -d . ClassWithoutModifierTest.java
ClassWithoutModifierTest.java:6: error: cannot find symbol
        var c = new ClassWithoutModifier();
                    ^
  symbol:   class ClassWithoutModifier
  location: class ClassWithoutModifierTest
1 error
```

just because `ClassWithoutModifier` is not visible outside of its package.

### 6.7.4 The `private` Modifier

The `private` modifier restricts the scope of a member of a class to the class itself. As we saw in the previous sections, it represents the keystone for the encapsulation. Private methods are also often used, and are invoked by other methods of the same class. Regarding the private instance variables, we have already noted previously that when encapsulated, they can still be used in the subclasses using the setter and getter public methods.

Finally, unlike the `public` modifier, the `private` modifier is not applicable to a class declaration.

Summarizing what has been said in these sections, we can refer to the following table. It shows the access modifiers and their scope (only for the members of a class):

| MODIFIER | SAME CLASS | SAME PACKAGE | SUBCLASS | EVERYWHERE |
|----------|------------|--------------|----------|------------|
| public | YES | YES | YES | YES |
| protected | YES | YES | YES | NO |
| *No modifier* | YES | YES | NO | NO |
| private | YES | NO | NO | NO |

## 6.8 The `static` Modifier

`static` is perhaps the most powerful Java modifier... maybe even too powerful! With `static`, the object-oriented programming finds a meeting point with the functional one, and its use must therefore be limited to situations of real and concrete usefulness. In other words, this modifier should not be understood as a shortcut to avoid creating objects. In fact, we will see that the static methods are very similar to the functional programming functions. The programmer, who comes with previous experience of this type of programming, could therefore be tempted to abuse this concept. Instead, we must not forget that Java was born as an object-oriented language, and it would be useless to study it without knowing how to exploit its potential.

We could translate the term `static` with "shared by all the instances of the class", or simply with "of the class". So, the encapsulation rules when we use this modifier are altered. We can encapsulate a static variable, but that variable will still be shared by all objects instantiated from the same class. In general, therefore, encapsulation does not apply to static variables (which, as we shall see shortly, should only be used in certain cases).

As aforementioned, a static member has the characteristic of being able to be used by means of a syntax such as:

```
ClassName.memberName
```

in place of:

```
objectName.memberName
```

We can use `static` to mark the methods and attributes of a class (therefore all the members of a class) and as we will see soon also the so-called *initializers*. It is not possible to apply this modifier to local variables, method parameters, constructors or classes. A class and its static members will share the same life cycle. In fact, just the use of a static member of a class (without instantiating the class), will cause the containing class to be loaded into memory.

> **We can mark the declaration of most of the components of a Java application with more than one modifier, regardless of the order in which they are placed. A variable declared `static` and `public` for example, has the same properties as a variable declared `public` and `static`.**

## 6.8.1 Static Methods

A **static method** is a method that is shared by all objects instantiated by the class in which it is declared. We can say that *a static method belongs to the class itself, and not to a particular instance*.

An example of a static method is the `sqrt()` method (which stands for "square root") of the Math class (package `java.lang`), which is called via the syntax:

```
Math.sqrt(number)
```

Math is therefore the name of the class and not the name of an instance of that class (we could guess from the fact that the name starts with a capital letter). The reason why the Math class declares all its methods as static is easily understandable. In fact, if we instantiate two different

**247**

objects from the Math class, obj1 and obj2, the two commands:

```
obj1.sqrt(4);
```

and

```
obj2.sqrt(4);
```

would produce exactly the same result (2). Actually, it does not make sense to instantiate two "mathematical" objects.

A method marked with static and public, can be considered a sort of function (it's no coincidence that, in the Math class, the square root function has been made public and static) and therefore this kind of approach to methods should be limited only to cases where the execution of the method does not depend on the characteristics of the object on which the method is called. A correctly declared static method could be one that does operations on a string passed as input. For example, the following method returns how many occurrences of the character character there are within the string string:

```
public class StringUtils {
    public static int countOccurrences(String string, char character) {
        int count = 0;
        for (int i = 0; i < string.length(); i++) {
            if (string.charAt(i) == character) {
                count++;
            }
        }
        return count;
    }
//We could add other methods that performs operations on strings
}
```

In this case, declaring the method as static is certainly a good choice. For example, in JShell we can execute this command (obviously after also having declared the StringUtils class):

```
jshell> StringUtils.countOccurrences("And it is sweet to shipwreck in such a sea",'e')
$3 ==> 4
```

To invoke the countOccurrences() method, we used the class name (it is useless to instantiate it). We passed a string as the first parameter and a character as a second parameter, and as we can see from the output, four occurrences were found.

## 6.8.2 Static Variables (Class Variables)

A **static variable**, being shared by all the instances of the class, will always have the same value for each object of a class.

**248**

An example is shown below:

```java
public class ExampleClass {
    public static int a = 0;
}

public class ExampleClassMain {
    public static void main (String args[]) {
        System.out.println("a = " + ExampleClass.a);
        ExampleClass obj1 = new ExampleClass();
        ExampleClass obj2 = new ExampleClass();
        obj1.a = 10;
        System.out.println("obj1.a = " + obj1.a);
        System.out.println("obj2.a = " + obj2.a);
        obj2.a=20;
        System.out.println("obj1.a = " + obj1.a);
        System.out.println("obj2.a = " + obj2.a);
    }
}
```

The output of this simple program will be:

```
a = 0
obj1.a = 10
obj2.a = 10
obj1.a = 20
obj2.a = 20
```

As we can see, if an instance modifies the static variable, it will also be modified for the other instance. In fact, it is shared by the two instances and resides right in the class. For example, a variable of this type could be useful for counting the number of objects instantiated by a class (we could do so, increasing it in a constructor):

```java
public class Counter {
    private static int counter = 0; // unnecessary initialization
    private int number;
    public Counter() {
        counter++;
        setNumber(counter);
    }
    public void setNumber(int number) {
        this.number = number;
    }
    public int getNumber() {
        return number;
    }
}
```

Notice how the instance variable number is set in the constructor of this class with the value of the static variable `counter`.

> **Unlike an ordinary instance variable, a static variable is initialized to the null value of its type when the class is loaded and not when the object is instantiated: it is not an instance variable.**

This means that `number` will represent the serial number of each instantiated object. For example, after this instruction:

```
Counter c1 = new Counter();
```

the static variable `counter` will be equal to 1 and the variable `c1.number` will also be equal to 1. Then if we instantiate another `Counter` object:

```
Counter c2 = new Counter();
```

then the static variable `counter` will be equal to 2. In fact, being shared by all the instances of the class, it's not reset anytime a new instance is created. Instead the variable `c1.number` will always be 1, while the variable `c2.number` will be 2.

The `static` modifier therefore disregards the concept of object and closely links the variables to the concept of class which, in turn, becomes something more than a simple means of defining objects. For this reason, we sometimes refer to static instance variables as **class variables**.

> **A variable marked as `static` and `public` can be considered a sort of "global variable". Global variables are a shortcut for programmers, but they are difficult to manage and, for this reason, their use is rightly considered an example of bad practice. This type of approach to variables should therefore be avoided. However, it is sometimes useful to use global constants, defined with `public`, `static` and `final`. For example, the `Math` class defines two public static constants: `PI` and `E` (see official documentation).**

 A static method can only use static variables (and of course local variables), but cannot use instance variables without using object references. In fact, a static method does not belong to any particular instance, and therefore could not "choose" an instance variable of a particular instance without explicitly referencing it. For example, the following class:

```
public class StaticMethod {
    private int instanceVariable;
    private static int classVariable;
    public static void main(String args[]) {
        System.out.println(instanceVariable);
    }
}
```

will produce the following error when compiled:

```
non-static variable instanceVariable cannot be referenced from a static context
        System.out.println(instanceVariable);
                           ^
1 error
```

 If we print the `classVariable` variable instead, the problem will not arise.

We have already unconsciously encountered a static variable, over and over again: the `System.out` variable. In fact, `out` is a static variable of the `System` class (belonging to the `java.lang` package). It is a variable of a type named `PrintStream`, which is a type of class that allows us to print a stream of data on a certain destination, and it is this class that declares the `print()` and `println()` methods that we have used so far (see official documentation). In particular, the `System.out` object represents the standard output of the system, that is, in the case of Windows, it represents the command prompt. That's why a call to `System.out.println()` prints the result at the command prompt.

## 6.8.3 Static Initializers and Object Initializers

The `static` modifier can also be used to mark a simple block of code defined within a class (but outside a method). We are talking about a new component (rarely used) that is called a **static initializer**. A static block defined within a class will have the characteristic of being called when the class itself is loaded into memory, even before a possible constructor. The syntax is simple, as shown in the following example:

```
public class StaticExample {
    private static int a = 10;
    public StaticExample(){
        a += 10;
    }
    static {
        System.out.println("static value = " + a);
    }
}
```

**251**

> **This block, as in the case of static methods, can use variables defined outside it if, and only if, declared as static.**

Let's suppose we create an object of this class using the following syntax:

```
StaticExample obj = new StaticExample();
```

This code fragment will produce the following output:

```
static value = 10
```

In fact, when instantiating an object from a class, first it must be loaded into memory. It is in this loading phase that the static block is executed, and consequently the output message is printed. The constructor is then called and will increase the static value again.

> **Even more static initializers can be added to a class; these will be executed sequentially from top to bottom.**

The use of a static initializer can actually be considered sporadic and linked to advanced design solutions.

### 6.8.3.1 When a class is loaded into memory

Java Specifications assert that a MyType class (or interface), is loaded into memory and initialized, before the first occurrence of any one of the following events:

- an instance of MyType is created (in case it is a class).

- A static method declared by MyType is invoked.

- A static field declared by MyType is assigned with a value.

- A static field declared by MyType is used and the field is not a constant variable.

- A reference to a static field causes initialization of only the class or interface that actually declares it, even though it might be referred to through the name of a subclass, a subinterface, or a class that implements an interface.

Also, there are two other events that deal with topics we haven't yet studied:

- an assert statement nested within MyType is executed (see section 9.6).

■■ Invocation of certain reflective methods in class `Class` and in package `java.lang.reflect` also causes class or interface loading and initialization (see section 12.4).

A class or interface will not be initialized under any other circumstance.

### 6.8.3.2 Object Initializers

There is also another type of initializer, but not a static one. It is called **instance initializer** (or **object initializer**) and is implemented by including code in a block of braces within a class (and outside a method). Its characteristic is to be executed when an object is instantiated, before the constructor. For example, if we instantiate the following class:

```
public class InstanceInitializer {
    public InstanceInitializer() {
        System.out.println("Constructor");
    }
    {
        System.out.println("Initializer");
    }
}
```

then this will be printed:

```
Inizializer
Constructor
```

Even the instance initializers are rarely used.

> **Multiple static and instance initializers can be placed in the same class. The initializers will be executed sequentially, depending on how they were ordered inside the file, but the static ones will always take precedence because they will be executed when the class is loaded.**

## 6.8.4 Static Import

In version 5 of Java, so-called **static imports** were introduced (along with many other features). With the `import` command, we can use types belonging to external packages in our code. In other words, it is possible to import the names of the classes (besides interfaces, enumerations and annotations) into our files, so that they can be used without having to specify the entire **fully qualified name**. For example, if we want to use the `DOMSource` class of the `javax.xml.transform.dom` package, we have two possibilities:

**1.** Import the class with this instruction:

```
import javax.xml.transform.dom.DOMSource;
```

and then use it in our source file using only the class name. For example:

```
DOMSource source = new DOMSource();
```

**2.** Or we can write the full package name every time we use it. For example:

```
javax.xml.transform.dom.DOMSource source =
    new javax.xml.transform.dom.DOMSource();
```

In some cases, however, we may wish to import into the file only what is declared static within a certain type, and not the type itself. For example, knowing that the Math class contains only static methods and constants, we may want to import, rather than the Math class, only its static members. To do this, use the following static import command:

```
import static java.lang.Math.*;
```

In this case, we have imported all the static members within the file. So, it will be legal to write, instead of:

```
double d = Math.sqrt(4);
```

just:

```
double d = sqrt(4);
```

without prefixing the class name before the static method. It is also possible (and preferable) to statically import only some specific members, for example:

```
import static java.lang.Math.PI;
import static java.lang.Math.random;
import static java.sql.DriverManager.getConnection;
import static java.lang.System.out;
```

Notice how importing static method names does not require us to specify parentheses for their arguments.

> **The use of static imports is not always advantageous and, in general, we do not recommend its use.**
> **All considerations and recommendations for using this feature of Java are treated in the eleventh chapter, in the section 11.4 entitled "More on Static Imports".**

### 6.8.5 When to Use static

You will surely have noticed that the use of static has been discouraged practically in every section. In fact, if we wanted to act as purists of Object Orientation, we should say that static is simply a word not to be used in Java programming. We could program anything without it. But static is not a representation of all that's evil! Certainly, we must avoid global variables, not create functions instead of methods, and not use static imports without reason. There are cases where programming problems can be solved in an elegant and functional way. For example, in the case of the instance counter, in section 6.8.2, a static variable allowed us to achieve our goal with minimum effort.

The public static constants (attributes declared public, final and static) then, are widely used. In fact, if we have an instance variable declared as final, and explicitly initialized when declared, then we should also declare it static, to prevent the overhead of being initialized every time an object is instantiated.

> If we want to initialize our constant using an argument of a constructor, then we should not use the static modifier, since every instance could have its constant value.

We have also seen that the static method sqrt() of the Math class is correctly defined (why instantiate an object of the Math class if we don't need it?). As for encapsulation (the main topic of this chapter), it is possible to create static attributes and to encapsulate them with the setter and getter methods (also declared as static), but we must keep in mind that there is a difference. Consider the following code:

```java
public class StaticEncapsulation {
    private static int staticAttribute = 0;
    public static void setStaticAttribute(int staticAttribute) {
        this.staticAttribute = staticAttribute;
    }
    public static int getStaticAttribute() {
        return staticAttribute;
    }
}
```

The code will not compile! The output of the compilation will be as follows:

```
StaticEncapsulation.java:4: error: non-static variable this cannot be referenced
  from a static context
        this.staticAttribute = staticAttribute;
        ^
StaticEncapsulation.java:4: warning: [static] static
```

```
    variable should be qualified by type name,
    IncapsulamentoStatico, instead of by an expression
          this.staticAttribute = staticAttribute;
               ^
1 error
1 warning
```

This is because the reference this refers to the current object and therefore cannot be used in the context of a static method, and this is reported as an error. A warning is also printed (it is not an error but only a warning by the compiler) that warns us that this refers to an object, but the attribute staticAttribute belongs to the class StaticEncapsulation, and it would be preferable to use the class to refer to the attribute.

The code will then compile if the setter method is modified as follows:

```
public static void setStaticAttribute(int staticAttribute) {
    StaticEncapsulation.staticAttribute = staticAttribute;
}
```

In fact, it is therefore possible to exploit the encapsulation for static variables, bearing in mind that, in this way, we will not encapsulate objects, but classes. An implementation of a very famous (and very useful) static encapsulation is the *Singleton design pattern* (see the next section).

 In section 6.3.3.4, we saw that it is useless to assign the value of this to another reference. In this section we have seen that it is not possible to use reference this in a static method. However, by assigning the value of this to a static reference, it will eventually allow us to use the current object from a static method (although it can hardly really be considered a useful practice). Let's consider the following example:

```
public class StaticThisTrick {
    private int id;
    private static StaticThisTrick stt;
    public StaticThisTrick(int id) {
        this.id = id;
        stt = this;
    }

    public String toString() {
        return"StaticThisTrick id=" + id;
    }

    public static void main(String args[]) {
        System.out.println(stt);
        new StaticThisTrick(1);
        System.out.println(stt);
        new StaticThisTrick(2);
```

```
            System.out.println(stt);
            new StaticThisTrick(3);
            System.out.println(stt);
        }
    }
```

Launching it, we will get the following output:

```
null
StaticThisTrick id=1
StaticThisTrick id=2
StaticThisTrick id=3
```

So, we used in the static method `main()` the reference `stt` that points to the current object. Since in the constructor we have assigned to the reference `stt` the value of `this`, after each instance creation the value of `stt` changes. Note that if we have not yet instantiated objects, the value of `stt` is set to its default value: `null`.

## 6.8.6 Singleton Design Pattern

**Design patterns** are standard design solutions applicable to different contexts. They represent an example of a high level of reuse, not of a method or of a class, but of a design solution (**conceptual reuse**). If a design problem occurs during the design phase of an application, most of the time there is no need to reinvent the wheel. A standard solution already exists (it has been found and formalized in the past by expert designers) and is applicable. It is enough to know it and implement it in our context (but it is not always simple!).

> **Online we will find Appendix D dedicated to the introduction of the design patterns.**

A great example of design pattern is the **Singleton** design pattern. If we need a class to be instantiated only once, and therefore all users of this class must always use the same instance, the solution is to apply the Singleton pattern. The classic implementation of the Singleton pattern consists of creating a class with:

1. a private constructor. This will imply that this constructor that must be called to instantiate an object, must be called only within the class itself;

2. a private and static variable of the same type as the class (usually called `instance`);

3. a public and static method (usually called `getInstance()`) that defines a simple logic to always return the same (unique) instance of the class itself.

Here is an example of the implementation of the Singleton pattern:

```
public class SingletonExample {
    private static SingletonExample instance;

    private SingletonExample() {
    }

    public static SingletonExample getInstance() {
        if (instance == null) {
            instance = new SingletonExample();
        }
        return instance;
    }
}
```

Note how the getInstance() method inside the class can call the constructor method (even if declared private) to instantiate the class itself. For the logic that it defines, an object will be created only the first time this method is called and assigned to the static attribute instance. From the second call on, this method will always return the same instance.

So, to get the only instance of the SingletonExample class, the other classes will have to use this syntax:

```
SingletonExample uniqueInstance = SingletonExample.getInstance();
```

and we will be sure that all these classes will always use the same SingletonExample instance. In Figure 6.9, we can see the class diagram showing the implementation of the Singleton pattern just described.

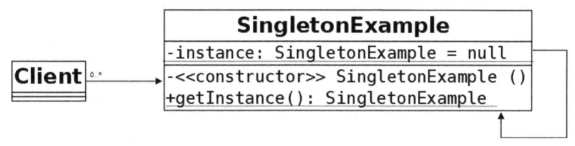

**Figure 6.9 - Class Diagram "Singleton Pattern".**

In the diagram of Figure 6.9 we can see two new elements of UML syntax. **Static variables and methods** are underlined in UML. The two arrows (lines with **direction**) on the diagram are called associations. **Associations** are relationships between classes, but more precisely, they represent relationships between objects. It may seem strange because the class diagram is a static diagram but it defines elements (associations) that represent dynamic relationships between objects. The information that associations give us, is about use. In the diagram, the arrow that starts from the `Client` class and ends in the `SingletonExample` class, indicates that the `Client` class objects at runtime will use an object of the `SingletonExample` class. The symbol `0..*` that can be observed at the source of the association next to the `Client` class, indicates a **multiplicity of the association**. This information makes it clear that the association refers to objects, since the class is always one and therefore it makes no sense to speak of several classes, if anything, of more objects. At the other end of the association, the multiplicity is not indicated, which means that the multiplicity of objects in the `SingletonExample` class, assumes the default value 1. Therefore, bearing in mind the direction and multiplicity, and the content that defines the `SingletonExample` class as a `Singleton`, this association must be read as "at runtime, multiple objects of type `Client` use only one object of type `SingletonExample`". Which means that each `Client` object uses a reference of the unique `SingletonExample` object.

The other association that we see in Figure 6.9 starts and ends in the same class, without specifying the multiplicity. It is called **reflexive association**, and implies that the `SingletonExample` class has a reference to itself. And indeed, `SingletonExample` has been implemented with a reference to itself within it.

It should be noted that the multiplicity and the direction of the associations are optional, because it's not certain that, at any given moment during development, we are sure of having clear information, and therefore of being able to make decisions that are certain.

The use of patterns also allows programmers to use a simplified terminology to talk about the code. Programmers often communicate using pattern terminology (for example "... this class is a Singleton ..."). In addition, some IDEs automate design pattern implementations automatically.

> **EJE also allows us to implement the Singleton pattern automatically. After creating a class, simply click on the** Insert ⟳ Singleton **menu or use the** CTRL-F9 **key combination.**

# Summary

In this chapter, the support offered by Java for **Object Orientation** was introduced. After a historical overview, some fundamental paradigms were listed: abstraction, reuse, encapsulation, inheritance and polymorphism. **Abstraction** consists of creating the programming entities (classes, methods, etc.) with an appropriate name and implementation. We can concentrate on the elements that most characterize the entity we are defining, and can thus make it easier to interact with the software. **Reuse** allows us to reuse classes, methods, packages, design solutions, concepts and more, without having to rewrite or reinvent them. Even though they are fundamental paradigms of object-oriented programming, abstraction and reuse are valid paradigms for functional programming as well. For this reason, they are often considered secondary paradigms, but the reader should keep in mind that their use is absolutely crucial for programming in Java, as we will try to demonstrate in this manual.

The **class diagram** defined by UML, helps us to represent the classes in a very readable and practical way. With association notation, we can also obtain information on the relationships between the objects instantiated by the classes.

**Encapsulation** ensures greater maintainability, robustness and reusability. Writing code to implement encapsulation is very simple (private variable and accessor and mutator methods), so much so that most development tools support a standard way to encapsulate the attributes of a class. It is also easy to understand when to apply this concept: practically always!

We have also introduced the reference this even if, for now, it does not seem to be an indispensable keyword to program. Its introduction, however, was useful to clarify some obscure points that could (even unconsciously) represent an obstacle to the complete comprehension of the topics. In fact, with this and the dot operator, we can refer methods and variables in the same class, and with the syntax this(), we can invoke one constructor from another to reuse the code.

The concept of **package** and the possibility of management "by hand" (that we could use if we worked from the command line without an IDE) were also defined. Although in real programming, the packages are always used, we have underlined how this can initially influence the learning curve for a reader who is only approaching Java programming, and wants to use all the constructs. However, using an IDE such as Eclipse or Netbeans, package usage is virtually transparent.

The **modules** will be explained in a separate chapter later, when the time is ripe to better appreciate the concepts. Meanwhile, we can note how the whole standard library has been reorganized as a result of the modules introduction in Java 9.

The meanings of the **access modifiers** and their applicability to the components of the Java language were then explained. The public modifier can be applied to methods, variables and classes, which then inherit the property to be used by any class. The protected modifier, instead, makes a method or variable accessible to the classes in the same package, and inherited in all subclasses, even if belonging to another package. If no modifier is provided to a variable or method, then these will only be accessible to classes in the same package. Finally, the private modifier makes a class member (method or variable) not accessible outside the class where it's defined.

Furthermore, a fundamental modifier, static, and its applicability to class members was explained. The static modifier, makes methods and variables *belong to the class*, and not to a specific object. For this reason, it is necessary to refer to them through the name of the class and not that of the object.

We took advantage of this to introduce a new type of component: the static and object **initializers**. A **static initializer** is composed of the static modifier and the block of code that follows it. It has the characteristic of being called only once when the class is loaded into memory. On the other hand, an **instance initializer** (or **object initializer**) is simply represented with a block of code, which will be called before the constructor, when an object is instantiated.

We also referred to the existence of **static imports** and we have so far discouraged their use. With these, we can import only the static members of other classes into a class. For an in-depth analysis of static imports, see the eleventh chapter. We also showed how the static modifier is suitable for solving particular problems, and that it is not a tool to be abused.

We took the opportunity to introduce design patterns and, in particular, the Singleton pattern. **Design patterns** allow us to use already consolidated design solutions to solve some typical programming problems. The **Singleton** pattern, in particular, allows us to create a class from which we can instantiate a single object. This way we are sure that all objects instantiated by other classes of the application will always deal with this unique object.

**Exercises, source code, appendices and other resources are available at** http://www.javaforaliens.com.

## Chapter Goals

Have the following goals been achieved?

| Goal | Achieved | Achievement Date |
|---|:---:|:---:|
| Understand the reasons for the birth of object-oriented programming (Unit 6.1) | O | |
| Know how to list the fundamental paradigms and concepts of object-oriented programming (Unit 6.2) | O | |
| Know how to create a basic class diagram (Units 6.2, 6.9) | O | |
| Know how to define and use the concepts of abstraction and reuse (Unit 6.2) | O | |
| Understand the use and usefulness of encapsulation (Units 6.3, 6.4, 6.5) | O | |
| Understand how the use the reference this (Unit 6.3) | O | |
| Understand when and how to use encapsulation (Units 6.4, 6.5) | O | |
| Understand how to use packages (Units 6.6, 6.7) | O | |
| Understand how to use access modifiers (Unit 6.7) | O | |
| Understand how to use the static modifier (Unit 6.8) | O | |
| Understand the concept of design pattern and be able to implement with code the Singleton pattern (Unit 6.8) | O | |

# 7

# Inheritance and Interfaces

**Goals:**

At the end of this chapter, the reader should be able to:

✔ Understand the definition, use and usefulness of inheritance (generalization and specialization) (Unit 7.1).

✔ Understand the consequences of the simultaneous use of encapsulation and inheritance (Unit 7.2).

✔ Understand and know how to use the super keyword (Unit 7.2).

✔ Understand and know how to use the abstract, final and the other modifiers (Units 7.2, 7.3).

✔ Understand and know how to use the interfaces (Unit 7.4).

✔ Know how to deal with various complex cases of multiple inheritance (Unit 7.4).

In this chapter, we will deal with **inheritance** and other related concepts. Here, we will not speak exclusively about programming but also of more abstract concepts; we should learn to have a designer vision. Anyone can program, just know how to use if and the for, and you can do everything! It's like that in theory. In practice you have to have clear rules and ideas before starting to program with your head down. What makes the difference between a good geek and a good developer is the quality of his work. A developer should be able to analyze and design his solution, creating simple and maintainable code. This is not a book about design, but we will try to tease your curiosity on the subject in order to try and make you understand its importance.

# 7.1 Inheritance

Like all the paradigms that characterize Object Orientation, the concept of **inheritance** is also inspired by something that exists in the real world. The term must be understood in the *Darwinian sense*. In the real world, we classify everything with classes and subclasses. For example, a dog is an animal, an airplane is a vehicle, a guitar is a musical instrument. In Java, inheritance is the feature that allow to group multiple classes that have common characteristics with the extensibility realationship. For example, the Dog class will extend the Animal class. The immediate result is the possibility of inheriting already written code, and therefore of managing sets of classes collectively because they have some characteristics in common. The rules for using inheritance correctly are simple and clear. But although inheritance is an easy topic to understand, it is not always used correctly.

## 7.1.1 The Keyword extends

The keyword extends will allow us to implement inheritance.
Consider the following classes that we do not encapsulate for simplicity:

```java
public class Book {
    public String title;
    public String author;
    public String publisher;
    public int numberOfPages;
    public int price;
    //. . .
}

public class JavaBook {
    public String title;
    public String author;
    public String publisher;
    public int numberOfPages;
    public int price;
    public final String SUBJECT = "Java";
    //...
}
```

We note that the Book and JavaBook classes represent two concepts similar and therefore they declare fields in common. Inheritance will allow us to relate the two classes with the following syntax:

```java
public class JavaBook extends Book {
    public final String SUBJECT = "Java";
    //. . .
}
```

In this way, the JavaBook class will inherit all the public fields of the extended class. Therefore, in the JavaBook class, there are also the public variables publisher, price, title, author and numberOfPages. These are already defined in the Book class, even if they have not been explicitly coded. The SUBJECT constant, instead, belongs only to the JavaBook class. In particular, we will say that JavaBook is a **subclass** of Book, and Book is a **superclass** of JavaBook. The first advantage is obvious, in this example we reused the code avoiding a "copy-paste", but the inheritance cannot be reduced to just writing fewer lines.

The UML notation that defines the extension relationship, is an arrow that goes from the subclass to the superclass. Figure 7.1 shows a class diagram of the **inheritance relationship** between the two classes.

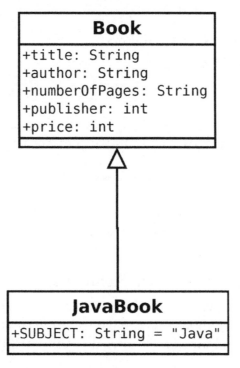

**Figure 7.1 - Class Diagram "Inheritance: JavaBook is a Subclass of Book".**

## 7.1.2 The Object Class

As we have already observed several times, the Java compiler often inserts, in the compiled bytecode, some instructions that the programmer has not inserted. This is to facilitate the developer both in learning and in coding.

We have also already stated several times that object-oriented programming is inspired by real-world concepts. All of the standard Java library has been designed and organized in such a way as to satisfy the object theory. Since reality is made up of objects (everything can be considered an object, existing as both concrete elements and abstract concepts), in the standard Java library, there is a class called Object that abstracts the concept of a generic object. It belongs to the java.lang package and is, in fact, the superclass of each class. It is at the top of the class hierarchy and therefore all classes inherit the members of Object (we can verify this by reading the description of the methods of any class in the documentation). If we define a class that does not extend other classes, it will automatically extend Object. This means that if we wrote:

```java
public class Art {
    //...
}
```

the compiler would translate this class as follows:

```java
public class Art extends Object {
    //...
}
```

> **In the real world, everything is an object so, in Java, all classes will extend Object.**

So, when we create our own class, it is inserted into the class hierarchy at the top of which there is the Object class. Indeed, each class inherits all the methods defined by the Object class, as we will see in the following chapters.

### 7.1.3 When to Use Inheritance: "Is a" Relationship

When we talk about inheritance, we often believe that to implement it, we need a couple of classes that declare fields in common. This could only be interpreted as an indication of inheritance. The decisive test must, however, be carried out through the so-called **"is a" relationship**.

In order to make proper use of inheritance, the programmer has to ask to himself only one simple question: "is an object of the candidate subclass also an object of the candidate superclass?".

If the answer to the question is positive, inheritance must be applied, if the answer is negative, inheritance should not be applied.

Indeed, if the application of inheritance depended solely on the fields in common between two classes, we could find extension relationships between classes such as Triangle and Trapezoid For example:

```
public class Triangle {
    public final int SIDES_NUMBER = 3;
    public float sideOneLength;
    public float sideTwoLength;
    public float sideThreeLength;
    //. . .
}

public class Trapezoid extends Triangle {
    public final int SIDES_NUMBER = 4;
    public float sideFourLength;
    //. . .
}
```

But a trapezoid is not a triangle! And for the "is a" relationship, this extension is not valid. The problem is that the construction of a program takes place step by step. If we incorrectly link two classes in terms of inheritance, we would, at first, write fewer lines of code, but the problems would arise later, when we try to exploit a trapezoid when using a triangle. The "is a" relationship keeps us safe from these inconveniences, and is a very simple test to do.

> **Note that the logical problems of an incorrect abstraction of our classes, could be amplified as the code grows, implementing inheritance and encapsulation. In the tenth chapter entitled "A Guided Example of Object-Oriented Programming" the veracity of the statement is demonstrated.**

Inheritance is therefore defined by the relation "is a", which applies to objects, not to classes.

## 7.1.4 How to Use Inheritance: Generalization and Specialization

These are two terms that define the processes that lead to the implementation of inheritance. We can talk about **generalization** if, starting from a certain number of classes, a superclass is defined which collects their common characteristics.

On the other hand, we talk about **specialization** when, starting from a class, we define one or more subclasses in order to obtain more specialized objects.

The usefulness of specialization is easy to highlight: suppose we want to create a MyButton class, whose instances are displayed as buttons to be used on a graphical interface. Starting from scratch, creating pixel by pixel is very complicated. If, instead, we extend the Button class of the java.awt package, we just have to add the code that will customize the MyButton.

In the last example of the previous section, we had the Triangle class and the Trapezoid class available. We noticed how the failure of the "is a" test discourages us from implementing inheritance. Yet, these two classes have fields in common and it does not seem to be an accidental event. In fact, both the `Triangle` and the `Trapezoid` are ("is a" relationship) both polygons. The solution to this problem is *natural*. Simply *generalize* the two abstractions into a Polygon class, which could be extended by the `Triangle` and `Trapezoid` classes. For example:

```java
public abstract class Polygon {
    private int sidesNumber;
    private int sideOneLength;
    private int sideTwoLength;
    private int sideThreeLength;
    //...
}

public class Triangle extends Polygon {
    public static final int SIDES_NUMBER = 3;
    public Triangle () {}
    //...
}

public class Trapezoid extends Polygon {
    public static final int SIDES_NUMBER = 4;
    private int sideFourLength;
    //...
}
```

If we had started from the `Polygon` class and then defined the two subclasses, we would have talked about *specialization* instead. Using the specialization process, it is also easy to think about other possible subclasses such as `Hexagon`, `Pentagon`, `Octagon`, `Square` and so on.

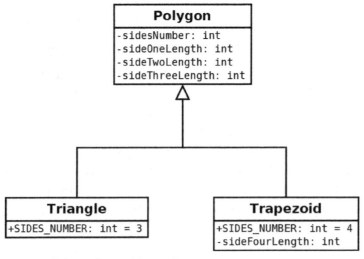

**Figure 7.2 - Class diagram of the polygon hierarchy.**

The `Polygon` class is therefore the most generic and, in a program that uses polygons, the only class that we probably will not create will be the `Polygon` class because it's too generic. In these cases, the `Polygon` class must be declared `abstract`, and this will imply that it cannot be instantiated (we would get a compile-time error if we tried). So, `Polygon` would remain important only to allow us to exploit the advantages of inheritance, but there will be no objects instantiated directly from this class. However, as mentioned, objects instantiated by its subclasses `Trapezoid` and `Triangle` can all be considered polygons!

In Figure 7.2, we have represented the hierarchy of the presented classes. For simplicity, we have omitted detailing the methods (remember that UML in this book is often used informally).

## 7.2 Inheritance Language Support

After understanding what is inheritance, it is necessary to evaluate its impact not only on how we are going to design our programs, but also how Java features support this fundamental object-oriented paradigm. In the next sections then, we will examine the impact that inheritance has on the concepts we already know, and we will introduce new inheritance-related features that we have not yet presented.

### 7.2.1 Inheritance-Encapsulation Relationship

Since encapsulation can be practically considered mandatory and inheritance a valuable tool for development, we must ask ourselves what causes the combined use of both paradigms? That is: what will we inherit from an encapsulated class? We have already stated, at the end of the previous chapter, that extending a class means inheriting non-private members. Let's therefore consider a `Recurrence` class obtained by specializing the `Date` class defined in the previous chapter as an example of encapsulation. It is excluded that the `Recurrence` class can access the day, `month` and `year` variables directly, as these will not be inherited. In fact, these variables had been declared `private` within the superclass `Date`. But since all the set and get methods are declared `public` in the superclass, they will be inherited and then made usable in the subclass as shown in Figure 7.3. So even if the `Recurrence` class does not explicitly own `Date`'s private variables, it is as if it possessed them, since it can still use them through its setter and getter methods.

As already stated in the previous chapter, a common mistake is to think that, in order to use a certain variable in a subclass, it is necessary to declare it `protected`, when it is more than sufficient to have the mutator (set) and accessor (get) methods available in the subclasses.

Furthermore, to declare an instance variable `protected` means to make it public to all the classes of the same package (see section 6.7). This means that the protected variable is directly accessible to all classes belonging to the same package and, except in rare cases, this is not the desired encapsulation level.

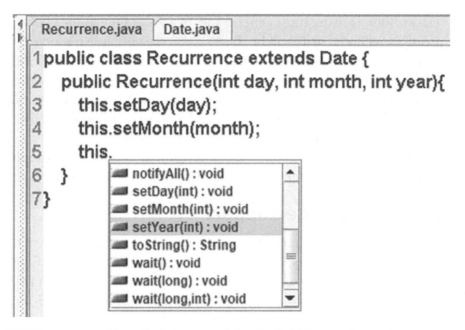

**Figure 7.3 - EJE: Recurrence Class that accesses inherited public members.**

## 7.2.2 Inheritance and Constructors

Inheritance is not applicable to constructors. Even when they are declared public, constructors are not inherited for a very simple reason: their name. Remember that a constructor has been defined in the second chapter as a special method, as it has the following properties:

1. it has the same name as the class to which it belongs;

2. it has no return type;

3. it is called automatically (and only) whenever an object of the class to which it belongs is instantiated, for that object;

4. it is present in every class.

With regard to the last point, we have also defined the *default constructor* as the constructor that is introduced into a class by the compiler at compilation time, in case the programmer did not explicitly provide it. We also stated that a constructor is usually used to initialize object variables at the time of the instance. For all this, if for example the JavaBook class inherited from the Book class a constructor, it would inherit a constructor called Book(). A constructor called a Book() in a class called JavaBook could never be called! In fact, to instantiate an object from the JavaBook class, it is mandatory to call a constructor named JavaBook(). For example, given the following code:

```
JavaBook javaBook = new JavaBook();
```

if, in its place, we wrote:

```
JavaBook javaBook = new Book();
```

we would create an object of the Book class, not an object of the JavaBook class (also obtaining a compile-time error).

The fact that constructors are not inherited from the subclasses is absolutely in line with the syntax of the language, but at the same time is in contradiction with the principles of object-oriented programming. In particular, the rule of abstraction seems to have been violated. In fact, when the developer decided to implement the inheritance mechanism, they had to test its validity through the so-called "is a" relationship. To the question: "can an object instantiated by the candidate subclass also be considered an object of the candidate superclass?" they have indeed answered affirmatively.

A book on Java, also being a book, must have all the characteristics of a book. In particular, the constructor must also be reused. Not being able to inherit it, however, abstraction seems to have been violated. Instead, it is precisely in such a situation that Java demonstrates its consistency. In fact, we can add another property to the constructor definition:

5. any constructor (even the default constructor), always invokes a superclass constructor as the first instruction.

For example, we add constructors to the Book and JavaBook classes:

```
public class Book {
    //. . .
    public Book(){
        System.out.println("Book created!");
    }
}

public class JavaBook extends Book {
    public JavaBook() {
        System.out.println("Book on Java created!");
    }
}
```

The reader, having learned that the constructors are not inherited, should conclude that the instance of a JavaBook, through a syntax of the type:

```
new JavaBook(); /* The assignment of a reference is not
   mandatory to instantiate an object */
```

would output the following string:

```
Book on Java created!
```

The output will instead be:

```
Book created!
Book on Java created!
```

In fact, the constructor `BookJava()` first invokes the constructor of the superclass `Book()` and then it is executed.

The mandatory call to a superclass constructor is made using the super keyword, which is introduced below.

## 7.2.3 The super Keyword

In the sixth chapter, we defined the keyword `this` as "implicit reference to the current object". We can define the super keyword as "implicit reference to the intersection between the current object and its superclass". This reference allows us to access the components of the superclass and in particular its constructor.

### 7.2.3.1 super *and Constructors*

The super keyword is closely linked to the concept of constructor. In fact, in every constructor, there is always a call to the superclass constructor, through a special syntax that uses the super reference. For example, in the JavaBook class, the constructor will be modified by the compiler in the following way:

```
public class JavaBook extends Book {
    public JavaBook() {
        super(); //implicit instruction if not provided by the programmer
        System.out.println("Book on Java created!");
    }
}
```

Here is how the constructor of the Book class is invoked by the constructor of the JavaBook class. We can explicitly do the call to super(), but if we do not do it, the compiler will add this instruction. The call to a superclass constructor is therefore inevitable!

> Note that the constructor of the Book **class will also call the constructor of its superclass** Object, **using an implicit** super() **command.**

Now suppose we want to equip the superclass Book with a constructor that sets the `title` variable. In fact, an object of type Book should have at least a `title`:

```
public class Book {
    //...
    public Book (String title) {
        this.title = title;
    }
}
```

This class will compile, but JavaBook will no longer compile:

```
JavaBook.java:1: error: constructor Book in class Book cannot be applied to given types;
public class JavaBook extends Book {
       ^
  required: String
  found: no arguments
  reason: actual and formal argument lists differ in length
1 error
```

We modify the superclass and the subclass does not compile anymore... strange! But not that strange, since they are linked by the "is a" relationship. Reading the error of the compiler, however, you can guess what happened. The subclass constructor has tried to call a superclass constructor that is not there: the constructor without parameters. In fact, if a constructor is added explicitly, no other default constructor is implicitly inserted. Then the super() instruction, automatically inserted in the subclass JavaBook, tries to call the superclass constructor without parameters (in fact no parameters have been specified between the brackets). To solve the problem, we must modify the constructor of JavaBook in such a way as to make it call the constructor of the superclass Book which takes the title as input. The following solution is the best:

```
public class JavaBook extends Book {
    public JavaBook (String title) {
        super(title);
    }
    //...
}
```

Therefore, we have inserted an explicit call to the superclass constructor that takes a string as input. It has also been natural to modify the list of subclass parameters, and this too can be considered an index of Java's coherence towards object-oriented paradigms.

> **Warning: the superclass constructor's call using** `super()`, **must be the first instruction of a constructor and cannot be inserted into a method other than a constructor.**

If we had more constructors in the superclass, we could choose which one to call. For example, if the Book class defines several constructors in the following way:

```
public class Book {
    //...
    public Book (String title, String author) {
        this(title); //call to the next constructor
        setAuthor(author);
    }

    public Book (String title) {
        this.title = title;
    }
    // Setter and Getter methods omitted
}
```

The JavaBook class could call the most appropriate constructor, depending on the case. For example:

```
public class JavaBook extends Book {
    public JavaBook (String title) {
        super(title);
    }

    public JavaBook (String title, String author) {
        super(title, author);
    }
    //   . . .
}
```

The call via super() to a superclass constructor or through this() to a constructor of the same class, can only be used as the first instruction in a constructor. If one of these instructions is not entered as the first instruction, the compiler will report an error. This implies that only one instruction between super() or this() will be present in a constructor. If we explicitly insert the this() command, then the call to super() cannot be placed in the same constructor. However, note that in cases like this, a constructor calls another constructor using the this() command. This other constructor, in turn, either calls a third constructor via another this() command, or calls a superclass constructor with the super()! In short, the superclass constructor will be called in any case sooner or later. For example, the following class that represents a character (font) to be used in an editor:

```
public class Character {
    private String type;
    private int size;

    public Character (String type) {
```

```
        this(type, 12);
    }

    public Character (String type, int size) {
        //Here a super() invocation will be inserted from the compiler
        setType(type);
        setSize(size);
    }
    //Accessor and mutator methods omitted...
}
```

declares a first constructor that invokes the second with the command this(). In the second constructor, however, the compiler explicitly inserts the super() command as the first statement. The call to a superclass constructor (which in this case is the Object class) has only been postponed.

> **We cannot even call a constructor using the super() or this() commands from an ordinary method. Only constructor can use these instructions.**

### 7.2.3.2 super *and Methods*

Since the references super and this can even call constructors, why can they not call ordinary methods? Of course, they can do it! The this reference is capable of calling methods, as we have already seen in the previous chapter. With the syntax:

```
this.methodName()
```

it was possible to call methods of the same class; but we said that the reference this, in these cases, is redundant since Java considers it implicit if a reference is not specified before the call of a method. So, write:

```
this.methodName()
```

It is equivalent to writing:

```
methodName()
```

With the following syntax, instead:

```
super.methodName()
```

it will be possible to invoke a superclass method from a subclass method. This makes sense in case of rewriting a method in a subclass, otherwise the superclass method would still be inherited in the subclass, and therefore it would be useless to use super. For example, consider the following classes:

```java
public class Person {
    private String name, surname;
    public String toString() {
        return name + " " + surname;
    }
    //accessor and mutator methods (set and get) omitted
}

public class Customer extends Person {
    private String address, phoneNumber;
    public String toString() {
        return super.toString()+ "\n"+
        address + "\nTel:" + phoneNumber;
    }
    //accessor and mutator methods (set and get) omitted
}
```

The Person class declares a method called toString(). It is one of the most popular methods, is declared directly by the Object class, and it should be the method responsible for representing the object on which the method is called with a string. So, the Person class is already **overriding** (rewriting) the method, causing the method to return a string consisting of the name and the surname.

The Customer class extends the Person class and also inherits the toString() method. But this method is, in turn, redefined to also print the new fields defined in the Customer class: address and telephone. To also print the name and surname, the toString() method of the Customer class first calls the toString() method of the Person superclass (reuse, to avoid duplication of code) and then concatenates the result with the address and telephone details. Remember that the string \n is equivalent to wrapping the text (new line key), as we saw in the third chapter.

> If the toString() **method was not rewritten, it would return a string with the** ClassName@AddressWithExadecimalFormat. **This is because being the** Object **class very generic, the Java creators decided that the** toString() **method should return reference information. Override will be fully explored in the next chapter.**

## 7.2.4 Inheritance and Initializers

The static and instance initializers seem to be inherited in some way, but it is not true inheritance, rather, the normal flow of execution. Let's demonstrate it clearly with an example.

Consider a class that defines two simple initializers (one static and one instance), as well as a constructor without parameters:

```java
public class ParentInitializer {
    public ParentInitializer () {
        System.out.println("ParentInitializer constructor");
    }
    {
        System.out.println("ParentInitializer initializer");
    }

    static {
        System.out.println("ParentInitializer static initializer");
    }
}
```

Let's extend `ParentInitializer` with the `ChildInitializer` class which declares, in turn, two other initializers and a `main()` method that auto-instantiates:

```java
public class ChildInitializer extends ParentInitializer {
    public ChildInitializer (){
        System.out.println("ChildInitializer constructor");
    }
    {
        System.out.println("ChildInitializer initializer");
    }

    static {
        System.out.println("ChildInitializer static initializer");
    }
    public static void main(String args[]) {
        new ChildInitializer();
    }
}
```

The resulting output will be as follows:

```
ParentInitializer static initializer
ChildInitializer static initializer
ParentInitializer initializer
ParentInitializer constructor
ChildInitializer initializer
ChildInitializer constructor
```

Note that, for both static and instance initializers, access modifiers are not valid, and therefore inheritance rules do not apply. What happens is that before the `ChildInitializer` class is loaded, the `ParentInitializer` class must be loaded into memory, which explains the first two lines of the output. Remember that, while the static initializers are invoked when the class is loaded into memory, instance initializers are called at the time of the object instance, before the constructor. In the example, it so happens that the `ChildInitializer` constructor is called, which, as we have seen, calls the `ParentInitializer` constructor. But before this is done, the `ParentInitializer` initializer runs. The same happens in the subclass where, before the constructor is called, the initializer is invoked, and here it is the output of the previous example.

> **Initializers are rarely used, but it is good to know how they are invoked in case of inheritance.**

## 7.2.5 Inheritance and Modifiers

In the next subsections, an overview is presented of the modifiers we already know, and their behavior in the event of inheritance. Let's start by summarizing the situation regarding access modifiers.

> **We will cover the `abstract` modifier separately in section 7.3.**
>
> **The other modifiers such as `volatile`, `synchronized`, `transient`, `strictfp`, `native` do not have interesting properties related to inheritance.**

### 7.2.5.1 Access Modifiers

The `private` modifier can be applied to variables and methods, and prevents those members from being inherited in a subclass.

The `protected` modifier, which can also be applied only to variables and methods, allows members to be inherited. For example, let's consider the following class (already encountered in the previous chapter) declaring a protected variable and a protected method:

```java
package com.cdsc.test;

public class ProtectedWithinClass  {
    protected int protectedVariable;

    protected void protectedMethod() {
        System.out.println("protected method invoked");
    }
}
```

The following subclass, while belonging to a different package, inherits and uses protected members:

```
package com.cdsc;

import com.cdsc.test.*;

public class ProtectedSubclassOutsidePackage extends ProtectedWithinClass {
    public void methodThatUsesProtected() {
        protectedMethod();
        System.out.println(protectedVariable);
    }
}
```

Also, a subclass belonging to the same package inherits and can use protected members:

```
package com.cdsc.test;

public class ProtectedSubclassWithinPackage extends ProtectedWithinClass {
    public void methodThatUsesProtected() {
        protectedMethod();
        System.out.println(protectedVariable);
    }
}
```

It is important to understand that only within the same package it is possible to access protected members of another class. A classic belief of many Java programmers is that instead it is possible to access protected members even in subclasses belonging to different packages. Actually, a subclass that does not reside in the same superclass package inherits the members protected by the superclass, but cannot, for example, instantiate an object from the superclass, and use a protected member. That is, if for example we add the following method to the class ProtectedSubclassOutsidePackage:

```
public void invalidMethod() {
    var pic = new ProtectedWithinClass();
    pic.protectedMethod();
}
```

we will get the following compile-time error:

```
error: metodoProtected() has protected access in ProtectedInClasse
        pic.metodoProtected();
           ^
1 error
```

Obviously, the same method in the ProtectedSubclassWithinPackage class would not have caused any problems during compilation.

However, when we *do not specify modifiers* before instance variables or methods, they will be inherited only in subclasses belonging to the same package. Instead, if we do not specify modifiers when we declare a class, it will be visible (and therefore extensible) only by classes belonging to the same package. In fact, if we declare the class:

```
package com.cdsc.test;

/* public */ class SuperclassInsidePackage {

}
```

the following subclass will not compile if we do not declare the SuperclassInsidePackage superclass as public:

```
package com.cdsc;

import com.cdsc.test.*;

public class SubclassInsideDifferentPackage extends SuperclassInsidePackage {

}
```

The output that follows is:

```
SubclassInsideDifferentPackage.java:5: error: cannot find symbol
public class SubclassInsideDifferentPackage extends SuperclassInsidePackage {
                                                    ^
  symbol: class SuperclassInsidePackage
1 error
```

Instead, the following class will compile because it belongs to the same package:

```
package com.cdsc.test;

public class SubclassInsidePackage extends SuperclassInsidePackage {

}
```

### 7.2.5.2 The static Modifier

The static modifier can be used with the import command, to import static members of a class, but, above all, it can be applied to variables, methods and even initializers. The import command has nothing to do with inheritance. Instead, variables and static methods are inherited, but because they belong to the class and not to objects, it is **inheritance between classes**.

> **Technically we are using the term *inheritance* incorrectly. There are differences and exceptions with classical inheritance that will be highlighted in the next pages.**

For example, let's consider the class:

```
public class ClassWithStaticMethod {
    public static void staticMethod() {
        System.out.println("This is a static method");
    }
}
```

It is possible to extend it and use the `staticMethod()` method without referring to it in this way:

```
public class SubclassWithStaticMethod extends ClassWithStaticMethod {
    public void aMethod() {
        staticMethod();
    }
}
```

We can also verify the inheritance for classes with the class:

```
public class ClassWithStaticMethodTest {
    public static void main(String args[]) {
        SubclassWithStaticMethod.staticMethod();
    }
}
```

### 7.2.5.3 The `final` *Modifier*

We have already seen how this modifier is used to declare constants in Java. But `final` can be used not only with variables, but also with classes and methods to influence inheritance rules. The term `final` must be understood in the sense of "non-modifiable". Indeed:

■■ a variable (both instance and local) declared as `final` becomes a constant;

■■ a method declared as `final` cannot be rewritten in a subclass (*override*, which will be explained below, cannot be applied). This means that it is inherited as it was declared in the superclass;

■■ a class declared as `final` cannot be extended.

For example, the `String` and the `Math` classes of the `java.lang` package are examples of classes declared `final`. Therefore, these classes cannot be extended because we would get an error in the compilation phase as follows:

```
jshell> class FinalClassExtendsTest extends String {}
|  Error:
|  cannot inherit from final java.lang.String
|  class FinalClassExtendsTest extends String {}
|                                      ^----^
```

**The following observation is not related to inheritance. However, we want to conclude the discussion about the** final **modifier.**

The final modifier can also be used for local variables and local methods parameters. In such cases, the values of these variables will not be locally modifiable. For example, the following code is compiled without errors:

```
public class LocalVariables {
    public static void main(String args[]) {
        System.out.println(new LocalVariables().finalLocalVariablesMethod(5,6));
    }
    public int finalLocalVariablesMethod(final int i,final int j) {
        final int k = i + j;
        return k;
    }
}
```

Declaring the parameters of a method as final is considered, by some, to be good programming practice. The modifier, in this case, emphasizes the fact that the parameters should not be modified. In fact, they are valued from the outside, and changing their value within the method means distorting their definition.

Since the first chapter we have always declared the main() method in the same way:

```
public static void main(String [] args) {}
```

Although useless, the final modifier can be used to declare the main() method. So the following declaration is also valid:

```
public final static void main(String [] args) {}
```

## 7.3 The abstract Modifier

The abstract modifier can be applied not only to classes but also to methods. It does not make sense to talk about abstract variables.

### 7.3.1 Abstract Methods

An abstract method does not implement its own code block and therefore is devoid of behavior. The definition of an abstract method does not have curly braces but ends with a semicolon. An example of an abstract method is the following:

```
public abstract void paintPicture();
```

This method cannot be invoked (as it is not defined) but can be subject to rewriting (override) in a subclass as we will see in depth in the next chapter dedicated to polymorphism.

An abstract method can be defined only within an abstract class. In other words, a class that also contains only one abstract method must be declared abstract.

## 7.3.2 Abstract Classes

A class declared as abstract cannot be instantiated. The programmer who intends to mark a class with the abstract modifier must be aware a priori that from that class we will never instantiate objects. But why create a class that cannot be instantiated? Because sometimes we need to create generic classes to be extended, and which represent a concept that is too generic to be instantiated in the context of a given program. The Polygon class of the example in section 7.1.4, for example, is an excellent candidate to become an abstract class. In fact, in a hypothetical use of the classes we have defined, we will never create objects from the Polygon class, but only from the Triangle and Trapezoid concrete classes:

```java
public class PolygonTest {
    public static void main(String args[]) {
        Triangle triangle = new Triangle(25, 2, 18);
        Trapezoid trapezoid = new Trapezoid(24, 11, 20, 17);
        System.out.println(triangle);
        System.out.println(trapezoid);
    }
}
```

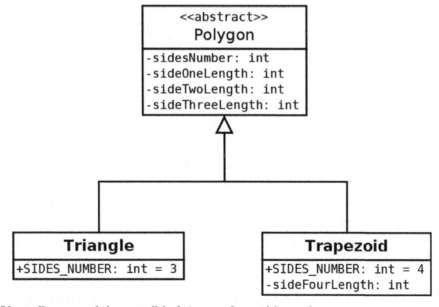

**Figure 7.4 - Class diagram of the possible future polygon hierarchy.**

Therefore, we can declare the `Polygon` abstract class as in Figure 7.4.

> **Note that the UML notation for the `abstract` modifier is quite open to criticism. In fact, it would be enough to write the name of the entity (class or method) in italics. This choice, however, means that the clarity of the diagram will depend on the type of font chosen to write the text (the problem does not arise if we use pen and paper for our diagrams). With some fonts, the difference between italics and non-italics styles is not clearly visible. For this reason, we have added a so-called stereotype <>. A stereotype allows us to label an entity with a significant word to characterize it. With the stereotype <> we have made it more evident that the `Polygon` class has been declared abstract.**

The `abstract` modifier is also an important design tool. In fact, by declaring an abstract class, we will also declare that this must be extended, and then we will direct the development towards the creation of subclasses of the abstract class. The advantage of thinking about programming with superclasses (and then for interfaces as we will see in the next section) rather than getting lost in the details of the subclasses, is great. In fact, interaction with the software will be easier if we think about abstractions rather than implementations.

Consider the following abstract class that defines the method presented in the previous section:

```java
public abstract class Painter {
    //. . .
    public abstract void paintPicture();
    //. . .
}
```

This class makes sense if inserted into a system in which the `Painter` object can be considered a concept too generic to define a new type to be instantiated. Suppose that, for our system, knowing the pictorial style of a `Painter` object is fundamental and, since there are no painters capable of painting with any kind of style among all the existing ones, it makes no sense to instantiate a `Painter` class. It would be correct to create in our system non-abstract subclasses of `Painter` like `ImpressionistPainter` and `NeorealistPainter`. These subclasses must redefine the abstract `paintPicture()` method (unless one also intends to declare the subclass abstract). Note that the `Painter` class could have concretely implemented the `paintPicture()` method

**284**

but, on a logical level, it would not be right to define it favoring one style rather than another. However, nothing prevents an abstract class from implementing all of its methods.

Let's take an example, talking about musical instruments:

```
public abstract class Instrument { //Abstract class
    public String name;
    public String price;
    public abstract void playFSharp(); /*Every instrument play a different
                                        * sound! Cannot define this method!
                                        */

    //. . .
}

public class Guitar extends Instrument { //Concrete class extends Instrument
    public void playFSharp() { // Override of the method
      //Method implementation for the Guitar.
    }
    // . . .
}

public abstract class WindInstrument extends Instrument { /*Abstract class that
                                                           * extends Instrument
                                                           */
    /* The playFSharp method inherithed is still abstract (no override) since is
     * too generic!
     */
    // . . .
}

public class Flute extends WindInstrument { /* Concrete class that extends
                                             * WindInstrument
                                             */
    public void playFSharp() {
      //Method implementation for the flute
    }
    //. . .
}
```

In this example, we saw the Instrument class as superclass of the concrete Guitar class (which redefines the playFSharp() method) and of the WindInstrument abstract class (which does not redefine the playFSharp() method that is inherited as abstract). Finally, the concrete Flute class extends WindInstrument (which in turn extends Instrument). So, the guitar is an instrument and the flute is a wind instrument, but it's also an instrument: it's all consistent!

The big advantage of implementing an abstract class is that it **forces** its subclasses to implement a behavior. At the design level, abstract classes are a fundamental tool.

> The `abstract` **modifier could be considered the opposite of the** `final`
> **modifier when used with classes. In fact, a** `final` **class cannot be ex-**
> **tended, while a class declared as** `abstract` **must be extended. It is not**
> **possible to use the** `abstract` **and** `final` **modifiers jointly for classes**
> **and methods, for clear logical reasons. Equally, it is not possible to**
> **jointly use the** `abstract` **and** `static` **modifiers for the methods.**

Unlike the real world, where a person could be a parent, a programmer, a book reader and a musician at the same time, in Java there is no such thing as **multiple inheritance**: a class can only extend one class at a time. This means that a `Person` class cannot be declared, as in the following example:

```
public class Person extends Programmer, Parent,
    Reader, Musician { // Not valid!
```

We only need to choose a superclass because, in Java after the extends clause, we can only specify just one class. The reasons why **multiple inheritance** has not been allowed in Java reside in previous experiences of other languages, which have had to overcome with complex stratagems the limits of the definition. However, since version 8 of Java, the interface concept has been revised to support other features as well. Today, with the interfaces, it is possible to have a *soft multiple inheritance*, which does not introduce the problems present in other languages. However, the rule that it is possible to extend only one class at a time remains valid.

## 7.4 Interfaces

From the design point of view, an interface is an evolution of the concept of abstract class. From the point of view of the code, it looks like a class without its internal implementation instead. In fact, an interface wants to represent what we called the *public interface* when talking about encapsulation, that is, that part of the object visible to the outside, which hides its internal implementation.

In the next pages, we will divide the explanation of the interfaces into two parts, pre-Java 8, and the current one.

### 7.4.1 Classical Definition (pre-Java 8)

Up until Java 7, an interface, by definition, could only have methods implicitly declared public and abstract and variables implicitly declared public, static and final. Here is a first simple example of an interface:

```
public interface Greeting {
    public static final String CIAO ="Ciao";
    public static final String BUONGIORNO ="Buongiorno";
    //. . .
    public abstract void greet();
}
```

We can equivalently write this interface by omitting all modifiers:

```
public interface Greeting {
    String CIAO ="Ciao";
    String BUONGIORNO ="Buongiorno";
    //. . .
    void greet();
}
```

In this case, Java works for us behind the scenes adding the modifiers that we have not written. So, CIAO and BUONGIORNO will always be static public constants, and the greet() method will still be implicitly declared public and abstract (in fact, the method ends with a semicolon). This means that it is not possible to use modifiers in contrast to those that Java expects. For example, if we tried to declare greet() as protected, we would get a compile-time error:

```
Greeting.java:5: error: modifier protected not allowed here
    protected void greet();
              ^
1 error
```

In any case, each member (variable or method) of an abstract class has public visibility.

> Like classes, interfaces should be written within files that have exactly the same name as the interface internally defined, and with the suffix .java. Then the Greeting interface of the example must be saved in a file named Greeting.java, although, as with classes, this is not mandatory. The naming conventions are the same that apply to classes. Also, the same access modifiers are used: public and the *default package visibility* (i.e. no modifier at all).

An interface cannot be instantiated (it is not a class) and cannot declare constructors. It makes sense to define an interface because it can be somehow extended. However, given that, without instantiating objects, programs do not work, we need classes to inherit from interfaces. But classes cannot extend classes using the extends keyword, but they can *implement* them. The implements keyword is used very similarly to extends, and produces the same result: to inherit the members of the implemented interface.

We could then use the example interface as follows:

```
public class GreetingImpl implements Greeting {
    public void greet(){
        System.out.println(CIAO);
    }
}
```

In practice, we have created a GreetingImpl class, and we have made it implement the Greeting interface. In this way, we inherited the members of the Greeting interface in the GreetingImpl class, and we were forced to redefine the inherited abstract method. If we had not done so, we would have inherited an abstract method, and then we would have to declare the GreetingImpl class as abstract.

A class can therefore extend only one superclass at a time, while it can implement an indefinite number of interfaces, effectively simulating what is called *multiple inheritance* (which will be dealt with in detail in the following sections). For example, the syntax for implementing two interfaces and extending a class is as follows:

```
[modifiers] class ClassName extends SuperClassName implements
    InterfaceName1, InterfaceName2 {
//. . . class code
}
```

> **Note that the extension declaration must always precede that of the implementation.**

But are there hierarchies between interfaces? Yes, indeed an interface can extend other interfaces. For example, the syntax to make an interface extend two other interfaces, is the following:

```
[modifiers] interface NameInterface1 extends InterfaceName1,
    InterfaceName2 {
//. . . interface code
}
```

Summarizing: a class can implement one or more interfaces, but it can extend a single class. An interface can extend one or more interfaces. However, an interface cannot extend a class.

### 7.4.2 Static Methods

From Java version 8 onwards, **static methods** can be defined within the interfaces. There has never been a particular reason (like, a technical problem) why it was never intended to include static methods within the interfaces. It simply did not seem in line with the interface concept as a *contract to be implemented*. So, today, we can write interfaces as follows:

```java
public interface StaticMethodInterface {
    static void staticMethod() {
        System.out.println("Static method invoked!");
    }
}
```

and call static methods directly through the interfaces:

```java
public class StaticMethodInterfaceTest {
    public static void main(String args[]) {
        StaticMethodInterface.staticMethod();
    }
}
```

Using the interfaces containing static methods, we betray the *contractual* nature for which it was defined. An interface like the previous one does not need to be implemented, in fact the static methods of an interface are not inherited. Therefore, the implements command does not inherit static methods. Interfaces of this type are simply used to define static and public methods, in practice they define functions. For example, if we consider the class:

```java
public class StaticMethodClass implements StaticMethodInterface {

}
```

then the following code:

```java
public class StaticMethodInterfaceTest {
    public static void main(String args[]) {
        StaticMethodClass.staticMethod();
    }
}
```

would produce a compile-time error:

```
StaticMethodInterfaceTest.java:3: error: cannot find symbol
        StaticMethodClass.staticMethod();
                         ^
  symbol:   method staticMethod()
  location: class StaticMethodClass
1 error
```

Ultimately, we must call the method using the name of the interface and not the name of its subclass:

```
public class StaticMethodInterfaceTest {
    public static void main(String args[]) {
        StaticMethodInterface.staticMethod();
    }
}
```

Before Java 8, to obtain structures with static methods, classes were always used - abstract or with private constructors (like the Math class we have already mentioned) or implemented as a Singleton (see section 6.8.6). Using an interface with static methods in place of a class does not seem to be a big advantage. For example, a class could declare a static initializer to execute code when it is first loaded into memory. In an interface, it is illegal to declare initializers.

 With version 9 of Java, it is also possible to create **private static methods**. Private static methods can only be called by static methods of the same interface, and are not inherited. We must use them simply as auxiliary methods for static methods.

### 7.4.3 Default Methods

Another new feature introduced by Java 8 was the ability to declare concrete methods within the interfaces. We speak of **default methods** because they are declared using the default keyword as a modifier. For example, consider the following code:

```
public interface Soloist {
    default void executeSolo() {
        //Major scale in C
        System.out.println("C D E F G A B");
    }
}
```

In this way, we can inherit this method in a possible subclass without having to rewrite the method (which is not abstract). The following class compiles without problems:

```
public class Musician implements Soloist {

}
```

The method executeSolo() can always be rewritten if necessary (but this is a topic that we will go into in more detail in the next chapter). However, having a default implementation can generally be very convenient.

**290**

 We can write more than one default method in an interface, and these can then coexist with abstract methods and static methods.

With version 9 of Java, it is also possible to create auxiliary **private methods** in the interfaces. As with static private methods, private methods can only be invoked by default methods declared in the same interface. We must not declare them as default methods, precisely because they are only intended as auxiliary methods and are not inherited. In fact, the following code:

```java
public interface PrivateMethodInsideInterfaceTest {
    default void defaultMethod() {
        privateMethod();
    }

    private default void privateMethod() {
        System.out.println("Private Method invoked");
    }
}
```

will fail compile time with the following error:

```
PrivateMethodInsideInterfaceTest.java:6: error: illegal combination
  of modifiers: private and default
    private default void privateMethod() {
                    ^
1 error
```

## 7.4.4 Functional Interfaces

The name "interface" has, in some sense, lost its original meaning, although it is always possible to use interfaces by declaring only abstract methods. In fact, with the introduction of private methods, interfaces are almost technically equivalent to abstract classes, apart from the fact that they cannot declare instance variables. Although interfaces can now implement abstract and concrete methods such as abstract classes, one should never forget the difference in purpose between the two concepts (see section 7.4.6). An interface should represent a *behavior* that more classes might take, and behavior cannot be instantiated. An abstract class should instead represent an overly abstract generalization to be instantiated. Furthermore, it must be noted that a class can extend only one abstract class, while it can implement many interfaces.

By definition, interfaces that contain a single abstract method are called **functional interfaces**. To indicate this, the acronym **SAM** is often used, which stands for **Single Abstract Method**. They are so called because it is as if they exist only to declare a function to be implemented. Functional interfaces are a good example of how interfaces should be used. There is also a new package that declares a series of functional interfaces: the **java.lang.function** package. Regarding the functional interfaces, we will return later to explain their applications, in particular in the seventeenth chapter in the second volume, dedicated to lambda expressions.

## 7.4.5 Multiple Inheritance

As we have already said, a class can implement multiple interfaces. So, in Java today, is possible to use a simplified version of that feature called *multiple inheritance*.

> We talk about "simplification" because the classes can inherit, from the interfaces, only their functional part (the methods) and not the data (apart from the static constants that an interface can declare). In other languages, however, there is complete multiple inheritance, which includes very complicated rules to manage the problems resulting from its implementation.

It was possible to implement multiple interfaces even before Java 8 but it inherited abstract methods that needed rewriting. It was all very simple even if we inherited two methods with the same name from different interfaces: it was always necessary to rewrite the method. With the advent of default methods, multiple inheritance has, therefore, taken on a different meaning than in the past. So, if we consider the following interfaces:

```java
public interface Reader {
    default void read(Book book) {
        System.out.println("I'm reading: " + book.getTitle() + " by "
            + book.getAuthor());
    }
}

public interface Programmer {
    default void program(String language) {
        System.out.println("I'm programming with " + language);
    }
}
```

we can create the following class that implements both interfaces and inherits their methods:

```java
public class WhosReading implements Reader, Programmer {

}
```

And here is an example of use:

```java
public class MultipleInheritanceTest {
    public static void main(String args[]) {
```

```
        var you = new WhosReading();
        var javaForAliens = new Book("Java for Aliens","Claudio De Sio Cesari");
        you.read(javaForAliens);
        you.program("Java");
    }
}
```

So far, there are no problems. But it will not always be that simple to implement multiple inheritance. There are a number of cases in which we need to know the rules to solve the problems that arise. Let's look at the various rules starting with the *Diamond Problem* case.

### 7.4.5.1 Diamond Problem

In the case, a class inherits - from two interfaces - two default methods with the same signature (name plus list of attributes) and the class must redefine the method. Consider, for example, the following interface that declares a default method:

```
public interface Soloist {
    default void executeSolo() {
        //Major scale in C
        System.out.println("C D E F G A B");
    }
}
```

Let's extend this interface twice with specializations that rewrite the default method:

```
public interface BluesSoloist extends Soloist {
    default void executeSolo() {
        //Blues scale in C
        System.out.println("C Eb F Gb G Bb C");
    }
}

public interface RockSoloist extends Soloist {
    default void executeSolo() {
        //Pentatonic scale in c
        System.out.println("C D E G A C");
    }
}
```

If we now try to create a class that implements both interfaces, for example:

```
public class Guitarist implements BluesSoloist, RockSoloist {

}
```

we will obtain a compile-time error:

```
Guitarist.java:1: error: class Guitarist inherits unrelated defaults for executeSolo()
  from types BluesSoloist and RockSoloist
public class Guitarist implements BluesSoloist, RockSoloist {
       ^
1 error
```

This is the famous *problem of diamond inheritance* (or, simply *diamond problem*).

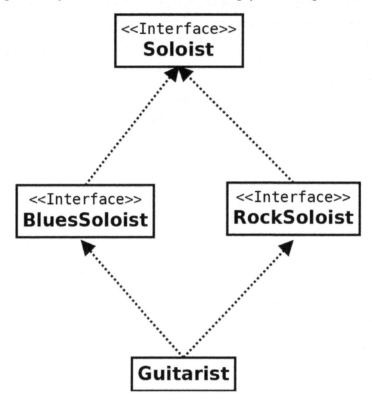

**Figure 7.5 - Diamond Problem described with UML.**

In the example, the compiler has reported an error to us, as it is not able to decide which of the two inherited implementations of the executeSolo() method should be considered the priority one.

> Note that, even if the Soloist interface did not exist, the problem would present itself in exactly the same way. But let's say that in finding ourselves in this situation, it is more probable that the Soloist interface has been defined.

The only solution we have to fix the name conflict is to redefine the method in order to specify its implementation again. For example, in the following class we create a completely new method that uses the implementations of both implemented interfaces:

```
public class Guitarist implements BluesSoloist, RockSoloist {
    public void executeSolo() {
        //Pentatonic scale + blues scale in C
        System.out.println("C D E G A C");
        System.out.println("C Eb F Gb G Bb C");
    }
}
```

This will be the output:

```
C D E G A C
C Eb F Gb G Bb C
```

In this case, we have duplicated code already written in the interfaces, but this can be avoided by using the super reference. In fact, with the following syntax, the same result is obtained:

```
public class Guitarist implements BluesSoloist, RockSoloist {
    public void executeSolo() {
        //Pentatonic scale + blues scale in C
        RockSoloist.super.executeSolo();
        BluesSoloist.super.executeSolo();
    }
}
```

The syntax of super in this case is different from the one we saw in section 7.2.3. The following call:

```
super.executeSolo();
```

would not have solved the ambiguity. So, we use the syntax specifying the type we want to be used:

```
SuperclassName.super.superclassMethodName
```

Having clarified the first rule, there are other possible situations that need to be managed when multiple inheritance is implemented.

### 7.4.5.2 Conflict Between an Abstract and a Concrete Method

If a class implements multiple interfaces, if there is a conflict between an abstract method inherited from the first interface and a concrete method inherited from another interface, we will have to solve the situation by redefining the method in the class as seen in the Diamond Problem case.

Although, therefore, it would have been plausible to inherit only the concrete method, the Java designers opted for uniformity. It does not affect how two peer interfaces conflict. If at least one interface provides an implementation to the conflicting method, the programmer must resolve the ambiguity with awareness. So if, in the previous example, the interface RockSoloist had defined as abstract the executeSolo() method, then the Guitarist class would have had to rewrite the method as in the case of the Diamond Problem.

### 7.4.5.3 Conflict Between Two Abstract Methods

In a class that implements multiple interfaces, if there is a conflict of names of only abstract methods, then we are in the pre-Java 8 situation, and the solution is to redefine the method in the sub-class (as seen for the solution to the Diamond Problem).

That is, if in the previous example, both the RockSoloist and BluesSoloist interfaces had defined the executeSolo() methods as abstract, then the Guitarist class would have inherited an abstract method that had to be rewritten. So, the solution described for the Diamond Problem is valid in this case too.

### 7.4.5.4 Conflict Between Redefined Methods

In case a class implements two interfaces where one extends the other, if in the class that implements them there is a conflict of names of inherited methods, then the implementation of the most specific interface will be inherited.

Therefore, considering the interfaces defined in the Diamond Problem case, if a new RockGuitarist class had implemented the Soloist and RockSoloist interfaces, as in the following example:

```
public class RockGuitarist implements Soloist, RockSoloist {

}
```

then the RockGuitarist class would have inherited the implementation of the RockSoloist interface, as it is more specific than that of Soloist (in fact, RockSoloist had redefined the Soloist method). Then the output of the following test class:

```
public class Show {
    public static void main(String args[]) {
        Guitarist guitarist = new Guitarist();
        guitarist.executeSolo();
        RockGuitarist rockGuitarist = new RockGuitarist();
        rockGuitarist.executeSolo();
    }
}
```

would be the following:

**296**

```
C D E G A C
C Eb F Gb G Bb C
C D E G A C
```

### 7.4.5.5 Class Always Wins

If a class inherits a signature conflict between a method inherited from an extended class and a method of the implemented interface, then the implementation of the class will be inherited, even if it is abstract (this rule is known as "**class always wins**"). For example, consider the following abstract class:

```
public abstract class AbstractGuitarist {
    public abstract void executeSolo();
}
```

which defines the method to executeSolo() as abstract. If we now try to compile the following GuitaristSoloist class that extends the AbstractGuitarist and implements the Soloist interface (which instead defines a default implementation to the executeSolo() method):

```
public class SoloGuitarist extends AbstractGuitarist implements Soloist {

}
```

we will have the following compile-time error:

```
SoloGuitarist.java:1: error: SoloGuitarist is not abstract and does not override
  abstract method executeSolo() in AbstractGuitarist
public class SoloGuitarist extends AbstractGuitarist implements Soloist {
       ^
1 error
```

Among the two definitions of the executeSolo() method, the abstract version of the AbstractGuitarist class was inherited, rather than the concrete version of the Soloist interface (class always wins). If, however, the AbstractGuitarist had somehow implemented the executeSolo() method, then the SoloGuitarist class would have been compiled without errors, inheriting the executeSolo() method of the AbstractGuitarist class.

Summarizing the five rules just seen: the inherited method must always be rewritten except in the last two cases (*conflict between redefined methods* and *class always wins*) where they respectively win the most specific interface and the class.

### 7.4.5.6 Multiple inheritance and static methods

For static methods, rules similar to those we have seen for abstract and default methods apply. For example, if we consider the following code included in a file called **StaticMethodsMITest.java**:

```
public class StaticMethodsMITest extends A3 implements I2 {
    public static void main(String args[]) {
        staticMethod();
    }
}
interface I1 {
    public static void staticMethod() {
        System.out.println("Interface I1");
    }
}
interface I2 extends I1 {
    public static void staticMethod() {
        System.out.println("Interface I2");
    }
}
class A3 {
    public static void staticMethod() {
        System.out.println("Abstract class");
    }
}
```

From the output we can verify that the rule "class always win" is valid:

```
java StaticMethodsMITest.java
Abstract class
```

We can verify the other rules by modifying this code. As we have seen in section 7.4.2, the static methods declared in the interfaces are not imported into the subclasses. So, if for example our StaticMethodsMITest class no longer extends the abstract class A3, but only implements the I2 interface (and consequently the I1 interface since I2 extends I1), by launching the **StaticMethodsMITest.java** file, we would get the following compile-time error:

```
cannot find symbol
        staticMethod();
        ^
  symbol:    method staticMethod()
  location: class StaticMethodsMITest
1 error
```

which indicates that the method was not actually inherited. So, the rule that applied to abstract and default methods, i.e. that the most specific method was inherited (in this case it would have been the I2 method), does not apply. In practice, the following options remain: we are obliged to rewrite the method in the class StaticMethodsMITest:

```
public static void staticMethod() {
    System.out.println("StaticMethodsMITest");
}
```

Or we can modify its `main()` method by explicitly calling the static method of the interfaces, for example:

```
public static void main(String args[]) {
    I2.staticMethod(); */
}
```

or:

```
public static void main(String args[]) {
    I1.staticMethod();
}
```

> Note that the `final` **modifier could be used in interfaces, to not allowing override of a static method in subinterfaces and subclasses.**

### 7.4.5.7 Multiple Inheritance and Constants

We have seen how to manage methods with multiple inheritance, but how does it work with constants? Let's consider the following code:

```
abstract class AbstractClass {
    public static final int VALUE = 1;
}
interface Interface {
    int VALUE = 2;
}
class Subclass extends AbstractClass implements Interface {
    public static void main(String args[]) {
        System.out.println(VALUE);
    }
}
```

If we tried to compile the file containing the previous code, we would get the following compile-time error:

```
error: reference to VALUE is ambiguous
        System.out.println(VALUE);
                           ^
  both variable VALUE in AbstractClass and variable VALUE in Interface match
1 error
```

Therefore, the rule "class always wins" does not apply when we are dealing with constants. So, we must always use a super-type reference for the constant, for example in the following way:

```
System.out.println(AbstractClass.VALUE);
```

## 7.4.6 Differences Between Interfaces and Abstract Classes

 It is not possible to instantiate neither abstract classes nor interfaces. Furthermore, the common advantage that both abstract classes and interfaces offer, lies in the fact that they can force subclasses to implement behaviors. A class that inherits an abstract method, in fact, must override the inherited method or be declared, in turn, abstract. Therefore, from the design point of view, these tools support data abstraction.

An obvious practical difference between the two concepts is what they can define. An interface can define static constants, static methods, default methods, private auxiliary methods (also static) and abstract methods. An abstract class is, instead, an ordinary class, but it cannot be instantiated and it can contain abstract methods (but this is not necessary).

Therefore an abstract class is usually nothing more than an abstraction that is too general to be instantiated in the context in which it is declared. A good example is the Vehicle class:

```
public abstract class Vehicle {
    public abstract void accelerate();
    public abstract void decelerate();
}
```

For example, each vehicle accelerates and decelerates and therefore all non-abstract classes extending Vehicle must rewrite the methods accelerate() and decelerate().

```
public class Plane extends Vehicle {
    public void accelerate() {
        // overrides the method of the Vehicle abstract class
    }
    public void decelerate() {
        // overrides the method of the Vehicle abstract class
    }
}
```

An interface, on the other hand, is usually not a true abstraction that is too general for the context, if anything it is a *behavioral abstraction*, which does not make sense to instantiate in the context itself. Interfaces often have names that recall adjectives and behaviors.

Considering the example of the Vehicle superclass of Plane, we could introduce a Flying interface (note how the name suggests a behavior rather than an abstract object) that will be implemented by the "flying classes". Now if the Flying interface is defined as follows:

```
public interface Flying {
    void land();
    void takeOff();
}
```

every class that has to abstract a concept of flying object (like an airplane or a bird) must implement the interface. We then rewrite the `Plane` class as follows:

```
public class Plane extends Vehicle implements Flying {
    public void land() {
        // overrides the method of the Flying interface
    }
    public void takeOff() {
        // overrides the method of the Flying interface
    }
    public void accelerate() {
        // overrides the method of the Vehicle abstract class
    }
    public void decelerate() {
        // overrides the method of the Vehicle abstract class
    }
}
```

The advantage of programming with abstract classes and interfaces will be explained in the next chapter dedicated to polymorphism.

## Summary

This chapter was mainly dedicated to the second fundamental paradigm of Object Orientation: **inheritance**. It is applied through the keyword `extends`, with the subclass that must extend the superclass. It is a clear and simple concept to learn and applicability is based on the "**is a**" relationship. For example, considering the `Trapezoid` and `Triangle` classes, once we realize that they have some common characteristics, we have to ask ourselves "is a trapezoid a triangle?" Obviously not, but as we have seen, both a trapezoid and a triangle are polygons, so it is advisable to create the superclass `Polygon`. That is, instead of using the process of **specialization** that leads to the creation of a subclass from a superclass, we must use the **generalization** process in this case, which consists of creating a superclass that collects elements common to several subclasses.

Various other topics related to inheritance have also been introduced. The `final` **modifier** prevents the extension of the classes from being applied or the rewriting of the inherited methods.

The `abstract` **modifier** is used for the opposite purpose, which is to force subclasses to extend abstract classes and rewrite abstract methods. An abstract class can have abstract methods but it is not mandatory that it has at least one. Abstract methods do not have a code block, and are defined in order to be implemented in subclasses. The Object **class** is the superclass of any class, directly or indirectly. In fact, any class that does not extend another class implicitly extends Object.

It has been highlighted that **inheritance and encapsulation coexist peacefully**, and that they validate each other. The private variables of a superclass are encapsulated in the superclass, and therefore can also be used in the subclass using the setter and getter methods. Furthermore, the correct use of abstraction is the basis for not making mistakes that would be amplified by encapsulation and inheritance.

**Constructors are not inherited**, but the **first instruction in a constructor is always a call to another constructor**. The super() syntax is inserted by the compiler when it is absent from a constructor. Consequently, the constructors of a superclass are always called by the constructors of a subclass. Calling another constructor of the same class using the this() command only implies that the call to super() is postponed. In fact, the constructors of the same class cannot all call each other, and at least one will not have, as a first instruction, a call of type this(). So, explicitly or implicitly, in at least one constructor, we will have a super() call.

Static methods are inherited at the class level, creating a kind of **class inheritance**.

The private **modifier**, applied to the members of a class, ensures that they are not inherited. Instead, the protected **modifier** causes members to be inherited by subclasses, but it is not necessary for variables if they are encapsulated, because protected variables are visible - as if they were public - to the classes of the package in which they are declared. **Not using modifiers** makes members of a class visible only within the same package, and therefore they will not be inherited by classes outside this package. If a class is not declared as public, and therefore does not declare modifiers, it is not visible outside the package in which it is declared. This implies that it cannot be extended by classes not belonging to the same package.

**Initializers** are executed when an object is loaded into memory, while **static initializers** are loaded when a class is loaded into memory. Since the subclasses depend on their superclass, then the initializers of a superclass, even if they are not inherited, are **still invoked** to be loaded into memory.

**Interfaces** should be created to represent behaviors. They cannot declare instance variables but only static and public constants. They can declare abstract methods, default methods and static methods. With version 9 of Java, they can also declare private auxiliary methods, both static and non-static. Private methods cannot be declared as default methods.

We can implement a kind of **multiple inheritance** in Java, implementing multiple interfaces that have default methods. It is possible to run into the famous **problem of diamond inheritance**, which occurs when the same method is inherited from two different interfaces. The rules in such cases can be summarized in the fact that the inherited method must always be rewritten except in two cases. If the two interfaces from which the method is inherited are linked by the extension relationship, then the subinterface method is taken into consideration, because it is more specific. Another case where there is no need to rewrite the method, is when we inherit the same method from a class and from an interface: "the **class** method **always wins**".

The **essential difference** between abstract classes and interfaces lies in the fact that abstract classes should represent concepts that are too general to be instantiated, while the interfaces should represent behaviors. A good example of the use of interfaces are **functional interfaces**, i.e. interfaces that declare a **single abstract method** (SAM).

> **Exercises, source code, appendices and other resources are available at http://www.javaforaliens.com.**

## Chapter Goals

Have the following goals been achieved?

| Goal | Achieved | Achievement Date |
|------|----------|------------------|
| Understand the definition, use and usefulness of inheritance (generalization and specialization) (Unit 7.1) | O | |
| Understand the consequences of the simultaneous use of encapsulation and inheritance (Unit 7.2) | O | |
| Understand and know how to use the super keyword (Unit 7.5) | O | |
| Understand and know how to use the abstract, final and other modifiers (Units 7.2, 7.6) | O | |
| Understand and know how to use the interfaces (Unit 7.4) | O | |
| Know how to deal with various complex cases of multiple inheritance (Unit 7.4) | O | |

# 8

# Polymorphism

> **Goals:**
>
> At the end of this chapter the reader should:
>
> ✓ Understand the meaning of polymorphism (Unit 8.1).
> ✓ Know how to use overload, override and polymorphism with methods (Units 8.2, 8.3).
> ✓ Understand and know how to use data polymorphism with its implementations: heterogeneous collections, polymorphic parameters and virtual invocations of methods (Unit 8.3).
> ✓ Know how to use the `instanceof` operator and object casting (Unit 8.3).

This chapter is entirely dedicated to the more complex paradigm of Object Orientation: **polymorphism**. This is a fairly broad and articulated topic that is used relatively rarely, considering the power it makes available to the developer. At the end of this chapter, however, the reader should fully understand its importance. If this is not the case, you can always go back to reading these pages in the future. One thing is certain: understanding polymorphism is much simpler than implementing it.

## 8.1 Polymorphism

**Polymorphism** (from the Greek "many forms") is another concept that has been imported into object-oriented programming from the real-world. It allows us to refer with a single term to different entities. For example, both a landline phone and a smartphone allow us to make phone calls, as both can be defined as telephones. Therefore, telephoning can be considered a polymorphic action (it has different implementations). Polymorphism in Java is a complex subject, which branches off into various sub-topics. Using a convention where we will represent the *concepts* with rectangles and *concepts that have a real implementation in Java* with ovals, we will try to schematize polymorphism and its expressions in Figure 8.1.

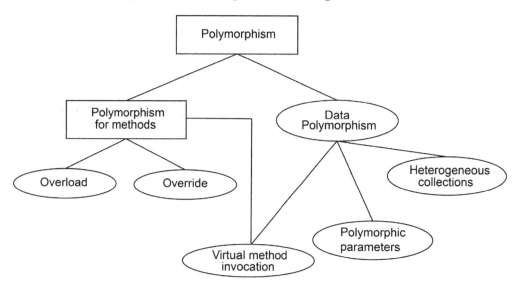

**Figure 8.1 - Polymorphism in Java.**

## 8.1.1 Reference Explained

Before starting to define the various aspects of polymorphism, we present a convention for defining a reference type variable. Defining precisely what a reference is and how it is represented in memory is not a simple matter. Usually a reference is identified with a *pointer* (even if it is not properly correct). In many texts dealing with other programming languages, a pointer is referred to as "a variable that contains an address". Actually, the definition of pointer changes from platform to platform!

So once again we use a convention. We can define a **reference** as a variable that contains two relevant pieces of information: the address in the memory and the *pointing range* defined by its type. Let's consider the already encountered Point class, modified with encapsulation:

```
public class Point {
    private int x;
    private int y;
    public void setX(int x) {
        this.x = x;
    }
    public void setY(int y) {
        this.y = y;
    }
```

```
    public int getX() {
        return x;
    }
    public int getY() {
        return y;
    }
}
```

For example, if we write:

```
Point obj = new Point();
```

we can suppose that the reference `obj` has a numerical value as an address, for example 10023823, and the `Point` class as a pointing range. In particular, what we have defined as a *pointing range* will ensure that the reference object can access the public interface of the `Point` class, that is, all public members (`setX()`, `setY()`, `getX()`, `getY()`) declared in the `Point` class. The address will make the reference point to a particular area of memory, where the object will reside. A representative diagram is shown in Figure 8.2.

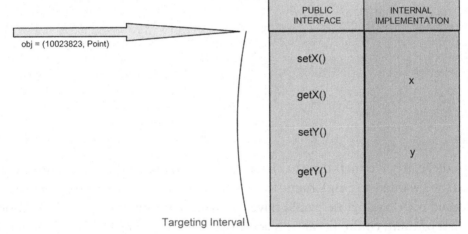

**Figure 8.2 - Reference Convention.**

# 8.2 Polymorphism for Methods

**Polymorphism for methods**, as far as it has been presented here, will allow us to use the same name for different methods. In Java, it finds its practical realization in two forms: **method overloading** and **method overriding**.

### 8.2.1 Overload

In one method, the pair consisting of the identifier and the parameter list is called the **signature** of the method.

In Java, a method is uniquely identified not only by its name, but also by its list of parameters, i.e. by its signature. Thus, methods with the same name can coexist in a class if they have a different signature. On the signature definition, is based one of the most popular Java features: **overloading**.

### 8.2.1.1 Method Overloading

With **method overloading**, the programmer can use the same name for different methods. But all of this will still have to make logical sense. For example, we could assign the same name to two methods that conceptually have the same functionality, but that satisfy this functionality differently. Here is a trivial example of method overloading:

```java
public class Arithmetic {
    public int sum(int a, int b) {
        return a + b;
    }
    public float sum(int a, float b) {
        return a + b;
    }
    public float sum(float a, int b) {
        return a + b;
    }
    public int sum(int a, int b, int c) {
        return a + b + c;
    }
    public double sum(int a, double b, int c) {
        return a + b + c;
    }
}
```

In this class, there are five methods that have the same name and execute sums, but in a different way. If we wanted to implement these methods with another language that does not support method overloading, we would have to invent a new name for each method. For example, the first of them could be called sumTwoInts(), the second sumOneIntAndOneFloat(), the third sumOneFloatAndOneInt(), the fourth sumThreeInts(), the fifth even sumOneIntOneDoubleAndOneFloat()! At this point the usefulness of the overload is evident. We note that the parameter list has three criteria of distinction based on:

- **parameter type** (example: sum(int a, int b) is different from sum(int a, float b));

- **the number of parameters** (example: sum(int a, int b) is different from sum(int a, int b, int c));

- **and parameter position** (example: sum(int a, float b) is different from sum(float a, int b)).

**308**

The identifiers we use for the parameters, on the other hand, are not criteria for distinguishing methods (example: sum(int a, int b) is not different from sum(int c, int d)). Furthermore, the return type is not part of the signature of a method, so it's not relevant for the overloading definition.

In some books, overload is not considered a polymorphic aspect of the language. In these books, polymorphism itself is defined differently than it has been defined in this context. As always, everything is relative to the area in which we're discussing. If we had found ourselves discussing object-oriented analysis and design rather than programming, we would also not have included overload as a polymorphism implementation. If we ignore the language, even though we are not, overload should not even exist. Furthermore, polymorphism has been defined by many authors as a consequence of the implementation of inheritance. Overload and inheritance have nothing in common. However, if we limit ourselves to considering the definition we gave of polymorphism (same name to different things), overloading should certainly be considered one of the implementations of polymorphism. Some authors prefer to define overload as "static polymorphism" to differentiate it from override (rewriting of methods in subclasses) which is labeled as "dynamic polymorphism".

Other overload examples that we have already used (more or less unconsciously) in this text, are the println() and print() methods of the System.out object. In fact, there are ten different println() methods, and nine versions of print(). It is possible to pass as parameters to these methods not only strings, but also integers, booleans, arrays of characters or even objects. You can try it as an exercise by consulting the documentation (hint: System.out is a PrintStream object belonging to the java.io package).

Note that even static methods can be overloaded. It is also possible to create mixed overloads with static and instance methods. For example, the following class compiles without errors:

```
public class MixedOverloadTest {
    public static void main(String args[]) {}
    public static void main() {}
    public void main(boolean b) {}
}
```

Having stated that a method is uniquely identified by its signature, a main() method should also be able to declare a return type other than void. Instead the main() method is a special method, and if it returns a return type other than void, this method could be compiled, but it will not be considered a "true" main() method. For example, if we had the following class:

```
public class MainCuriosityTest {
    public static double main(String[] args) {
        double d = .1; // same as double d = 0.1;
        System.out.println(d);
        return d;
    }
}
```

it is possible to compile it, but we cannot launch it, since it does not contain a main() method correctly declared. If we added a correctly declared main() method inside the previous class, we would get a compile-time error, because we would have two methods with the same signature:

```
error: method main(String[]) is already defined in class MainCuriosityTest
    public static void main(String args[]) {
                       ^
1 error
```

### 8.2.1.2 Constructor Overloading

We have already seen another example of overload in the second chapter, when we introduced the constructors, and also in the sixth chapter where we saw how a constructor can invoke another constructor using the keyword this. It seemed natural to create more constructors in the same class with different parameter lists but, actually, we were already using the overload unknowingly. Below is a simple example of **constructors overloading**:

```
public class Customer {
    private String name;
    private String address;
    private int phoneNumber;
    public Customer() {
        // constructor explicitly inserted (this is not the default constructor)
    }
    public Customer(String name) {
        this.name = name;
    }
    public Customer(String name, String address) {
        this(name);
        this.address = address;
    }
```

```
    public Customer(String name, String address, int phoneNumber) {
        this(name, address);
        this.phoneNumber = phoneNumber;
    }
    // . . .
}
```

### 8.2.1.3 Overload Ambiguity

 If, in a class, there are overloaded methods that take objects as input, it is possible to invoke them with the null value as an argument. How can the compiler understand which method to call in this case? In general, it cannot understand it, and returns an error when compiling. For example, compiling the following class:

```
public class NullOverloadTest {
    public void overloadedMethod(String string) {
        System.out.println("overloadedMethod(String string)");
    }

    public void overloadedMethod(Integer integer) {
        System.out.println("overloadedMethod(Integer integer)");
    }

    public static void main(String args[]) {
        var nullOverloadTest = new NullOverloadTest();
        nullOverloadTest.overloadedMethod(null);
    }
}
```

we will get the following compile-time error:

```
error: reference to overloadedMethod is ambiguous
        nullOverloadTest.overloadedMethod(null);
                         ^
  both method overloadedMethod(String) in NullOverloadTest a
nd method overloadedMethod(Integer) in NullOverloadTest match
1 error
```

In fact, it is not possible to choose whether to call the method that takes the string as input, or the one that takes the Integer object as input.

If, instead, an inheritance relationship exists between the types that represent the parameter to which we pass the value null, the compiler will compile the code without errors and choose to call the method with the most specific type. For example, if these two methods existed in the previous class:

```
    public void overloadedMethod(Object object) {
        System.out.println("overloadedMethod(Object object)");
    }
```

```
    public void overloadedMethod(String string) {
        System.out.println("overloadedMethod(String string)");
    }
```

it will be possible to launch the file and get the following output:

```
overloadedMethod(String string)
```

since `String` is a subclass of the `Object` class.

## 8.2.2 Varargs

As already mentioned, when we presented the concept of method in second chapter, the so-called **varargs** (abbreviation of **variable-length argument lists**) can be used as arguments of the methods. With varargs, it is possible to make a method accept an unspecified number of arguments (including the possibility of passing zero parameters), thus avoiding an overload of methods. The syntax of varargs makes use of **ellipses** (the suspensive dots "..."). For example, the following class could replace with a single method, the overload of methods of the `Arithmetic` class presented in section 8.2.1.1:

```
public class ArithmeticVarArgs {
    public double sum(double... doubles) {
        double result = 0.0D;
        for (double tmp : doubles) {
            result += tmp;
        }
        return result;
    }
}
```

In fact, the following code is valid:

```
var obj = new ArithmeticVarArgs();
System.out.println(obj.sum(1,2,3));
System.out.println(obj.sum());
System.out.println(obj.sum(1,2));
System.out.println(obj.sum(1,2,3,5,6,8,2,43,4));
```

The following is the output of the previous lines of code:

```
6.0
0.0
3.0
74.0
```

Note that the output of the method will be of the double type (unless casting).

When using varargs there is an important constraint: it is possible to declare a single varargs argument per method, and this must occupy the last position in the list of parameters.

So, for example the following method:

```
public void m(String... strings, int... integers) {
    // code omitted
}
```

will cause the following compile-time error:

```
error: varargs parameter must be the last parameter
    public void m(String... strings, int... integers) {
                  ^
1 error
```

### 8.2.2.1 Varargs vs Arrays

Varargs, within the method where they are declared, are considered as arrays. So, as with arrays, we can derive their size with the `length` variable and use them within loops. The advantage of using varargs as the last argument of a method in place of an array, essentially lies in the fact that to call a method that declares variable arguments, we do not need to create an array. For example, if we had an array instead of varargs as the parameter for the sum() method:

```
public double sum(double[] doubles) {
    double result = 0.0D;
    for (double tmp : doubles) {
        result += tmp;
    }
    return result;
}
```

to invoke the method, we would have had to write something like the following lines of code:

```
double[] doubles = {1.2D, 2, 3.14, 100.0};
System.out.println(obj.sum(doubles));
```

or use the array syntax presented in the third chapter:

```
System.out.println(obj.sum(new double[]{1.2D, 2, 3.14, 100.0}));
```

In short, using varargs in place of arrays as parameters of a method is undoubtedly more convenient.

Actually, an array can also be passed to a variable argument. In fact, the lines of code above would work in the same way even if the sum() method accepted a varargs as an argument. So, if we have methods whose last argument is an array, it

**313**

is preferable to convert this last argument to varargs. In any case, the pre-existing code would not be affected.

 If we declared in the same class both methods sum() we've written so far (one that takes as a parameter a varargs of double, and another that takes as parameter an array of double), we will get the following compile-time error:

```
error: cannot declare both sum(double[]) and sum(double...) in ArithmeticVarArgs
    public double sum(double[] doubles) {
                      ^
1 error
```

which highlights the conceptual equivalence between an array and a varargs.

 Given that a varargs is equivalent to an array within the method in which it is declared, it is also possible to define the main() method as follows:

```
public static void main(String... args) {}
```

### 8.2.2.2 Varargs vs Overload

 Varargs give the illusion of using overload even if we talk about something different. In fact, the varargs must be declared by specifying a certain type of data (for example, double or String) and the number of values to be passed is undefined (it can also be zero). With overload, we can specify a fixed number of parameters and different types.

For example, let's consider again the Customer class that declared a constructor overload defined in section 8.2.1. With varargs, we could create a single constructor such as the following:

```java
public class CustomerVarArgs {

    private String name;
    private String address;
    private String phoneNumber;

    public CustomerVarArgs(String... par) {

        if (par != null) {

            if (par[0] != null) {
                this.name = par[0];
            }

            if (par[1] != null) {
                this.address = par[1];
```

```
        } if (par[2] != null) {
            this.phoneNumber = par[2];
        }
    }
}
//  . . .
}
```

It seems obvious that the overload is a better solution in this case.

## 8.2.3 Override

The **override**, and this time there is no doubt, is considered a very important feature of object-oriented programming and is, by some, superficially identified with the same polymorphism. The override (which we could translate as "rewriting") is the object-oriented term that is used to describe the characteristic that the subclasses have, to redefine a method inherited from a superclass. Naturally, there will be no override without inheritance. A subclass is always more specific of the extended class, and therefore it may inherit methods that need to be redefined to work properly in the new context.

For example, suppose that a redefinition of the Point class (which by convention we assume is two-dimensional) declares a distanceFromOrigin() method that calculates the distance between a point of given coordinates and the origin of the Cartesian axes. This method, if inherited within a subclass ThreeDimensionalPoint, needs to be redefined to calculate the desired distance, also taking into account the third coordinate. Let's see what has just been described with coding:

```java
public class Point {
    private int x, y;
    public void setX(int x) {
        this.x = x;
    }
    public int getX() {
        return x;
    }
    public void setY(int y) {
        this.y = y;
    }
    public int getY() {
        return y;
    }
    public double distanceFromOrigin() {
        int tmp = (x*x) + (y*y);
        return Math.sqrt(tmp);
    }
}
```

```java
public class ThreeDimensionalPoint extends Point {
    private int z;

    public void setZ(int z) {
        this.z = z;
    }

    public int getZ() {
        return z;
    }

    public double distanceFromOrigin() {
        int tmp = (getX()*getX()) + (getY()*getY()) + (z*z); // x and y are
        return Math.sqrt(tmp);                               // not inherited
    }
}
```

For those who do not remember how to calculate the geometric distance between two points: if we have the points P1 and P2 with coordinates respectively (x1,y1) and (x2, y2), the distance between them will be given by:

$$d(P1,P2) = \sqrt{(x1 - x2)^2 + (y1 - y2)^2}$$

If P2 coincides with the origin, it has the coordinates (0,0) and therefore the distance between a point P1 and the origin will be given by:

$$d(P1,P2) = \sqrt{(x1)^2 + (y1)^2}$$

> The sqrt() **method of the** Math **class (package** java.lang**) returns the result of the square root of the parameter passed as** double **(the reader is always encouraged to consult the documentation). Remember that it was possible to invoke it with the syntax** ClassName.methodName **name instead of** objectName.methodName **since it's a static method.**

The square of x and y was obtained by multiplying the value by itself. As an exercise, you can explore the documentation of the Math class to look for the presence of a method to raise numbers to power (sorry for the implicit spoiler...).

> Watch out! **Abstracting a two-dimensional point by creating a class named** Point **and inserting the** distanceFromOrigin() **method into the same class, are choices that seem acceptable. But are we not then . . .**

> . . . violating the paradigm of abstraction? Should the class not be called TwoDimensionalPoint? Is it right for a point to have a method for calculating distance from another point? Points do not calculate distance in the real world, if anything, it might be useful to create a Ruler class! The discussion continues in the tenth chapter entitled "A Guided Example of Object-Oriented Programming".

Observe how we have redefined the block of code of the distanceFromOrigin() method in the ThreeDimensionalPoint subclass. We have introduced the third coordinate to be taken into account so that the distance calculation can be performed correctly.

> Note that we have direct access to the z variable (without using the setter or getter method), since it is defined as private in the same class as the method that is using it.

### 8.2.3.1 Override Rules

So, the override seems simple to implement, but it is actually not that obvious: there are rules to follow:

1. the method rewritten in the subclass must have the same signature (name and parameters) of the superclass method;

2. the return type of the subclass method must coincide with that of the original method, or it must be of a type that extends the type of return of the superclass method;

3. the redefined method in the subclass should not be less accessible than the original superclass method.

As for the **first rule**, assuming that the name of the subclass method must be identical to that of the superclass, if we are talking about different signatures, we're talking about a different list of parameters. In cases like this, we would be facing an overload in place of an override. In fact, not being rewritten with the same signature, we would also inherit the superclass method in the subclass, and there would be two methods with the same name and a different parameter list. For example, suppose the Point class defines the setCoordinates() method:

```java
public void setCoordinates(int x, int y) {
    setX(x);
    setY(y);
}
```

**317**

In the ThreeDimensionalPoint subclass we would probably write:

```
public void setCoordinates(int x, int y, int z) {
    super.setCoordinates(x, y);
    setZ(z);
}
```

But this method has a different parameter list than the one defined in the Point class, and therefore it is not the same method, it is not an override. As a result, the setCoordinates() method of the Point class will also be inherited in the ThreeDimensionalPoint subclass.

With the **second rule**, it is clear that the return type is also a discriminant (unlike the overload where it was not). In particular, the return type of a method can also coincide with a subclass of the return type of the original method. In this case, we talk about **covariant return type**.

For example, keeping in mind the relationship of inheritance that exists between the classes Point and ThreeDimensionalPoint, if in the Point class, the following method was present:

```
public Point processPoint() {
    //...
}
```

then it would be legal to implement the following override in the ThreeDimensionalPoint class:

```
public ThreeDimensionalPoint processPoint() {
    //...
}
```

Finally, for the **third rule** the situation is quite clear. For example, if an inherited method is declared as protected, it cannot be redefined as private, if anything, as public.

> There is also another rule, that will be dealt with in the ninth chapter, dedicated to exception management. Moreover, in the twelfth chapter, we will see how to implement the (sort of) "covariant parameters" of a method, with a strategy based on generic types.

### 8.2.3.2 Override *Annotation*

One of the sneakiest mistakes a programmer can make is to miss an override. That is, to redefine incorrectly a method that we want to rewrite in a subclass, perhaps by typing a lowercase letter rather than a capital letter, or by mistaking the number of input parameters. In such cases, the compiler will not report errors, since it cannot guess the overriding attempt in progress. So, for example, the following code:

```
public class ThreeDimensionalPoint extends Point {
    public double distancefromOrigin() { //it should be distanceFromOrigin()!
        //...
    }
}
```

will be compiled correctly, but there will be no overrides in ThreeDimensionalPoint. The trouble is, that the problem will only occur when the application is running and it is not easy to identify the error.

We mentioned in the second chapter the concept of annotation. An **annotation** allows us to *annotate* any type of component of a Java program: from variables to methods, from classes to annotations themselves. With the term *annotate* we mean to qualify, to mark. That is, if for example, we write down a class, we will allow a software (for example, the Java compiler) to realize that this class has been marked, so that it can implement a certain behavior accordingly. The topic is quite complex and we will study it in the sixteenth chapter, which is entirely dedicated to annotations. However, the most intuitive example of annotation defined in the standard library, concerns the problem of the implementation of the override that we were considering. The Override annotation exists in the java.lang package. This can be (and should be) used to mark the methods that want to be an override of inherited methods. For example:

```
public class ThreeDimensionalPoint extends Point {
    @Override
    public double distancefromOrigin() { //it should be distanceFromOrigin()!
        //...
    }
}
```

> We can note how using an annotation requires the use of a character that we have never encountered in Java syntax: @.

If we mark our method with Override, when we violate some override rule, as in the previous code, then we get a compile-time error:

```
method does not override a method from its superclass
    @Override public double distancefromOrigin() {
    ^
  1 error
```

Getting an error in the compilation phase is much better than having it at runtime.

### 8.2.3.3 Override and static

In the previous chapter, for static methods, we talked about a kind of inheritance for classes. Static methods are inherited in subclasses, and we can rewrite them. However, it is not possible

**319**

to annotate the static methods with `Override`. For example, if we try to compile the following code:

```
class SuperClass {
    public static void main(String args[]) { }
}

class SubClass extends SuperClass {
    @Override
    public static void main(String args[]) { }
}
```

we will obtain a compile-time error:

```
error: static methods cannot be annotated with @Override
    @Override
    ^
1 error
```

Furthermore, we cannot rewrite an inherited static method in the subclass by redefining it as a non-static method, nor can we inherit a non-static method, and redefine it in a subclass as static. The following code indeed:

```
class SuperClass {
    public static void main(String args[]) { }
}

class SubClass extends SuperClass {
    public void main(String args[]) { }
}
```

causes the following compile-time error:

```
error: main(String[]) in SubClass cannot override main(String[]) in SuperClass
    public void main(String args[]) { }
                ^
  overridden method is static
1 error
```

while the code:

```
class SuperClass {
    public static void main(String args[]) { }
}

class SubClass extends SuperClass {
    public void main(String args[]) { }
}
```

causes the error:

```
error: main(String[]) in SubClass cannot override main(String[]) in SuperClass
    public static void main(String args[]) { }
                      ^
  overriding method is static
1 error
```

## 8.3 Polymorphism for Data

**Data polymorphism** essentially allows the assigning of a superclass reference to an instance of a subclass. For example, taking into account that ThreeDimensionalPoint is a subclass of Point, it will be absolutely legal to write:

```
Point obj = new ThreeDimensionalPoint();
```

In fact, the reference obj will target an address that validates its pointing range. In practical terms, the public interface of the created object (consisting of the setX(), getX(), setY(), getY(), setZ(), getZ() and distanceFromOrigin () methods) contains the public interface of the Point class (consisting of the methods setX(), getX(), setY(), getX() and distanceFromOrigin()) and so the reference object will "think" to be pointing to a Point object. If we want to represent this situation graphically, we could do it as in Figure 8.3.

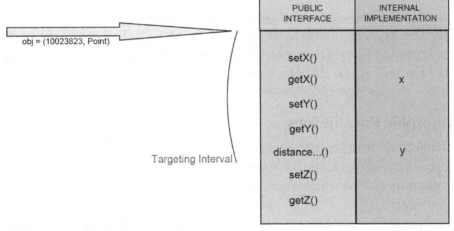

**Figure 8.3 - Polymorphism for Data.**

However, this kind of data approach has a limitation. A superclass reference will not be able to access the fields declared for the first time in the subclass. In the example, we would get an error when compiling if we tried to access the accessor and mutator methods of the third z co-

**321**

ordinate of the `ThreeDimensionalPoint` through the reference `obj`. That is, when coding the following line:

```
obj.setZ(5);
```

it would produce an error during compilation, since `obj` is a reference that has a pointing range defined by the `Point` type.

> **Note that in the real world we continuously use polymorphism for data, when we refer to a three-dimensional point with the term "point", or to a smartphone, with the term "telephone".**

 We note that, when using data polymorphism, the special word `var` is not appropriate. In fact, if we write:

```
Point obj = new ThreeDimensionalPoint();
```

it is not the same as:

```
var obj = new ThreeDimensionalPoint();
```

because in the second case, the type of the `obj` reference will be automatically inferred as of `ThreeDimensionalPoint` type.

> **Usually the reader tends now to ask himself: "OK, I understand what polymorphism for data means, but what's the use?". After reading this chapter we will have the answer.**

## 8.3.1 Polymorphic Parameters

We know that parameters in Java are always passed by value to methods. This implies that passing a reference parameter to a method means passing the numeric value of the reference, in other words, its address. This address could include an object instantiated by a subclass, thanks to data polymorphism.

In a method, a parameter of the reference type is called a **polymorphic parameter** when, even though it's a reference of a given type, it can point to an object instantiated from a subclass. Thus, by exploiting data polymorphism, a parameter of a method can point to different objects. This is the case of the `println()` method which takes a parameter of `Object` type.

```
Point p1 = new Point();
System.out.println(p1);
```

We have already seen that all classes (including the Point class) are subclasses of the Object class. So, we can invoke the println() method, passing it as a parameter rather than an instance of Object, a Point instance like p1. But we can pass an instance of any class to the println() method that takes an Object as input, since the polymorphism for data is valid, and each class is a subclass of Object.

To fulfill the purpose of "printing an object", the println() method will call the toString() method on the parameter passed as input. This method certainly exists, having been declared in the Object class, as we will see in section 7.2.3.2. Many classes in the standard Java library override this method, returning descriptive strings of the object. If we pass to the println() method a parameter of an object of a class that does not redefine the toString() method, it would be called the toString() method inherited from the Object class (as in the case of the Point class). An implementation of the toString() method for the Point class could be as follows:

```
@Override
public String toString() {
    return "(" + getX() + "," + getY() + ")";
}
```

## 8.3.2 Heterogeneous Collections

A **heterogeneous collection** is a collection composed of different objects (for example an array of Object that actually stores other types of objects). The possibility of exploiting heterogeneous collections is also guaranteed by data polymorphism. In fact, a declared array of Object could contain any type of object:

```
Object arr[] = new Object[3];
arr[0] = new Point();      //arr[0], arr[1], arr[2]
arr[1] = "Hello World!";   //are references of type Object
arr[2] = new Date();       //that targets objects created from subclasses
```

which is equivalent to writing:

```
Object arr[] = {new Point(), "Hello World!", new Date()};
```

Here is an example to understand the usefulness of these concepts. For the sake of simplicity, we will omit the setter and getter methods in our classes. Let's imagine that we want to create a system that establishes the salaries of a company's employees, considering the following classes:

```
public class Employee {
    private String name;
    private int salary;
```

```
        private int number;
        private String birthDate;
        private String hireDate;
        // setter and getter methods omitted
    }

public class Programmer extends Employee {
        private String knownLanguages;
        private int yearsOfExperience;
        // setter and getter methods omitted
    }

public class Manager extends Employee {
        private String workingTime;
        // setter and getter methods omitted
    }

public class SalesAgent extends Employee {
        private String [] customerPortfolio;
        private int commissions;
        // setter and getter methods omitted
    }
    ...
```

Our goal is to create a method that establishes employee salaries. We could now use a heterogeneous collection of employees and a polymorphic parameter to fix the problem in a simple, fast and elegant way. In fact, we could declare a heterogeneous collection of employees as follows:

```
Employee [] arr = new Employee [180];
arr[0] = new Manager();
arr[1] = new Programmer();
arr[2] = new SalesAgent();
...
```

 Polymorphism for data can be exploited even with arrays. For example, we can also use an Employee array reference to point to a Programmer array instance. It will not be a heterogeneous collection (unless the Programmer class is, in turn, extended from other classes), but only a Programmer array instance that is pointed to by an Employee array type reference:

```
Employee [] programmers = new Programmer[60];
```

 With the term **collection**, we mean an implementation from a set of classes and interfaces (called *Collections Framework*) defined in the Java standard library, which represent collections of objects. Compared to arrays, collections are resizable and have very specific features. For example, the classes that implement the List interface have the characteristic of being ordered, and an index is associated with each element. On the other hand, the classes that implement the Set interface have the feature of not allowing duplicates. The most used collection is probably the ArrayList, which extends the List interface. Just to give us an idea of what we are talking about, below is shown how to create and fill an ArrayList of strings:

```java
var arrayList = new ArrayList();
arrayList.add("ArrayList");
arrayList.add("implements");
arrayList.add("List");
```

The implementations of the Collections Framework are by default heterogeneous. For example, we can add to the arrayList object above instantiated, also objects of any type:

```java
arrayList.add(new Point(42,47));
arrayList.add("A string");
arrayList.add(new Employee());
```

The topic "Collections" (which is very important) will be presented and deepened in the thirteenth and eighteenth chapters in the second volume.

### 8.3.3 instanceof operator

Among the Java operators there is a binary operator that can be useful when dealing with data polymorphism: instanceof. Using this construct, we can check the real type a reference is pointing to:

```java
public void payEmployee(Employee emp) {
    if (emp instanceof Programmer) {
        emp.setSalary(1500);
    }
    else if (emp instanceof Manager) {
        emp.setSalary(3000);
    }
    else if (emp instanceof SalesAgent) {
        emp.setSalary(1000);
    }
    System.out.println(emp.getClass().getName() + " - Salary = " + emp.getSalary());
        //. . .
}
```

Now we can call this method within a foreach loop (of 180 iterations), passing all of the elements of the heterogeneous collection, and thus reach our purpose:

```
//...
for (Employee employee : arr) {
    payEmployee(employee);
    //...
}
```

In particular, the instanceof operator has, as its operands, a reference (the first operand) and a type (the second operand). This operator returns true if the first operand is a reference that points to an object instantiated from the second operand or an object instantiated from a subclass of the second operand type. If one of these two conditions do not occur, it returns false.

This implies that if the payEmployee() method is written as follows:

```
public void payEmployee(Employee emp) {
    if (emp instanceof Employee) {
        emp.setSalary(1000);
    } else if (emp instanceof Programmer) {
    //...
```

all employees would be paid the same way. In fact, even if emp was a Programmer's reference, the check of the first if would have been verified, since if emp is a Programmer, for inheritance, it is also an Employee.

The instanceof operator returns a compile-time error if the second operand is incompatible with the first one. For example, the following code:

```
public class InstanceofTest {
    public static void main(String args[]) {
        InstanceofTest test = new InstanceofTest();
        System.out.println(test instanceof ArrayList);
    }
}
```

will cause the following compile-time error:

```
incompatible types: InstanceofTest cannot be converted to ArrayList
        System.out.println(test instanceof ArrayList);
                           ^
1 error
```

In fact, it is impossible that an object of InstanceofTest type is also of ArrayList type. Because we can't extend two classes.

If instead the type of one of the two operands is an interface, no error will be reported (unless the type of the other parameter is a class declared final, as we will see in the last example of this section). For example, the following code will not cause problems when compiling:

```
System.out.println(test instanceof Runnable);
```

Runnable **is an interface that is implemented in the** Thread **class. We will study these types in the fifteenth chapter in the second volume.**

Indeed, at runtime the compiler cannot know if the test reference of type InstanceofTest, specified as the first operand, points to an object instantiated by its subclass that also implements the Runnable interface (specified as second parameter). For example, the following class could exist:

```
class InstanceofTestRunnable extends InstanceofTest implements Runnable {
    public void run() {}
}
```

The rule applies to both operands. In fact, also the following snippet (where the type of the first operand is an interface) does not create problems in compilation:

```
Runnable r = new Thread();
System.out.println(r instanceof ArrayList);
```

Even more so, even if both types of the two operands of the instanceof operator are interfaces, no error will be reported. For example, the following snippet compiles without errors:

```
List list  = new ArrayList();
System.out.println(list instanceof Runnable);
```

Finally, if the two operands of the instanceof operator are of a different type, and if one of the two operands is a class declared final, we will always get a compilation error. In fact, a final class, such as the String class, cannot be extended, and therefore it does not make sense to use the instanceof operator. For example:

```
String s = "reH Dunmo' law' tlhIngan";
System.out.println(s instanceof Runnable);
```

will cause the following compile-time error:

```
error: incompatible types: String cannot be converted to Runnable
        System.out.println(s instanceof Runnable);
                           ^
1 error
```

**If both operands are of the same type (for example** String**), no error will be returned, but in this case, it would be completely superfluous to use the** instanceof **operator.**

There is no need to do nullity checks on the first argument of the instanceof operator. If the first argument is null, (remember that the second argument is a type) then the operator will return false.

### 8.3.4 Objects Casting

In the previous example, we observed that the instanceof operator allows us to check which type of instance, a reference is pointing to. But we already know that data polymorphism means that a superclass reference pointing to an object instantiated from a subclass, cannot access the members declared in the subclasses themselves. However, there is the possibility of re-establishing full accessibility to the members of the object through the **objects casting** mechanism.

Let us return to the example just presented. Suppose that the salary of a programmer depends on the number of years of experience. In this situation, after checking that the reference emp is pointing to an instance of Programmer using the instanceof operator, we will need to access the yearsOfExperience variable. If we tried to access it using the syntax:

```
emp.getYearsOfExperience();
```

we would certainly get an error when compiling. But if we used the mechanism of objects casting, we would overcome this last obstacle. This can be implemented by declaring a Programmer reference and pointing it to the memory address where the reference emp is pointing, using the casting to confirm the pointing range. The new reference, being the right one, will allow us to access any member of the Programmer instance.

Object casting uses a syntax very similar to casting between primitive data:

```
if (emp instanceof Programmer) {
    Programmer pro = (Programmer) emp;
    //...
```

We are now able to access the yearsOfExperience variable through the syntax:

```
//...
if (pro.getYearsOfExperience() > 2)
//...
```

As usual, we try to clarify the ideas by trying to schematize the situation with a graphical representation. Let's take a look at Figure 8.4.

In Figure 8.4, we can see how the two references have the same numeric value (address) but different pointing range. The accessibility of the object depends on this.

If we try to assign the emp address to the reference pro without using the casting, we get an

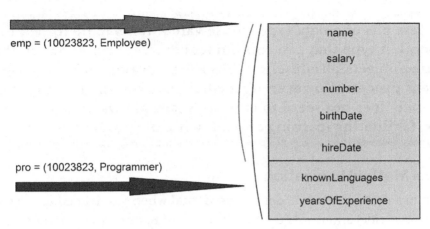

emp = (10023823, Employee)

pro = (10023823, Programmer)

| name |
| salary |
| number |
| birthDate |
| hireDate |
| knownLanguages |
| yearsOfExperience |

**Figure 8.4 - Two different types of access to the same object.**

error in the compilation phase and a related message that asks for an explicit casting. Once again, the behavior of the compiler confirms the robustness of the language. The compiler cannot determine if a given object resides at a certain address rather than another at runtime. It is only running that the Java Virtual Machine can take advantage of the instanceof operator to resolve the doubt.

 Note that object casting should only be used after checking its validity with a check based on the instanceof operator. The risk lies in compiling the program correctly, and then seeing it fail at runtime with an exception of type ClassCastException.

The exceptions will be discussed in the next chapter, and the ClassCastException is one of the most frequently encountered exceptions.

 Object casting should not be considered a standard programming tool, but rather as a useful means of solving design problems. An ideal object-oriented design would do without object casting. As far as we are concerned, within a project, the need for casting leads us to think of "forcing", and maybe it would be better to find a solution through updating the design. However, there are cases in which the use of this tool is inevitable.

 Once again, let's look at another aspect that led to Java being defined as a simple language to learn. Casting is a topic that also exists in other languages and concerns the types of primitive numerical data. It is realized by truncating the . . .

... **excess bits of a data type whose value wants to be forced to enter into another type that can contain less data. We note that, in the case of casting objects, absolutely no bits are truncated, so it is a completely different process! However, if we abstract from the types of data, the difference does not seem to exist and Java allows us to use the same syntax, facilitating learning and allowing the programmer to use it.**

### 8.3.5 Virtual Method Invocation

An invocation to a method m can be defined as **virtual** when m is defined in a class A, redefined in a subclass B (override) and invoked on an instance of B, through a reference of A (polymorphism for data). When the m method is invoked in a virtual way, the compiler "thinks" of invoking the method m of the class A. The redefined method in class B is actually invoked. A classic example is the toString() method of the Object class. We have already mentioned that it is overridden in many classes of the standard library. Consider the Date class of the java.util package. In it, the toString() method is rewritten in such a way as to return information about the Date object (day, month, year, hour, minutes, seconds, day of the week, summer time...). Consider the following code fragment:

```
...
Object obj = new Date();
String s1 = obj.toString();
...
```

Reference s1 will point to a string that contains information about the Date object, the only instantiated object. We can see the schematization in Figure 8.5.

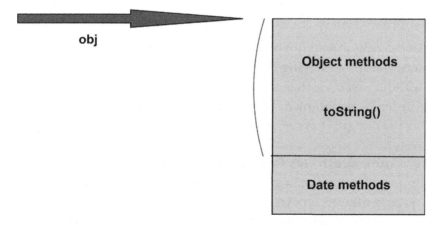

**Figure 8.5 - The method space of a Date object that overrides toString() of the Object class.**

The reference obj can only access the public interface of the Object class and therefore also the toString() method. The reference however, points to a memory area where an object of the Date class resides, in which the toString() method has a different implementation than the one that provides the Object class.

> **Note that the toString() method had already been called in a virtual way in the example of the polymorphic parameters section.**

## 8.3.6 Example of Use of Polymorphism

Let's suppose we have the following classes available:

```java
public abstract class Vehicle {
    public abstract void accelerate();
    public abstract void decelerate();
}

public class Plane extends Vehicle {
    @Override
    public void accelerate() {
        //. . .
    }
    @Override
    public void decelerate() {
        //. . .
    }
}

public class Car extends Vehicle {
    @Override
    public void accelerate() {
        //. . .
    }
    @Override
    public void decelerate() {
        //. . .
    }
    public void setReverseGear() {
        //. . .
    }
    //. . .
}

public class Ship extends Vehicle {
    @Override
    public void accelerate() {
```

```
        //. . .
    }
    @Override
    public void decelerate() {
        //. . .
    }
    public void throwAnchor() {
        //. . .
    }
    //. . .
}
```

The Vehicle abstract superclass defines the methods accelerate() and decelerate(), which are then redefined in more specific subclasses such as Plane, Car, and Ship.

 Note that the methods have been declared as abstract. Indeed, how does a vehicle accelerate? Like a ship or a plane? The right answer is that there is no answer! It is indefinite. A vehicle can certainly accelerate and decelerate but, in this context, we cannot say how. The most correct solution therefore appears to declare the methods as abstract.

Consider the following class which uses overload:

```
public class Traveler {
    public void travel(Car a) {
        a.accelerate();
        //. . .
    }
    public void travel(Plane a) {
        a.accelerate();
        //. . .
    }
    public void travel(Boat n) {
        n.accelerate();
        //. . .
    }
    //. . .
}
```

Although the overload represents a remarkable solution for the encoding of the Traveler class, we notice repetitions in the code blocks of the three methods. In fact, taking advantage of a polymorphic parameter and a virtual method invocation, the Traveler class could be codified in a more compact and functional way:

```
public class Traveler {
    public void travel(Vehicle v) { //polymorphic parameter
        v.accelerate(); //virtual invocation of the method
        //. . .
    }
    //. . .
}
```

The following code fragment uses the previous classes:

```
Traveler claudio = new Traveler();
Car fiat500 = new Car();
// we should have created also a Boat or a Plane
claudio.travel(fiat500);
```

Note the clarity and versatility of the code. We have fallen into a highly extensible context: if we wanted to introduce a new Vehicle (suppose the Bicycle class) it would suffice to code it without touching what has been written so far!
The following code is also a good example:

```
Traveler claudio = new Traveler();
Plane piper = new Plane();
claudio.travel(piper);
```

 We have seen that if we invoke a method of an object using a reference of a super-class, the rewritten method of the class with which the object was instantiated will be invoked, and not the method of the class of the reference we are using. In fact, with the following snippet:

```
Vehicle piper = new Plane();
piper.accelerate();
```

we will invoke the accelerate() method redefined in the Plane class, and not the original method of the Vehicle class (which among other things was abstract).
The situation changes if we try to access variables, or public constants (both static and non-static), that we are going to overwrite in the subclasses (there is no override for the attributes of a class). For example, if we consider the following classes:

```
abstract class Pet {
    public final String name = "Generic Pet";
}

class Dog extends Pet {
    public final String name = "Dog";
}
```

the following code:

```
Pet pet = new Dog();
System.out.println(pet.name);
Dog dog = new Dog();
System.out.println(dog.name);
```

will cause the following output:

```
Generic Pet
Dog
```

which implies, that even if the name constant has been rewritten in the Dog subclass, to access it we need a reference of the same class. In fact, through the Pet superclass reference, we can access the Pet class constant.

## 8.3.7 Polymorphism and Interfaces

Data polymorphism also works with interfaces. This means that we can use references of interfaces to point to objects that implement these interfaces. In the previous chapter, we said that interfaces can be defined to abstract behaviors and adjectives, and then be implemented in concrete classes. In the previous chapter, we defined the Flying interface in the following way:

```
public interface Flying {
    void land();
    void takeOff();
}
```

Every class that has to abstract a concept of flying object (like a plane, a helicopter or a bird) must implement the interface. So, we rewrote the Plane class as follows:

```
public class Plane extends Vehicle implements Flying {
    @Override
    public void land() {
        // overrides the method of the Flying interface
    }
    @Override
    public void takeOff() {
        // overrides the method of the Flying interface
    }
    @Override
    public void accelerate() {
        // overrides the method of the Vehicle abstract class
    }
    @Override
    public void decelerate() {
        // overrides the method of the Vehicle abstract class
    }
}
```

**334**

We could then create polymorphic parameters to take advantage of the `Flying` interface:

```
public class ControlTower {
    public void authorizeLanding(Flying v) {
        v.land();
    }

    public void authorizeTakeOff(Flying v) {
        v.takeOff();
    }
}
```

In this way we can pass to these methods flying objects created by classes that implement the `Flying` interface.

 As we saw in section 8.2.3.3, it is not possible to redefine a static method as a non-static method. We have also seen that it is not even possible to declare a method that overrides a non-static method as static. The same situation exists even when an interface is extended by another interface. A static method declared in an interface cannot be rewritten in a subinterface as a default method. Obviously, a default method cannot be rewritten in a subinterface as a static method.

### 8.3.8 Polymorphism and Constructors

We have already seen in the previous chapter that there is no inheritance of constructors, even if the instance of a subclass, thanks to the `super()` command, will always cause a call to a superclass constructor. In any case, since there is no inheritance, it makes no sense to speak of *override of constructors*, or constructor polymorphism. But there is a situation that concerns the constructors and the order in which they are executed with respect to the initialization of the attributes, to be taken into account, and which we will explain below.

 Consider the following situation: we have a superclass that declares a constructor that invokes a certain method defined within the same class. Let us also suppose that we have defined a subclass that overrides the inherited method. If we instantiate the subclass, its constructor will in any case invoke the superclass constructor. The latter will not invoke the method defined in the superclass, but the method rewritten in the subclass, since in any case we are instantiating an object from the subclass. This could cause an error at runtime if the subclass method used specific variables of the subclass and that are not defined in the superclass. For example, the following code compiles correctly:

```
abstract class Tool {
    public Tool () {
        doWork();
    }
}
```

```
        public void doWork() {
            System.out.println("Working...");
        }
    }
    class Hammer extends Tool {
        String data ="nail";
        public Hammer () {
            //implicit call to super();
        }
        @Override
        public void doWork() {
            System.out.println("Hammering on "+ data);
        }
    }
    public class ToolsTest {
        public static void main(String[] args) {
            Tool tool = new Hammer();
        }
    }
```

but at runtime we will get the output:

```
Hammering on null
```

in fact, the data variable is used before it is initialized in the subclass, and therefore still has a null value. In this case, we got a wrong output, but references with null values, can easily lead the runtime to be interrupted by NullPointerException exceptions, which is caused by the use of a null reference.

> **Exceptions are the main topic of the next chapter, and the NullPointerException is the most frequent exception.**

For example if the doWork() method was rewritten in the subclass:

```
public void doWork() {
    if (!data.isEmpty()) {
        System.out.println("Hammering on "+ data);
    }
}
```

then the program would cause the following output:

```
Exception in thread "main" java.lang.NullPointerException
        at Hammer.doWork(ToolsTest.java:17)
        at Tool.<init>(ToolsTest.java:3)
        at Hammer.<init>(ToolsTest.java:12)
        at ToolsTest.main(ToolsTest.java:24)
```

**336**

# Summary

In this chapter, we have mainly explored Java's support for **polymorphism** by dividing it into various sub-topics. Polymorphism is divided into polymorphism for methods and for data. **Polymorphism for methods** is a concept that finds its implementation in Java via overload and override.

**Overload** allows us to create methods with the same name (but a different parameter list) in the same class. The pair name-parameter list, is called the method **signature**. An alternative to overloading can sometimes be the use of methods that exploit **varargs**, but we must evaluate the cost and benefit from time to time.

**Override** allows us to rewrite the methods inherited from superclasses in the subclasses. Compared to the original superclass method, the rewritten method must have the same signature, the same return type and must not be less accessible. The Override annotation allows us to mark the rewritten methods in such a way as to declare to the compiler that we are rewriting an inherited method. In this case, the compiler will check for us if we are correctly applying the override, returning a possible error if needed.

**Data polymorphism** itself has an implementation in Java. With it, a superclass reference can point to an object instantiated by a subclass. The real usefulness of data polymorphism is evidenced by the use of polymorphic parameters, virtual invocations of methods, and heterogeneous collections.

With the instanceof operator, we can check if a certain reference actually points to a certain type. After verifying with the instanceof operator what type a reference points to, we can also use **object casting** to get a reference of the verified type.

A **heterogeneous collection** is a collection of data, for example, an array that contains different objects. As for the arrays, this means that the array is declared of a given type, but is then populated by objects instantiated by subclasses of this type. There are classes in the standard Java library (see the thirteenth and the eighteenth chapters in the second volume) that are called **collections**, which are potentially heterogeneous. The *collections* are actually much more used than arrays, because they are resizable and have utility methods and properties.

**Polymorphic parameters** are parameters of declared methods of a given type, which then, at runtime, can point to objects instantiated by subclasses of this type.

Furthermore, the simultaneous use of data polymorphism and override gives rise to the possibility to use **virtual method invocation**. With a single instruction that invokes a method on a certain class, we can then dynamically invoke methods rewritten on objects instantiated by subclasses.

All of the programming tools we have seen in this chapter are very useful and their correct use must become one of the fundamental objectives for the reader. Anyone can tweak with Java, but there are other more suitable languages for tweaking.

Development with Java must be accompanied by the search for design solutions to facilitate programming. If you do not want to do this, maybe Java is not the right language to learn. It will certainly not be easy to correctly use the powerful tools of object-oriented programming. Although we could be clear on all of the topics they have studied so far, it is not a given that we'll be able to create a program starting from scratch. Indeed, it is highly improbable that we will succeed if we have no previous programming experience. Certainly, it can help a lot knowing an object-oriented methodology (see the online appendix entitled "Bibliography") or at least UML (to which two of the online appendices are dedicated), but there's no substitute for experience. The advice for the novices is, therefore, to try to create their own personal project (something that could be useful), naturally not too complicated, and to perform all of the exercises provided by the book. In this way, he will *touch by hand* the difficulties of design, and even if the project could never be completed, at least he will start to experience, he will make mistakes and will learn to correct them.

> **Exercises, source code, appendices and other resources are available at http://www.javaforaliens.com.**

## Chapter goals

Have the following goals been achieved?

| Goal | Achieved | Achievement Date |
|---|:---:|:---:|
| Understand the meaning of polymorphism (Unit 8.1) | O | |
| Know how to use overload, override and polymorphism with methods (Units 8.2, 8.3) | O | |
| Understand and know how to use data polymorphism with its implementations: heterogeneous collections, polymorphic parameters and virtual invocations of methods (Unit 8.3) | O | |
| Know how to use the instanceof operator and object casting (Unit 8.3) | O | |

# Exceptions and Assertions

> **Goals:**
>
> At the end of this chapter, the reader should:
> - ✓ Understand the differences between exceptions, errors and assertions (Unit 9.1).
> - ✓ Know how to handle the various types of exceptions with `try - catch` blocks (Units 9.2, 9.3).
> - ✓ Know how to create custom exception types and manage the propagation mechanism with the keywords `throw` and `throws` (Units 9.2, 9.3).
> - ✓ Know how to use the `try-with-resources` construct (Unit 9.3).
> - ✓ Understand assertions and know how to use them (Unit 9.4).

The concepts related to exceptions, errors, assertions and the corresponding management, allow the developer to write robust software, that is, that it will work correctly even in unexpected situations. In the pages that follow, we will talk not only of the fundamental syntax part of Java, but also of design. In particular, the mechanism of propagation of exceptions is a feature of the language that cannot be ignored. Assertions, on the other hand, are rarely used, but they are an excellent tool for writing working code.

## 9.1 Exceptions, Errors and Assertions

Of the three topics discussed in this chapter, the most important is certainly the management of exceptions, a real cornerstone of the language.

You can define an **exception** as an unexpected situation that can occur during an application flow. You can handle an exception in Java by learning to use five simple keywords: `try`, `catch`, `finally`, `throw`, and `throws`. It will also be possible to create custom exceptions and decide not only how, but also in which part of the code to manage them, thanks to an extremely powerful propagation mechanism. This concept is implemented in the Java library using the Exception class and its subclasses. An example of an exception that could occur within a program is a division between two numerical variables in which the divisor variable has a value of 0. As it is known, in fact, this operation cannot be performed.

It is instead possible to define an **error** as an unforeseen situation that indicates serious problems. Most such errors are abnormal conditions, and unlike exceptions, errors are not solvable. This concept is implemented in the Java library using the Error class and its subclasses. An example of error that a program could cause, is the termination of memory resources. This condition is not remediable.

Furthermore, it is possible to define an **assertion** as a condition that must be verified, that will allow the developer to consider a piece of code to be correct. Unlike exceptions and errors, assertions are a tool for testing software robustness. They can be enabled during development and testing, and possibly disabled during the release phase. Thus, the execution of the software will not undergo any kind of slowing down. This concept is implemented by the keyword assert. For example, an assertion could assert that in a division the divider variable must be different from 0. If this condition does not occur, the code execution will be interrupted by the assert command.

## 9.2 Throwable Hierarchy

In the standard Java library, there is a class hierarchy that relates the Exception class and the Error class to each other. Both of these classes in fact, extend the Throwable superclass, as can be seen in Figure 9.1.

As already mentioned, we must not confuse the concept of error (a problem that a program cannot solve) and the concept of exception (non-critical problem that can be handled). The fact that both the Exception class and the Error class extend a class called Throwable is due to the mechanism by which the Java Virtual Machine reacts when it encounters an error or an exception. In fact, if our program *throws* an exception during runtime, the JVM instantiates an exception class object related to the problem issued, and throws the newly-instantiated exception (via the throw keyword). If our code does not *capture* (via the catch keyword) the exception, the JVM exception handler will interrupt the program, generating, as output, detailed information about what happened. For example, suppose that, during execution, a program tries to perform a division by zero between integers. The JVM will create an ArithmeticException object (appropriately initialized) and launch it. In practice, it is as if the JVM executed the following lines of code:

```
ArithmeticException exc = new ArithmeticException();
throw exc;
```

Everything happens behind the scenes and will be transparent to the developer.

We will study the `throw` keyword in section 9.3.5.3

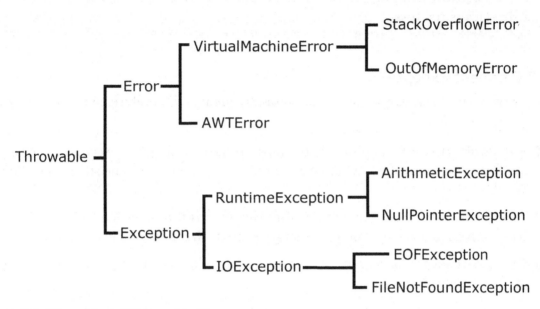

**Figure 9.1 - Hierarchy for Throwable Classes.**

## 9.2.1 Checked and Unchecked Exceptions

A further categorization of exceptions is represented by the definition of *checked exceptions* and *unchecked exceptions*. We refer to the `RuntimeException` (and its subclasses) as an **unchecked exception**. All other exceptions (that is, all those that do not extend `RuntimeException`), are called **checked exceptions**. If we use a method that launches a checked exception without handling it, the compilation will fail (that's why we call it a checked exception). Instead it is possible to compile without error a method that launches an unchecked exception, without necessarily handling it. This means that when we use code that could throw a checked exception, the compiler will force us to handle it (if we don't write the code that handles the exception, we will get a compile-time error). The possible launch of an unchecked exception will never be reported as an error by the compiler (this is why the unchecked exception extend `RuntimeException`). For example, if in our code a division is made between two numeric variables, the divisor could also take the value 0, causing an unchecked exception of `ArithmeticException` type.

But the compiler won't force us to handle the `ArithmeticException` every time we perform a division. We will return to the topic in the next sections.

> **Also the subclasses of `Error` can be treated as if they were unchecked exception. In fact, it is possible to compile code that can generate an error, without managing it. Furthermore, handling an error could be sometimes useless.**

## 9.2.2 Frequent Exceptions

There are some types of exceptions that are more frequent and therefore better known by Java developers. These are:

- `NullPointerException`: probably the most frequent among the exceptions. For example, it is launched by the JVM when a method is called on a reference that instead points to `null`.

- `ArrayIndexOutOfBoundsException`: this exception is thrown when trying to access an array with an index that is too high compared to its size, or less than zero.

- `ClassCastException`: very insidious exception; it is launched at runtime when we try to cast to a wrong class type.

These exceptions all belong to the `java.lang` package and are *unchecked exceptions*, i.e. exceptions that can occur at runtime without any compiler warning.

Instead we will often deal with *checked exception* when using some standard libraries. For example, if we use packages like `java.io`, we will often have to handle exceptions like `IOException` and its subclasses `FileNotFoundException`, `EOFException`, etc. Subclasses of `IOException` are also `SocketException` and its subclass `ConnectException`, which however belong to the package `java.net` (see Chapter 20). In the `java.sql` library it is very often necessary to handle the `SQLException` (see Chapter 21).

## 9.2.3 Custom Exceptions

However, it is probable that, sometimes, new types of exceptions must be defined. In fact, for a particular program, it could be an exception to execute a division with the value 5 as the divisor. More likely, a program that must automatically manage reservations for a theater, may want to throw an exception when we try to reserve a place no longer available. In this case, the solution is to extend the `Exception` class and optionally add members and override methods such as `toString()`. The following is an example:

```
public class BookingException extends Exception {
    public BookingException() {
        // The Exception constructor invoked initialize
        // the private variable message
        super("Problem with the booking");
    }
    @Override
    public String toString() {
        return getMessage() + ": sold-out!";
    }
}
```

Our exception contains information about the problem and represents a correct abstraction. Obviously, we could have also added other methods and attributes.

> **Note that we have created a checked exception. If we want to create an unchecked exception, we have to extend the** `RuntimeException` **class (or one of its subclasses).**

# 9.3 Exception Handling Mechanism

As already stated above, the developer has some keywords to handle exceptions: `try`, `catch`, `finally`, `throw` and `throws`. In the next subsections we will see how to use these keywords, how to use custom exceptions, how to manage the propagation of exceptions, and in general the impacts that exception handling has on our programming.

### 9.3.1 `try` - `catch` Blocks

If we need to develop a piece of code that can potentially trigger an exception, we can surround it with a `try` block followed by one or more `catch` blocks. For example, let's consider the following class:

```
public class Exc1 {
    public static void main(String args[]) {
        int a = 10;
        int b = 0;
        int c = a/b;
        System.out.println(c);
    }
}
```

This class can be compiled without problems, but it will generate an exception during its execution, due to the fact that performing a division by zero is impossible. In this case, the JVM, after interrupting the program, will produce the following output:

```
Exception in thread "main" java.lang.ArithmeticException: / by zero at Exc1.main(Exc1.java:6)
```

This is a message that is certainly very explanatory, as it has highlighted:

- the type of exception (java.lang.ArithmeticException);

- a descriptive message (/ by zero);

- the method in which the exception was launched (at Exc1.main);

- the file in which the exception was launched (Exc1.java);

- the line in which the exception was launched (: 6).

> **Note that the ArithmeticException class is an unchecked exception. In fact, the previous code can be compiled even though no type of exception management is present.**

The only problem is that the program ended prematurely. Using the try and catch keywords, it will be possible to handle the exception in a personalized way, ending the program without it being abruptly interrupted:

```java
public class Exc2 {
    public static void main(String args[]) {
        int a = 10;
        int b = 2;
        try {
            int c = a/b;
            System.out.println(c);
        } catch (ArithmeticException exc) {
            System.out.println("Division by zero...");
        }
    }
}
```

When the JVM executes this code, it will encounter the division by zero in the first row of the try block and will launch the ArithmeticException exception, which will be captured in the catch block that follows it. So, the line that was supposed to print the variable c will not be executed. Instead, the line that prints the string "Division by zero..." will be executed, with which we have handled the exception and allowed our program to end in a natural way. As you will surely have noticed, the syntax of the try - catch blocks can be rather strange, but soon we will get used to it because it is present several times in practically all Java programs. In particular, the catch block must declare a parameter (as if it were a method) of the type of the exception to be captured. In the previous example, the reference exc pointed to the exception that the JVM had instantiated and launched. In fact, through it, we can find information about the exception itself.

### 9.3.1.1 Exceptions as Information Containers

The easiest way to get information about what happened is to invoke the printStackTrace() method on the exception.

```
int a = 10;
int b = 0;
try {
    int c = a/b;
    System.out.println(c);
} catch (ArithmeticException exc) {
    exc.printStackTrace();
}
```

The printStackTrace() method will output the above informational messages, which the program would have produced if the exception had not been handled, but without interrupting the program itself.

> **Usually this method is used only for debugging purposes, not in professional applications, where its use is discouraged.**

From the Throwable class, other methods are inherited such as toString(), getMessage(), and getCause() (which we will present shortly). For example, if we redefine the previous catch block by invoking the getMessage() method on the exception:

```
} catch (ArithmeticException exc) {
    System.out.println(exc.getMessage());
}
```

we would get the following output:

```
/ by zero
```

If instead we redefine it by invoking the toString() method on the exception:

```
} catch (ArithmeticException exc) {
    System.out.println(exc);// equivalent to System.out.println(exc.toString());
}
```

we would get a slightly different output:

```
java.lang.ArithmeticException: / by zero
```

But in general, an exception represents a container of information on the event that triggered the problem. Each subclass of Exception could declare particular methods and attributes.

## 9.3.2 Catching Exceptions

It is essential that we declare via the catch block, an exception of the right type. For example, the following code fragment:

```
int a = 10;
int b = 0;
try {
    int c = a/b;
    System.out.println(c);
} catch (NullPointerException exc) {
    exc.printStackTrace();
}
```

would produce an unhandled exception and therefore an immediate termination of the program. In fact, the try block, never launched a NullPointerException, but an ArithmeticException.

### 9.3.2.1 Handle more exceptions

As for the methods, even for the catch blocks, the parameters can be **polymorphic**. For example, the following code fragment:

```
int a = 10;
int b = 0;
try {
    int c = a/b;
    System.out.println(c);
} catch (Exception exc) {
    exc.printStackTrace();
}
```

contains a catch block that would handle any type of exception, being Exception the superclass from which any other exception descends. The reference exc is, in this example, a polymorphic parameter.

It is also possible to follow a try block with more catch blocks, as in the following example:

```
int a = 10;
int b = 0;
try {
    int c = a/b;
    System.out.println(c);
} catch (ArithmeticException exc) {
    System.out.println("Division by zero...");
} catch (NullPointerException exc) {
    System.out.println("Null reference...");
} catch (Exception exc) {
    exc.printStackTrace();
}
```

In this way, our program would be more robust and would handle different types of exceptions. In the worst case, that is, if the `try` block throws an unexpected exception, the last `catch` block would handle the problem.

The order of the `catch` blocks is essential. If we had:

```
int a = 10;
int b = 0;
try {
    int c = a/b;
    System.out.println(c);
} catch (Exception exc) {
    exc.printStackTrace();
} catch (ArithmeticException exc) {
    System.out.println("Division by zero...");
} catch (NullPointerException exc) {
    System.out.println("Null reference...");
}
```

the last two catch blocks would be superfluous and the compiler would report the error as follows:

```
D:\Exc2.java:12: exception java.lang.ArithmeticException has already been caught
        catch (ArithmeticException exc) {
        ^
D:\Exc2.java:15: exception java.lang.NullPointerException has already been caught
        catch (NullPointerException exc) {
        ^
```

## 9.3.2.2 Multi-catch

There are cases in which the content of the catch blocks is identical, although they catch different exceptions, for example:

```
int a = 10;
int b = 0;
```

```
try {
    int c = a/b;
    System.out.println(c);
} catch (ArithmeticException exc) {
    System.out.println(exc.getMessage());
} catch (NullPointerException exc) {
    System.out.println(exc.getMessage());
} catch (Exception exc) {
    exc.printStackTrace();
}
```

To avoid redundancy, it is possible to declare in a single catch, more than one parameter as shown below:

```
int a = 10;
int b = 0;
try {
    int c = a/b;
    System.out.println(c);
} catch (ArithmeticException | NullPointerException exc) {
    System.out.println(exc.getMessage());
} catch (Exception exc) {
    exc.printStackTrace();
}
```

The symbol "|" is used to separate the names of the exception classes, but a single reference is declared (exc). This reference is implicitly declared as final. This type of cumulative exception handling is called **multi-**catch, and was first introduced with Java Version 7.

### 9.3.3 The finally Clause

It is possible to follow a try block, in addition to catch blocks, another block defined by the finally keyword, for example:

```
public class Exc4 {
    public static void main(String args[]) {
        int a = 10;
        int b = 0;
        try {
            int c = a/b;
            System.out.println(c);
        } catch (ArithmeticException exc) {
            System.out.println("Division by zero...");
        } catch (Exception exc) {
            exc.printStackTrace();
        } finally {
            System.out.println("Operation attempt");
        }
    }
}
```

What is defined in a `finally` block is executed anyway, whether the exception is thrown or not. If the `try` block ends by not throwing exceptions or throwing exceptions unhandled from one of the `catch` blocks following the `try` block, then the `finally` block is executed directly. If instead the `try` block ends by launching an exception handled by one of the `catch` blocks following the `try` block, then the `finally` will be executed after the end of the execution of the `catch` code that captured the exception. A `finally` block is very useful when there are critical operations that must be performed whatever happens. So, the output of the previous program is:

```
Division by zero...
Operation attempt
```

If instead the variable b was set to 2 rather than 0, the output would be:

```
5
Operation attempt
```

There can be only one `finally` block for each `try` block, and it must always be the last block (it cannot precede a `catch` block).

> A `try` **block can also be directly followed by a** `finally` **block (without a** `catch` **blocks). The** `finally` **block will certainly be executed after the execution of the** `try` **block, whether the exception is thrown or not. However, if the exception were thrown and not managed with a** `catch` **block, the program would end abnormally.**

### 9.3.3.1 Closing Closeable Objects

A classic example (more significant than the previous one) in which the word `finally` is used, concerns a topic we will discuss in Chapter 21: JDBC, i.e. the software interface with which a Java program can interact with a database.

> A *database* **represents a data archive, structured in order to rationalize the management, updating and retrieving of information. There are different types of databases, but here, what we will refer to is the** *relational database*, **where the information is organized in** *tables* **related to each other.**

Consider for example the following code:

```java
public void selectFromDB() {
    Connection conn = null;
    Statement stmt = null;
    ResultSet rs = null;
    try {
        conn = DriverManager.getConnection(url, username, password);
        stmt = conn.createStatement();
        rs = stmt.executeQuery("SELECT * FROM PERSON");
        while (rs.next()) {
            System.out.println(rs.getString(1));
    } catch (SQLException e) {
        e.printStackTrace();
    } finally {
        if (rs != null) {
            try {
                rs.close();
            } catch (SQLException e) {
                e.printStackTrace();
            }
        }
        rs = null;
        if (stmt != null) {
            try {
                stmt.close();
            } catch (SQLException e) {
                e.printStackTrace();
            }
        }
        stmt = null;
        if (conn != null) {
        try {
            conn.close();
        } catch (SQLException e) {
            e.printStackTrace();
        }
        conn = null;
    }
    }
}
```

The previous method attempts to execute a *query* to a database, through the JDBC interfaces of the java.sql package. In the example, stmt is a Statement object that we need to execute a command, and conn is a Connection type object. The executeQuery() command is called on the Statement object and takes as input a so-called *SQL query*. **SQL (Structured Query Language)** is the standard language which allows us to interact with the database. It has its own syntax. In this case, with the SELECT * FROM PERSON command, we requested from the database all the contents of a *table* called Person. If there are problems (for example, due to incorrect SQL syntax), the JVM will launch a SQLException, which will be caught in the corresponding catch block. If there are no problems, the program will print the results obtained from the query on the screen. In any case, after the attempted query, the connection to the database must be closed, as well as the other *closable objects* such as the object stmt of Statement type, and the object rs of ResultSet type. If these objects were not closed, they would never be deleted from the memory by the Garbage Collector (for more details on JDBC please see Chapter 21). To make sure that these objects are closed, we have written the necessary code within the finally block.

> **Note that if we try to call the close() method on closable objects, we are forced to handle the SQLException. This exception is a checked exception, and the close() methods are declared in such a way as to force the programmer to handle this exception (as we will see in detail when we discuss the keyword throws later). In the finally block, therefore, it is possible to observe a very verbose code, with nested try - catch blocks. As we will see in the next section, however, it is possible to avoid writing so much code.**

### 9.3.4 Try-with-Resources

Since version 7 of Java, some classes and interfaces (including Connection) have been updated to support the so-called try-**with-resources** mechanism. This allows the automatic closing of objects that would need to be closed once used.

The syntax provides the declaration of the object (or objects) to be closed automatically as a sort of parameters of the try block. The following is an example (equivalent to the previous one):

```
try(Connection conn =
    DriverManager.getConnection(url, username, password);
    Statement stmt = conn.createStatement();
    ResultSet rs = stmt.executeQuery("SELECT * FROM PERSON")) {
    while (rs.next()) {
        System.out.println(rs.getString(1));
    }
} catch (SQLException e) {
    e.printStackTrace();
}
```

The *closable* objects conn, stmt and rs, are therefore declared as if they were parameters of the try block (which here should be called try-with-resources block). When the block ends its execution, the three resources will be automatically closed. This will happen either in the positive case (the code is executed correctly), or in the negative case (for example an exception is thrown). Exactly as if the commands to close the resources were inside a `finally` clause. This is a big advantage.

### 9.3.4.1 Closeable Objects

Not all objects are closeable. In particular, objects that can be closed are objects that implement the `AutoCloseable` interface (package `java.lang`) or the `Closeable` interface (package `java.io`). For example, the following class is closable:

```java
public class CloseableResource implements AutoCloseable {
    @Override
    public void close() {
        System.out.println("close() method invoked");
    }
    @Override
    public String toString() {
        return "CloseableResource";
    }
}
```

So, it can be used in a try-with-resources construct as follows:

```java
public class TryWithResourceTest {
    public static void main(String args[]) {
        try (var closeableResource = new CloseableResource()) {
            System.out.println("I'm going to close: "+ closeableResource);
        }
        catch (Exception exc) {
            exc.printStackTrace();
        }
    }
}
```

the output of which will be:

```
I'm going to close: CloseableResource
close() method invoked
```

### 9.3.4.2 Effectively Final Variables

With Java 9, a lot of things have changed compared to the past. Now, we can also use final variables in the round brackets of the try-with-resources or variables actually not modified that are called **effectively final variables**. With "variables that are not actually modified", we mean variables that, even if they are not declared final, are not modified. The compiler is able to distinguish whether a variable is actually unmodified or not. So, the main() method of the previous example can be written in an equivalent way as follows:

```
public static void main(String args[]) {
    var closeableResource = new CloseableResource();
    try (closeableResource) {
        System.out.println("I'm going to close: "+ closeableResource);
    }
    catch (Exception exc) {
        exc.printStackTrace();
    }
}
```

Thus, the construct of try-with-resources becomes more concise and readable.

> **A local variable declared as a resource to be closed in a try-with-resources construct is implicitly final.**

### 9.3.4.3 Suppressed Exceptions

Even with a try-with-resources block it is possible to declare an arbitrary number of catch blocks and one finally block, as if it were an ordinary try.

 > **These blocks will be executed only after the resources have been closed. So, pay attention to not use closed objects. A typical mistake is to use the closed resources within these blocks, thus causing other exceptions!**

If, during the execution of the try block an exception was thrown, this will be considered a priority with respect to any exceptions automatically launched by the try-with-resources block (if there were any problems in closing the resources used). In this case, the JVM will launch the internal application exception from the try block, and declare as **suppressed** the exceptions launched during the automatic closing of the objects used. However, these exceptions will be set as attributes of the launched application exception, and can be accessed by calling the getSuppressed() method on the exception object that is launched.

For example, let's extend the ResourceClosable class, with the following class:

```java
public class AlmostCloseableResource extends CloseableResource {
    private Number number;

    @Override
    public void close() {
        super.close();
        number = Double.valueOf(.1);
        Integer integer = (Integer)number;
    }

    public void launchException() {
        number = Integer.valueOf("Something is really wrong!");
    }

    @Override
    public String toString() {
        return "AlmostCloseableResource";
    }
}
```

In this extension we have overridden the methods `close()` and `toString()`, and added a new `launchException()` method. The `close()` method invokes the `close()` method of the super-class it is rewriting, via the super reference. Then it assigns to the number instance variable of Number type, a Double object that is returned by the call to the static method `valueOf()` of the Double class.

> **Number is the superclass of Double and also of other wrapper classes like Integer (see official documentation).**

A primitive double value is passed as input to this method (.1 which is equivalent to the value 0.1) which is then correctly converted into a Double object. In the next line, however, a ClassCastException will be thrown, an exception that is thrown when we cast objects to illegal types. In fact, we try to cast the Integer type, an object that at runtime will be actually a Double type. Therefore, the `close()` method will not be completed correctly at runtime, because a ClassCastException will be thrown.

The `launchException()` method instead, will throw an exception of NumberFormatException type. This exception represents a string formatting error. In fact, the `valueOf()` static method of the Integer class is invoked, which should convert the argument of String type that it takes as input, and return an Integer object. But in the string passed as input, there is no integer value to be converted, but a literal sentence, which therefore does not respect the format that the method expected. This is why this method will launch the NumberFormatException.

So, let's consider the following test class:

```java
public class TryWithResourceSuppressedTest {
    public static void main(String args[]) {
        try (var almostCloseableResource = new AlmostCloseableResource()) {
            System.out.println("I'm going to close: " + almostCloseableResource);
            almostCloseableResource.launchException();
        }
        catch (Exception exc) {
            exc.printStackTrace();
            Throwable[] suppressedExceptions = exc.getSuppressed();
            for (Throwable exception : suppressedExceptions) {
                System.err.println("SUPPRESSED EXCEPTION: " + exception.toString());
            }
        }
    }
}
```

This will produce the following output when launched:

```
I'm going to close: AlmostCloseableResource
close() method invoked
java.lang.NumberFormatException: For input string: "Something is really wrong!"
      at java.base/java.lang.NumberFormatException.forInputString(
 NumberFormatException.java:68)
      at java.base/java.lang.Integer.parseInt(Integer.java:658)
      at java.base/java.lang.Integer.valueOf(Integer.java:989)
      at AlmostCloseableResource.launchException(AlmostCloseableResource.java:11)
      at TryWithResourceSuppressedTest.main(TryWithResourceSuppressedTest.java:5)
      Suppressed: java.lang.ClassCastException:
 class java.lang.Double cannot be cast to class java.lang.Integer
 (java.lang.Double and java.lang.Integer are in module java.base of loader 'bootstrap')
            at AlmostCloseableResource.close(AlmostCloseableResource.java:7)
            at TryWithResourceSuppressedTest.main(TryWithResourceSuppressedTest.java:3)
SUPPRESSED EXCEPTION: java.lang.ClassCastException:
 class java.lang.Double cannot be cast to class java.lang.Integer
 (java.lang.Double and java.lang.Integer are in module java.base of loader 'bootstrap')
```

Analyzing the code of the TestTryWithResourceSuppressed class and its output, we can see that after printing the message:

```
I'm going to close: AlmostCloseableResource
```

exploiting the override of the toString() method of the AlmostCloseableResource class, the launchException() method is immediately called, and this throws the NumberFormatException. Immediately after, the try-with-resources construct, tries to automatically close the almostCloseableResource object by invoking its close() method. In fact, the following is printed:

```
close() method invoked
```

However, the `close()` method also throws an exception (`ClassCastException`), but this is suppressed to give priority to the exception that was launched within the try-with-resources block. In fact, from the output we can note that first the information regarding the `NumberFormatException` exception is printed, and then the flow executes the `catch` block which goes to print the suppressed exceptions. Without this `catch` block, we would not have had information on any suppressed exceptions.

## 9.3.5 Exception Propagation

At this point, some readers may be wondering why one should use the mechanism of exceptions rather than simple `if` constructs. Actually, we will see that exception objects can be used to transport information about a problem towards the *calling methods*, i.e. the methods that invoke the method in which an exception is thrown. Exception handling therefore brings with it a type of event-based programming, which allows us to create well-abstract methods that have a precise return type and which must not take into account any exceptions that may arise. Exceptions follow a different execution flow that is defined with particular characteristics of the language, as we will see in the next sections.

### 9.3.5.1 Launching Exceptions: the throw keyword

Let's go back to the problem statement defined in section 9.2.3, where we imagined we wanted to create a program that should automatically manage reservations for a theater. This application may wish to launch an exception when we try to book a seat that is no longer available. We therefore created the following unchecked exception:

```
public class BookingException extends Exception {
    public BookingException() {
        // The Exception constructor invoked initialize
        // the private variable message
        super("Problem with the booking");
    }
    @Override
    public String toString() {
        return getMessage() + ": sold-out!";
    }
}
```

However, the JVM cannot automatically launch a `BookingException` in case we try to reserve a place that is no longer available. The JVM, in fact, knows when to launch an `ArithmeticException` but does not know when to launch a `BookingException` (that is been created by us). In this case, it is the developer that has to launch the exception. In fact, the keyword `throw` allows the throwing of an exception through the following syntax:

```
BookingException exc = new BookingException();
throw exc;
```

or equivalently (since the exc reference would then no longer be usable):

```
throw new BookingException();
```

A throw statement causes an immediate exit from the running method.
The launch of the exception should follow a conditional check such as the following:

```
if (availableSeats == 0) {
    throw new BookingException ();
}
```

Further we have to handle the exception with a catch block, as follows:

```
try {
    //seats availability check
    if (availableSeats == 0) {
        //throw the exception
        throw new BookingException();
    }
    //method that realize the booking
    //if no exception is thrown
    availableSeats--;
} catch (BookingException exc) {
    System.out.println(exc.toString());
}
```

> With the throw command we can launch any Throwable sub-class, not necessarily a custom exception. For example the java.lang.IllegalArgumentException, is often thrown when an invalid argument is passed as input to a method.

As we mentioned in section 4.4.2, the throw statement can also be used within a switch expression, after the arrow notation ->. For example, we could write:

```
availableSeats = switch(availableSeats) {
    default -> availableSeats-1;
    case 0 -> throw new BookingException();
};
```

and everything would work as before.
You will have surely noticed that the previous code does not represent a good example of

handling the exception: having to use the `if` condition, the use of the exception seems super-fluous. In fact, it is! But there must be a reason why it is possible to create custom exceptions and to be able to launch them.

### 9.3.5.2 Exception Propagation

This reason is the **propagation of the exception** to the calling methods. The power of exception handling is essentially due to this propagation mechanism. In practice, it is possible not to handle an exception in the method where it is thrown. At that point the calling method (i.e. the method that called the method that throws the exception) can handle the exception with a `try` - `catch` construct, or allow the exception to propagate again. To understand this mechanism better, let us rely on an example as usual. Suppose we have the following class:

```
public class BoxOffice {
    private int availableSeats;
    public BoxOffice() {
        availableSeats = 100;
    }
    public void book() {
        try {
            //seats availability check
            if (availableSeats == 0) {
                //throw the exception
                throw new BookingException();
            }
            //method that realize the booking
            //if no exception is thrown
            availableSeats--;
        }
        catch (BookingException exc) {
            System.out.println(exc.toString());
        }
    }
}
```

The `BoxOffice` class simplistically abstracts a virtual box office that allows us to reserve seats in a theater. Now, let's consider the following executable class (with `main()` method) that uses the `BoxOffice` class:

```
public class BookingManager {
    public static void main(String [] args) {
        var boxOffice = new BoxOffice();
        for (int i = 1; i <= 101; ++i) {
            boxOffice.book();
            System.out.println("Seat booked n° " + i);
        }
    }
}
```

For classes like that, the fact that the exception is managed within the BoxOffice class is a problem. In fact, the output of the program will be:

```
Seat booked n° 1
Seat booked n° 2
...
Seat booked n° 99
Seat booked n° 100
Problem with the booking: sold-out!
Seat booked n° 101
```

This is a contradiction! Managing exceptions is always an operation to be performed, but we do not always have to handle exceptions where they occur. In this case, the ideal action would be to handle the exception in the BookingManager class, rather than in the BoxOffice class:

```
public class BookingManager {
    public static void main(String [] args) {
        var boxOffice = new BoxOffice();
        try {
            for (int i = 1; i <= 101; ++i) {
                boxOffice.book();
                System.out.println("Seat booked n° " + i);
            }
        }
        catch (BookingException exc) {
            System.out.println(exc.toString());
        }
    }
}
```

All this is possible thanks to the Java exception propagation mechanism. We must avoid handling the exception in the book() method of the BoxOffice class, so that the exception propagates to the calling method, which in this case coincides with the main() method of the BookingManager class.

### 9.3.5.3 The throws *keyword*

To compile the BoxOffice class, however, it is not enough to remove the try - catch block from the book() method, but we also have to add the throws clause in the method declaration to explicitly inform the compiler that we could throw a BookingException in this method:

```
public void book() throws BookingException {
    //seats availability check
    if (availableSeats == 0) {
        //throw the exception
        throw new BookingException();
    }
```

**359**

```
        //method that realize the booking if no exception is thrown
        availableSeats--;
    }
```

In this way, we will get the correct output:

```
Seat booked n° 1
Seat booked n° 2
...
Seat booked n° 99
Seat booked n° 100
Problem with the booking: sold-out!
```

If we did not use the throws clause in the method declaration, the compiler would not compile the previous code. An error message would have been printed, to make us know that the method book() could throws the BookingException exception (which is obvious to the compiler due to the presence of the keyword throw) and that this is not handled. But a checked exception must be always caught in a catch block, or declared to be thrown with the throws clause. In fact, the error message returned would be the following:

```
BoxOffice.java:5: unreported exception BookingException;
   must be caught or declared to be thrown
```

 This message is further proof of the robust features of Java. With the throws clause in the method declaration, it is as if we're warning the compiler that we are aware that the method can throw the BookingException at runtime, and we will handle the exception in another part of the code.

So, if a hypothetical callingMethod() method wants to use the methodToCall() method, which declares with a throws clause the possible launch of a given type of exception, the callingMethod() method should handle the exception with a try - catch block that includes the call to the methodToCall(), or it should declare a throws clause to the same exception in its declaration too. For example, this applies to the main() method of the BookingManager class.

 We need to add the throws clause because our exception is a checked exception (having extended the Exception class and not the RuntimeException class). In case we had used an unchecked exception, the throws clause would not have been necessary (but if we wanted, we could use it to force the . . .

. . . caller method to handle the unchecked exception). This is the main difference between a checked and an unchecked exception. In fact, in section 9.2.1 we stated that "if we use a method that launches a checked exception without handling it, the compilation will fail (that's why we call it a checked exception)".

Many standard library methods are declared with a throws clause. For example, many methods of the java.io package classes declare throws clauses to the IOException (input-output exception). This means that if we use these methods, we must handle somewhere the IOException.

You can also declare more than one exception in the throws clause, separating the various types with commas, as in the following example:

```
public void book() throws BookingException, NullPointerException {
    //...
}
```

Before the advent of version 7, the following code:

```
public void rethrowException(String exceptionName)
    throws FirstException, SecondException {
    try {
        if (exceptionName.equals("First")) {
            throw new FirstException();
        } else {
            throw new SecondException();
        }
    } catch (Exception e) {
        throw e;
    }
}
```

Given:

```
class FirstException extends Exception { }
class SecondException extends Exception { }
```

. . .

. . . would not have been valid for compiling. Although it was evident that the method `rethrowException` raised one of the two exceptions `FirstException` or `SecondException`, having used a `catch` block that raises an `Exception`, it was also necessary to replace (or at least add) the `throws` clause `Exception`. Java 7 has eliminated this behavior by introducing a compilation analysis that verifies the veracity of the `throws` clause.

### 9.3.5.4 Overriding Methods: Another Rule

Although many developers consider checked exceptions to be useless and carefully avoid using them in their own programs, the Java designers conceived them as part of a method's interface. In fact, when we talked about overriding a method in the previous chapter, we listed three **rules**.

1. The method rewritten in the subclass must have the same signature (name and parameters) of the superclass method.

2. The return type of the subclass method must match that of the superclass method, or it must be of a type that extends the return type of the superclass method.

3. The redefined method in the subclass should not be less accessible than the original superclass method.

Now we have to introduce another one:

4. When overriding a method, we cannot specify `throws` clauses on exceptions that the superclass method does not include in its `throws` clause. However, it is possible for the overriding method to declare a `throws` clause for exceptions that are subtypes of exceptions defined by the superclass method in its `throws` clause.

Let's try to explain this rule with an example:

```
public class BaseClass {
    public void method() throws java.io.IOException {
    }
}
class CorrectSubclass1 extends BaseClass {
    public void method() throws java.io.IOException {
    }
}
```

```
class CorrectSubclass2 extends BaseClass {
    public void method() throws java.io.FileNotFoundException {
    }
}
class CorrectSubclass3 extends BaseClass {
    public void method() {
    }
}
class NotCorrectSubclass extends BaseClass {
    public void method() throws java.sql.SQLException {
    }
}
```

The BaseClass class includes a method that declares an IOException in its throws clause. The CorrectSubclass1 class overrides the method and declares the same IOException in its throws clause. The class CorrectSubclass2 overrides the method and declares a FileNotFoundException, which is a subclass of IOException in its throws clause. The CorrectSubclass3 class overrides the method and does not declare throws clauses. Finally, the NotCorrectSubclass class overrides the method and declares a SQLException in its throws clause, and this is illegal.

Note that the above rule applies only to checked exceptions, that is, to exceptions that are not subclasses of RuntimeException. This means that a method that overrides an inherited method can add unchecked exceptions in its throws clause that were not present in the throws clause of the original method. For example, the following class will also be correctly compiled:

```
class CorrectSubclass4 extends BaseClass {
    @Override
    public void method () throws java.lang.NullPointerException {}
}
```

In fact, a new unchecked exception is added to the throws clause of the overriding method (NullPointerException), and the checked exception (IOException), that was declared in the throws clause of the original method, is removed. Of course, it can also remove from its throws clause any unchecked exceptions that were present in the throws clause of the original method.

### 9.3.5.5 Warnings

When we compile a Java file, the compiler, in addition to correctly compiling or giving errors, may also return **warnings**. For example, by compiling the BookingException class (and, in general, any class that extends Throwable) with any IDE (Eclipse, Netbeans or even EJE), we will get the following output:

```
BookingException.java:1: warning: [serial] serializable class BookingException has no definition of
    serialVersionUID
public class BookingException extends Exception {
       ^
1 warning
```

This is not an error. The class has been compiled and the **.class** file has been created. The compiler is only *warning us* that this file has been defined in a potentially dangerous way. In particular, we have been told that our class is serializable and has not defined a serialVersionUID. At this point in the book, we do not yet have the knowledge necessary to understand exactly the meaning of this warning. However, at least a partial explanation is needed, although it will probably be clear after dealing with the topic of serialization. The Throwable class implements an interface called Serializable. This is defined in the java.io package of the standard library. It is an interface that does not declare methods, but if implemented, it allows the objects that implement it to be *serialized*. For example, a serializable object can be stored in a file, or sent through a network. Now, we will not discuss the technicalities of serialization (which will be dealt with in detail in the twentieth chapter regarding Input-Output), since our goal is only to understand the meaning of this warning. Suffice it to know that if a class is serializable, we are being asked by the compiler to define an attribute named serialVersionUID. This may be necessary if our class were to be used in distributed environments (i.e. if the objects in the class were to be used by different virtual machines traveling through a network). In cases like these, there should be a copy of the serializable class on different machines. This means that, without the explicit declaration of the serialVersionUID ensuring that the two versions are compatible, the reading of the serializable object could fail and an InvalidClassException could be launched. To solve this warning, we can declare the serialVersionUID, for example, as follows:

```
private static final long serialVersionUID = 8144963013726442881L;
```

Note that we can specify any access modifier, even if we usually prefer private, since there is no reason to expose this attribute to the outside. However, it is mandatory that it must be declared as a static and final long type. The value to assign to serialVersionUID is arbitrary, it would be good to generate a unique one as in the example, but also the 1L value would be fine! IDEs such as Eclipse and Netbeans have facilities that allow automatic generation of these values.

Another possibility to solve the warning, but if we are sure that this class should not be serialized, the only valid thing to do is to use the SuppressWarning annotation on the class itself as follows:

```
@SuppressWarnings("serial")
public class BookingException extends Exception {
```

In this case, it is as if we had recommended the compiler not to worry about the warning, because the risk is controlled. Where we compile directly from the command line in the following way:

```
javac BookingException.java
```

no warning will be launched. In fact, in order for our warnings to be reported, we must fill in with the **-Xlint:all** (or simply with **-Xlint**) option:

```
javac –Xlint:all BookingException.java
```

It is also possible to specify which type of warning must be reported, for example, with the following command:

```
javac –Xlint:serial BookingException.java
```

only warnings will be reported on the missing `serialVersionUID`.

For more information on compiler options, see the JDK tool documentation. In general, also with the IDEs, it should be possible to set an option so that the compiler does not signal warnings.

> **For EJE, go to** File ⇨ Options ⇨ Java Tab **and deselect the warning check box.**

## 9.3.6 More on Exception Handling

In this section we have collected some features of exception handling that not all Java programmers know. These features can be used in particular scenarios, but all in all quite frequent.

### 9.3.6.1 More on entering a `finally` block

In section 9.3.3, we stated that a `finally` clause is executed when a `try` block ends without throwing exceptions (immediately caught in some `catch` block), or after a catch block that was executed following an exception thrown in the `try` block.

> **It is also possible to avoid** `catch` **blocks, and have just a** `finally` **block that follows a** `try` **block. In this case, the** `finally` **block will certainly be executed after the** `try` **block is executed, both if the exception is thrown, and if it is not thrown. However, if the exception were launched, and not handled with a** `catch` **block, the program would terminate abnormally.**

Having said that, we have to consider that both a try block and a catch block can end with the following scenarios:

- A return command is executed, and ends the method in which our construct resides.

- An unchecked exception like a NullPointerException, or a ClassCastException, is thrown by the JVM.

- An exception is thrown explicitly using the throw command.

- The code block is executed entirely without encountering one of the conditions illustrated in the previous points.

In all these scenarios, the finally block will definitely be executed.

> However, there is another scenario, which is the only one that will not the finally **clause to be executed: the** System.exit() **method is invoked. This method causes the immediate termination of the program.**

 But what happens if, within the finally clause, one of the scenarios described above takes place? For example, a finally block could be executed following the execution of a return command encountered within the try block, and from the same finally clause, an exception could be thrown. What will happen? Will the method return the value specified in the try block, or will it throw the exception thrown in the finally block? As we can guess, the finally block will always have priority. And therefore, the return command of the try block will have no effect.

### 9.3.6.2 Exceptions Caused by Other Exceptions

With version 1.4 of the language, a new feature has been introduced. The Throwable class was modified to support a simple wrapping mechanism. Often, in fact, it is necessary for the developer to capture a certain exception in order to launch another. For example:

```
try {
    //...
} catch(AnException e) {
    throw new AnotherException();
}
```

In such cases, however, the information in the first exception (in the example AnException) is lost.

**Before version 1.4, it was therefore necessary to create a custom exception that could contain another one as an instance variable. For example:**

```
public class WrapperException {
    private Exception otherException;
    public WrapperException(Exception otherException) {
        this.setOtherException(otherException);
    }
    public void setOtherException(Exception otherException) {
        this.otherException = otherException;
    }
    public Exception getOtherException() {
        return otherException;
    }
    //...
}
```

**With this type of exception, we can include one exception into another, like this:**

```
try {
    //...
} catch(AnException e) {
    throw new WrapperException(e);
}
```

**But with version 1.4, we no longer need to create a custom exception to get wrapper exceptions.**

In the Throwable class, the getCause() and initCause(Throwable) methods and two new constructors, Throwable(Throwable) and Throwable(String, Throwable) have been introduced. It is therefore now possible, for example, to code the following instructions:

```
try {
    //...
} catch(ArithmeticException exc) {
    throw new SecurityException(exc);
}
```

Where we caught an exception exc of ArithmeticException type, and we throw a SecurityException that wraps exc. Somewhere else in the code we can retrieve the ArithmeticException from the SecurityException by code like the following:

```
try {
    //...
} catch(SecurityException se) {
    ArithmeticException ae = (ArithmeticException)se.getCause();
    //...
}
```

> **It is also possible to concatenate an arbitrary number of exceptions.**

### 9.3.6.3 Loading Classes: ExceptionInInitializerError

 We have seen that the exceptions are launched and handled within methods. However, there is the possibility that these are not launched in a method, but within a static initializer, or during the initialization of a static variable, i.e. during the class loading. In these two scenarios, the exceptions launched are automatically wrapped in an ExceptionInInitializerError. For example, let's consider the following code:

```
public class StaticIntializerTest {
    public static void main(String args[]) throws Throwable {
        new StaticIntializerExample();
    }
}

class StaticIntializerExample {
    static int a;

    static {
        a = getValue(10);
    }

    static int getValue(int a) {
        if (a == 10) {
            throw new IllegalArgumentException("The argument " + a + " is not valid");
        }
        return 10;
    }
}
```

The StaticIntializerTest class instantiates the StaticIntializerExample class. We already know that, instantiating a class, first means load it into memory, and that static variables and static blocks are first initialized (in the order in which they are placed in the class). The StaticIntializerExample class declares a static variable a that is initialized within a static block. The static method getValue() is invoked within it, which launches an IllegalArgumentException. Note that the main() method does not handle the exception, in fact it is declared with the throws Throwable clause. Then the program, once launched, will end abruptly showing the following output:

```
Exception in thread "main" java.lang.ExceptionInInitializerError
    at StaticIntializerTest.main(StaticIntializerTest.java:3)
Caused by: java.lang.IllegalArgumentException: The argument 10 is not valid
    at StaticIntializerExample.getValue(StaticIntializerTest.java:14)
    at StaticIntializerExample.<clinit>(StaticIntializerTest.java:9)
    ... 1 more
```

As we can see, an ExceptionInInitializerError has been launched, but the IllegalArgumentException, has been reported as the real cause of the problem.

> **Note that we would have obtained the same result if the variable a had been initialized directly without a static block in the following way:**
> ```
> static int a = getValue(10);
> ```

ExceptionInInitializerError is an error, not an exception. In fact, the class was not loaded into memory, and this problem cannot be solved. However, it would have been possible to catch the error, for example, like this:

```java
public class StaticIntializerTest {
    public static void main(String args[]) throws Throwable {
        try {
            new StaticIntializerExample();
        }
        catch (Throwable exc) {
            System.out.println("Cannot initialize class: " + exc.getCause());
        }
    }
}
```

getting the following output:

```
Cannot initialize class: java.lang.IllegalArgumentException: The argument 10 is not valid
```

**369**

# 9.4 Introduction to Assertions

When assertions were introduced in version 1.4 of Java, for the first time, the list of keywords was changed with the addition of a new one: `assert`, which had never happened in previous major releases.

An **assertion** is an instruction that allows us to test any behaviors expected in an application. Each assertion requires a boolean expression which the developer believes should be verified at the point where it is declared. If the verification is negative, we must state that there's an error in the implementation of the code, or in jargon, a *bug*. Assertions can therefore be a useful tool to make sure that the written code behaves as expected. The developer can disseminate the code of assertions in order to test the robustness of the code in a simple and effective way. Finally, the developer can disable the reading of assertions by the JVM in the software release phase, so that the execution is not slowed down. Many developers think that using assertions is one of the most successful techniques to find bugs. Yet assertions are relatively seldom used in the context of Java programming. Maybe for some they are out of fashion, but the reality is that most people are not very clear how they should be used. Furthermore, assertions also represent an excellent tool for documenting the internal behavior of a program, and helps maintainability.

There are two types of syntax for using assertions:

1. `assert boolean_expression;`

2. `assert boolean_expression: printable_expression;`

With the first syntax, when the application executes the assertion `boolean_expression`, if the value of the expression is `true`, the program continues normally, but if the value is `false`, an `AssertionError` error is thrown. For example, the instruction:

```
assert b > 0;
```

is semantically equivalent to:

```
if (!(b>0)) {
    throw new AssertionError();
}
```

Apart from the elegance and the compactness of the `assert` construct, the difference between the two previous expressions is remarkable. Assertions represent, rather than an instruction, a tool to test the veracity of the assumptions made by the developer in their application. If the condition asserted by the programmer is `false`, the application will terminate immediately, showing the reasons via a stack-trace (`printStackTrace()` method above). In fact, something occurred that was not foreseen by the developer themselves. It is possible to disable the reading of the assertions by the JVM once the product has been released, in order that its execution is not slowed down. This highlights the difference between assertions and all other application instructions: assertions can be disabled, while the other instructions cannot.

With respect to syntax 1), syntax 2) allows us to also specify an explanatory message by means of a printable expression. For example:

```
assert b > 0: b;
```

or:

```
assert b > 0: "the value of b is " + b;
```

or:

```
assert b > 0: getMessage();
```

or also:

```
assert b > 0: "assert b > 0 = " + (b > 0);
```

printable_expression can be any expression that returns some value (so it is not possible to invoke a method with void return type). The syntax 2) therefore allows us to improve the stack-trace of the assertions.

> JUnit is probably the most popular software for running automated tests. Among the authors are two computer gurus, Kent Beck, author of the *Test Driven Development* (*TDD*) process and the Extreme Programming methodology, and Erich Gamma, historical co-author of the first book on Design Pattern. In particular, JUnit was created to do *unit tests*, or to create software that automatically tests each of the classes we create. The great advantage of this approach is that, at the end of a working day (but also at the beginning or during), it will be possible to test the correctness of our classes with a simple click, and obtain a report on the regression bugs of our project that may be created with development on a daily basis. JUnit is completely based on assertions, and existed before assertions were introduced in Java. In fact, the authors created methods, such as assertEquals() or assertTrue(), to verify the correctness of the code. We will briefly introduce JUnit at the end of the next chapter. For more information on JUnit, see: http://junit.org/.

## 9.4.1 Design by Contract

The mechanism of assertions owes its success to a design technique known as **Design by Contract**, developed by Bertrand Meyer. This technique is a fundamental feature of the programming language developed by Meyer himself: Eiffel (for information **http://www.eiffel.com**). But it is possible to design by contract, fairly easily, with any programming language. The technique is based, in particular, on three types of assertions: *preconditions*, *postconditions* and *invariants* (the invariants in turn are divided into *internal*, *class*, on the *flow of execution* types).

With a **precondition**, the developer can specify what the state of the application should be at the time an operation is invoked. In this way, it is made explicit who is responsible for testing the correctness of the data. The use of the assertion reduces both the danger of completely forgetting controls and carrying out too many controls (because they can be enabled and disabled). Since we tend to use assertions in testing and debugging, we should never confuse the use of assertions with that of exception handling. In section 9.4.3, rules to follow for the use of assertions will be explained.

With a **postcondition**, the developer can specify what the application state should be at the time an operation is completed. Postconditions are a useful way of saying what to do, without saying how. In other words, it is another method to separate interface and internal implementation.

Finally, the concept of **invariant** can be used, which if applied to a class, allows us to specify constraints for all instantiated objects. These may be in a state that does not respect the specified constraint (called an *inconsistent state*) but only temporarily during the execution of some method, at the end of which the state must return to being consistent.

Design by contract is a design technique rather than a programming one. It allows us, for example, to test the consistency of inheritance. A subclass, in fact, could weaken the preconditions and fortify postconditions and class invariants in order to validate the extension. We recommend that you take a look at the bibliography if interested in learning more about design by contract.

> **If your requirement is to use pre-existing code created with a version of Java prior to version 1.4, you should consult Appendix J.**

## 9.4.2 Notes for Running Programs that Use the Word `assert`

As repeatedly stated, it is possible, at runtime, to enable or disable assertions. As usual, we must use options, this time applying them to the **java** command: **-enableassertions** (or more briefly **-ea**) to enable assertions, and **-disableassertions** (or **-da**) to disable them. For example:

```
java -ea MyProgramWithAssertions
```

enables the JVM to read the `assert` constructs while

```
java -da MyProgramWithAssertions
```

disables assertions so as to not slow down the application. Since assertions are disabled by default, the previous command is equivalent to the following:

```
java MyProgramWithAssertions
```

The following rules apply to both enabling and disabling:

1. if we do not specify arguments after the assertion enablement (or disablement) options, assertions will be enabled (or disabled) in all classes of our program (but not in the standard library classes used). This is the case with the previous examples.

2. By specifying the name of a package followed by three dots, we enable (or disable) assertions in that package and all its subpackages. For example, the command:

```
java -ea -da:mypackage... MyProgram
```

will enable assertions in all classes except those in the `mypackage` package; specifying only the three dots, on the other hand, will enable or disable assertions in the default package (that is, the folder from which the command is launched).

3. By specifying only the name of a class, we enable (or disable) assertions in that class. For example, the command:

```
java -ea:... -da:MyClass MyProgram
```

will enable assertions in all classes of the default package, except in the `MyClass` class.

You can also enable (or disable) the assertions in the standard library classes that we want to use through the **-enablesystemassertions** (or more briefly **-esa**) and **-disablesystemassertions** (or **-dsa**) options. The above rules also apply to these options.

 **In some critical programs, it's possible that the developer wants to ensure that assertions are enabled. With the following block of static code:**

...

```
...

static {
    boolean assertsEnabled = false;
    assert assertsEnabled = true;
    if (! assertsEnabled)
        throw new RuntimeException ("Asserts must be enabled!");
}
```

**it is possible to guarantee that the program is executable only if assertions are enabled. The block in fact, first declares and initializes the boolean variable assertsEnabled to false, and then changes its value to true if assertions are enabled. If assertions are not enabled, the program ends with the launch of the RuntimeException, otherwise it continues. Recall that the static block is executed (see Chapter 6) only once, when the class containing it is loaded. For this reason, the static block should be inserted in the main() class to be sure to get the desired result.**

### 9.4.3 When to Use Assertions

Not all developers may be interested in using assertions. An assertion cannot be reduced to a concise way of expressing a regular condition. An assertion is, instead, the fundamental concept of a design methodology aimed at making the programs more robust. However, when the developer decides to use this tool, it should be of interest to use it correctly. So, let's see some advices.

#### 9.4.3.1 First Piece of Advice

It's often recommended (even in official Java documentation) not to use preconditions to test the correctness of parameters of public methods. It is instead recommended to use preconditions to test the correctness of the parameters of private methods, protected or with visibility at the package level. This depends on the fact that a non-public method has the possibility of being called by a limited, known, correct and working context. This implies the presumption that our calls to the method are correct, and it is therefore right to reinforce this concept with an assertion. Suppose we have a method with package visibility like the following:

```
public class InstancesFactory {
    Object getInstance(int index) {
        assert (index == 1 || index == 2);
        switch (index) {
            case 1:
                return new Instance1();
            case 2:
                return new Instance2();
        }
    }
}
```

The `InstancesFactory` class implements a custom solution based on the pattern called **Factory Method** (for information on the concept of pattern, see Appendix D).

If this method can only be called from classes that belong to the same package of the `InstancesFactory` class, it should never happen that the `index` parameter is different from 1 or 2, because that would be a bug.

If instead the `getInstance()` method was declared as `public`, the situation would be different. In fact, a possible check of the index parameter should be considered ordinary, and therefore to be managed by throwing an exception:

```
public class InstancesFactory {
    public Object getInstance(int index) throws Exception {
        if (!(index == 1 || index == 2)) {
            throw new Exception("Wrong index: " + index);
        }
        switch (index) {
            case 1:
                return new Instance1();
            case 2:
                return new Instance2();
        }
    }
}
```

In this case, the use of an assertion would not guarantee the robustness of the program, but only its interruption if assertions were enabled at runtime, being unable to control, a priori, that the method is invoked in the correct way. Consequently, a precondition of this type would violate the object-oriented concept of public method.

### 9.4.3.2 Second Piece of Advice

The use of assertions is not recommended where we want to test the correctness of data entered by a user. Assertions should test the consistency of the program with itself, not the consistency of the user with the program. Any incorrect input from a user should be managed by exceptions, not assertions. For example, let's modify the Date class we talked about in Chapter 6 to explain encapsulation:

```
public class Date {
    private int day;
    //...
    public void setDay(int day) {
        assert (day > 0 && day <= 31): "Invalid day";
        this.day = day
    }
    //...
```

where the day argument of the setDay() method was passed by a user through an interface object, which represented a graphical user interface (code 6.2 bis):

```
...
Date aDate = new Date();
aDate.setDay(interface.getConfirmedDay());
aDate.setMonth(interface.getConfirmedMonth());
aDate.setYear(interface.getConfirmedYear());
...
```

As you will have guessed, the use of the assert keyword is incorrect. In fact, if assertions were enabled during the execution of the application and the user entered an incorrect value to initialize the day variable, the application would be interrupted with an AssertionError! If assertions were not enabled, no control would prevent the user from entering incorrect values. The ideal solution would be to handle the situation through an exception, for example:

```
public void setDay(int day) throws RuntimeException {
    if (!(day > 0 && day <= 31)) {
        throw new RuntimeException("Invalid day");
    }
    this.day = day;
}
```

Clearly, the condition can be easily improved.

### 9.4.3.3 Third Piece of Advice

The use of assertions is well suited to postconditions and invariants. By **postcondition**, we mean a condition that is checked just before the execution of a method ends (the last instruction). The following is an example:

```
public class Connection {
    private boolean isOpen = false;
    public void open() {
```

```
        // . . .
        isOpen = true;
        // . . .
        assert isOpen;
    }
    public void close() throws ConnectionException {
        if (!isOpen) {
            throw new ConnectionException("Impossible to close open connections!");
        }
        // . . .
        isOpen = false;
        // . . .
        assert !isOpen;
    }
}
```

We divide the **invariants** into internal invariants, class invariants and execution flow invariants. By **internal invariants**, we mean assertions that test the correctness of the flows of our code. For example, the following code block:

```
if (i == 0) {
    //...
} else if (i == 1) {
    //...
} else { // we know that i must be equal to 2
    //...
}
```

can become more robust with the use of an assertion:

```
if (i == 0) {
    //...
} else if (i == 1) {
    //...
} else {
    assert i == 2 : "Warning!!! i = " + i + "!";
    //...
}
```

Such a type of invariant is most likely used within a default clause of a switch construct. Often the developer underestimates the construct by omitting the default clause, because it assumes that the flow certainly passes through a certain case. Assertions are very useful for validating our assumptions. For example, the following code block:

```
switch(carType) {
    case Car.SPORTS:
        //...
    break;
```

```
        case Car.LUXURY:
            //...
        break;
        case Car.UTILITY:
            //...
        break;
}
```

can become more robust with the use of an assertion:

```
switch(carType) {
        case Car.SPORTS:
            //...
        break;
        case Car.LUXURY:
            //...
        break;
        case Car.UTILITY:
            //...
        break;
        default:
            assert false : "Car type not expected : " + carType;
}
```

By **class invariants**, we mean particular internal invariants that must be true for all the instances of a certain class, in every moment of their life cycle, except during the execution of some methods. At the beginning and at the end of each method, however, the state of the object must return consistently. For example, an object of the following class:

```
public class Scale {
    private double weight;
    public Scale() {
        resetHand();
        assert handOnZero();// class invariant
    }
    private void setWeight(double grams) {
        assert grams > 0; // pre-condition
        weight = grams;
    }
    private double getWeight() {
        return weight;
    }
    public void weigh(double grams) {
        if (grams <= 0) {
            throw new RuntimeException("Grams <= 0! ");
        }
        setWeight(grams);
        showWeight();
        resetHand();
```

```
        assert handOnZero(); // Class invariant
    }
    private void showWeight() {
        System.out.println("The weight is " + weight + " grams");
    }
    private void resetHand() {
        setWeight(0);
    }
    private boolean handOnZero() {
        return weight == 0;
    }
}
```

could, after each weighing, reset the hand of the scale (note that only the two public methods end with an assertion).

By **execution flow invariants**, we mean assertions placed in areas of the code that should never be reached. For example, if we have code commented this way:

```
public void method() {
    if (flag == true) {
        return;
    }
    // The flow don't have to reach this point!
}
```

we could replace the comment with an `assert false` statement:

```
public void method() {
    if (flag == true) {
        return;
    }
    assert false;
}
```

## 9.4.4 Conclusions

In this chapter we have grouped together topics that may seem similar, and we have explained their differences. The underlying concept is that using exception handling is critical to building robust applications. Assertions represent a convenient mechanism to test the robustness of our applications. Exception handling is not advisable, it is mandatory! Assertions are very often unjustly snubbed. In fact, we need to have some experience to fully exploit their potential. Design by contract is a complex subject that must be studied thoroughly in order to obtain better results. However, even the use of simpler concepts such as postconditions can improve the robustness of our applications.

# Summary

In this chapter, we first distinguished the concepts of exception, error, and assertion. The **hierarchy of classes** that can be thrown in Java starts from the Throwable class, which is extended by Error and Exception. We have categorized the exceptions and errors with an overview of the main classes. In addition, we have divided the types of exceptions into **unchecked** (all subclasses of RuntimeException) and **checked** (all other exceptions). The mechanism underlying the management of exceptions has been presented, along with the five keywords that allow it to be managed. try – catch - finally blocks let us handle exceptions locally. throw - throws couples, instead, support the (robust) propagation of exceptions.

By extending the Exception class (or its subclasses), we can create our own **custom exceptions**. These usually need to be thrown by us with the throw command (and if they are checked exceptions they must also be declared with the throws keyword).

The possibility of abstracting the concept of exception with objects and the possibility of exploiting the call-stack mechanism (**error-exception propagation**) allow the creation of object-oriented, simple and robust applications at the same time, without having to worry about designing a return type that also contemplates the possibility of specifying a problem.

The try-**with-resources** construct guarantees us simplicity and robustness in cases where we deal with objects that implement the Closeable or AutoCloseable interface.

The **override** implementation is also based on the definition of the throws clause. In fact, a method that overrides cannot use in its throws clause, checked exceptions that were not present in the throws clause of the original method. However, we can use a subclass of the class declared in the throws clause of the original method in the clause of the overriding method.

We also mentioned the concept of **warning** to clarify some doubts that could be presented by compiling the examples presented.

**Assertions** can be declared in a synthetic way or also specifying a possible error message. They have the characteristic of being enabled or disabled at the time of the execution of the program, and are provided with different usage options to be specified from the command line. We have also introduced their use within the **design by contract**, introducing the concepts of preconditions, postconditions and invariants.

**Preconditions** are used at the beginning of a method, and are used to test the input if the method is not public.

**Postconditions** are instead positioned at the end of the method, and are used to test the correctness of the method results.

On the other hand, **invariants** can be within the code of a method and are divided into class invariants, internal invariants and the execution flow.

By **internal invariants**, we mean assertions that test the correctness of the flows of our code. They are often found within algorithms for testing intermediate situations.

By **class invariants**, we mean particular internal invariants that must be true for all the instances of a certain class, in every moment of their life cycle, except during the execution of some methods.

By **execution flow invariants**, we mean assertions placed in areas of the code that should never be reached.

**Exercises, source code, appendices and other resources are available at http://www.javaforaliens.com.**

## Chapter Goals

Have the following goals been achieved?

| Goal | Achieved | Achievement Date |
|------|----------|------------------|
| Understand the differences between exceptions, errors and assertions (Unit 9.1) | O | |
| Know how to handle the various types of exceptions with try-catch blocks (Units 9.2, 9.3) | O | |
| Know how to create custom exception types and manage the propagation mechanism with the keywords throw and throws (Units 9.2, 9.3) | O | |
| Know how to use the try-with-resources construct (Unit 9.3) | O | |
| Understand assertions and know how to use them (Unit 9.4) | O | |

# 10

# A Guided Example to Object-Oriented Programming

> **Goals:**
>
> At the end of this chapter, the reader should:
>
> ✓ Know what it means to develop an application in Java using the object-oriented programming paradigms (Units 10.1, 10.2, 10.3).
> ✓ Understand what it means to test your software automatically with JUnit (Unit 10.4).
> ✓ Be introduced to the usefulness of the "Java Logging" API (Unit 10.4).

This chapter will be useful to newbies, and to all those who have difficulty with object orientation. In the following pages, we will simulate the creation of a simple program, step by step. The emphasis will be on the choices and reasoning that must be carried out when planning objects. In this way, we will provide an example of how to deal with the problems of object-oriented programming, at least for the first few times. This is a didactic approach, and the final solution will not be an example of a good design solution. Rather, it will serve to understand the reasoning that must guide us during the various stages of development. The example presented in this chapter is oriented to the programmer, and not to other roles such as analyst, designer, architect, etc. To have a more global view of the software development cycle, please refer to the fifth chapter. In the second part of this chapter, we will address important topics such as *testing* and we will introduce some basic concepts of *logging*. Like Chapter 5, this chapter is designed to bring the reader closer to the development of *real software*, this time focusing more on programming than on other aspects of the software development cycle.

# 10.1 Why This Chapter?

This chapter was introduced to give the reader a small but important experience, aimed at the correct use of the paradigms of object-oriented programming. When approaching Object Orientation, the most difficult goal is not understanding the definitions which, as we have seen, are derived from the real world, but using it in the right way within an application.

What the reader might probably lack, is the ability to write a program, which is probably the most important topic! Let's take an example: if someone asked you to write an application that simulates an address book, or a card game, or any other application, you will soon ask yourself some questions: "which classes will be part of the application?", "where is inheritance used?", "where is polymorphism used?" and so on.

These are questions that are very difficult to answer because, for each of them, there are many answers, all of which seem valid. If we were to decide which classes defined the application that simulates an address book, we could decide to create three classes (AddressBook, Person, and the class that contains the main() method), or five (Address, Search, AddressBook, Person, and the class that contains the main() method) or more. In-depth reflections on the various situations that could arise in using this application (so-called use cases) would probably suggest the coding of other classes. A solution with many classes would probably be more functional, but it would require too much implementation effort for an application that could be called "simple". On the other hand, an implementation that makes use of a small number of classes would force the developer to insert too much code into too few classes. This would also be a less object-oriented approach, since our application will not simulate the real world as it is.

The best solution will be *absolutely personal*, because it is guaranteed by common sense and experience.

It has already been mentioned that an important support for solving these problems is guaranteed by knowing object-oriented methodologies, or at least by knowing UML (see Appendices F and G and the various chapters of the book which introduce examples for the various diagrams). Here, however, where our main goal is to learn a programming language, it is not advisable or feasible to introduce other complex topics. The study of the language cannot solve all our problems but it can be a useful support for the study of Object Orientation. An example exercise will now be presented. The reader can try to solve it, or study the solution. With this exercise, we aim to make careful observations on the choices made, and then draw important conclusions. The solution will be presented with an **iterative and incremental approach** (at each iteration in the development process, the software will be increased), as it is based on the model of modern object-oriented methodologies. In this way, all the steps performed in creating the program will be discussed.

## 10.2 Case Study

**Goal (problem statement):**

Create an application that can calculate the geometric distance between points. Points can be on two- or three-dimensional references.

> With this exercise, we will not make a useful application; its purpose is purely didactic. We won't follow a methodology, but will create a solution with coding. Then we'll try to make it better.

## 10.3 Case Study Resolution

Below is one of the many possible solutions. We must not consider it as a solution to be imitated, but it must be considered just as an opportunity to study and reflect on how to create better applications in the future.

### 10.3.1 Step 1

We identify the classes that the application surely cannot do without (those that, in Chapter 5, we defined as **key abstractions**). It seems clear that the classes that define the **domain** of this application must be essential components. Let's code the Point and ThreeDimensionalPoint classes using encapsulation, inheritance, constructor overloading and code reuse:

```java
public class Point {
    private int x, y;
    public Point() {
        //Constructor without parameters
    }
    public Point(int x, int y) {
        this.setXY(x, y); //this is optional
        //code reuse
    }
    public void setX(int x) {
        this.x = x; //this is mandatory
    }
    public void setY(int y) {
        this.y = y; //this is mandatory
    }
    public void setXY(int x, int y) {
        this.setX(x); //this is optional
        this.setY(y);
    }
    public int getX() {
```

```
            return this.x; //this is optional
        }
    public int getY() {
            return this.y; //this is optional
        }
    }

public class ThreeDimensionalPoint extends Point {
    private int z;
    public ThreeDimensionalPoint() {
        //Constructor without parameters
    }
    public ThreeDimensionalPoint(int x, int y, int z) {
        this.setXYZ(x, y, z); //Code reuse
    }
    public void setZ(int z) {
        this.z = z; //this is mandatory
    }
    public void setXYZ(int x, int y, int z) {
        this.setXY(x, y); ///Code reuse
        this.setZ(z); //this is optional
    }
    public int getZ() {
        return this.z; //this is optional
    }
}
```

 Let's make a first observation: in order to use inheritance *legally*, we have violated the rule of abstraction. In fact, we assigned the Point identifier to a class that should have been called TwoDimensionalPoint. It would make sense to call the class Point, only where the context of the application was clear and more restrictive. For example, in a painting application, the Point class would make sense. When the context is, instead, so abstract as in our example, why should a point have two dimensions?

Remember that, to implement the inheritance mechanism, the developer must check its validity through the so-called "is a" relationship (see section 7.1.3). By violating abstraction, we have been able to validate inheritance. In fact, we asked ourselves: "is a three-dimensional point a point?" The affirmative answer allowed us to implement the specialization of the Point class. If we had followed the rule of abstraction, we could not have implemented inheritance between these two classes, since we would have to ask: "is a three-dimensional point a two-dimensional point?" In this case, the answer would have been negative. This choice was made, not because it facilitates the continuation of the application, but just to see how the development becomes more difficult if we start violating the basic rules. Despite the simplicity of the problem, the power of language will allow us to complete the task. At the same time, we will see how to force the code to meet the requirements. In general, however, it is good to try to follow all the rules that we can in the initial stages of development, relegating any *forcing* to resolving malfunctions in the final stages of development.

> **The coding of two classes like these was obtained by making several changes. Getting optimal solutions on the first try is not realistic! This observation will also apply to the next steps.**

## 10.3.2 Step 2

Let's identify the functionalities of the system. It has been requested that our application should calculate the distance between two points. Let's make some reflections before we begin to code. We distinguish two types of calculating the distance between two points: between two two-dimensional points and two three-dimensional points. We exclude, a priori, the possibility of calculating the distance between two points of which one is two-dimensional and the other three-dimensional. At this point, it seems reasonable to introduce a new class (for example the Ruler class) with the responsibility of performing these two types of calculations. Although it seems to be the right solution, we opt for another implementation strategy: we assign the same classes Point and ThreeDimensionalPoint the responsibility for calculating the distances among their instances. Note that abstracting these classes, by inserting in their definitions methods called distance(), represents another obvious violation of the rule of abstraction itself. In fact, in this way, we could say that we mean an object as a point able to calculate, itself, the geometric distance that separates it from another point. And all this does not represent a real situation at all. This further violation of the abstraction of these classes will allow us to evaluate its consequences and, at the same time, to verify the power and the coherence of object-oriented programming.

> **Remember that the geometric distance between two two-dimensional points is given by the square root of the sum of the square of the difference between the first coordinate of the first point and the first coordinate of the second point, and the square of the difference between the second coordinate of the first point and the second coordinate of the second point. So, given a point $P_1$ with coordinates $x_1$ and $y_1$, and a point $P_2$ with coordinates $x_2$ and $y_2$, their distance is calculated as follows:**

The following is the new coding of the Point class, which should then be extended by the

ThreeDimensionalPoint:

```java
public class Point {
    private int x, y;
    //omitting the rest of the class
    public double distance(Point p) {
        //square of the difference of the x of the two points
        int tmp1 = (x - p.x)*(x - p.x);
        //square of the difference of the y of the two points
        int tmp2 = (y - p.y)*(y - p.y);
        //square root of the sum of the two squares
        return Math.sqrt(tmp1 + tmp2);
    }
}
```

> **Even though not technically mandatory, in terms of the reuse paradigm, we could call the p.getX() and p.getY() methods rather than directly using the instance variables p.x and p.y. In Chapter 6, in fact, we saw that even the getter methods can implement an algorithm before returning the variable (even if the standard of implementation of the getter methods does not provide algorithms). In that case, we would reuse the possible algorithm, and if this evolves, we should not modify the call to the getter method.**

We note how in a future main() method, it would be possible to write the following code fragment:

```java
//creation of a point with coordinate x = 5 and y = 6
Point p1 = new Point(5,6);
//creation of a point with coordinate x = 10 and y = 20
Point p2 = new Point(10,20);
//call of the distance() method on the p1 object
double dist = p1.distance(p2);
//print of the result
System.out.println("The distance is " + dist);
```

We have already achieved an encouraging result!

### 10.3.3 Step 3

Note that the distance() method inherited in the ThreeDimensionalPoint subclass, needs an override to make sense. But here, the previous violations of the abstraction paradigm, begin to show us the first inconsistencies. In fact, the distance() method in the ThreeDimensionalPoint class, having to calculate the distance between two three-dimensional points, should take as input an object of ThreeDimensionalPoint type, in the following way:

```java
public class ThreeDimensionalPoint extends Point {
    private int z;
    //omitting the rest of the class

    @Override
    public double distance (ThreeDimensionalPoint p) {
        //square of the difference of the x of the two points
        int tmp1=(getX()-p.getX())*(getX()-p.getX());
        //square of the difference of the y of the two points
        int tmp2=(getY()-p.getY())*(getY()-p.getY());
        //square of the difference of the z of the two points
        int tmp3=(z-p.z)*(z-p.z);
        //square root of the sum of the three squares
        return Math.sqrt(tmp1+tmp2+tmp3);
    }
}
```

In this situation, however, we would be faced with an overload rather than an override! In fact, in the ThreeDimensionalPoint class there will be the distance(ThreeDimensionalPoint p1) method, and the distance(Point p1) method inherited from the Point class in this class. The latter, however, as we have noted previously, should not be available in this class, since it would represent the possibility of calculating the distance between a two-dimensional and a three-dimensional point.

The best solution then seems to force an override. We can rewrite the distance(Point p1) method. However, we must consider the reference p as a polymorphic parameter (see section 8.3.1) and use object casting (see section 8.3.4) within the code block to ensure the correct behaviour of the method:

```java
public class ThreeDimensionalPoint extends Point {
    private int z;
    //omitting the rest of the class

    @Override
    public double distance(Point p) {
        if (p instanceof ThreeDimensionalPoint) {
            //square of the difference of the x of the two points
            int tmp1=(getX()-p1.getX())*(getX()-p1.getX());
            //square of the difference of the y of the two points
            int tmp2=(getY()-p1.getY())*(getY()-p1.getY());
            //square of the difference of the z of the two points
            int tmp3=(z-p1.z)*(z-p1.z);
            //square root of the sum of the three squares
            return Math.sqrt(tmp1+tmp2+tmp3);
```

```
            }
        else {
            return -1; //distance not valid!
        }
    }
}
```

As anticipated, we used advanced language features to solve problems that arose from not correctly designing our solution by ignoring the abstraction rule. The distance(Point p) method should now work correctly. Finally, it is absolutely advisable to make some stylistic changes to our code, in order to ensure a better functional abstraction, and a better readability of the code:

```
public class ThreeDimensionalPoint extends Point {
    private int z;
    //omitting the rest of the class

    @Override
    public double distance(Point p) {
        if (p instanceof ThreeDimensionalPoint) {
            //Call to a private method using casting
            return this.calculateDistance((ThreeDimensionalPoint)p);
        }
        else {
            return -1; //distance not valid!
        }
    }
    private double calculateDistance(ThreeDimensionalPoint p1) {
        //square of the difference of the x of the two points
        int tmp1=(getX()-p1.getX())*(getX()-p1.getX());
        //square of the difference of the y of the two points
        int tmp2=(getY()-p1.getY())*(getY()-p1.getY());
        //square of the difference of the z of the two points
        int tmp3=(z-p1.z)*(z-p1.z);
        //square root of the sum of the three squares
        return Math.sqrt(tmp1+tmp2+tmp3);
    }
}
```

> Java also has powerful exception management, which is one of the strong points of the language (see Chapter 9). It would certainly be better to raise a custom exception rather than return a negative number, in case there is an error. You could try to implement a solution based on exceptions as an exercise.

## 10.3.4 Step 4

Now we can start writing the class containing the `main()` method. The name to be assigned should coincide with the name of the application itself. We'll opt for the `GeometricTest` identifier because, rather than considering this as a complete application, we prefer to think of it as a test for a core of working classes (`Point` and `TreeDimensionalPoint`) that can be reused in a real application.

```java
public class GeometricTest {
    public static void main(String args[]) {
        //...
    }
}
```

Usually, when we start learning a new programming language, one of the first topics that the aspiring developer learns to manage is input/output operations. When approaching Java, the output command remains mysterious for a while:

```java
System.out.println("String to print");
```

and an instruction that allows us to acquire input data remains unknown for a long time! This is due to a very precise reason: the classes that allow us to perform input/output operations are part of the `java.io` package of the standard library. This package has been designed with a very specific philosophy, based on the *Decorator design pattern* (for information about Design Patterns see Appendix D, for information on the Decorator pattern see Chapter 20). The result is initial difficulties in approaching the subject, but these are offset by simplicity and effectiveness once the concepts on which it is based are understood. For example, an aspiring programmer may find it difficult to understand why, to print a string on the screen, the Java creators have implemented such a complex mechanism (`System.out.println()`). For a Java programmer, it is very easy to use the same methods to perform complex output operations, such as writing to a file or sending messages over the network. We refer the reader to Chapter 20 regarding input/output for details. Meanwhile, we will use the mechanism based on the arguments of the `main()` method, already presented in section 3.6.7.

So, let's code our main class, calling it `GeometricTest`. We use the `main()` arguments and a standard library method (`Integer.parseInt()`) to get an integer from a string:

```
public class GeometricTest {
    public static void main(String args[]) {
        //Get integers from strings
        int p1X = Integer.parseInt(args[0]);
        int p1Y = Integer.parseInt(args[1]);
        int p2X = Integer.parseInt(args[2]);
        int p2Y = Integer.parseInt(args[3]);
        //Creating two points
        Point p1 = new Point(p1X, p1Y);
        Point p2 = new Point(p2X, p2Y);
        //Print the distance
        System.out.println("the distance is " + p1. distance(p2));
    }
}
```

We can now compile and run the application, for example by writing from the command line:

```
java GeometricTest 5 6 10 20
```

that will produce the following output:

```
the distance is 14.866068747318506
```

To run this application, we are obliged to specify four arguments from the command line, in order to not get an exception. Otherwise, at runtime, the Java Virtual Machine will encounter variables with undefined values such as `args[0]`.

## 10.3.5 Step 5

We can improve our application in such a way that it can also calculate the distance between two three-dimensional points. We first introduce an algorithm to check if the right number of arguments has been specified: if there are four parameters, the distance between two two-dimensional points is calculated, if there are six parameters, the distance between two three-dimensional points is calculated. In all other cases, an explanatory message is presented and the execution of the program ends, preventing any exceptions at runtime.

```
public class GeometricTest {
    public static void main(String args[]) {
        /* Declaring the local variables */
        Point p1 = null, p2 = null;
        /* testing if this program has been called specifying the
        right number of arguments from the command line*/
```

```
        if (args.length == 4) {
            //Get integers from strings
            int p1X = Integer.parseInt(args[0]);
            int p1Y = Integer.parseInt(args[1]);
            int p2X = Integer.parseInt(args[2]);
            int p2Y = Integer.parseInt(args[3]);
            //Creating two points
            p1 = new Point(p1X, p1Y);
            p2 = new Point(p2X, p2Y);
        }
        else if (args.length == 6) {
            //Get integers from strings
            int p1X = Integer.parseInt(args[0]);
            int p1Y = Integer.parseInt(args[1]);
            int p1Z = Integer.parseInt(args[3]);
            int p2X = Integer.parseInt(args[4]);
            int p2Y = Integer.parseInt(args[5]);
            int p2Z = Integer.parseInt(args[6]);
            //Creating two points
            p1 = new ThreeDimensionalPoint(p1X, p1Y, p1Z);
            p2 = new ThreeDimensionalPoint(p2X, p2Y, p2Z);
        }
        else {
            System.out.println("insert  4 or 6 arguments");
            System.exit(0); // Application exit
        }
        //Print the distance
        System.out.println("the distance is " + p1.distance(p2));
    }
}
```

The `Point` and `ThreeDimensionalPoint` **classes now seem to be reusable "behind" other applications... or maybe not...**

## 10.4 Introduction to Testing and Logging

But are we sure that the code we have written is correct? Are we really sure that the classes in our simple application work in any scenario? Is it possible that they behave in an unexpected way in certain scenarios?

Well, we can never say that! In fact, the perfect application does not exist. Perhaps in simple applications such as ours, it is possible to succeed in not introducing malfunctions but, in a real application, an unexpected behaviour (a *bug*) is always possible and probably unavoidable.

How can we then create an application that does not have any bugs (or at least that does not present important bugs)? There are several approaches that make it possible to drastically reduce software malfunctions. There are programming and software development cycle techniques that have been designed to reduce and manage bugs. There are also real methodologies that promise "zero bug" code, but we believe it is sufficient for this book to limit ourselves only to introducing a relatively simple technique to learn and experiment: *Unit Testing*. Later, we will also briefly introduce *Logging*.

### 10.4.1 Unit Testing in Theory

Before starting to describe what a **unit test** is, let's start by defining what a **test** is. There are various types of tests, the most famous are:

■ **Unit Test**: should ensure that every unit works correctly.

■ **Integration Test:** should ensure that the various components of the software work correctly together when connected.

■ **System Test**: should be done using the same interface that the end user will use.

We will only focus on the first type of test: unit tests.

> **There are other types of tests which however, it does not seem appropriate to introduce in this book.**

The unit test is a technique that has existed for years and has found its definitive success at the same time as the rise of free and open source software called *JUnit* (for information and download, see **http://www.junit.org**).

 **The Unit Test's great fame was also propitiated by the success of some methodological processes such as "Extreme Programming" (XP), whose main author (Kent Beck) is also one of the creators of JUnit. XP is today relatively little used, surpassed by other methods such as Scrum (for information** https://www.scrum.org/resources/what-is-scrum**). But historically XP was one of the first processes to embrace the agile manifesto** (http://agilemanifesto.org/iso/it/manifesto.html)**.**

This software is integrated as a plug-in in most professional development tools like Eclipse and Netbeans. The idea behind unit testing is really simple. If our code has to work, let's test it *class by class*, by designing and writing **test cases**, that is, the *code that tests our code*! Often the first idea that comes to mind after reading the previous sentence is: "What? Write the tests before the program itself?" and the second one is "but if I have to write some code to ensure that my software will not contain bugs, who assures me that the code of my tests does not, in turn, have bugs?" Yes, these questions are absolutely justified, but that's not all! You have to know that it is the belief and practice of many developers, especially those who practise (or sometimes think of practising) agile processes, to always write the tests before and then the class to implement. How is it possible? Does the world now turn backwards? But if you think about it, it's not so strange ... let's take a moment to think about the history of programming languages. At the dawn of programming, developers programmed using punched cards with a language called *Assembly*. This language allows access to the system on which it is developed, in an unlimited way, and although it is a very powerful language, it is also a very dangerous language. In fact, is also a favourite language of virus developers. To make a long story short, then other languages were born with less and less permissive compilers, COBOL, C, C++ and finally Java (and later others). The robustness of Java is also guaranteed by its compiler which, as we have seen several times in previous chapters, is also very "strict" in situations that compilers of other languages do not check at all. The theory of Unit Test is, after all, inspired by this simple theory: if we want robust classes, we have to first create a small compiler for the class itself! Does everything not seem more rational now? Well, then, let's try to understand, in practice, how to create and use our unit tests. Maybe we will learn to avoid introducing bugs in the tests we write.

If we want to write small compilers for our classes, we have to create classes that verify that, what is written (or maybe what we want to write), functions properly.

> **A unit test could be created before the class to be tested. In this way, it will also represent an element that designs the class itself. However, it is useful to write unit tests, even after creating the class to be tested.**

For each class of our application it is good practice to create another test class. For each method of our class, we need to create a variable number of methods (*test cases*) in the test class, each of which calls the method to be tested with different inputs, and verifies that the output is as expected. So, the number of possible bugs that the method to test could generate in our application, goes down as the number of verified test cases increases.

## 10.4.2 Unit Test in Practice with JUnit

For example, let's take our `Point` class. We could call our test class `PointTest`. Then we try to test the only non-trivial method of this class, the `distance()` method. We have already asserted that, for each method to be tested, we must identify a variable number of test cases. That is, we will have to pass different inputs verifying that the output of the method is the expected one. The fact that the possible inputs of the method are practically infinite does not mean, however, that we have to create an endless number of test cases! To be able to design all the tests that will allow us to consider the method as working and robust, we can use a simple technique: **equivalence classes**. If we want to simplify the concept, we can say that we have to try to create a test case for each *class of equivalence* for methods input. By "equivalence class" we mean: given the set of all possible test cases of the method, it is possible to group these cases into subgroups (called equivalence classes) whose elements are linked by an equivalence relation, that is, from a certain point of view these elements are equivalent. This means, for example, that if we want to verify that the distance of the point with coordinates $x = 1$ and $y = 1$ from the point with coordinates $x = 1$ and $y = 2$ is 1, it will be useless to verify that the distance from the point with coordinates $x = 1$ and $y = 3$ is 2. These two tests are bound by an **equivalence relation** (that of belonging to the same abscissa) and therefore are part of the same equivalence class. If we choose to only implement the first case, then we have to write the following code:

```
import org.junit.Assert;
import org.junit.Test;

public class PointTest {
    @Test
    public void testDistanceOnX() {
        Point p1 = new Point(1,1);
        Point p2 = new Point(1,2);
        double distance = p1.distance(p2);
        Assert.assertTrue(distance == 1);
    }
}
```

Using JUnit is particularly simple. As we can see, we essentially used the @Test annotation and the static method assertTrue() of the org.junit.Assert class.

Our test class does not have a main() method. It can simply contain various methods which, if annotated by @Test, will be automatically invoked by JUnit when the command is executed:

```
java org.junit.runner.JUnitCore PointTest
```

Note that we are passing the name of our PointTest class as an argument to the JUnitCore class, which belongs to the org.junit.runner package. This command will only work if the junit.jar file is included among the values that can be associated with the CLASSPATH variable. For information on setting the classpath, refer to Appendix E. If we use an IDE such as Eclipse, just run JUnit from the appropriate menu.

With the last instruction of the method:

```
Assert.assertTrue(distance == 1);
```

JUnit will generate a success message or an error report, depending on whether the condition `distance == 1` is verified or not.

If you had a test class in mind, you probably conceived it with two small differences: a `main()` method, required to run a class, and instead of the final method statement, a simple `System.out.println(distance)` to print the result. Not bad, except for the fact that there is a need for the human eye to verify the correctness of the test. With JUnit, we can automate these checks with assertions.

> JUnit was born when, at the time, Java did not support the `assert` keyword (see Chapter 9). So, when we talk about assertions in JUnit, we mean a series of test methods that have names like `assertTrue()` or `assertEquals()`, which have the task of deciding whether or not a certain condition (or assertion) is verified.

In this way, we can create a series of test methods in a test class. This test class can also be performed in the future, perhaps when our classes have been modified. In this way, we will only have to verify that the tests are successful, without having to read the written code to understand what it had to do. For example, if, in a few months, we modify the `distance()` method, to test its correctness, it will be enough to re-run our test class. In the event of an error, the output of JUnit will allow us to investigate the problem.

> It is also possible to run a set of test classes with a single command.

Let's now design other test cases to verify the correctness of the `distance()` method. To identify test cases, it is sometimes useful to think about situations that, if it depended on us, we would always try to avoid. For example, an interesting test case could be the one that passes to the method instead of an object of type `Point`, a `null` value. Another case could be to calculate the distance between two points with the same coordinates. We could also verify the robustness of our solution by passing an object of type `TreeDimensionalPoint` (polymorphic parameter) to the `distance()` method. Let's write these tests, enriching the `PointTest` class:

```
import org.junit.Assert;
import org.junit.Test;
```

```
public class PointTest {
    @Test
    public void testDistanceOnX() {
        Point p1 = new Point(1,1);
        Point p2 = new Point(1,2);
        double distance = p1.distance(p2);
        Assert.assertTrue(distance == 1);
    }

    @Test
    public void testDistanceWithNull() {
        Point p1 = new Point(1,1);
        Point p2 = null;
        double distance = p1.distance(p2);
        Assert.assertTrue(distance == -1);
    }

    @Test
    public void testDistanceFromTheSamePoint() {
        Point p1 = new Point(1,1);
        Point p2 = new Point(1,1);
        double distance = p1.distance(p2);
        Assert.assertTrue(distance == 0);
    }

    @Test
    public void testDistanceFromAThreeDimensionalPoint() {
        Point p1 = new Point(1,1);
        Point p2 = new ThreeDimensionalPoint(1,2,2);
        double distance = p1.distance(p2);
        Assert.assertTrue(distance == -1);
    }
}
```

For now, let's just do these tests. In Figure 10.1, we can see the result of the execution of our test, using Eclipse, which includes JUnit with a GUI.

As we can see, there are problems! 50% of our tests failed, and we only created a few tests! In particular, the test called testDistanceWithNull(), even ended with an unexpected exception (a NullPointerException, see Chapter 9).

> **As an exercise, you should try to solve the problems highlighted by JUnit.**

It is possible that the reader who has no work (or academic) experience of programming, has no idea what it means to develop software. We only have a few lines available but there are large books that describe these topics. So, for those who don't have real development experience, it

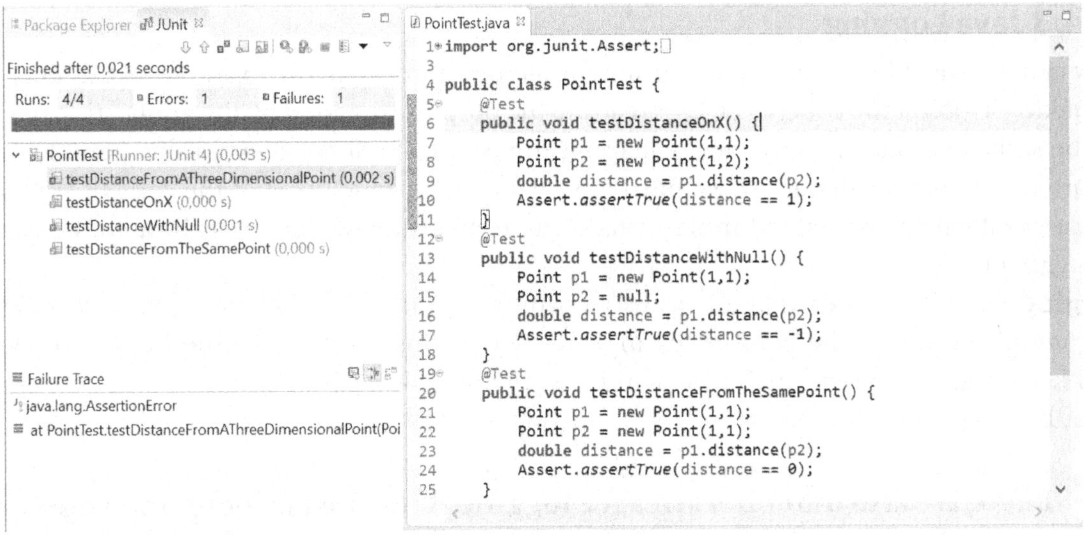

**Figure 10.1 – JUnit Output on Eclipse.**

is important to know that, when a project starts, it is very likely that you will not be the only developer. There will be other people to share information, techniques and knowledge with, and not all of them will be developers, but everyone has tasks and responsibilities (see Chapter 5). The developer's responsibility should not be limited to creating software starting from requirements. It is also important to be sure that the written code works, is documented, and that it is clear what objectives were to be implemented. All developers who can or will have access to the code in the future, must be able to use the code. When unit tests are done, they also make explicit the objectives of a class.

This is not to say that you must necessarily test all the classes you create. You probably do not feel the need (even if the last example should make you reflect on this) and you probably would like to program in a less "extreme" way. You are not obliged to test every class, and maybe you should not have so much time, it is very often too expensive to write so many test cases. But having automated tests that allow you to test the regression of the software (the more code you introduce, the greater the chance of introducing bugs), is, however, a benefit worth having. So, we would like to suggest the creation of test cases, at least, on all the most important features, if you do not want to test class by class. In this case, however, we cannot say we're using "unit tests", but JUnit is still a very useful tool.

> Remember that to find the bugs, the IDE makes available the fundamental tool called *debugger*, which we introduced in Chapter 5.

**399**

### 10.4.3 Java Logging

How can we find a bug? It is likely that for simple programs (like the example in this chapter), just taking a look at the code, or at least reading the outputs provided by the application or tests, can be sufficient. But when we face real applications, it will not be so easy to find and fix bugs. Before we can use the debugger, we need to understand in which part of the code the problem resides. Only after understood more or less where the cause of the bug is located, we can set debugging points.

**Logging** is the technique that allows us to print *information about the instructions that the application is running* on the console, or in a file. To do this, we can use the library known as **Java Logging**, defined within the java.util.logging package, included in the module named java.logging.

> There are also other libraries for logging. The most famous and widely used is undoubtedly *log4j*, whose second version can be downloaded at https://logging.apache.org/log4j/2.x/. Many developers prefer log4j, since it was born before Java logging, and for some it is more complete and performs better. However, Java Logging is an official library, so we chose to use it to present this topic.

**Log outputs** can be printed on standard output (the console, just like with System.out. println()), but also in a file or on a network stream. The essential advantage over a simple printout is that, with Java Logging, it is possible to associate a **severity level** with the message to be printed, and consequently to filter their print. In fact, it is possible to determine which messages should be printed, specifying severity levels at runtime.

> We can also filter the printing by specifying the package name or the name of the individual classes.

For example, let's consider the following code:

```
import java.util.logging.*;
import java.io.*;

public class LoggingExample {
    private final static Logger LOGGER = Logger.getLogger(LoggingExample.class.getName());
    public static void main(String args[]) throws IOException {
        configureLog();
        LOGGER.info("Level INFO Log");
```

```
        LOGGER.finest("Level FINEST Log");
    }
    private static void configureLog() throws IOException {
        Handler fileHandler = new FileHandler("file.log");
        Logger.getLogger("LoggingExample").addHandler(fileHandler);
        Logger.getLogger("LoggingExample").setLevel(Level.INFO);
    }
}
```

> **We have omitted instructions to handle exceptions in order to have a simpler code.**

This class initially declares a static constant LOGGER of type Logger, which is created starting from the name of the class, with the getLogger() factory method. Note that, in this case, we could also write:

```
Logger.getLogger("LoggingExample");
```

in place of:

```
Logger.getLogger(LoggingExample.class.getName());
```

> **The code that we used in the example that does not use a string (always subject to typos), is still recommended. There, we use a technique called *Reflection*, which will be presented in Chapter 13.**

The main() method first calls the configureLog() method, and then invokes the printing methods for the log, the first associated with the INFO level and the second associated with the FINEST level. The configureLog() method creates a FileHandler object with the name of a file that will be created to host log messages. Then the fileHandler object is linked with the LOGGER using the addHandler() method. In this way, the log will be printed in a file called **file.log**. Furthermore, the log level is set as INFO, using the setLevel() method.

The LOGGER object has methods for each log level. Java Logging defines seven levels listed in the following table in order of priority, together with the corresponding Logger class method to use:

| Level | Logger Method |
|-------|---------------|
| SEVERE | severe() |
| WARNING | warning() |

| INFO | info() |
|------|--------|
| CONFIG | config() |
| FINE | fine() |
| FINER | finer() |
| FINEST | finest() |

> **The logger methods are overloaded in order to pass an exception as a second parameter, whose information will be included in the log record. Furthermore, in addition to the methods listed, it is also possible to use the** log() **method in an equivalent way, taking advantage of the fact that the level can be specified as a parameter. For example:**
>
> ```
> LOGGER.severe("Level SEVERE Log", exception);
> ```
>
> **is equivalent to writing:**
>
> ```
> LOGGER.log(Level.SEVERE, "Level SEVERE Log", exception);
> ```

The LoggingExample class, when executed, prints a file called **file.log** in XML format. This format (which we will discuss in detail in Chapter 22) allows us to specify information using **tags**, constructs that may contain other tags. The output contained in the **file.log** file is as follows:

```xml
<?xml version="1.0" encoding="windows-1252" standalone="no"?>
<!DOCTYPE log SYSTEM "logger.dtd">
<log>
<record>
  <date>2019-01-22T16:36:25.987742600Z</date>
  <millis>1548174985987</millis>
  <nanos>742600</nanos>
  <sequence>0</sequence>
  <logger>LoggingExample</logger>
  <level>INFO</level>
  <class>LoggingExample</class>
  <method>main</method>
  <thread>1</thread>
  <message>Log Level INFO</message>
</record>
</log>
```

Even without knowing XML, it is possible to interpret this output. Within the record tag (which is opened with <record> and closed with </record>), some information is defined. Included in this information, we can distinguish the message tag, which contains the log string (INFO level) that we had specified with the instruction:

```
LOGGER.info ("Log at INFO level");
```

Instead, the FINEST type log will not be printed in the file, since FINEST has the lowest priority level with respect to INFO, as we have seen in the table.

In order to see both logs printed, we should specify in the configureLog() method the Level.FINEST level for the LoggingExample class.

The argument is quite long, and we will not go further into it, for the reasons specified above. But of course, it is easy to predict that the level of an application's log can be changed even during the runtime of the application. In this way, we can decide when to enable or disable certain levels, in order to investigate any unexpected behaviour in our applications.

## Summary

In this chapter, we have seen an **example** of how we can write an application step by step. The purpose of this chapter was to simulate the development of a simple application and the problems that may arise during development. The problems were solved one by one, sometimes even by forcing solutions. It has been pointed out that when we don't follow some rules (for example abstraction), it naturally leads to problems. In addition, we tried to understand how we can implement some object-oriented features with concrete examples.

Chapters 6, 7 and 8 of this first volume, are dedicated exclusively to the support that Java offers to Object-Orientation. But of course, it does not end there! There are many other topics to be studied, such as the advanced features of the language. It is essential to understand that the work of a programmer who knows Java at a medium level, but who has a good OO method for development, is worth much more than the work of a programmer with a formidable Java preparation level, but without a good OO method. The advice is, therefore, to improve your knowledge on Object Orientation as soon as possible, even if, being topics of a more abstract level, we must first feel ready to study them for a gain of some kind. As always, the best way to learn certain arguments is by practising. Being close to an experienced person (mentor) while developing is, from our point of view, the best way to grow fast. The theory to be learned is indeed very huge, but the most complicated thing, is to put the described techniques correctly into practice. An additional difficulty to overcome, is the point of view of authors of the various methodologies. It is not rare to find in two texts of different authors, an opposing advice for solving the same type of problem. As already stated, therefore, the reader must develop a critical eye towards their studies; such an approach to the study of OO requires, therefore, a discrete experience of development.

In the final part of the chapter, we also mentioned **testing** practices (using the **JUnit** tool). We have seen that creating the tests first, and then the classes that these tests have to test, is not such a strange idea. Just consider the test classes as mini compilers for our classes. JUnit uses the **assertion** concept, which allows us to write code that asserts what conditions must be verified for a certain test to be passed. The great advantage of writing a test suite to test all of our classes (or even some) is that, once written, we can also run it every day to check if our development has caused some regression in the software (bugs). It will actually work as a class compiler. This approach is very useful, especially for a software company with many developers.

Finally, we only introduced the concept of **logging**, talking about the **Java Logging** framework. It allows us to print **log messages** that contain information about the instructions that the application is running, which can be enabled or disabled based on a level that can also be set at runtime. In this way, we can decide to easily read only the log messages that most interest us.

> **Exercises, source code, appendices and other resources are available at http://www.javaforaliens.com.**

# Part II Conclusions

The second part of the book ends here. While in the first part, almost exclusively, programming topics were presented, in this second part, we tried to concentrate on the theoretical part, while also thinking about analysis and design. The goal is to direct you to practices that lead you to create better code, that is easy to modify and with which it is easy to interact. As you can imagine, practice will be the best ally. In fact, only by directly facing the issues described, will one realize how much one can really influence the fact that software can be considered a success or not.

## Chapter Goals

Have the following goals been achieved?

| Goal | Achieved | Achievement Date |
|---|---|---|
| Have in mind what it means to develop an application in Java using the object-oriented programming paradigms (Units 10.1, 10.2, 10.3) | O | |
| Understand what it means to test your software automatically with JUnit (Unit 10.4) | O | |
| Be introduced to the usefulness of the "Java Logging" API (Unit 10.4) | O | |

# Part III
## Java Language Advanced Features

Part III will present the reader with the most important advanced features of the language. Some concepts are developed to a very high degree and, in general, the concepts themselves are, on average, more complicated than those seen so far. Even seemingly simple topics like enumerations present us with rather complex situations.
Part III consists of two chapters:

1. In the eleventh chapter, we will talk about enumerations and their advanced features. In addition, we will present nested types and therefore also internal classes and anonymous classes, topics that can lead to many complex scenarios.

2. Part III concludes with the last chapter of this first volume, where *generic programming* is introduced. At the same time, key implementations of the *Collections* library are also presented, as well as all advanced features such as type erasure, wildcards, bounded wildcards and parameters, generic methods, intersection types, wildcard capture, helper methods, covariant parameters and so on.

The advanced features of Java will evolve later when we will also define other types of programming such as *multi-threaded*, *functional* and meta-programming. The next two chapters are preparation for those that come afterwards which will allow us explore some of the most important standard Java libraries.
As always, we recommend that the reader carries out all of the proposed exercises.

# 11

# Enumerations and Nested Types

> **Goals:**
>
> At the end of this chapter, the reader should:
>
> ✓ Understand what nested types are (Unit 11.1).
> ✓ List the basic properties of nested classes (Unit 11.1).
> ✓ Know how to define and use anonymous classes (Unit 11.2).
> ✓ Understand how to use enumerations (Unit 11.3).
> ✓ Understand how to use the advanced features of enumerations (Unit 11.3).
> ✓ Understand when to use `static` imports (Unit 11.4).

In Chapter 2, we introduced the fundamental components of Java programming, but we limited ourselves to the indispensable concepts. We only mentioned the other fundamental components of Java programming in the last section of the second chapter, since analyzing the topic was still premature.

Now the time has come to introduce enumerations, which, like classes and interfaces (and as we will see, annotations), are usually saved in files with the suffix **.java**. The concept of an enumeration is not complicated, but the advanced features will need some explaining.

In this chapter, we will explore two main topics: nested types and enumerations. A knowledge of nested types is required prior to making an advanced definition of enumerations. Both topics are simple enough to learn if we limit their use to the basics. They become much more complex when we want to apply the advanced features of these new definitions. The properties of nested types are particularly tricky and not well-known to most Java programmers. More common, instead, are anonymous classes which, up to Java 7, represented the most dynamic, concise and functional way of writing Java code.

The second part of the chapter is probably more interesting. We will define enumerations with the support of simple examples. After presenting the reasons why enumerations constitute a real strong point of Java, we will present their properties, the advanced features (specific methods, overrides through anonymous classes, constructors, etc.), their relationship with object-oriented paradigms, and with programming elements such as `switch` construct and `static` imports. Furthermore, we will try to understand what the compiler does for us, and we will see how all enumerations also extend the `java.lang.Enum` class, inheriting its methods.

# 11.1 Nested Classes

A **nested class** is a class that is defined within another class. A nested class has some properties, and there are different scenarios to analyze in order to use a nested class correctly. For example, we can mark a nested class with some modifiers that cannot be used with ordinary classes, for example `protected` and `static`. From a nested class it is possible to access the members of the class in which it is defined. We can also define a nested class within a method. Further when we compile a class that contains a nested class, two files will be created, one for the external class, and one for the internal class, which will be called respectively: **OuterClassName.class** and **OuterClassName$InnerClassName.class**.

> **The name of the nested class must be different from the name of the class that contains it.**

Some topics that concern nested classes, can be particularly complex, and all in all, the nested classes are used relatively rarely. In fact, there are only a few development niches (for example the one relating to graphic interfaces) where they are extensively used.

 Note that in the title of this chapter we talked about **nested types** because the same concepts that we will present in particular for classes, can also be generalized for interfaces, enumerations and annotations. Let's start talking about nested classes, which are not static, called *inner classes*.

### 11.1.1 Nested Classes: Definition

A **nested class** (or even an **inner class** if it is not declared as static) is just a class defined within another class. For example:

```java
public class Outer {
    private String message = "In the class ";
    private void printMessage() {
        System.out.println(message + "Outer");
    }
    /* the inner class can use the members declared by the containing class*/
```

```
    public class Inner {
        // inner class
        public void method() {
            System.out.println(message + "Inner");
        }
        public void callMethod() {
            printMessage();
        }
        //. . .
    }
    //. . .
}
```

The advantage of implementing one class within another is primarily about saving code. In fact, the inner class has access to instance and static members of the outer class, even when declared private. In the example, the method() method of the Inner inner class uses the private message instance variable, which is, however, defined in the Outer external class. The same goes for the method called callMethod() in the Inner inner class, which calls the external class printMessage() method.

Nested classes can declare instance members (variables and methods), but not static members. The only static members allowed are constants. In fact, if, for example, we declare a static variable in the following way in the Inner inner class:

```
    public static String staticVariable = "Inner";
```

we will get the following compile-time error:

```
Outer.java:9: error: Illegal static declaration in inner class Outer.Inner
        public static String staticVariable = "Inner";
                      ^
    modifier 'static' is only allowed in constant variable declarations
1 error
```

If, instead, we also add the final modifier to the variable, making it constant:

```
    public final static String staticVariable = "Inner";
```

the code will compile correctly.

## 11.1.2 Nested Classes: Properties

 We have seen that a nested class is declared within another class. In particular, in the example, an inner class was declared at the same level as the instance members. We will see, however, in section 11.1.2.4, that we can declare nested classes, even within methods (*local nested classes*). Actually, an inner class is not simply a class declared within another class, it has different properties than an ordinary class.

### 11.1.2.1 Access Modifiers and Scope

Ordinary classes can only use public as an access modifier or not use modifiers (*default modifier*), and we saw in the sixth chapter how this implies that this class is accessible outside the package in which it is declared, or not. So, it is not possible for an ordinary class to use protected and private modifiers.

Instead, nested classes can be declared using all access modifiers as if they were instance members of a class. This implies that instances of a nested class follow the rules of modifiers as described in section 6.7. For example, if we declare a private nested class, it will be instantiable only within the class that contains it while a nested class declared as public, can also be instantiated outside the class that contains it but with a very particular syntax as we will see in the next section.

### 11.1.2.2 Instantiating Nested Classes

 Let's consider the following class which contains two nested classes, one of which is public (PublicInner) and one private (PrivateInner), along with an instance method (printPrivateInstance()):

```java
public class OuterInstances {
    //Public nested class
    public class PublicInner {
        private String name = "PublicInner";
        public void printName() {
            System.out.println(name);
        }
    }
    //Private nested class
    private class PrivateInner {
        private String name = "PrivateInner";
        public void printName() {
            System.out.println(name);
        }
    }
    //Instance OuterInstances method
    private void printPrivateInstance() {
        PrivateInner privateInner = new PrivateInner();
        privateInner.printName();
    }
}
```

In the printPrivateInstance() method the PrivateInner nested class is instantiated in the usual way, and its method printName() is called. But outside the OuterInstances class, the PrivateInner nested class is not visible. Furthermore, instantiating a nested class outside the class that contains it is not trivial at all. In fact, a nested class, being declared within a class that contains it, cannot exist without it. To refer to a nested class, we need to use a syntax of the type: ExternalClassName.InternalClassName.

In particular, if we wanted to instantiate an inner class outside the class in which it is defined, we need to take certain steps. Referring to the previous example, we need to:

1. instantiate the external class (in which the inner class is declared):

   ```
   OuterIstances outerIstances = new OuterIstances();
   ```

2. declare the object we want to instantiate from the inner class through the external class (using the dot operator):

   ```
   OuterIstances.PublicInner publicInner;
   ```

3. instantiate the object from the inner class through the object instantiated by the external class (note the call to the new operator invoked using the dot operator):

   ```
   publicInner = outerIstances.new PublicInner();
   ```

The output of the compilation of the following file:

```
public class OuterInstancesTest {
    public static void main(String args[]) {
        OuterInstances outerInstances = new OuterInstances();
        outerInstances.printPrivateInstance();
        OuterInstances.PublicInner publicInner = outerInstances.new PublicInner();
        publicInner.printName();
    }
}
```

will be:

```
PrivateInner
PublicInner
```

We first instantiated the OuterInstances class. Then on this object we invoked the method printPrivateInstance() which printed the name variable of the PrivateInner private nested class. Finally, we instantiated the PublicInner public nested class with the syntax described above.

 In the printPrivateInstance() method of OuterInstances, to instantiate the PrivateInner class, we can also use as an alternative syntax:

```
OuterInstances.PrivateInner privateInner = new OuterInstances.PrivateInner();
```

since the PrivateInner inner class cannot exist without the OuterInstances class that

**411**

contains it. This last syntax, although more verbose, seems more correct than the one we used in the example. We could also use the following syntax:

```
OuterInstances.PrivateInner privateInner = new PrivateInner();
```

while the following would be invalid:

```
PrivateInner privateInner = new OuterInstances.PrivateInner();
```

since it is the right side of the assignment that "commands".
In fact, the following statement is also valid:

```
var privateInner = new OuterInstances.PrivateInner();
```

### 11.1.2.3 The this Reference

In the methods of an inner class, we can use the this reference. With it we can refer to the members of the inner class and not the class that contains it. To reference a member of the external class the following syntax should be used:

```
ExternalClassName.this.memberName
```

This clarification is important if there is a possibility of ambiguity between members of the internal class and members of the external class. In fact, it is possible to have an internal and an external class that declare a member with the same identifier (say, an instance variable named foo). Within the methods of the inner class, if we do not specify a reference for the variable foo the reference this will be implicitly used. Therefore, the instance variable of the inner class will be referenced. To reference the variable of the external class, it is therefore necessary to use the syntax:

```
ExternalClassName.this.memberName
```

For example, the output of the following code:

```java
public class Outer2 {
    private String string = "outer";
    public class Inner2 {
        private String string = "inner";
        public void methodInner() {
            System.out.println(Outer2.this.string + " " + this.string);
        }
    }
    public static void main(String [] args) {
        Outer2 outer = new Outer2();
        Outer2.Inner2 inner = outer.new Inner2();
        inner.methodInner();
    }
}
```

will be the following:

```
outer inner
```

> The previous rules are also applied to other data structures not yet addressed such as interfaces, enumerations and annotations. Not only will it be possible to create internal classes, internal interfaces, internal enumerations and internal annotations in a class, but an enumeration or an annotation can also be created within an interface (with some exceptions). However, we are talking about programming practices that are now negligible.

### 11.1.2.4 Local Classes

A nested class can also be defined within a method and it is called a **local class**. It is possible to also declare a local class in a block of code of a construct, like that of an `if` or a `for`, and it will be accessible only within the block of code in which it was declared.

> Also note that it is not possible to declare the `Inner` local class marked with a modifier such as `private`, `protected` or `public`. Being within a method, such a declaration would not make sense.

Like all nested classes, a local class will have access to all static and instance members of the class. Local variables, on the other hand, will be accessible only if declared as `final` or are effectively unmodified (*effectively final*). For example, the following code:

```java
public class Outer {
    private String stringOuter = "JAVA";
    public void methodOuter() {
        int intLocal = 7;
        class Inner {
            public void methodInner() {
                System.out.println(stringOuter + " " + (++intLocal));
            }
        }
    }
}
```

will produce a compile-time error, as the expression ++intLocal tries to assign a new value to a local variable of the method (so it is certainly not *effectively final*).

 Up to Java 7, it was still mandatory to declare the variable with the `final` modifier. The rule has been made more flexible to allow a more gradual introduction of lambda expressions in Java 8 (see Chapter 17).

Naturally, we would have gotten an error even if we had modified the value of the variable in the method outside of the nested class.

Note that if that variable is a reference, then even when declaring it `final`, we can always modify its internal structure. For example, consider the `StringBuilder` class, already encountered in Chapter 5, which represents an editable string. The following example compiles without errors, despite the internal structure of the local variable `sbLocal` being modified internally, with the call to the `append()` method:

```java
public class Outer {
    public void methodOuter () {
        StringBuilder sbLocal = new StringBuilder("Andrea");
        class Inner {
            public void methodInner() {
                sbLocal.append("Simone");
            }
        }
    }
}
```

However, in the method `methodInner()`, a statement that reassigns the reference to another object :

```java
sbLocal = new StringBuffer("Simone");
```

would cause a compilation error.

 Taking advantage of what we have just said, we can overcome the limit that continues to exist for primitive variables. For example, referring to the first example of this section where the `intLocal` variable was not effectively final, we can package the value of `intLocal` in an array (which is an object) of size 1, as in the following code:

```java
public class Outer {
    private String outerString = "JAVA";
    public void methodOuter() {
        int intLocal = 7;
```

```
        int array [] = {intLocal};
        class Inner {
            public void methodInner() {
                System.out.println(outerString + " " + (++array[0]));
            }
        }
    }
}
```

An array is an object, and so we fall back to the previous case concerning the reference. Indeed, we modify the internal structure of the array object, without changing its pointing.

### 11.1.2.5 Static Nested Classes

 It is possible to declare a **static nested class**. In this case, however, it is automatically considered a **top-level class**. This means that it will no longer be defined as an *inner class* and will not have the property of being able to access the members (variables and methods) of the instance in which it is defined. Instead, the nested class can only access static declared members of the class that contains it. In fact, as we have already said, an *inner class* is defined as a nested class that is not static.

A nested class can declare static members only if it is declared as static (we have already noticed that instead the inner classes can declare static variables only if they are also declared final, or they can only declare static constants). Consider for example, the following class:

```
public class OuterStatic {
    public static class InnerStatic {
        public String field ="Instance Variable";
        public static String staticField ="Static variable";
    }
}
```

In the OuterStatic class we declared the static nested class InnerStatic, which declares an instance variable (field) and a static variable (staticField). In the following class instead, first we print the static variable directly, and then we instantiate the static nested class:

```
public class OuterStaticTest {
    public static void main(String args[]) {
        System.out.println(OuterStatic.InnerStatic.staticField);
        OuterStatic.InnerStatic innerStatic = new OuterStatic.InnerStatic();
        System.out.println(innerStatic.field);
    }
}
```

In practice, a static nested class has been defined as a top level class because it is as if it were an ordinary class, whose type has a syntax like the following:

```
ExternalClass.NestedClass
```

**415**

In fact, the `InnerStatic` static nested class that we saw in the previous example actually belongs to the `OuterStatic` class and is referred to as `OuterStatic.InnerStatic`. Therefore, to instantiate the static nested class, the syntax we saw for inner classes is not required. It is the same syntax we usually use for ordinary classes, only that the type of the object is `OuterStatic.InnerStatic`.

### 11.1.2.6 Abstract Nested Classes

A nested class can also be declared `abstract`, and can be extended. Consider the following example:

```java
public class OuterAbstract {
    public abstract class InnerAbstract {
        public abstract void abstractMethod();
    }
    public static abstract class InnerStaticAbstract {
        public abstract void abstractMethod();
    }
//  public abstract static void test();
}
```

The `OuterAbstract` class declares two nested abstract classes: `InnerAbstract` and `InnerStaticAbstract`. The latter is also declared `static`.

The last line of the `OuterAbstract` class is a comment, which shows the declaration of a method marked with the `abstract` and `static` modifiers. If this line were not inside a comment, we would have a compilation error, since a pair of `abstract` and `static` modifiers is not compatible for a method (see section 7.6.2). Instead, in the example, we have seen that `abstract` and `static` can be used to mark a nested class.

### 11.1.2.7 Nested Classes Extended Outside the Containing Class

In the previous section we defined two abstract classes in the `OuterAbstract` class. We can create other inner classes that extend these abstract classes within the `OuterAbstract` class, in the following way:

```java
public class InnerAbstractImpl extends InnerAbstract {
    @Override
    public void abstractMethod() {
    }
}
public static class InnerStaticAbstractImpl extends InnerStaticAbstract {
    @Override
    public void abstractMethod() {
    }
}
```

> The `InnerStaticAbstractImpl` **inner class was declared** `static`, **but even a non-static class could have extended** `InnerStaticAbstract`.

Now consider the following class which declares an inner class and a static nested class:

```
public class OuterInheritance {
    public class InnerInheritance {
        public void method() {
            System.out.println("InnerInheritance");
        }
    }
    public static class InnerStaticInheritance {
        public void method() {
            System.out.println("InnerStaticInheritance");
        }
    }
}
```

We can also extend the nested classes of the previous example outside of the `OuterInheritance` class. As regards the `InnerStaticInheritance` static nested class, since it is a top-level class, it can be extended it in the following way:

```
public class InnerStaticInheritanceSubClass extends OuterInheritance.InnerStaticInheritance {
    // code omitted
}
```

If, on the other hand, we want to extend the non-static `InnerInheritance` class, the situation changes: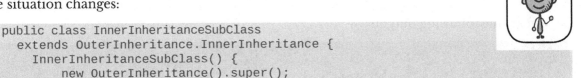

```
public class InnerInheritanceSubClass
    extends OuterInheritance.InnerInheritance {
    InnerInheritanceSubClass() {
        new OuterInheritance().super();
    }
}
```

We were forced to add a constructor that instantiates the `OuterInheritance` class which includes the inner class `InnerInheritance` that we are extending. Through the `super()` call, we explicitly invoke the `OuterInheritance` constructor. This is because we cannot access an inner class without an instance of the external class.

### 11.1.2.8 Deeper Nested Classes

It is also possible to create classes nested within nested classes. For example, the following code declares a `Level1Class` class, which contains a `Level2Class` inner class, which in turn declares a Level3Class inner class:

```java
public class Level1Class {
    private int levelVariable = 1;
    class Level2Class {
        private int levelVariable = 2;
        class Level3Class {
            private int levelVariable = 3;
            private void testThis() {
                System.out.println(Level1Class.this.levelVariable);
                System.out.println(Level2Class.this.levelVariable);
                System.out.println(this.levelVariable);
            }
        }
    }
}
```

The Level3Class class that is nested in the Level2Class class, which is in turn nested in the Level1Class class, declares a testThis() method that accesses all three levelVariable variables declared in the three classes, using the reference this as already seen in section 11.1.2.3. To instantiate the Level3Class class, of course, we need to instantiate first Level1Class, then the Level2Class inner class, and finally Level3Class:

```java
Level1Class l1 = new Level1Class();
Level1Class.Level2Class l2 = l1.new Level2Class();
Level1Class.Level2Class.Level3Class l3 = l2.new Level3Class();
```

then invoking the testThis() method:

```java
l3.testThis();
```

we will get the following output:

```
1
2
3
```

> **After compilation will be created the files:**
> Level1Class.class, Level1Class$Level2Class.class **and**
> Level1Class$Level2Class$Level3Class.class.

## 11.1.3 When to Use Nested Classes

From the object-oriented point of view, usually, a constraint or requirement should not recommend the implementation of a nested class. This means that in general, we can always code without nested classes from a design point of view. The advantage lies, above all, in saving code in certain situations (such as when we have to create an event handler for a graphical interface, as explained in Chapter 23 dedicated to GUIs). It may be desirable to create a nested class only in cases where there is a strong exclusive interoperable relationship between two classes, so as to create a two-way dependency between the two. For example, a Car class may need a Mechanic class to perform repairs. A mechanic must have access to the Car to be able to repair it (biunivocal dependence). Assuming that we fit into a very specific context where a mechanic always has a particular car to handle, then it might seem valid to declare the Mechanic class as an inner class. In fact, the solution, without a nested class, would require the coding of the following classes:

```java
public class CarNoInner {
    private String engineState;
    private MechanicNoInner mechanic;

    public CarNoInner () {
        mechanic = new MechanicNoInner(this);
    }

    public void setEngineState(String engineState) {
        this.engineState = engineState;
    }

    public String getEngineState() {
        return engineState;
    }
}

public class MechanicNoInner {
    private CarNoInner car;

    public MechanicNoInner (CarNoInner car){
        this.car = car;
    }

    public void repairEngine() {
        car.setEngineState("good");
    }
}
```

Instead, by creating Mechanic as an internal class, the situation is simplified a lot:

```java
public class Car {
    private String engineState;

    public class Mechanic {
```

**419**

```
                    public void repairEngine() {
                        engineState = "good";
                    }
                }
            }
```

The negative side of this approach is that, if the `Mechanic` class will then also be used outside the `Car` class, it will always be necessary to instantiate a car to instantiate a mechanic, as explained previously, with the following syntax:

```
Car car = new Car();
Car.Mechanic mechanic = car.new Mechanic();
```

# 11.2 Anonymous Classes: Definition

 The **anonymous classes** are particular inner classes, in fact they are declared inside other classes. Very often, they are declared within methods (**local anonymous classes**), and, of course, do not have a name.

> **Like nested classes, anonymous classes were introduced after the birth of the language: in Version 1.2.**

## 11.2.1 Syntax

When declaring an anonymous class, one must also instantiate it. This means that once an object is instantiated (with the syntax highlighted in bold in the next example), an anonymous class is implicitly defined. But how can an unnamed class be instantiated? What is the name of the constructor of a class that has no name? The syntax at first sight can be confusing:

```
public class Outer4 {
    private String message = "In the class ";

    public void methodWithClass(final int a) {
        //Definition and creation of the anonymous class
        ExistingClass ec = new ExistingClass() {
            @Override
            public void method() {
                System.out.println(message + "anonymous number " + a);
            }
        }; //note the ";"
        ec.method();
    }
}
```

```
//Superclass of the anonymous class
public class ExistingClass {
    public void method() {
        System.out.println("In the existing class");
    }
}
```

In practice, the syntax is the following:

```
SuperType identifier = new SuperType() {
    [class_redefinition]
};
```

To define an anonymous class, an object is instantiated from a certain class, then a code block is opened and this is redefined as if we were extending it, but without assigning a name to this extension.

An anonymous class must therefore definitely extend another class (in the example, extending ExistingClass) and exploit a reference (thanks to the data polymorphism) and a constructor (by definition the anonymous class has no name and therefore has no constructor). In fact, the anonymous class in the example uses the reference ec of type Existingclass to refer to an object of its anonymous subclass, and like all the subclasses implicitly always calls the constructor of the superclass (Existingclass). In this case we have overridden the method() method defined in Existingclass.

**An anonymous class can be instantiated only once, so in some respects it can be considered an implementation of the Singleton pattern (see section 6.8.6).**

We can see a certain similarity to the alternative syntax for the instance of an array that we saw in section 3.6.4, where the array was declared and instantiated, and then its elements were defined as follows:

```
String strings [] = new String[] {"HelloWorld.java", "HelloWorld.java"};
```

## 11.2.2 Non-Denotable Type

Therefore, anonymous classes are not defined using the class keyword as we have done so far. Together with other data structures that we will see later, anonymous classes belong to the category of so-called **non-denotable types**. Non-denotable types have already been defined in section 3.7.3, as types whose name we cannot explicitly declare in the code, but which the compiler is able to define internally, thanks to its inference capacity. In the case of anonymous classes, it is obvious that this is a non-denotable type since we are talking about unnamed classes.

It should therefore be noted that an anonymous class is defined by the instance of its (unique) object, but note that the class that has no name and this object are two different things. The object we instantiate is just an object. The anonymous class instead, is defined internally by the compiler, but it is not possible to instantiate it again, at most we can declare an identical one. In the example we saw earlier, the instance had the identifier ce, while the anonymous class has no identifier. Therefore, we can clearly distinguish the anonymous class from its instance.

## 11.2.3 Anonymous Classes vs Inner Classes

An anonymous class (not its instance) is defined by the compiler as if it were an inner class. In fact, anonymous classes are declared within other classes, and for this reason they can themselves be considered particular inner classes. This means that the compiler internally creates an anonymous class as it does with an inner class. For this reason, an anonymous class has the same properties as an inner class, except for those that require the use of the class name (see section 11.2.3.2), and are used for the same purposes (especially for handling events on graphical interfaces).

We also note that similarly to the inner classes, if we compile a class that contains an anonymous class, two files will be created: `ExternalClassName.class` and `ExternalClassName$1.class`. And if we introduce a second anonymous class, the file `ExternalClassName$2.class` will be created, and so on for any other anonymous classes.

Unlike inner classes, however, the declaration of an anonymous class also requires that:

1. an object is instantiated together with the class declaration;
2. there must be a superclass or a superinterface that the constructor will use (only virtually in the case of an interface). If a class does not have a name, it cannot have a constructor.

### 11.2.3.1 Anonymous Classes and Modifiers

We have seen that anonymous classes can be declared within another class at the level of instance members. Can we then use modifiers in the same way as nested classes? In theory, yes, but this time the modifiers will mark the instance of the anonymous class, and not the anonymous class itself. So, for example an instance of an anonymous class can be declared `private`, and therefore be available only within the class in which it is defined.

Even if we declare locally an anonymous class (local anonymous class), a possible modifier such as `final`, will refer only to the instance of the anonymous class.

Actually, every anonymous class is implicitly declared `final`. In fact, the inheritance is implemented using the keyword `extends` followed by the name of the class, but an anonymous class has no name, and therefore it is not possible to extend it.

An anonymous class cannot be declared `abstract`. A class becomes abstract if the `class` keyword preceding the class name is marked with the `abstract` modifier. But an anonymous class has no name and does not use the `class` keyword.

For the same reason we cannot declare an anonymous class `static`. However, we can declare the instance of the anonymous class to be static.

### 11.2.3.2 Properties in Common with the Inner Classes

The anonymous classes share certain properties with the nested classes:

1. they have access to both instance and static members of the class in which they are declared.

2. They can declare instance members, but not static members, at most only static constants.

3. The `this` reference used within the anonymous class, points to the anonymous class itself. To access the reference `this` of the class in which the anonymous class is defined, the syntax `ExternalClassName.this` must be used (see section 11.1.2.3).

4. Finally, like the inner classes, even anonymous classes can be declared within methods (**local anonymous classes**), and even in this case there is the constraint of being able to access local variables and parameters only if they are declared `final`, or if they are effectively non-modifiable (*effectively final*). Assuming, therefore, that the `Outer4` class has been defined, the following code is valid:

```
public class Outer4 {
    private String message ="In the class ";

    public void methodWithClass(final int a) {
        ExistingClass ec = new ExistingClass() {
            @Override
            public void method() {
                System.out.println(message + "anonymous number " + a);
            }
        } ;
        ec.method();
    }
}

//Superclass of the anonymous class
public class ExistingClass {
    public void method() {
        System.out.println("In the existing class");
    }
}
```

**423**

### 11.2.3.3 Anonymous Classes and Inheritance

We previously stated that the rules for inner classes also apply to the other nested types (interfaces, enumerations and annotations). As with anonymous classes, it is only possible to extend classes or interfaces, but not enumerations or annotations. In fact, enumerations and annotations cannot be extended.

To declare an anonymous class, it is mandatory to exploit a superclass and its constructor. If a class does not have a name, it cannot have its own constructor. Actually, we can also exploit a *superinterface*. In this case, we will exploit a "virtual constructor" since an interface does not define constructors (we will see an example in the next section).

If we consider, for example the `Flying` interface, introduced in Chapter 7, adding the new `glide()` method:

```
public interface Flying {
    void glide();
    void takeOff();
    void land();
}
```

then it will be possible to create *instances that are not immediately identified,* using the following syntax:

```
public class FlyingAnonymousTest {
    public static void main(String args[]) {
        Flying ufo = new Flying() {
            @Override
            public void takeOff() {
                System.out.println("An undentified flying object is taking off");
            }
            @Override
            public void glide() {
                System.out.println("An undentified flying object is gliding");
            }
            @Override
            public void land() {
                System.out.println("An undentified flying object is landing...");
            }
        };
        //Let's use the object from the anonymous class.
        ufo.takeOff();
        ufo.glide();
        ufo.land();
    }
}
```

Note how it seems to instantiate objects directly from the interface, which is implemented concurrently with the object instance. Note also that the syntax seems to make us use the constructor of an interface! But we know that interfaces do not have constructors, so with the syntax:

```
new Flying() { //...
```

we are using a *virtual* constructor.

> **It is, of course, also possible to extend abstract classes. As we have already stated, an anonymous class cannot itself be abstract, so if it extends an abstract class, it must necessarily redefine all its abstract methods.**

## 11.2.4 Anonymous Local Classes and `var`

 Note that an anonymous class is always declared with the purpose of overriding one or more methods of the extending class. If, in the example, we had defined a new method (not inherited) in the anonymous class, we would not have been able to invoke it without a reference of the anonymous class type (which, however, cannot exist!). For example, if, in the previous example, we had defined the anonymous class in this way:

```
//...
//Declaration and instance of the anonymous class
ExistingClass ec = new ExistingClass() {
    @Override
    public void method() {
        System.out.println(message+"anonymous");
    }

    public void nonInvocableMethod() {
        System.out.println("There is no reference for an anonymous class: "
          + "this method cannot be called!");
        }
    };
}
```

given what we said previously, since the previous one is a class with no name (non-denotable type), we cannot obtain a reference of the class itself, but only use one of the class that it extends.

With the introduction of the word `var`, we can get around this.

> This is possible only in cases where the anonymous class is declared within a method (*local anonymous class*). In fact, for local variables, the word var can only be used instead of the type.

In the following example:

```java
public class VarAnonymousTest {
    public static void main(String args[]) {
        var testObject = new Object() {
            String name ="This can be used with var!";
            void test(String test){
                System.out.println(test);
            }
        } ;
        testObject.test(testObject.name);
    }
}
```

we can see that we have been able to use both the variable and the method that we defined ex-novo in the local anonymous class. So, in this case the introduction of the word var, besides representing a tool to reduce the verbosity of Java, has allowed us to overcome a limit of the language.

## 11.2.5 When to Use Anonymous Classes

 A particularly useful aspect of anonymous classes is when they are declared when passing a parameter in a method. This is probably the most useful way to use them. We are talking here about creating specializations created on the fly with some methods overriding. For example, consider the following Pilot class that declares a method that takes a Flying object as input:

```java
public class Pilot {
    private String name;

    public Pilot (String name) {
        this.name = name;
    }

    public void go(Flying flying) {
        flying.takeOff();
        flying.glide();
        flying.land();
    }
```

```
    public void setName(String name) {
        this.name = name;
    }

    public String getName() {
        return name;
    }

    @Override
    public String toString(){
        return getName();
    }
}
```

We can use anonymous classes dynamically, as in the following example:

```
public class PilotTest {
    public static void main(String args[]) {
        Pilot pilot = new Pilot("Simone");
        pilot.go(new Flying() {
            @Override
            public void takeOff() {
                System.out.println("An undentified flying object is "
                    + "taking off");
            }
            @Override
            public void glide() {
                System.out.println("An undentified flying object is gliding");
            }
            @Override
            public void land() {
                System.out.println("An undentified flying object is "
                    + "landing...");
            }
        } );
    }
}
```

In this case, we can change the implementation of the methods on the fly, without perhaps having declared the class, and without ever having given a reference to the created object. It is a way of working that is less object-oriented, but very useful. We can say that we have passed, to a method, the code to be executed! This is really very powerful, let's try to understand why.

One of the so-called "anti-patterns" of programming (the opposite of patterns, and something to avoid) is the so-called "copy-paste". Of course, it is convenient to avoid writing the same piece of code twice, but if we are doing it, we must realize that we are doing, a priori, something somehow wrong: we should even feel guilty! This is because we are actually paving the way for potential bugs. In fact, if one day we fix a bug,

**427**

modifying one of the two pieces, we will probably not do it in the other one and it will remain bugged. After all, one of the fundamental paradigms of Object Orientation, and good programming in general, is *reuse*. Our aim must therefore be to avoid copy-paste as much as we can.

For example, if we find ourselves having to rewrite a piece of code into two different classes, it is possible that these two classes may be in an inheritance relationship. If the Pilot and Person class declare the properties (private attributes with accessor and mutator methods) name, surname and id, it is clear that Pilot can extend the Person class.

On the other hand, if two classes share a fragment of identical code in two different methods, it is very likely that that piece of code can be abstracted into a method to be invoked and perhaps moved to a third utility class.

If the piece of code in common is in two methods of the same class, then it might be possible to extrapolate this piece of code in a private method that is simply invoked by the two original methods.

> **This last refactoring technique (see Chapter 5) can be automated using an IDE like Eclipse or Netbeans, by selecting the piece of code to be included in the private method, and pressing the menu called Extract Method (Introduce Method on Eclipse). The IDE will take care of creating the private method (allowing us to choose some details like the name), and will replace the selected code with the call to the new private method in the rest of the class.**

And if this piece of code in common differs slightly (perhaps on only one line) from another? In some cases, it is still possible to abstract the code fragment into a method, making the code fragment different, depending on a parameter passed to the new method. Let's try to explain better with an example. For example, consider the following Movie class:

```java
public class Movie {
    private String name;
    private String genre;
    private int reviewsAverage;

    public Movie (String name, String genre, int reviewsAverage) {
        this.name = name;
        this.genre = genre;
        this.reviewsAverage = reviewsAverage;
    }

    // getter and setter methods omitted
}
```

Let's write a `VideoStore` class, which contains two methods that are practically the same except for one line of code (highlighted in bold):

```java
public class VideoStore {
    private Movie[] movies;

    public VideoStore() {
        movies = new Movie[10];
        loadMovies();
    }

    public void setFilms(Movie[] movies) {
        this.movies = movies;
    }

    public Movie[] getFilms() {
        return movies;
    }

    public Movie[] getSciFiMovies() {
        Movie [] sciFiMovies = new Movie[10];
        for (int i = 0, j= 0; i< 10;i++) {
            if ("SciFi".equals(movies[i].getGenre())) {
                sciFiMovies[j] = movies[i];
                j++;
            }
        }
        return sciFiMovies;
    }

    public Movie[] getNiceMovies() {
        Movie [] niceMovies = new Movie[10];
        for (int i = 0, j= 0; i< 10;i++) {
            if (movies[i].getReviewsAverage() > 3) {
                niceMovies[j] = movies[i];
                j++;
            }
        }
        return niceMovies;
    }

    private void loadMovies() {
        // code for loading some movies omitted
    }
}
```

The `getSciFiMovies()` and `getNiceMovies()` methods that filter sci-fi movies and movies with a review average of more than 3, are virtually identical except for the names of the local variables (which are just names and, anyway, we could have called them the same) and the check of the if clause. The algorithm is not trivial because, in the for loop, we have defined two indices that are incremented at different times: i to be scrolled through the movies array (instance variable), while j for the array to be filled and returned. It seems to be an insurmountable obstacle to avoid copy-paste and, in most cases, the average Java programmer leaves the code like that, putting the program at risk.

With the following class, we print science fiction movies:

```java
public class VideoStoreTest {
    public static void main(String args[]) {
        VideoStore videoStore = new VideoStore();
        System.out.println("\nSciFi movies:");
        Movie[] sciFiMovies =  videoStore.getSciFiMovies();
        for (Movie movie: movies) {
            if (movie != null) {
                System.out.println(movie);
            }
        }
    }
}
```

The solution consists in using anonymous classes. First, we must create a simple interface that abstracts the concept of filter:

```java
public interface MovieFilter {
    boolean filter(Movie movie);
}
```

Then we can replace the two similar methods of the VideoStore class with the following:

```java
public Movie[] getFilteredMovies(MovieFilter movieFilter) {
    Movie [] filteredMovies = new Movie[10];
    for (int i = 0, j= 0; i< 10;i++) {
        if (movieFilter.filter(movies[i])) {
            filteredMovies[j] = movies[i];
            j++;
        }
    }
    return filteredMovies;
}
```

Note that, in the previous code, we highlighted the virtual invocation of a method. In fact, the filter() method is abstract and invoked on a reference of an interface. So, taking advantage of what we learned in Chapter 8, to filter our movies we can use the following code:

```java
//...
System.out.println("Nice movies:");
```

**430**

```
Movie[] niceMovies = videoStore.getFilteredMovies(new MovieFilter() {
    public boolean filter(Movie movie) {
        return movie.getReviewsAverage() > 3;
    }
});
//...
System.out.println("\nSciFi movies:");
Movie[] sciFiMovies = videoStore.getFilteredMovies(new MovieFilter() {
    public boolean filter(Movie movie) {
        return "SciFi".equals(movie.getGenre());
    }
});
//...
```

In this way, we have passed, on the fly, the code to be executed to the method as a parameter! And we avoided copy-paste. We can also invent new filters by defining them on the fly.

This solution is very advanced and flexible, perhaps it is the most complex we have seen so far, so much so, that many Java programmers have never used it! This type of solution is also widely used for handling events on graphical user interfaces, as can be seen in Chapter 22.

The negative side of this approach to programming is is the lack of readability, and we need to write a lot of code. But with the introduction of lambda expressions in Java 8, we will see in Chapter 17 that it will be possible to achieve the same result with less effort and a much more compact and powerful syntax.

## 11.3 Enumeration Types

 **Enumerated types** or more simply **enums**, are one of the fundamental components of Java programming that we have not yet introduced. This is a new type of data structure, which is added to the classes, interfaces and annotations (which we will delve into a dedicated chapter), and then can be saved in files with the suffix .java. This time, instead of using class or interface, we will use the keyword enum. Enumerations are data structures similar to classes, but with particular properties. Let's start with an example:

```
public enum MyEnumeration {
    ONE, TWO, THREE;
}
```

We have just defined an enum called MyEnumeration, defining three of its **elements** (also called **values**) that are called ONE, TWO and THREE. It's like we've defined a new type. In fact, an enumeration is transformed by the compiler into a class that extends the abstract Enum class (package java.lang). The elements of this enum are implicitly of the MyEnumeration type and therefore the type should not be specified. They are simply defined by separating them with commas.

These are static constants, but we must not declare them neither `final` nor `public` nor `static` because, implicitly, in an enum they are already. Note that, in the example, after the list of values, the ";" is not necessary, but it is recommended. In fact, it will become necessary if other elements are defined in the enumeration, such as methods.

Each element of `MyEnumeration` is of type `MyEnumeration`. This is the most difficult characteristic of the enum to understand at first. Therefore, once an enumeration is defined, all its possible instances are defined. We cannot instantiate another `MyEnumeration`, in addition to those defined by `MyEnumeration` itself. This is why it seems to be more correct to define its elements as *values* of the enumeration. Since these are constants, Java convention (see Chapter 3) recommends defining the elements of an enumeration with uppercase characters. Recall that the underscore character ("_") can be used as a word separator. Furthermore, the enumerations must be defined with the same convention as the classes. The syntax of an enum is not only limited to what we have just seen. There are many other features that an enumeration can do, for example implement interfaces, define constructors, methods, etc.

## 11.3.1 Inheritance and Enumerations

An enum cannot be extended, nor can it extend another enum or another class. In fact, enumerations will be transformed by the compiler into classes that extend the `java.lang.Enum` class. This means that we will inherit different methods from the `java.lang.Enum` class, which we can safely invoke on the elements of the enum. For example, the `name()` method is defined to return the name of the element, so:

```
System.out.println(MyEnumeration.ONE.name());
```

will print:

```
ONE
```

The `toString()` method also returns the same result, so the statement:

```
System.out.println(MyEnumeration.ONE);
```

produces exactly the same output (since the `println()` method calls the `toString()` method on the input object). It is also possible to override the methods of `java.lang.Enum` (we'll soon see how), including the `toString()` method. On the other hand, the `name()` method cannot be overridden, because it is declared `final`.

Enum also declares a complementary method to `toString()`: the static method `valueOf()`, which, passing as input a string, returns the corresponding value of the enumeration. For example:

```
MyEnumeration element = MyEnumeration.valueOf("ONE");
System.out.println (element);
```

will print:

```
ONE
```

Furthermore Enum defines the final ordinal() method. This method returns the position index within the enum of one of its elements. As usual, the index starts from zero and this method can be used within loops.

Enumerations also define the values() method. This method returns an array containing all the elements of the enumeration, in the order in which they were declared. We can use this method to iterate over the values of an enumeration. This practice could be useful when we do not know the enumeration we're using. For example, by using an enhanced for loop, we can print the contents of MyEnumeration:

```
for (MyEnumeration myEnumeration : MyEnumeration.values()) {
    System.out.println(myEnumeration + " is in position " + myEnumeration.ordinal());
}
```

The output of the previous example is:

```
ONE   is in position 0
TWO   is in position 1
THREE  is in position 2
```

As we have already stated, enumerations are transformed by the compiler into classes that extend the java.lang.Enum class. In particular, each enum implicitly extends the abstract class java.lang.Enum (which is not an enumeration). That's why they can take advantage of, or override, Enum's methods.

> **Beware that the compiler will not allow the developer to create classes that directly extend the Enum class. It is a special class created specifically to support the concept of enumeration.**

An enumeration cannot extend other enums or classes. In fact, since a class can extend only one class, an enumeration being transformed by the compiler to a class that extends java.lang.Enum, cannot extend other classes.

## 11.3.2 Polymorphism and Enumerations

It is, however, possible for an enum to implement one or more interfaces. In fact, we can declare in an enum all the methods we want, including those to be implemented by an interface. This means that, if we want to exploit the data polymorphism, we can only do it through the use of interfaces or an enum reference. For example, let's consider the following interface:

```
public interface Numerator {
    void printIndex();
}
```

Let's rewrite the enumeration by making it implement the previous interface:

```
public enum MyEnumeration2 implements Numerator {
    ONE, TWO, THREE;
    @Override
    public void printIndex() {
        System.out.println("index: " + this.ordinal());
    }
}
```

and we can use the data polymorphism using the `Numerator` interface in the following way:

```
Numerator n = MyEnumeration.TWO;
n.printIndex();
```

which will print:

```
index: 1
```

We can also use a reference of type `java.lang.Enum` to use the polymorphism for data:

```
Enum e = MiaEnumeration.ONE;
```

But with a reference of type `java.lang.Enum`, we will not be able to call the `printIndex()` method as previously seen, because of the rules of data polymorphism.

> **The last instruction will be completed, but a warning from the compiler will be reported. The `Enum` class that is defined using a "generic type" has not been used correctly. We will explain this topic in more detail in the next chapter.**

Being unable to extend an enum, it cannot be declared as `abstract`. So, when we implement an interface in an enum, we will have to implement all inherited methods.

## 11.3.3 Methods, Variables, Constructors and Nested Types within an Enumeration

In an enum, it is also possible to create variables, methods and constructors. However, the latter are implicitly declared as `private` and cannot be used except in the context of the enumeration itself. For example, with the following code, the `MyEnumeration` enum is redefined for the third time:

```
public enum MyEnumeration3 {
    ZERO(), ONE(1), TWO(2), THREE(3);
    private int value;
    private MyEnumeration3() {
    }
    MyEnumeration3(int value) {
      setValue(value);
    }
    public void setValue(int value){
      this.value = value;
    }
    public int getValue(){
      return this.value;
    }
    @Override
    public String toString() {
      return ""+value;
    }
}
```

Note how the constructor is used when the elements of the enum are defined.

The following rules apply to enumerations.

1. **Any declaration must be placed after the declaration of the enumeration elements**. If we put any statement before the list of elements, we will get an error when compiling. The declaration of the elements must explicitly end with a "; ", and it is a good habit to always do it that way.

2. **It is possible to declare any number of constructors (using overload) which will be implicitly considered** private. In the example, we have two constructors, for one of which we have specified (although redundant) the private modifier. If we explicitly declared a public or protected constructor, we would get an error when compiling. For the rest, the same rules applied to class constructors apply. As for the classes, if we do not insert constructors, the compiler will add one without parameters (the default constructor). Also, as with the classes, the default constructor will not be inserted when we explicitly insert one, as in the previous example.

3. **When constructors are explicit, as in this case, the values of the enum can use them**. Just look at the example code. The values ONE, TWO and THREE use the constructor that takes an input of type integer (the syntax is intuitive). The ZERO value, on the other hand, uses the constructor without parameters. Two empty brackets are explicitly used, which underline how the ZERO value is using the constructor without parameters. This

**435**

syntax is absolutely superfluous (the round brackets could be omitted) and is only mentioned because represents a valid syntax. If, in the example, we had a single constructor (the one that takes an integer as the input parameter) all the elements of the enum would have been obliged to use that single constructor.

4. **An enum constructor cannot access a** `static` **field that is not** `final`. So, if we tried to compile the following class without removing the comment symbols (/* and */) around the `final` modifier for the PREFIX constant:

```java
public enum NatureElements {
    HEART("Heart"), FIRE("Fire"), WATER("Water"), AIR("Air");
    static  /* final */ String PREFIX ="The element is ";
    String name;
    NatureElements(String string) {
        name = prefix + string;
    }
    @Override
    public String toString() {
        return name;
    }
}
```

we would get the following compile-time error:

```
NatureElements.java:6: error: illegal reference to static field from initializer
        name = PREFIX + string;
                 ^
1 error
```

5. **It is possible to declare nested types (classes, interfaces, enumerations and annotations) within an enumeration, exactly as we do in classes, in interfaces (and in annotations)**. No particular attention should be paid to this aspect, just remember to put them after the values of the enum. For example, we can also declare an enum within an enum, as follows:

```java
public enum MyEnum {
    ENUM1(), ENUM2;
    public enum MyEnum2 {a,b,c}
}
```

> On the contrary, it is not possible to do the opposite: in an inner class, it is not possible to declare an enumeration.

### 11.3.4 When to Use an enum

 We cannot say that enumerations allow us to create code that we cannot create with classes. If anything, we can say that it will allow us to create more robust code in some cases. It is recommended to use enumerations whenever we a need to declare a finite number of values in order to manage the flow of an application. Let's take an example. Before the advent of Java enumerations, it was often necessary to create symbolic constants to represent values. These constants were often defined as integers or strings. Sometimes, constants were collected within dedicated interfaces. For example:

```java
public interface Action {
    public static final int FORWARD = 0;
    public static final int BACK = 1;
    public static final int STOP = 2;
}
```

Besides the fact that interfaces could be used for more object-oriented purposes, the fundamental reason why this approach is considered inadvisable is that, at the compilation level, it is not possible to specify constraints that prevent the user from using a type incorrectly. Consider, for example, the following code:

```java
public void execute(int action) {
    switch (action) {
        case Action.FORWARD:
            foForward();
        break;
        case Action.BACK:
            goBack();
        break;
        case Action.STOP:
            stop();
        break;
    }
}
```

No compiler could detect that the following statement is not valid:

```java
object.execute(3);
```

We can add a default clause to the switch construct, where the problem can be handled in some way, but this will only be useful at runtime, and not during compilation. A more robust implementation of the previous code may require the use of a class such as the following:

```java
public class Action {
    private String name;
    public static final Action FORWARD = new Action("FORWARD");
```

```
    public static final Action BACK = new Action("BACK");
    public static final Action STOP = new Action("STOP");
    public Action(String name) {
        setName(name);
    }
    public void setName(String name) {
        this.name = name;
    }
    public String getName() {
        return this.name;
    }
}
```

In this case, the execute() method could be modified in such a way so as to replace the switch construct with an if construct:

```
public void execute(Action action) {
    if (action == Action.FORWARD) {
        goForward();
    }
    else if (action == Action.BACK) {
        goBack();
    }
    else if (action == Action.STOP) {
        stop();
    }
}
```

Unfortunately, however, even in this case, the problem remains (even if an abstraction with a class seems better than that with an interface). It is always possible to pass null to the execute() method. Any check we want to insert can only fix the problem at runtime. In cases like this, the use of an enumeration brings widespread approval. In fact, if we create the following enumeration:

```
public enum ActionEnum {
    FORWARD, BACK, STOP;
}
```

without changing the code of the execute() method (we can also use an enum type as a test expression of a switch construct), we will have fixed the problem.

## 11.3.5 Nested Enumerations (in Classes) or Member Enumerations

As already stated, enumerations can also be nested into classes. For example, we can write code like this:

```
public class Volume {
    public enum Level {HIGH, MEDIUM, LOW};
```

```
        // implementation of the class omitted. . .
    }
```

If we want to print an enumeration element within the class with the `toString()` method, we can use the following syntax:

```
System.out.println(Level.HIGH);
```

If we are outside the class, we should use this syntax:

```
System.out.println(Volume.Level.HIGH);
```

Note that a nested enum is implicitly static. In fact, the following code is valid:

```
public class Volume {
    public enum Level {HIGH, MEDIUM, LOW};
    // implementation of the class . . .
    public static void main(String args[]) {
        System.out.println(Level.HIGH);
    }
}
```

If `Level` was not static, we could not have used it in a static method like `main()`. Encapsulation can also be used, but as with static constants, there are no major dangers, since their value cannot change.

Note how `static` imports, described in section 6.8.4, are a good fit for importing the values of enumerations, or even the types inserted into enumerations. In fact, in both cases we are talking about static elements. Assuming the `Volume` class belonging to the `music` package is declared:

```
package music;

public class Volume {
    //...
```

For example, in another class we could import the `HIGH` value of the `Level` nested enum within the `Volume` class, with the following syntax:

```
import static music.Volume.Level.HIGH;

public class StaticImportTest {
    public static void main(String args[]) {
        System.out.println(HIGH);
    }
}
```

Note that the result of the `toString()` method, called on the `HIGH` element, will be printed.

**439**

> Static **imports were introduced at the same time as enumerations, in Version 5 of the language. It seems that** static **imports had, above all, the task of supporting the introduction of enumerations, trying to reduce verbosity. In section 11.4 we will deepen the topic.**

## 11.3.6 Enumerations and Specific Methods of the Elements

 But is it really impossible to extend an enum? Not exactly! In fact, it is possible for certain enumerations to be extended by their own elements, using the syntax of anonymous classes. We can define the methods in the enumeration and override them with its elements. Consider the following CardinalPoints enumeration:

```java
public enum CardinalPoints {
    NORTH {
        @Override
        public void test() {
            System.out.println("method of the NORTH element");
        }
    } ,
    SOUTH, WEST, EAST;
    public void test() {
        System.out.println("method of the enum");
    }
}
```

A method called test() has been defined, and this should print the string method of the enum. But the element NORTH, with a syntax similar to that of anonymous classes, also declares the same method, subjecting it to overriding. In fact, the compiler will turn NORTH into an anonymous class, which will extend CardinalPoints. So, the instruction:

```java
CardinalPoints.NORTH.test();
```

will print:

```
method of the NORTH element
```

while the instruction:

```java
CardinalPoints.SOUTH.test();
```

will print:

```
method of the enum
```

since the element SOUTH did not override test().

**440**

### 11.3.7 Switch and enum

In Chapter 4, we introduced the switch construct. Now that we know more about enumerations, let's try to understand how this concept can be used in the construct. If a switch construct defines an enumeration as a *test expression*, all instances of that enumeration can be possible constants for the case clauses. For example, keeping in mind the Level enumeration above, let's consider the following code fragment:

```
switch (getLevel()) {
    case HIGH:
        System.out.println(Level.HIGH);
    break;
    case MEDIUM:
        System.out.println(Level.MEDIUM);
    break;
    case LOW:
        System.out.println(Level.LOW);
    break;
}
```

The test expression is of type Level and the constants of the case clauses are the elements of the enumeration itself. Note how the elements do not need to be referenced with the name of the enumeration, as follows:

```
case Level.HIGH:
    System.out.println(Level.HIGH);
break;
case Level.MEDIUM:
    System.out.println(Level.MEDIUM);
break;
case Level.LOW:
    System.out.println(Level.LOW);
break;
```

in fact, the compiler is able to infer by itself the elements of the type specified by the test expression.

Although in a switch construct based on an enum it is not possible for the default clause to be executed during runtime (this is one of the advantages of an enum, compared to the "old" approaches) it is still a good idea to use one. In fact, the enumeration can easily have additions over time. This is especially true if the code is shared among multiple programmers. In this case, there are two approaches to be recommended. The first one is softer and consists in managing any kind of new types in general. For example:

```
default:
```

```
        System.out.println(getLevel());
```

The second method is certainly more robust, as based on the assertions:

```
default:
    assert false: "value of the enumeration is new: " + getLevel();
```

Note that the assertion should bring out the problem during testing if the enumeration `Level` has been expanded with new values.

In case we do not want to implement the `default` clause, if we use an IDE like Eclipse its compiler can still help when the enumeration involved in the `switch` evolves. In fact, if all the enumeration cases are not included in a switch, for example:

```
case HIGH:
    System.out.println(Level.HIGH);
break;
case MEDIUM:
    System.out.println(Level.MEDIUM);
break;
```

then, when compiling, the compiler will signal us a warning.

In section 4.4.7 called "Exhaustiveness", we have seen how a `switch` expression that does not cover every possible value of a certain enumeration with its case clauses, causes a compilation problem.

## 11.4 More on `static` imports

Static **imports** should only be used carefully. The real usefulness of this feature is limited only to a few situations. On the other hand, a programmer misinterpreting the use of this mechanism can easily make things more complicated!

Static imports allow us to import only what is static within a class. The syntax is:

```
import static packageName.ClassName.staticMemberName
```

It is advisable to use `static` imports when we are only interested in static members of a certain class, but not in its instances. The immediate benefit that the programmer receives is being able to use statically-imported members, without referencing them with the class name (lower verbosity). For example, we can statically import the `System.out` object:

```
import static java.lang.System.out;
```

In this way it will be possible to write in our code:

```
out.println("25774");
```

in place of:

```
System.out.println("25774");
```

In the event that other variables named out are not declared or statically-imported into our file, there is no technical problem that prevents us from using static import. In this way we will be able to write less boring and repetitive code like System.out within our class.

> **The usefulness of this functionality is real if and only if the statically-imported member is used several times within the code.**

We can also import all static members of a class using a wildcard, which is the usual asterisk symbol. For example, with the following code:

```
import static java.lang.Math.*;
```

we import all the static members of the Math class. So, within our code we will be able to call the various static methods of Math without referencing them with the name of the class that contains them. For example, supposing that x and y are the coordinates of a two-dimensional point, the calculation of the distance of the point from the origin, before the advent of static imports, could be coded as follows:

```
Math.sqrt(Math.pow(x,2) + Math.pow(y,2));
```

but it is possible to achieve the same result with less effort using a static import:

```
sqrt(pow(x,2) + pow(y,2));
```

We can also statically import a static method. In this case, only the name of the method is specified and not the eventual list of arguments. For example:

```
import static java.sql.DriverManager.getConnection();
```

 Static nested classes can also be statically-imported. For example, we can import the nested static class LookAndFeelInfo of the class UIManager (a class that contains information on the look and feel of a Swing application, see Chapter 23) with the following syntax:

```
import static javax.swing.UIManager.LookAndFeelInfo;
```

In this case, since it is a static nested class and therefore referenceable with the name of the class that contains it, it would be possible to also import it in the traditional way with the following syntax:

```
import javax.swing.UIManager.LookAndFeelInfo;
```

However, a static import highlights the fact that the nested class is static and perhaps, in such situations, its use is more appropriate.

## 11.4.1 Using static Imports

The question is: are we sure that the use of static imports always represents an advantage? The answer is: it depends! Styles and tastes in the world of programming are sometimes subjective. There are those who find it useful to avoid referencing static variables because, in this way, they write less code and find this practice sufficiently expressive. It is not our preference, as repeatedly stressed in this text. We prefer a long and explanatory name to a short and ambiguous one. If we are not used to reading all the imports of a class (which can also be many), it is easy to think that an unreferenced statically-imported member is just a member declared within the class (see also section 11.4.2.1). We could waste time and concentration in such a situation. However, there are some situations that fully justify the use of static imports.

### 11.4.1.1 Enumerations

A case where the use of static imports is actually useful, is when using enumerations. For example, consider the TigerNewFeature enum defined below:

```
package com.claudiodesio.jfa;

public enum TigerNewFeature {
    ANNOTATIONS, AUTOBOXING, ENUMERATIONS, FOREACH,
    FORMATTING, GENERICS, STATIC_IMPORTS, VARARGS
}
```

**The elements of this enumeration represent the most important features introduced in Java 5, whose nickname was "Tiger". This is why the enumeration is called** TigerNewFeatures.

Also consider a method addUpdates() of a hypothetical class JavaProgrammer:

```
package com.claudiodesio.jfa;
import java.util.*;

public class JavaProgrammer {
    private List updates;

    private String name;

    public JavaProgrammer(String name, TigerNewFeature... features) {
        this.name = name;
        updates = new ArrayList();
        addUpdates(features);
    }
    //...
    public void addUpdates(TigerNewFeature... features) {
        for (TigerNewFeature update : features) {
            updates.add(update);
        }
    }
}
```

Using the same method addUpdates(TigerNewFeature... features), we can add more TigerNewFeature enumeration elements, as follows:

```
JavaProgrammer pro = new JavaProgrammer("Claudio",
   TigerNewFeature.VARARGS, TigerNewFeature.FOREACH,
   TigerNewFeature.ENUMERATIONS, TigerNewFeature.GENERICS);
```

In this case, the use of a static import is certainly appropriate:

```
import static com.claudiodesio.jfa.TigerNewFeature.*;
//...
JavaProgrammer pro = new JavaProgrammer("Claudio", VARARGS, FOREACH,
   ENUMERATIONS, GENERICS);
```

In fact, we have avoided unnecessary repetitions and streamlined the code. At the same time, readability does not seem to have worsened.

### 11.4.1.2 Abstraction

Another situation where the use of static imports is fully justified, is strictly linked to the concept of abstraction (see Chapter 6). Often it happens to have an interface that defines several static constants (it is often code that already exists). Consider, for example, the following interface:

```
package application.db.utility;
public interface SQLConstants {
    String GET_ALL_USERS = "SELECT * FROM USERS";
```

```
        String GET_USER = "SELECT * FROM USERS WHERE ID = ?";
        // Other constants...
}
```

This interface can make sense in some contexts. In fact, it defines string type constants containing all the SQL commands that a certain application defines. This facilitates the reuse of these commands in various classes.

Now suppose we need to create a class that repeatedly uses the constants of this interface: the solution usually used in these cases is to implement the interface:

```
package application.db.logic;
import application.db.utility.*;
import java.sql.*;
import java.util.*;

public class DBManager implements SQLConstants {
    public Collection getUsers() throws SQLException{
        Collection users = null;
        Statement statement = null;
        //...
        ResultSet rs = statement.executeQuery(GET_ALL_USERS);
        //...
        return users;
    }
    // Other methods...
}
```

However, the most correct solution would be to use the interface, not implement it. If we implement it, it would be like we were saying that DBManager "is a" SQLCostants (see section 7.1.3). A correct solution could be the following:

```
package application.db.logic;
import application.db.utility.*;
import java.sql.*;
import java.util.*;

public class DBManager {
    public Collection getUsers() throws SQLException{
        Collection users = null;
        Statement statement = null;
        //...
        ResultSet rs = statement.executeQuery(SQLConstants.GET_ALL_USERS);
        //...
        return users;
    }
    // Other methods...
}
```

Considering that we haven't reported all the methods (there could be dozens) the last solution forces the programmer to write code that is a bit too repetitive. Although inaccurate, the first solution has a considerable programmatic advantage and low impact when it comes to analytical error. After all, we are inheriting static constants, not concrete methods. So, the situation is this: the second is the most correct solution, the first solution is the more convenient!

Well, in this case, using `static` imports seems the most appropriate solution:

```
package application.db.logic;
import static application.db.utility.SQLConstants.*;
import java.sql.*;
import java.util.*;

public class DBManager {
    public Collection getUsers() throws SQLException{
        Collection users = null;
        Statement statement = null;
        //...
        ResultSet rs = statement.executeQuery(GET_ALL_USERS);
        //...
        return users;
    }
    // Other methods...
}
```

The third solution is correct and convenient.

## 11.4.2 Impact on Java

The introduction of `static` imports in Java 5 was probably due to the introduction of enumerations. It seemed like it was a feature introduced to say: "enumerations are fantastic and, if we use `static` imports, we will also avoid writing the repetitive code that characterizes the syntax".

A negative consequence of the incorrect use of `static` imports, is the loss of identity when it comes to the statically-imported members. The elimination of the reference, on the one hand, can simplify the code to be written, but on the other hand, it could give rise to ambiguity. This can essentially happen in two situations: when statically importing members with the same name from different types, or with the *shadowing* of the variables imported with local and instance variables or the methods imported with the instance methods.

### 11.4.2.1 Ambiguity

In the event that we statically import methods with the same name as other methods already present within our classes, the overload rules apply (see Chapter 8). So, if we statically import methods with the same name as those defined in our classes, we need to make sure we have different signatures (in particular parameter lists)

for them. Otherwise the compiler will report the error "ambiguous reference to the method" if they were used within the code without reference, as well as static imports allow. In this case, to solve the compilation problem it is mandatory to reference the methods. The same also applies to the variables. Consider the following example:

```
import static java.lang.Math.*;
import static javax.print.attribute.standard.MediaSizeName.*;

public class AmbiguousVariables {
    public static void main(String args[]) {
        System.out.println(E);
    }
}
```

Compiling the previous file will result in the following output:

```
error: reference to E is ambiguous
        System.out.println(E);
                           ^
  both variable E in Math and variable E in MediaSizeName match
1 error
```

It is therefore mandatory to reference the constant E because it is present as a static variable, both in the Math class and in the MediaSizeName class, in order to eliminate ambiguity and not get an error in compilation, for example in the following way:

```
System.out.println(Math.E);
```

Note that the error is reported only because the constant E was used. If we had used other static members of the Math and MediaSizeName classes, we would not have obtained compilation errors. Even if we explicitly only imported the two variables E, as follows:

```
import static java.lang.Math.E;
import static javax.print.attribute.standard.MediaSizeName.E;
```

the compiler would have reported the error only where we use the constant E.

### 11.4.2.2 Shadowing

Another problem caused by not referencing statically-imported variables is known as *shadowing*.

The **shadowing** phenomenon occurs when we declare a local variable with the same name as a variable that has a broader scope, like an instance variable. As already seen in the second chapter, within the method where the local variable is declared, the compiler considers the local variable *more important*. In such cases, to use the instance variable, it is mandatory to reference it with the reference this. The shadowing affects not only the instance variables but also the statically-imported ones, as the following example shows:

**448**

```
import static java.lang.System.out;
//...
    public void print(PrintWriter out, String text) {
        out.println(text);
    }
```

Within the `print()` method, the reference out is not `System.out`, but an argument of type `PrintWriter`. Now consider the following code:

```
import static java.lang.Math.pow;
public class Shadowing {
    public static double pow(double d1, double d2){
        return 0;
    }
    public static void main(String args[]) {
        System.out.println(pow(2,2));
    }
}
```

Due to the shadowing effect, the local method pow() will be considered a priority compared to the statically-imported method. So, we can come to the conclusion that statically importing a member of a class, appears to be an operation that should be managed carefully.

## Summary

A **nested class** is a class defined within another class. Nested classes can easily access the members (even the static ones) of the class that contains them. However, they cannot declare static members. With nested classes, we can use access specifiers, with the same rules used for members of a class.

If a nested class is not declared static, it is also called an **inner class**. On the other hand, static nested classes become **top-level classes**, and they will not have the property to access the instance variables of the class in which they are defined, but they can declare static members, and access the static members of the class in which they are declared.

If we want to instantiate a nested class (suppose we call it Inner) from outside the class that contains it (suppose we call it Outer), we need to do this by using a special syntax. First, we instantiate an object of the outer class (suppose this object is called object OuterClass), then we must instantiate the inner class as follows:

```
Outer.Inner inner = outer.new Inner();
```

Using the reference this inside a nested class involves referencing the current object of the nested class. If we want to use a reference to point to the instance of the object instantiated by the outer class, we must use the syntax: OuterClass.this. A nested class can also be declared

**449**

within a method (or in general in a code block) and, in this case, it is called a **local class**. In this case the local variables will be accessible only if declared **final or not actually modified (effectively final)**. The nested classes can be declared abstract.

An **anonymous class** is a nested class without a name. It has all the properties of an inner class, it must also be instantiated when it is declared and it must be subclassed by an existing class which the constructor will use. It can be used to pass code dynamically to a method.

**Enumerations** are particular data structures that also define all of their elements (a finite number of elements). These elements are implicitly declared public, final and static, just as the constructors are implicitly declared private. Enumerations are transformed by the compiler into classes that extend the java.lang.Enum class, from which they inherit the methods. For this reason, they cannot extend other classes but may eventually implement interfaces to exploit the polymorphism. They may contain other **nested enumerations**, and there are often nested enumerated within classes. We can declare methods in the enumeration and any element can override the declared method within the enumeration, thus creating specific methods for the enumeration elements. The switch construct supports enumeration testing, and the static import statement can be useful for limiting the verbosity of code that uses enumerations. We have also deepened the topic of static **imports** and understood how to recognize the problems of *ambiguity* and *shadowing*.

> **Exercises, source code, appendices and other resources are available at http://www.javaforaliens.com.**

## Chapter Goals

Have the following goals been achieved?

| Goal | Achieved | Achievement Date |
|---|:---:|:---:|
| Understand what nested types are (Unit 11.1) | O | |
| List the basic properties of nested classes (Unit 11.1) | O | |
| Know how to define and use anonymous classes (Unit 11.2) | O | |
| Understand how to use enumerations (Unit 11.3) | O | |
| Understand how to use the advanced features of enumerations (Unit 11.3) | O | |
| Understand when to use static imports (Unit 11.4) | O | |

# 12

# Generic Types

> **Goals:**
>
> At the end of this chapter, the reader should:
>
> ✔ Understand and know how to use generic types (Unit 12.1).
> ✔ Understand automatic type inference and raw types, and manage compiler warnings (Unit 12.1).
> ✔ Understand erasure and how inheritance is applied with generic types (Unit 12.2).
> ✔ Know how to use wildcards and bounded parameters (Units 12.2, 12.3, 12.4).
> ✔ Know how to create your own generic types (Unit 12.3).
> ✔ Know how to create generic methods (Unit 12.3).
> ✔ Know how to create intersection types (Unit 12.3).
> ✔ Know how to manage wildcard capture with helper methods (Unit 12.3).
> ✔ Know how to create covariant parameters (Unit 12.4).

It is normal for the code to have bugs. However, there are bugs that can be solved by intercepting them during compilation. This can be done if the language supports tools such as **generic types** (also called **generics**). In addition to allowing the compiler to identify possible bugs at compile time, the generics allow us to write less verbose code, avoiding dangerous casting of types, and allowing us to create generic (i.e. generics-based) algorithms. Therefore, we'll introduce a new type of programming: **generic programming**. When generic types were introduced in Version 5 of the language, they really changed the way we write Java code. With generics, Java programming became more powerful and robust, and today the standard library is based on many classes, interfaces and generic methods. By far the biggest use of generic types is certainly in the context of the use of collections. In this chapter, we will briefly introduce some collections that will serve as an example, but then we will study them further in

Chapter 14, dedicated to the `java.util` library. However, the use of generics is not limited to collections.

## 12.1 Generics and Type Parameters

A class (or an interface) can be declared as a **generic type**, adding one or more **type parameters** to the definition. The syntax uses angle brackets that surround type identifiers:

```
class ClassIdentifier <T1, T2,... Tn> {
    //...
}
```

For example, let's consider the following `Container` class that contains an object:

```
public class Container {
    private Object object;

    public void setObject(Object object) {
        this.object = object;
    }

    public Object getObject() {
        return object;
    }
}
```

This class seems simple and well done, but it will not be that simple to manage. In fact, we will set the `object` object with an instance of a `String`, or `Date`, or any other subclass of the `Object` class, since creating an instance of `Object` is not useful. When this instance is retrieved using the `getObject()` method, we will be forced to convert it to use it (casting). This operation is however potentially dangerous, because it could also recover a different type from what we expect. For example, in a program, we could write pieces of code that use this class in an incompatible manner. In a part of the code, we could insert an object of type `Integer` inside a `Container` type object using the `setObject()` method, and then elsewhere try to retrieve a `String` object using the `getObject()` method. In cases like this the Java Virtual Machine will launch a `ClassCastException` at runtime. In general, to use this class we should write instructions like the following:

```
Container container = new Container();
container.setObject("String");
// container.setObject(new Integer(1));
String object = (String)container.getObject();
System.out.println(object);
```

Note that a string casting was required when retrieving the object. If we had set an `Integer` object in the container (using the single-line comment for the second line and not for the third line) we would have obtained a `ClassCastException`. To avoid the exception, we could have used the `instanceof` operator:

```
Object object = container.getObject();
if (object instanceof String) {
    String string = (String)object;
    //...
} else if (object instanceof Integer) {
    Integer integer = (Integer)object;
    //...
} else if //...
```

but the code would become more verbose and prone to error.

To make our code more robust, we need to transform a generic class as follows:

```
public class GenericsContainer<T> {
    private T object;

    public void setObject(T object) {
        this.object = object;
    }

    public T getObject() {
        return object;
    }
}
```

Note that in place of `Object` now there is the **type parameter** T, which does not represent an existing type. This will be replaced with a real type when a `GenericsContainer` is instantiated. For example:

```
GenericsContainer<String> container = new GenericsContainer<>();
container.setObject("String"); //we can pass only strings
String object = container.getObject();//no cast needed
System.out.println(object);
```

In this example, it is as if we had used the `String` class in the whole class definition in place of the T parameter. So, the `setObject()` method will only accept strings; if we tried to pass other types, we would get a compile-time error. Also, we do not need to cast to `String` to retrieve the object using the `getObject()` method. Ultimately, for the `container` object, it is as if the `GenericsContainer` class had been declared as follows:

```
public class GenericsContainer<String> {
    private String object;

    public void setObject(String object) {
```

```
        this.object = object;
    }

    public String getObject() {
        return object;
    }
}
```

Only the type T parameter with the String type has been replaced.

The magic of the generic GenericsContainer class is that it can also be parameterized with any other type. For example:

```
GenericsContainer<Integer> container2 = new GenericsContainer<Integer>();
container2.setObject(new Integer("1"));
Integer object2 = container2.getObject(); //no cast needed
System.out.println(object2);
```

Strangely, a generic type in some ways should be considered a more specific type!

> **By convention, when declaring a type parameter, we use an identifier consisting of a single uppercase letter, which should represent the initial of a symbolic name (in this case, T means "Type"). In particular, the standard library often uses: E for "Element", K for "Key", N for "Number", V for "Value", T for "Type", and S, U, V for the second, third and fourth type.**

## 12.1.1 Generics and Collections

The most classic use of generic types is with the classes and interfaces of the **Collections framework**. By the word **framework**, we mean a micro architecture that provides extensible types within a specific domain. In software architecture theory, a framework is an example of **horizontal partitioning**, in other words a part of the reusable and extensible software. Here is, for example, how the List interface is declared:

```
public interface List<E> extends Collection<E>
```

As already stated in the previous section, the generic type E defined for List objects, is not an existing type, but only a generic identifier replaceable with any other type.

> **Note how the List interface extends the Collection interface that is also declared generic.**

Since the `List` interface is a generic type, we can parameterize it with the type parameter we want. For example, we could instantiate its most famous implementation, the `ArrayList` subclass with the following syntax:

```
List<Car> list = new ArrayList<Car>();
```

This means that we can only add `Car` type objects to this collection. In fact, the `add()` method used to add elements to the list is declared as follows:

```
public boolean add(E o)
```

So, once the `list` object has been instantiated by parameterizing it with the `Car` type, the type parameter `E` changes to `Car`, and therefore the parameter of the `add()` method also becomes `Car`. That is, for the `list` object, it is as if the `add()` method was declared as follows:

```
public boolean add(Car o)
```

Even if a class is defined as generic, the use of type parameters is not mandatory. The compiler of an IDE, however, will raise a warning in case of non-use (as we will see in detail in section 12.1.6). This is to allow backward compatibility with the code written before the advent of Java 5, where the generics simply did not exist.

So, suppose we have created an `ArrayList` in which we want to insert only strings. We will be obliged to use a casting when the strings are extracted from the `ArrayList` even if the type is known a priori. For example, let's consider the following code:

```
ArrayList list = getListOfStrings();
int size = list.size();
for (int i = 0; i < size; i++) {
    String string = (String)list.get(i);
}
```

If we remove the cast, we would get a compile-time error like the following:

```
incompatible types
found  : java.lang.Object
required: java.lang.String
String string = list.get(i);
^
```

In fact, the compiler cannot know a priori what kind of objects may have been put in the `ArrayList` as elements. Furthermore, in order to have robust code, we should always guarantee a priori that only strings are inserted, perhaps with a control like this:

```
if (input instanceof String) {
    list.add(input);
}
```

As already noted, without a control like the previous one, we could face one of the most insidious unchecked exceptions at runtime: the `ClassCastException`.

When we use a generic type without specifying the parameters, as we just did with the `ArrayList` class, the type is called **raw type**. It will be useful to know when we read the warning and error messages of the compiler (see section 12.1.6).

Fortunately, generics allow us to declare a list by specifying that it will only accept strings with the following syntax:

```
List<String> strings;
```

In addition, we must also assign to `strings` an instance that accepts the same type of elements, that is `String`:

```
List<String> strings = new ArrayList<String>();
```

but from Java 7 onwards, we can write this as (thanks to the automatic inference explained in section 12.1.5):

```
List<String> strings = new ArrayList<>();
```

to avoid unnecessary verbosity.

> **Note that the sharp brackets <> are usually called "the diamond".**

At this point, we have a list that accepts only strings (no other types). For example, the following code:

```
List<String> strings = new ArrayList<>();
strings.add("It's possible to add String");
```

will compile, but the following instruction:

```
strings.add(new Date());
```

will cause the following compile-time error:

```
cannot find symbol
symbol : method add(java.util.Date)
location: interface java.util.List<java.lang.String>
strings.add(new Date());
^
```

When an object is instantiated by a class that implements `List`, the compiler replaces all occurrences of `E` with the type specified between the angle brackets. In fact, for the `strings` object of the last example, the method add(E o) is recognized as add(String o). Here, the error message is explained. Therefore, the problems that are highlighted during the compilation phase will avoid other more serious problems during the execution of the program.

Parameterization of a generic type occurs not for the whole class, but only for that particular instance. So, we can create multiple lists with different parameters, as in the following example:

```
List<String> strings = new ArrayList<>();
List<Integer> ints = new ArrayList<>();
List<Date> dates = new ArrayList<>();
```

In general, all classes and interfaces such as Map, Iterator, Set, etc. of the Collections framework, support generics.

## 12.1.2 Primitive Types and Autoboxing-Autounboxing

Generics cannot be applied to primitive data types. So, the following code:

```
List<int> ints = new ArrayList<int>();
```

will return the error message:

```
found    : int
required: reference
        List<int> ints = new ArrayList<int>( );
            ^
```

Fortunately, the following syntax:

```
List<Integer> ints = new ArrayList<Integer>();
```

will allow us to easily add primitive integers. In fact, in Java, thanks to the double feature of **autoboxing-autounboxing**, the primitive types and the corresponding *wrapper types* can be used interchangeably. For example, it is possible to write:

```
Integer integer = 1;
Double d = 3.0D;
Boolean bool = true;
```

but also:

```
char c = new Character('c');
byte b = new Byte((byte)1);
```

or perform operations like:

```
int i = 29;
```

```
Short s = new Short ((short)7);
Float f = 74.0F;
double d2 = i*f-7;
```

> **We will deepen the discussion on both autoboxing-autounboxing and wrapper classes in Chapter 14, dedicated to the** `java.lang` **library.**

For this reason, it is allowed to write:

```
ints.add(1);
```

and also:

```
int integer = ints.get(0);
```

> **Note that the** `Byte, Short, Integer , Float, Double` **and** `Long` **classes (and others like** `BigDecimal`**), all extend the abstract class** `Number`**.**

## 12.1.3 The `Iterator` Interface

In addition to `List`, all classes and all interfaces in the Collections framework support generic types. More or less what we saw for `List` is valid for all the other collections and, in particular, for `Iterator`. `Iterator` is an often-used interface of the Collections framework that allows us to iterate over a collection. Usually, the call to the `iterator()` method on the used collection, returns a concrete implementation, that we point with an `Iterator` reference. It abstracts the concept of **iterator**: a cursor that sequentially selects the elements of the collection. The `hasNext()` method returns a `boolean`, depending on whether there are still items to be processed in the collection. The `next()` method, on the other hand, returns the next object selected by the iterator. For example, the following code:

```
List<String> strings = new ArrayList<>();
strings.add("Autoboxing & Auto-Unboxing");
strings.add("Generics");
strings.add("Static imports");
strings.add("Enhanced for loop");
//...
Iterator i = strings.iterator();
while (i.hasNext()) {
    String string = i.next();
    System.out.println(string);
}
```

will produce the following output:

```
found    : java.lang.Object
required: java.lang.String
            String string = i.next();
                            ^
1 error
```

The problem is, that we must also declare the Iterator as generic in the following way:

```
Iterator<String> i = strings.iterator();
while (i.hasNext()){
    String string = i.next();
    System.out.println(string);
}
```

> **Be careful not to use** Iterator **as generic on a non-generic** Collection.
> **We risk an exception at runtime if the collection has not been filled**
> **as expected. On the other hand, generics should really prevent these**
> **types of problems by reporting them during compile-time.**

## 12.1.4 The Map Interface

A Map is a collection that associates keys to its elements. Maps cannot contain duplicate keys and each key can be associated with only one value. Maps are very different to lists. They are not ordered like lists, but allow a read access (thanks to the key) that is faster than a list.

The Map interface declares two type parameters (which are separated by a comma). The following is how it is declared:

```
public interface Map<K,V>
```

This time, the two parameters are called K and V, respectively, initials for "Key" and "Value". In fact, both the keys and the values can be parameterized for the map. The most used implementation of the Map interface is the HashMap class. Below is a snippet of code that declares a generic map, with an Integer key parameter and String value parameter:

```
Map<Integer, String> map = new HashMap<Integer, String>();
```

Thanks to the autoboxing-autounboxing feature, we can use integer primitives to add the key. For example, the following code:

```
map.put(0, "generics");
```

```
map.put(1, "metadata");
map.put(2, "enums");
map.put(3, "varargs");
for (int i = 0; i < 4; i++) {
    System.out.println(map.get(i));
}
```

initializes the map and prints the values with a loop on its keys.

 It is also possible to create nested generics; for example, the following code is valid:

```
Map<Integer, ArrayList<String>> map = new HashMap<>();
```

This is a map that associates an arraylist of strings to an integer key. In order to derive an element of the nested arraylist, we can use the following code:

```
String s = map.get(key).get(number);
```

where both key and number are integers. Note how we did not even use a cast.

## 12.1.5 Automatic Type Inference

Java 7 introduced a small syntax change for the creation of generic types. The **type inference for generic instance creation** (that we will only call it **type inference**). Based on the name, it would seem to be something very complex. Actually, it is a simple subject, which, among other things, we have already mentioned.

 **Like all of the changes that influenced the syntax of Java 7, this was also proposed by Java users and was part of the so-called "Project Coin" project, whose goal was to simplify the developer's life: writing less means risking less. The tendency to make Java less verbose thanks to automatic compiler inferences, has not been turned off, for example, with the introduction in Java 8 of topics such as lambda expressions.**

But what is automatic inference? Let's take a simple example. Let's consider the following statement:

```
ArrayList<String> arrayList;
```

To instantiate this ArrayList, before the advent of Java 7 we had to write:

```
ArrayList<String> arrayList = new ArrayList<String>();
```

**460**

now it is possible to use the **diamond operator**, i.e. it is possible to omit the parameters for the instantiated object, as in the following example:

```
ArrayList<String> arrayList = new ArrayList<>();
```

The compiler is able to infer the type of parameter for the object instance, because it can read the reference to which it is assigned. So, since the reference arrayList has been declared as ArrayList<String>, then the assigned object will also be of the same type. As we've already asserted, the pair of empty sharp brackets is called "the diamond". Another more significant example could be:

```
Map<String, List<String>> hashMap = new HashMap<String, List<String>>();
```

which can now be rewritten as:

```
Map<String, List<String>> hashMap = new HashMap<>();
```

Note that we can use the diamond operator even when invoking a method. For example, the following code:

```
ArrayList<Number> arrayList = new ArrayList<>();
arrayList.addAll(new ArrayList<>());
```

is correctly compiled by the compiler.

 Up to Version 8 of Java, because of a limitation on the representation of anonymous classes by the JVM, it was not possible to use diamond notation when defining anonymous classes. In Java 9, this limitation has been overcome, and now we can use the diamond operator even when defining an anonymous class.

For example, the DiamondAnonymousClass class declares an anonymous class that extends ArrayList and overrides the add() method so that duplicates cannot be added:

```java
public class DiamondAnonymousClass {
    List<Integer> list = new ArrayList<>() {
        @Override
        public boolean add(Integer i) {
            if (contains(i)) {
                return false;
            }
            return super.add(i);
        }
    };
    //...
}
```

## 12.1.6 Raw Types and XLint

We have seen how automatic inference is possible thanks to the assignment of an object to a reference. In fact, the compiler will use the type parameter declared by the reference to infer the parameter of the assigned object. But if the reference does not declare a parameter, then automatic inference cannot take place. In particular, we said that, when using a generic type without specifying the type parameter, then we're talking about **raw type**. The raw type is compatible with legacy code, where there were no generic types, but the type-safety of generics is lost. In fact, we have already highlighted that the use of raw type will give rise to compilation-time warnings. For example, the following code:

```
List strings = new ArrayList();
strings.add("Lambda");
strings.add("Streams API");
strings.add("Date and Time API");
strings.add("JavaFX");
Iterator i = strings.iterator();
while (i.hasNext()) {
    String string = (String)i.next();
    System.out.println(string);
}
```

will have a positive build result, but will result in the following output:

```
Note: Generics1.java uses unchecked or unsafe operations.
Note: Recompile with -Xlint:unchecked for details.
```

These **warnings** (also called **notes**, or **lints** as defined in the specifications) warn the developer that there are unsafe or uncontrolled operations, and we are prompted to recompile the file with the `-Xlint` option (which, as we saw in section 9.3.5.5, is equivalent to the `-Xlint:all` option), to get more details. Following the suggestion of the compiler, we recompile the file with the requested option. Then the output will be:

```
D:\javac -Xlint Generics1.java
D:\Generics1.java:5: warning: [rawtypes] found raw type: List
        List strings = new ArrayList();
        ^
  missing type arguments for generic class List<E>
  where E is a type-variable:
    E extends Object declared in interface List
D:\Generics1.java:5: warning: [rawtypes] found raw type: ArrayList
        List strings = new ArrayList();
                           ^
  missing type arguments for generic class ArrayList<E>
  where E is a type-variable:
    E extends Object declared in class ArrayList
D:\Generics1.java:6: warning: [unchecked] unchecked call to add(E) as a member of the
```

```
raw type List
        strings.add("Lambda");
                   ^
  where E is a type-variable:
    E extends Object declared in interface List
D:\Generics1.java:7: warning: [unchecked] unchecked call to add(E) as a member of the
 raw type List
        strings.add("Streams API");
                   ^
  where E is a type-variable:
    E extends Object declared in interface List
D:\Generics1.java:8: warning: [unchecked] unchecked call to add(E) as a member of the
 raw type List
        strings.add("Date and Time API");
                   ^
  where E is a type-variable:
    E extends Object declared in interface List
D:\Generics1.java:9: warning: [unchecked] unchecked call to add(E) as a member of the
 raw type List
        strings.add("JavaFX");
                   ^
  where E is a type-variable:
    E extends Object declared in interface List
D:\Generics1.java:10: warning: [rawtypes] found raw type: Iterator
        Iterator  i = strings.iterator();
        ^
  missing type arguments for generic class Iterator<E>
  where E is a type-variable:
    E extends Object declared in interface Iterator
8 warnings
```

This time, the raw types are marked with a warning, with a brief explanation in the classic Java style. As we can see, these warnings are of two types: rawtypes and unchecked. There are actually various types of warnings, of which the unchecked are considered the most relevant. So, we can get a synopsis of all of the non-standard compiler options (i.e. that could change in the future) by running the command:

```
javac -X
```

We will find out that concerning Xlint, there are the following types:

```
-Xlint:<key>(,<key>)*
        Warnings to enable or disable, separated by comma.
        Precede a key by - to disable the specified warning.
        Supported keys are:
          all                   Enable all warnings
          auxiliaryclass        Warn about an auxiliary class that is
                                hidden in a source file, and is used from
                                other files.
          cast                  Warn about use of unnecessary casts.
          classfile             Warn about issues related to classfile
                                contents.
          deprecation           Warn about use of deprecated items.
          dep-ann               Warn about items marked as deprecated in
```

| | |
|---|---|
| | JavaDoc but not using the @Deprecated annotation. |
| divzero | Warn about division by constant integer 0. |
| empty | Warn about empty statement after if. |
| exports | Warn about issues regarding module exports. |
| fallthrough | Warn about falling through from one case of a switch statement to the next. |
| finally | Warn about finally clauses that do not terminate normally. |
| module | Warn about module system related issues. |
| opens | Warn about issues regarding module opens. |
| options | Warn about issues relating to use of command line options. |
| overloads | Warn about issues regarding method overloads. |
| overrides | Warn about issues regarding method overrides. |
| path | Warn about invalid path elements on the command line. |
| processing | Warn about issues regarding annotation processing. |
| rawtypes | Warn about use of raw types. |
| removal | Warn about use of API that has been marked for removal. |
| requires-automatic | Warn about use of automatic modules in the requires clauses. |
| requires-transitive-automatic | Warn about automatic modules in requires transitive. |
| serial | Warn about Serializable classes that do not provide a serial version ID. Also warn about access to non-public members from a serializable element. |
| static | Warn about accessing a static member using an instance. |
| try | Warn about issues relating to use of try blocks (i.e. try-with-resources). |
| unchecked | Warn about unchecked operations. |
| varargs | Warn about potentially unsafe varargs methods |
| none | Disable all warnings |

So, if when compiling our file with the -Xlint option, we get too many warnings, we can filter the list of warnings for the type we are interested in, specifying a sub-option. For example, by specifying -Xlint:unchecked we will see only unchecked type warnings listed.

> The list of potential warnings also includes other types not necessarily linked to generic types, as we already noted in the section 9.3.5.5, dedicated to warnings.

It is also possible to avoid receiving warnings during compilation, where it is considered that it is right not to use parameters for generic types, using the SuppressWarnings standard annotation (introduced in the ninth chapter and deepened in the sixteenth chapter). However, the best solution is to apply parameterization wherever possible.

> **What is stated in this section does not only apply to collections, but to all generic types, even those created by us.**

## 12.2 Inheritance and Generic Types

Inheritance can also be used for generic types. When we talk about inheritance, we also talk about data polymorphism, which is just a consequence of it. In fact, the Collections framework classes are generic and implement generic interfaces or extend other generic classes. For example, we used data polymorphism in the previous examples:

```
List<String> strings = new ArrayList<>();
```

List is actually an interface implemented by ArrayList. The type parameter, however, must be the same. In fact, in the next two sections, we will see why class hierarchies do not consider a hierarchy between type parameter to be valid for the purpose of implementing inheritance and polymorphism for data.

### 12.2.1 Inheritance and Type Parameter

Generic types also form hierarchies, but these hierarchies are not based on the declared type parameters. For example, the following code is valid:

```
ArrayList <Integer> arrayList = new ArrayList<>();
List <Integer> list = arrayList;
```

the following code, on the other hand, is not valid:

```
ArrayList <Number> list = arrayList;
```

In fact, if Number is a superclass of Integer, it does not authorize us to consider the generic type ArrayList<Number> a superclass of ArrayList<Integer>. Therefore, the following instruction is not valid either:

```
ArrayList<Number> list = new ArrayList<Integer>;
```

The reason why it is not possible for the type parameter to be the basis of a hierarchy, becomes evident with an example. Suppose we have an `ArrayList` of `Integer` objects:

```
List<Integer> ints = new ArrayList<Integer>();
```

If the inheritance also depends on the type parameter, we could assign a reference of type `List<Object>` to an object of type `List<Integer>`, since `Integer` is a subclass of `Object`, and we could write:

```
List<Object> objs = ints;
```

But using JShell, we can verify that we will return a compile-time error:

```
jshell> List<Integer> ints = new ArrayList<Integer>();
ints ==> []

jshell> List<Object> objs = ints;
|  Error:
|  incompatible types: java.util.List<java.lang.Integer> cannot be
|    converted to java.util.List<java.lang.Object>
|  List<Object> objs = ints;
|                      ^--^
```

In fact, if it were valid to assign an object of type `List<Integer>` to a reference of type `List<Object>`, then it would also be valid to write:

```
objs.add("A string in an Integer generic type?");
```

But, this way, we would have added a string in a type parameterized with `Integer`, and that therefore should only contain integers! It seems evident that inheritance (and therefore data polymorphism) cannot be determined by the type parameter.

## 12.2.2 Type Erasure

The technical reason why inheritance is not based on the generic type, depends on the concept of **type erasure,** usually referred to as just **erasure**. The management of generic types is only handled at compilation level. Remember that generics (along with many other features such as enumerations, annotations, the enhanced for loop, varargs, etc.) were introduced in Version 5 of Java, trying to impact as little as possible on what was there before. To make the introduction of generics possible, an additional task has been assigned to the compiler. In fact, the compiler transforms Java code into pre-Java 5 code before transforming it into bytecode. So, during the execution, the instructions:

```
ArrayList<Integer> arrayList = new ArrayList<Integer>();
ArrayList<Number> list = arrayList;
```

will be read by the JVM as if the generic types were not there (hence the term "erasure"):

```
ArrayList arrayList = new ArrayList();
ArrayList list = arrayList;
```

But, at this point, it would no longer be possible to have information on the compatibility of the elements of the two lists. This is why the compiler does not allow parameter-based inheritance: at runtime: parameters no longer exist.

> Erasure is one of the consequences of the deep-rooted philosophy of Java to always be compatible with previous versions. The goal is to allow developers to migrate without having to throw all the code written previously. This is not always 100% possible. So, when we migrate from one version of Java to the next, sometimes we need to retouch some details of our code.

## 12.2.3 Wildcard

In the light of what we have just seen, we need to stop for a moment to reflect on what the consequences of erasure can be. Suppose we have the following method that uses a raw type:

```
public void printList(ArrayList al) {
    Iterator i = al.iterator();
    while (i.hasNext()) {
        Object o = i.next();
        System.out.println(o);
    }
}
```

The compilation of this code will be successful, but warnings will be reported. Although it is possible to disable warnings with a compilation option (option -Xlint:none of the **javac** command see section 9.3.5.5), it would certainly be better to avoid them, rather than suppressing them. The simplest solution would be the following:

```
public void printList(ArrayList<Object> al) {
    Iterator<Object> i = al.iterator();
    while (i.hasNext()) {
        Object o = i.next();
        System.out.println(o);
    }
}
```

Unfortunately, the use of the generic type, due to the erasure, will simply imply that this method will only accept generic types that have, as input parameter, `Object` (and not for example `String`). So, the instruction:

```
twd.printList(new ArrayList<String>());
```

where `twd` is an object of the class containing the method `printList()`, will produce the following compile-time error:

```
TestWildCardError.java:25: error: cannot find symbol
        twd.printList(list);
           ^
  symbol:   method printList(ArrayList<String>)
  location: variable twd of type TestWildCard
1 error
```

What was meant to be a polymorphic parameter, therefore, proved to be a programming error. But what can we do if we do not actually want to decide on the fly the type parameter of the arraylist to be passed to the `printList()` method? For this purpose, there is a special syntax for generics that uses **wildcards**, represented by question marks. In particular, we are talking about **unbounded wildcards** (in contrast to the *bounded wildcards* that we will see in section 12.3.2). The following code represents the only real solution to the problem:

```
public void printList(ArrayList<?> al) {
    Iterator<?> i = al.iterator();
    while (i.hasNext()) {
        Object o = i.next();
        System.out.println(o);
    }
}
```

Using generics, this method will not generate any kind of warning during compilation and will accept any type of parameter for the arraylist input parameter.

 Since the compiler cannot check the correctness of the type parameter when a wildcard is used, it will refuse to compile any statement that attempts to add or set elements in the arraylist. Thus, the use of wildcards turns generic types into *read-only*. This means that the arraylist cannot be changed within this method. For example, if we add this instruction within the method:

```
al.add("");
```

we will get a compile-time error. This phenomenon is known as **wildcard capture**, and can be overcome thanks to stratagems based on helper methods, as we will see in section 12.3.5.

## 12.3 Create Our Own Generic Types

As we have already seen, we can define our generic types as in the following example:

```
public class OwnGeneric<E> {
    private List<E> list;
    public OwnGeneric() {
        list = new ArrayList<E>();
    }
    public void add(E e) {
        list.add(e);
    }
    public void remove(int i) {
        list.remove(i);
    }
    public E get(int i) {
        return list.get(i);
    }
    public int size() {
        return list.size();
    }
    public boolean isEmpty() {
        return list.size() == 0;
    }
    @Override
    public String toString() {
        StringBuilder sb = new StringBuilder();
        int size = size();
        for (int i = 0; i < size; i++) {
            sb.append(get(i) + (i != (size - 1) ? "-" : ""));
        }
        return sb.toString();
    }
}
```

The implementation of the toString() method probably needs some additional observations. First, let's note the use of the StringBuilder class. This is a class that represents a modifiable string, and has methods for concatenating and doing other operations with strings. Furthermore, the implementation of the for loop can be cryptic at first sight. In fact, using the ternary operator does not help readability. First of all, we note that within the for loop, there is only one expression. This adds a string to the sb object of type StringBuilder via the append() method. The parameter of this method consists of what is returned by the get() method, concatenated with the result of the ternary operator included in round brackets. This operator will return a dash ("-") to separate the various elements extracted from the collection if and only if, the value of i is different from the size of the collection -1 (i.e. after the last element there will not be a dash). In this way, the resulting output will have the correct formatting.

 Note how the parameter has been defined with an E, as used in the documentation. However, although it is preferable to use a single capital letter to define the parameter, we can use any valid word for Java syntax.

With the following code, instead, we use our generic type:

```
OwnGeneric<String> own = new OwnGeneric<String>();
for (int i = 0; i < 10; ++i) {
    own.add("" + (i));
}
System.out.println(own); //will be called the toString() method
```

The output will be:

```
0-1-2-3-4-5-6-7-8-9
```

> **With regard to the generic class we have just created, it is not possible to declare the instance variable list as static in the following way:**
>
> private static List <E> list = new ArrayList <E> ();
>
> **In fact, this would prevent the various instances of the class from using different parameters (since they must be shared for the definition of static).**

## 12.3.1 Bounded Parameters

The toString() method defined in OwnGeneric, prints the values of the internal variable list separated by dashes ("-"). In the example of the OwnGeneric class, the generic type was String and the toString() method formatted integers in a readable way, separating them with dashes. But we could also use the class as follows:

```
public class TestOwnGenericWithMinus {
    public static void main(String args[]) {
        OwnGeneric<String> own = new OwnGeneric<>();
        own.add("-");
        own.add("--");
        own.add("---");
        System.out.println(own);
    }
}
```

The execution of this last class will produce the following output which, in all likelihood, is not the desired one:

```
---------
```

We can create our own generic types with parameters that specify certain types (**bounded parameters**). The bounded parameters are very useful because they restrict the field of choice of the parameter to a hierarchy of classes, where using any parameter could lead to unexpected situations. For example, if we define the OwnGeneric class in the following way:

```
public class OwnGeneric <E extends Number> {
```

we can use only subclasses of numbers as parameters (for example Float, Integer ...).
So, if we tried to instantiate an OwnGeneric object with a string parameter, we will get an error as shown below:

```
jshell> OwnGeneric<String> own = new OwnGeneric<>();
|  Error:
|  type argument java.lang.String is not within bounds of type-variable E
|  OwnGeneric<String> own = new OwnGeneric<>();
|             ^----^
|  Error:
|  incompatible types: cannot infer type arguments for OwnGeneric<>
|      reason: inference variable E has incompatible bounds
|          equality constraints: java.lang.String
|          upper bounds: java.lang.Number
|  OwnGeneric<String> own = new OwnGeneric<>();
|                               ^----------^
```

> **Most of the time, we can use bounded parameters on classes created by us. In this way, we can protect ourselves from unexpected situations. Sometimes, it is convenient to create an interface (also completely empty) to use as a bounded parameter, that must be implemented by all the classes to be used.**

A direct consequence of the use of bounded parameters, is the creation of *covariant parameters* as input of the methods, as we will see in section 12.3.5.

## 12.3.2 Bounded Wildcard

The OwnGeneric class declared a generic type E, and this is used as a parameter in its methods. Now, instead, suppose we want to create a method that takes, as input, a generic type with a restricted (bounded) parameter. Suppose, however, that we're using a non-generic class, and therefore do not have a type parameter to be exploited, like E in the OwnGeneric class. If we do not have a parameter, how can we restrict the type parameter of a method? We just have to use a wildcard, that we will restrict as we did with the parameters in the previous section. In this case, we're talking about a **bounded wildcard**:

```java
public void print(List<? extends Number> list) {
    for (Iterator<? extends Number> i = list.iterator(); i.hasNext( ); ) {
        System.out.println(i.next());
    }
}
```

To this method we can only pass lists with a type parameter that is a subclass of Number. In this case, we used what is called an **upper bounded wildcard**.

We can also use **lower bounded wildcards** using, instead of the keyword extends, the keyword super. For example, the following method:

```java
public static void loadList(List<? super Integer> list) {
    int size = list.size();
    for (int i = 1; i <= size; i++) {
        list.add(i);
    }
    System.out.println(list);
}
```

allows us to fill and print a list filled with Integer, Number (which is, however, an abstract class and therefore cannot be instantiated) or Object.

Bear in mind that the parameters of a method can be of three types:

■■ a parameter that contains data to be used (an "IN" parameter): for example the printList() method;

■■ a parameter to be updated (an "OUT" parameter): for example the loadList() method;

■■ a parameter that contains data to be used and which must be updated.

The guidelines for using wildcards are as follows:

■■ use an upper bounded wildcard for type 1 parameters;

■■ use a lower bounded wildcard for type 2 parameters;

■■ use an unbounded wildcard if the type 1 variable is to be used by means of methods of the Object class (for example toString());

■■ do not use a wildcard for type 3 parameters.

### 12.3.3 Generic Methods

There is also a special syntax that does not use the wildcard:

```
public <N extends Number> void print(List<N> list) {
    for (Iterator<N> i = list.iterator(); i.hasNext( ); ) {
        System.out.println(i.next());
    }
}
```

where, with the instruction

```
<N extends Number>
```

inserted before the return type of the method, we are declaring, locally, a parameter called N, which must extend Number. This parameter will be usable within the whole method. This syntax may be preferable when, for example, the parameter <N> is often used within the method code (otherwise we are obliged to write <? extends Number> several times). This is an example of a *generic method.*

**Generic methods** are just methods that define their own type parameters. The syntax is the same as that used for generic types, but the visibility of the parameters is limited to the definition of the method itself, be it static, a constructor or an ordinary method. The type parameters must precede the return type of the method. In the case of a constructor method, must precede the name of the constructor. For example, the following class:

```
public class GenericMethod {
    public static <N extends Number> String getValue(N number) {
        String value = number.toString();
        return value;
    }
    public static void main(String args[]) {
        String value = GenericMethod.getValue(new Integer(25));
        System.out.println(value);
    }
}
```

declares the generic method getValue(), which declares an N parameter bounded to Number (which, therefore, could be used with any subclass of Number). Notice also how the number input parameter of the method is of type N (which is only visible within the getValue() method). In the main() method, the getValue() method is called using an Integer type object with a value of 25 (but it's also possible to pass the integer value 25 thanks to the autoboxing-unboxing rules).

There are also **generic constructor methods**. In particular, those that allow us to use a parameter for a constructor, where this parameter is different from the type parameter declared for the class. Let's make another example. Consider the

**473**

following class:

```
public class AdvancedInference<Boolean> {
    public <E> AdvancedInference(E e) {
        System.out.println(e);
    }
    //...
}
```

We have specified, for the generic constructor, a type parameter E different from that defined for the class (which was of type Boolean). In versions prior to Java 7, it was already possible to write:

```
AdvancedInference<Boolean> test = new AdvancedInference<Boolean>("");
```

In fact, the <Boolean> syntax represents the type parameter of the class, while the String value passed to the constructor will set the parameter E, which the constructor method takes as input. From Java 7 on, it is possible to instantiate this class in the following way:

```
AdvancedInference<Boolean> test = new AdvancedInference<>("");
```

In fact, the diamond operator will allow the inference of the class parameter (Boolean), while the String value passed to the constructor will set the parameter E, which the constructor takes as input.

 Equivalent to this syntax, we can also write:

```
AdvancedInference<Boolean> test3 =
    new <String>AdvancedInference<Boolean>("");
```

which also specifies the type parameter of the constructor <String>. This syntax is valid and compared to that previously seen, it is more verbose, but perhaps, more complete.

### 12.3.4 Intersection types

 From Java 8 onwards, it is possible to use a new *non-denotable type*: the **intersection type**. Until Java 7, if we had the need to have a certain type that inherit from multiple types, the only solution was to create this type. Today with intersection types, by exploiting bounded generic types, we can avoid creating this type.

> **The intersection types can be defined and used even without the generic types as we will see later.**

### 12.3.4.1 Example

For example, let's reconsider the classes and interfaces declared in Chapter 8, in particular the Flying interface:

```
public interface Flying {
    void land();
    void takeOff();
}
```

The Vehicle abstract class:

```
public abstract class Vehicle {
    public abstract void accelerate();
    public abstract void decelerate();
}
```

The Plane class:

```
public class Plane extends Vehicle implements Flying {
    @Override
    public void land() {
        // overrides the method of the Flying interface
    }
    @Override
    public void takeOff() {
        // overrides the method of the Flying interface
    }
    @Override
    public void accelerate() {
        // overrides the method of the Vehicle abstract class
    }
    @Override
    public void decelerate() {
        // overrides the method of the Vehicle abstract class
    }
}
```

And the Traveler class:

```
public class Traveler {
    public void travel(Vehicle v) { //polymorphic parameter
        v.accelerate(); //virtual invocation of the method
        //. . .
    }
}
```

Suppose we want to make the method travel() take as input an object that implements the Flying interface and simultaneously extends the Vehicle class. Before the advent of Java

Version 8, we were forced to create an abstract class like the following:

```
public abstract class FlyingVehicle extends Vehicle implements Flying {
}
```

Then we had to change the `travel()` method of the `Traveler` class, as follows:

```
public  void travel(FlyingVehicle t) { //polymorphic parameter
    t.accelerate(); //virtual invocation of the method
    t.takeOff();
    //. . .
}
```

Instead, from Java 8 onwards, it is possible to use an intersection type by exploiting a particular syntax for bounded parameter types. We can rewrite the `travel()` method as a generic method (see previous paragraph) in the following way:

```
public <T extends Vehicle & Flying> void travel(T t) { //polymorphic parameter
    t.accelerate(); //virtual invocation of the method
    t.takeOff();//virtual invocation of the method
    //. . .
}
```

We have highlighted the intersection type declaration in bold. With this syntax we declare a non-denotable type that must extend the `Vehicle` class and implement the `Flying` interface, using the & character.

> **The creation of the `FlyingVehicle` class is now superfluous because replaced by the intersection type.**

To invoke this method, it is necessary to pass as input an object that extends the `Vehicle` and implements `Flying`, such as an instance of the `Plane` class:

```
Plane piper = new Plane();
Traveler claudio = new Traveler();
claudio.travel(piper);
```

If, instead, we create the following `Balloon` class which implements `Flying` but does not extend `Vehicle`:

```
public class Baloon implements Flying {
    public void land() {
    }
    public void takeOff() {
    }
}
```

if we instantiate an object and pass it to the `travel()` method :

```
Traveler claudio = new Traveler();
Flying baloon = new Baloon();
claudio.travel(baloon);
```

we would get the following compilation error:

```
error: method travel in class Traveler cannot be applied to given types;
        claudio.travel(baloon);
                ^
   required: T
   found: Flying
   reason: inference variable T has incompatible bounds
     lower bounds: Vehicle,Flying
     lower bounds: Flying
   where T is a type-variable:
     T extends Vehicle,Flying declared in method <T>travel(T)
1 error
```

which warns us that a `Balloon` type object is not a vehicle!

### 12.3.4.2 Multiple Intersection

Intersection types can also intersect more than two types. For example, if we consider the following `Electric` interface:

```
public interface Electric {
}
```

we could create a generic intersection type like this:

```
<T extends Vehicle & Flying & Electric>
```

The previous syntax implies the definition of a non-denotable type that implements the `Electric` and `Flying` interfaces, and extends the `Vehicle` class.

### 12.3.4.3 Assignment of Intersection Types

If we consider the following class which returns an intersection type:

```
public class FlyingVehiclesFactory {
    public  <T extends Vehicle & Flying> T getFlyingVehicle() {
        return (T) new Plane();
    }
}
```

It is possible to assign the intersection type returned with a `Vehicle` type reference:

```
var factory = new FlyingVehiclesFactory();
Vehicle vehicle = factory.getFlyingVehicle();
```

```
vehicle.accelerate();
//vehicle.takeOff(); does not compile!
```

but in this case, it will not be possible to call the methods defined in the Flying interface. Same thing if we assign the intersection type using a Flying type reference:

```
Flying flying = factory.getFlyingVehicle();
//flying.accelerate(); does not compile!
flying.takeOff();
```

we can only call the methods defined in Flying, but not those defined in Vehicle. It is possible, however, to use the word var to assign the intersection type, so we will be able to call both the methods declared in Vehicle, and those in Flying:

```
var vehicleFlying = factory.getFlyingVehicle();
vehicleFlying.accelerate();
vehicleFlying.takeOff();
```

In this case, once again the word var made us overcome a limit of language.

## 12.3.5 Wildcard Capture

 In section 12.2.3, we saw that a collection parameter, parameterized with a wild-card, made the collection not modifiable within the method. In fact, we can quickly check with JShell, that the following code does not compile:

```
jshell> public class WildCardTest {
   ...>     void test(List<?> list) {
   ...>         list.set(0, list.get(0));
   ...>     }
   ...> }
|  Error:
|  incompatible types: java.lang.Object cannot be converted to capture#1
   of ?
|         list.set(0, list.get(0));
|                     ^---------^
```

In fact, list is parameterized with a wildcard but, within the code of the method, we are trying to insert an object that the compiler deduces is an Object. Yet, the list could be parameterized at runtime by strings, as in the following example:

```
List<String> param = new ArrayList<>();
param.add("string 1");
param.add("string 2");
param.add("string 3");
```

```
WildCardTest wct = new WildCardTest();
wct.test(param);
```

Even if `param` is parameterized with strings, the compiler fails to correctly infer the type parameter within the `test()` method. In particular, if we take the definition of wildcard itself, consider the elements of the collection as `Object`, and an `Object` cannot be put in a list that will be parameterized only at runtime (in our case, with strings). The compiler is telling us that, since the wildcard can be initialized with any type, at runtime, the collection can be parameterized with this type, and therefore we cannot assume a priori that it can be initialized with an `Object`. This phenomenon of *limited inference* is known as **wildcard capture**. We talk about **capture type** and it is another example of a non-denotable type.

### 12.3.5.1 Helper Methods

One way to solve the situation is to create a *helper method.*

A **helper method** is a generic method (see section 12.3.3) which defines a parameter for the collection to be used in order to update the collection itself. For example, the following implementation is valid:

```
public class WildCardTest {
    void test(List<?> list) {
        testHelper(list);
    }
    //Metodo helper
    private <T> void testHelper(List<T> list) {
        list.set(0, list.get(0));
    }
}
```

By using the `T` parameter of a generic method, we were able to update the collection that could not be updated in the previous implementation. In this case, within the `testHelper()` method, the compiler uses the `T` parameter (and not the wildcard) which is parameterized as a string at runtime. If, at runtime, `List<T> list` is parameterized with a string, then the instruction `list.get(0)` will return a string.

> The helper method technique also has a convention for the name of the auxiliary method, which should be of the format `originalMethodNameHelper()` type, which is the `originalMethodName` with the addition of `Helper` at the end of the name.

We will be able to exploit this technique when we find compile-time error messages that clearly report *capture* errors.

## 12.4 Covariant Parameters

 When we talked about the rules governing override in Chapter 8, we mentioned the **covariant return types**, applying which, it is possible to override methods whose return type is a subclass of the return type of the original method. For example, bearing in mind the relationship of inheritance that existed between the `Point` and `ThreeDimensionalPoint` classes if, in the `Point` class, the following method was present:

```java
public Point processPoint() {
    //...
}
```

it would be valid to implement the following override in the `ThreeDimensionalPoint` class:

```java
@Override
public ThreeDimensionalPoint processPoint () {
    //...
}
```

However, the overriding rules do not allow us to also have input parameters of a method that are covariant. This means that if, in the `Point` class, the `distance()` method is present, it measures the distance of the current point from another point:

```java
public class Point {
    public double distance(Point otherPoint) {
        //...
    }
}
```

and if we try to override this method in its subclass, specifying as input, instead of a `Point`, a `ThreeDimensionalPoint` (which we define as a **covariant parameter**):

```java
public class ThreeDimensionalPoint extends Point {
    @Override
    public double distance(ThreeDimensionalPoint otherPoint) {
        //...
    }
}
```

we will obtain a compile-time error:

```
Error:
method does not override or implement a method from a supertype
  @Override
  ^-------^
```

In order to override a method, the signature of the rewritten method must be identical to the signature of the extended method. When they do not match, we get two different methods in the subclass, and we then have overload and not override (see Chapter 8). We cannot, therefore, talk about the existence of covariant parameters in the strict sense. With generic types, however, it is possible to implement a stratagem to use covariant parameters. We're talking about a trick (or it would be better to call it a pattern) that is not trivial. In the following sections, in fact, we will study probably the most complex example presented so far.

## 12.4.1 Covariant Parameters Problem

Consider the following two interfaces:

```
interface Food {
    String getColor();
}
interface Animal {
    void eat(Food food);
}
```

It's easy to implement the Food interface in the Grass class:

```
public class Grass implements Food {
    public String getColor() {
        return "green";
    }
}
```

Just as it's easy to implement the Animal interface in the Carnivore class:

```
public class Carnivore implements Animal {
    public void eat(Food food) {
        //a carnivore could eat herbivores
    }
}
```

And yet, we implement both the Animal interface and the Food interface, in the Herbivore class (given that an herbivore could be the food of a carnivore):

```
public class Herbivore implements Food, Animal {
    public void eat(Food food) {
        //a herbivore could eat grass
    }

    public String getColor() {
        //. . .
    }
}
```

The problem is that, in this way, both a carnivore and an herbivore could eat anything; a carnivore could feed on grass. But this is far-fetched. We could solve the situation by using internal controls on the methods that, through the `instanceof` operator and the possible launch of a custom exception (`FoodException`) at runtime, impose the right constraints on our classes. For example:

```java
public class Carnivore implements Animal {
    public void eat(Food food) throws FoodException {
        if (!(food instanceof Erbivoro)) {
            throw new FoodException("A carnivore should " +
                "eat herbivores!");
        }
        //...
    }
}

public class Herbivore implements Food, Animal {
    public void eat(Food food) throws FoodException {
        if (!(food instanceof Grass)) {
            throw new FoodException("A herbivore should eat grass!");
        }
        //...
    }

    public String getColor() {
        //...
    }
}

public class FoodException extends Exception {
    public FoodException(String msg) {
        super(msg);
    }
    //...
}
```

In addition to the overriding rules on exceptions (see Chapter 9), in order to correctly compile our classes, we will also have to redefine the `Animal` interface so that the overridden `eat()` method defines a `throws` clause for launching a `FoodException`. The redefinition of the `Animal` interface is:

```java
interface Animal {
    void eat(Food food) throws FoodException;
}
```

Our classes are now better abstractions, but a problem will only be detected when the application is running. For example, the following code will compile correctly, and then raise an exception at runtime:

```
public class AnimalsTest {
    public static void main(String[] args) {
        try {
            Carnivore tiger = new Carnivore();
            Food grass = new Grass();
            tiger.eat(grass);
        } catch (FoodException exc) {
            exc.printStackTrace();
        }
    }
}
```

Here is the output:

```
FoodException: A carnivore should eat herbivores!
    at Carnivore.eat(Carnivore.java:4)
    at AnimalsTest.main(AnimalsTest.java:6)
```

## 12.4.2 Bounded Parameter Solution

 The best solution, however, would be to make the polymorphic parameter of the eat() method more specific, defining it as a Grass type for the Herbivore class, and of the Herbivore type for the Carnivore class. Ultimately, we would like to use the covariant parameters in the eat() method. In fact, in this way, the previous code would fail at compile-time, and this would be a great advantage. Let us first try to see how to declare the covariant parameters that would solve our problems:

```
public class Carnivore implements Animal {
    public void eat(Herbivore herbivore) {
        //...
    }
}
public class Herbivore implements Food, Animal {
    public void eat(Grass grass) {
        //...
    }

    public String getColor() {
        //...
    }
}
```

Unfortunately this code will not compile, because we have not implemented, in either class, the eat() method that takes as parameter a Food type object. In fact, the Carnivore class implements a method eat() that takes as input an object of type Herbivore, while the Herbivore class defines a method eat() that takes as input an object of type Grass. Therefore, inheriting

**483**

the abstract method eat() which takes as input an object of type Food, in non-abstract classes, we get compile-time errors:

```
Error:
Carnivore is not abstract and does not override abstract method eat(Food) in Animal
public class Carnivore implements Animal {
^------------------------------------------...
Error:
Herbivore is not abstract and does not override abstract method eat(Food) in Animal
public class Herbivore implements Food, Animal {
^------------------------------------------...
```

To achieve our goal, however, we can take advantage of the generic types. Let's redefine the Animal interface, parameterizing it with a *bounded parameter* in the following way:

```java
interface Animal <F extends Food> {
    void eat(F food);
}
```

Now we can redefine the Carnivore and Herbivore classes using for the Carnivore class a bounded parameter H that limits the type parameters to the Herbivore subclasses and, for the Herbivore class, a bounded parameter G that restricts the type parameters to the subclasses of Grass:

```java
public class Carnivore<H extends Herbivore> implements Animal<H> {
    public void eat(H herbivore) {
        //a carnivore could eat herbivores
    }
}
public class Herbivore<G extends Grass> implements Food, Animal<G> {
    public void eat(G grass) {
        //a herbivore could eat grass
    }

    public String getColor() {
        //. . .
    }
}
```

The previous code is correctly compiled and imposes the right constraints on the created hierarchies. Let's consider the following class with the main() method that correctly uses the classes Carnivore, Herbivore and Grass:

```java
public class AnimalsTest {
    public static void main(String[] args) {
        Animal<Herbivore> tiger = new Carnivore<Herbivore>();
        Herbivore<Grass> herbivore = new Herbivore<Grass>();
        Grass grass = new Grass();
```

**484**

```
        herbivore.eat(grass);
        tiger.eat(herbivore);
    }
}
```

We can see that the Tiger object is parameterized with the Herbivore type. This means that it is only possible to pass Herbivore objects (or any subclasses) to its eat() method. A similar logic is valid for the Herbivore object that is parameterized with a Grass type: this implies that it is possible to pass to its eat() method only objects of the Grass type (or of any subclasses).

> **Now, the eat() method of the Animal interface no longer has to define the throws clause in order to launch a FoodException. On the contrary, the FoodException class is no longer necessary.**

If, instead, we try to make a carnivore eat grass, this time we will get an error in the compilation and not at the runtime:

```
jshell> Carnivore<Grass> tiger = new Carnivore<Grass>();
|   Error:
|   type argument Grass is not within bounds of type-variable E
|   Carnivore<Grass> tiger = new Carnivore<Grass>();
|                    ^---^
|   Error:
|   type argument Grass is not within bounds of type-variable E
|   Carnivore<Grass> tiger = new Carnivore<Grass>();
|                                              ^---^
```

The bounded parameter of the Carnivore class, in fact, binds us to use only correct parameters. In conclusion, with bounded parameters, we have succeeded in implementing the covariant parameters of the methods!

> **In the previous examples, we could safely use the diamond operator. We did not do it just to make the examples more readable.**

## Summary

**Generic types** are types that can be used by setting a parameter at the time of their creation as objects. Generic types usually define methods that use this parameter, and the type of the parameter can change from object to object. The big advantage is that we can avoid execution exceptions (bugs) due to the ClassCastException. With generics, we can understand these types of problems in the compilation phase.

The functionality known as **automatic inference** allows us to make the code less verbose, avoiding writing where the type parameter of an instance of a generic type is superfluous. The pair of angle brackets is called the **diamond operator**. From Java 9 onwards, the diamond operator can be used even when defining anonymous classes.

The generic types that are instantiated without specifying the type parameters are called **raw type**, and their use generates exceptions during compilation. With the **-Xlint** option, we can filter any compiler warnings.

The **Collections framework** contains some of the most used classes by Java programmers, implemented as generic types. After evaluating the parameterization of **lists**, **maps** and **iterators** with generics, we tried to understand what the compiler's job behind the scenes is. **Autoboxing-unboxing** allows the use of wrapper classes as parameters of generic types instead of primitive types, in a transparent manner.

The **inheritance** of generic types is not based on the type parameter. In fact, **erasure** deletes the type parameter at compile-time (this is to maintain the compatibility of the new code with pre-Java 5 code). So, the type parameter cannot technically have a role in defining inheritance.

With **wildcards**, we can generalize the parameters of a generic type. The wildcard replaces the Object type which, for the rules of erasure, does not support inheritance and therefore the data polymorphism. It is used when it is not known, a priori, the type of parameter that will be used.

We can also create **custom generic types**, simply by defining parameters to the right of the type declaration, and possibly using these parameters within the defined methods.

With **bounded parameters**, we can limit the parameters of a certain generic type, thus restricting the possible types of parameters that can be used to instantiate objects.

In the same way, with **bounded wildcards**, we can limit the parameters passed to the methods so that they are subclasses of a certain type.

**Generic methods** are very useful for specifying the parameter only locally and using it within the method code.

**Intersection types** are non-denotable types that can be created by exploiting bounded parameter types, and represent non-denotable types that implement multiple types. They can be referenced by the word var, to obtain a reference capable of invoking the members of any inherited class or implemented interface.

The **helper methods**, are auxiliary methods to solve the problem of **wildcard capture**, that is the impossibility of adding an element to a generic type that has, as a parameter, a wildcard. A **helper method** is a generic method that defines the type parameter that can be used to modify the collection parameterized with wildcards. We pass this collection to the method that will modify the collection.

**486**

Finally, we have seen how it is possible to use **parameters of covariant methods**, using a complex pattern based on bounded parameters.

> **Exercises, source code, appendices and other resources are available at http://www.javaforaliens.com.**

# Part III Conclusions

Here ends the third part of the book. Now that we also know the enumerations, the nested types and the generic types (and all the related topics), we can finally study the fundamental libraries starting from Part IV. In fact, in the documentation of these libraries, it is taken for granted that the reader already knows these arguments. For example, the *Date and Time* library uses enumerations, as the *Collections* library makes great use of generic types. It should now be easier to understand hot to use of these APIs.

## Chapter Goals

Have the following goals been achieved?

| Goal | Achieved | Achievement Date |
|---|:---:|:---:|
| Understand and know how to use generic types (Unit 12.1) | O | |
| Understand automatic type inference and raw types, and manage compiler warnings (Unit 12.1) | O | |
| Understand erasure and how inheritance is applied with generic types (Unit 12.2) | O | |
| Know how to use wildcards and bounded parameters (Units 12.2, 12.3, 12.4) | O | |
| Know how to create your own generic types (Unit 12.3) | O | |
| Know how to create generic methods (Unit 12.3) | O | |
| Know how to create intersection types (Unit 12.3) | O | |
| Know how to manage wildcard capture with helper methods (Unit 12.3) | O | |
| Know how to create covariant parameters (Unit 12.4) | O | |

# Java Version New Feature Index

List of pages where new features are present for any Java version.

# Word Index

## Symbols

## A

Made in the USA
Las Vegas, NV
26 February 2021